THE T
OF JI

OR

THE NUN SANCTIFIED
BY THE VIRTUES
OF HER STATE
VOLUME I
By
St Alphonsus M Liguori, CSSR
Bishop of Saint Agatha, and Founder of the Congregation of
the Most Holy Redeemer.

TRANSLATED FROM THE ITALIAN.
EDITED BY
Rev Eugene Grimm
Priest of the Congregation of the
Most Holy Redeemer
1888

St Athanasius Press
All Rights Reserved 2014

ISBN-13: 978-1484984192

ISBN-10: 1484984196

St Athanasius Press
133 Slazing Rd
Potosi, WI 53820
melwaller@gmail.com
(email is the best way to reach us)
www.stathanasiuspress.com

Specializing in Reprinting Catholic Classics

Check out our other Titles
at the end of the book!

CONTENTS

THE APOSTOLIC BENEDICTION

REVEREND FATHER:

As the centenary of the death of the illustrious Founder of the Congregation of the Most Holy Redeemer drew near, you conceived the pious and appropriate plan of shedding a new lustre on his memory by translating all his works into English and publishing them. The Holy Father, therefore, who has at heart the spiritual advancement of the faithful, as well as the exaltation of the holy Doctor, has most graciously accepted the nine volumes thus far published, which you wished to present to him. While bestowing upon you well-deserved praise for your useful 3 labor, and thanking you for the gift inspired by your filial love, he gives you from his heart the blessing which you humbly asked for in your letter, complying also with the request of the Most Rev. Archbishop of Baltimore.

As the bearer of this, I wish you all happiness in the Lord.

I am, Reverend Sir,

Your obedient servant,

M. CARD. RAMPOLLA.

ROME, June 4, 1888,

APPROBATION

By virtue of the authority granted me by the Most Rev. Nicholas Mauron, Superior-General of the Congregation of the Most Holy Redeemer, I hereby sanction the publication of the work entitled "The True Spouse of Jesus Christ," being Volumes X. and XI. of the new and complete edition in English of the works of St. Alphonsus de Liguori, called " The Centenary Edition."

ELIAS FRED. SCHATER,

Sup. Prov. Baltinwrcnsis.

BALTIMORE, MD., March 13, 1888.

NOTICE

SAINT ALPHONSUS had reached the age of sixty-four years when he published THE TRUE SPOUSE OF JESUS CHRIST, which appeared in 1760. At that time of life he joined to the learning and sanctity that distinguished him a consummate experience; in a word, he united in himself all that could be desired in order to treat in a masterly manner of all the delicate matters that are spoken of in this work. This he has done in a superior manner, which has been justly appreciated not only in Italy, but in the whole Catholic world, as is proved by the numerous translations of his book, and by the success that they have met with.

We have endeavoured to give to our labor all the care that is due to the work and its venerated author, as well as to those persons that will be able to profit by it. To the True Spouse of Jesus Christ, which numbers twenty- four chapters, we have added various little works that have reference to the same subject. Besides the Abstract of the Virtues, the Spiritual Maxims, and the Aspirations of Love, which belong to the work as an appendix, the work contains: an Exhortation to a religious that she may make progress in the love of her divine Spouse Jesus Christ; an Exhortation addressed to the nuns of the Most Holy Re- deemer; an Exhortation to religious communities to introduce the per- petual adoration before the Blessed Sacrament; a Familiar Discourse to a young person taking the religious habit; a Sermon at the reception of the religious habit, heretofore unpublished; Rules for the Monastery of Mary, Queen of Heaven, at Airola; Notes on the life and death of Sister Teresa Mary de Liguori, and lastly, one hundred and fifty Spiritual Letters. These two volumes of the writings of St. Alphonsus contain, therefore, all that properly regards the religious

The saint himself tells us that his book is suitable not only to nuns, but also to all members of the religious state, in that which refers to the observance of the vows, regular discipline, and the perfection of their state. As for the practice of Christian virtues, the work will be found highly useful even for seculars. We add that this volume should with greater reason be serviceable to ecclesiastics, especially to those that are charged with the difficult task of directing souls in the spiritual life; they may draw therefrom lights that may not perhaps be found as clear and as sure elsewhere.

We fear, however, that some persons may find in some passages things that at first sight are of such a nature as to astonish and to displease them, for the author at times inveighs forcibly against abuses that have happily became rare or are at the present time even unknown in our country. Hence we think that we are obliged to ask them to consider well the circumstances. When St. Alphonsus wrote his work many communities in Italy and elsewhere had relaxed in spirit. Many abuses indeed existed, especially in the kingdom of Naples, and should be ascribed to the character or the manners of the country, and also to the excessive interference of the government in ecclesiastical affairs. This intermeddling often hindered the action of the Superiors, even of the Sovereign Pontiff, and favoured disorder. Yet other countries and other epochs have also their defects and their trials. The spectacle of what occurred then in Italy should awaken attention to what may perhaps be out of order among ourselves.

But you will say, " Would it not be better not to know the evil, and not to think of it?" Ah ! undoubtedly, if we were not always exposed to evil, if we had not continually to fear it and to take precautions in order to avoid it. Should 4 we wait till the evil is revealed by a sad experience ? The saints did not thus understand this; they did not cease to remind us of it by showing us the precipices yawning at our feet and the enemies that are besieging us, and by pointing out to us the neces- sary means to escape the danger and to resist the assaults to which we are always exposed.

Furthermore, if this book has been written for all the religious, it will have a twofold interest for the Superiors: it will inspire them with zeal and with vigilance, on which depend the maintenance of regular observances, and consequently the salvation of the Community and their own salvation. They should know not only the evil that exists, in order to remedy it, but even the evil that is possible, in order to prevent it, and hinder it from penetrating; they should even suspect it, says our saint. One day he had given utterance to very forcible language in a monastery. He was afterwards told that the nuns believed that he had in his address entered too much into details; this remark made him smile, and he answered: "What should I have told them ? Should I have told them that they are saints ? When one preaches, one preaches for every one, and one may suppose things that do not exist."
Finally, we may say to every religious that has the happiness of living in a house in which reigns exact observance: The example of so many

Communities that have fallen into a deplorable tepidity after having begun with the greatest fervor, should induce you to give continual thanks to God for the advantage that you enjoy, and to do all you can to attain its continuance, well knowing that the least abuse that succeeds in insinuating itself may in time bring about great ruin.

LIVE JESUS, MARY, JOSEPH, AND
ST. ALPHONSUS!

THE AUTHOR'S PREFACE.

THIS work, as appears from the title, is intended particularly for Nuns. However, only a small portion of it is directed exclusively to them; the remainder, but especially what regards the observance of the vows of religion, regular discipline, and the perfection of the religious state, is equally suited to Religious of all denominations; and what regards the Christian virtues, will be found highly useful even for seculars.

To each chapter I have annexed prayers, replete with pious affections, knowing that such prayers are very acceptable to Religious who seek perfection. For, as St. Denis the Areopagite says, "Divine love consists in the affections of the heart more than in the knowledge of the understanding." In human sciences, knowledge excites love; but in the science of the saints, love produces knowledge. He that loves God most, knows him best. Besides, it is not lofty and fruitless conceptions, but works, that unite the soul to God, and make it rich in merits before the Lord.

CHAPTER I.

THE MERIT OF VIRGINS WHO HAVE CONSECRATED THEMSELVES TO GOD.

1. They become like the Angels, and are the Spouses of Jesus Christ.

VIRGINS who have the happiness of dedicating themselves to the love of Jesus Christ by consecrating to him the lily of their purity, are, in the first place, as dear to God as his angels. They shall, says the Redeemer, be like the angels of God in heaven. Such is the immediate fruit of the virtue of chastity. Hence St. Ambrose says, that "Whoever preserves this virtue is an angel, and that whoever violates it is a demon." Baronius relates that when a certain virgin, called Georgia, was at the point of death a great multitude of doves was seen hovering about her; that when her body was brought to the church they flew to that part of the roof which corresponded to the place where the corpse had been put, and remained there till after the interment. By all who saw them, these doves were regarded as angels paying respect and homage to the body of the virgin. Chastity is justly styled an angelic and celestial virtue. "Because," says St. Ambrose, "This virtue has ascended even to the heavens, and thence taken an example to be imitated on earth; and because only in heaven, the residence of its spouse, it is practiced in all its perfection."

Besides, a virgin that consecrates herself to Jesus Christ becomes his spouse. Hence, writing to his disciples, St. Paul did not hesitate to say: I have espoused you to one husband, that I may present you as a chaste virgin to Christ." I have promised to present to Jesus Christ your souls as so many chaste spouses. In the parable of the virgins, Jesus himself wished to be called their spouse: They went out to meet the bridegroom .... they went in with him to marriage. The Redeemer, whenever he speaks of virgins, calls himself their spouse; but where he speaks of others, he calls himself master, pastor, or father. Hence that elegant verse of St. Gregory Nazianzen," and chaste virginity is adorned by Christ her spouse. These espousals are perfected in faith. And I will espouse thee to me in faith? Jesus Christ has, in a special manner, merited for mankind the gift of virginity, and is therefore followed by virgins whithersoever he goeth. The Mother of God once said to a soul, that a spouse of Jesus Christ ought to have a great esteem for all virtues, but that purity, by which she is principally assimilated to her divine spouse, should hold the first place in her heart. St. Bernard assured us that all just souls are spouses of the Lord. But St. Anthony of Padua adds that virgins consecrated to God are his spouses in a special manner. Hence St. Fulgentius calls Jesus Christ the only spouse of all consecrated virgins.

A young person desirous of settling in the world, will, if she be prudent, in the first place carefully inquire into the circumstances and dispositions of all who pretend to her affections, and will diligently seek to ascertain who of these is most deserving of her heart; and from whom she may expect the greatest happiness in this life. A religious, on the day of her profession, is espoused to Jesus Christ; for in the ceremony of profession the bishop says to the novice about to be professed: I spouse thee to Jesus Christ; may he preserve thee inviolate. Receive, then, as his spouse, the ring of faith, that, if thou serve him with fidelity, he may give thee an eternal crown. Let us, then, ask the spouse of the Canticles who is this divine bridegroom. Tell me, O sacred spouse, what are the qualities of thy beloved, the only object of thy affection, who renders thee the happiest of women? What manner of one is thy beloved of the beloved, O thou most beautiful among women? She will answer: My beloved is white and ruddy, chosen out of thousands. My beloved is rendered white by his innocence, and ruddy by the ardor with which he loves his spouses. In a word, he is so loving, so perfect in all virtues, and at the same time so courteous and affable, that he is of all spouses the most dear and amiable. "There is nothing," says St. Eucherius, "More glorious, nothing more beautiful, nothing more magnificent, than he is." "These happy virgins, then," says St. Ignatius, Martyr, "Who are consecrated to Jesus Christ, may be assured that they have obtained the most beautiful, the most noble, the most opulent and most amiable spouse that can be found in heaven or on earth."

Hence Blessed Clare of Montevallo used to say that her virginity was so dear to her, that rather than lose it she would be content to suffer the pains of hell during her whole life. Hence, as we learn from St. Ambrose, the glorious virgin St. Agnes, when to her was offered for husband the son of the Roman Prefect, justly answered that she had found a better spouse.

St. Domitilla, the emperors niece, through a love of virginity refused the hand of Count Aurelian; and when it was argued that she might lawfully marry him, because, although a Gentile, he would allow her to remain a Christian, she replied: "If to a young woman were offered the choice of a monarch or a peasant, which would she prefer? If I marry Aurelian, I must renounce the nuptials of the King of heaven, and would not that be the extreme of folly? You may, therefore, tell the count that I cannot accede to his proposal." Thus she preserved her virginity, which she had consecrated to Jesus Christ; and rather than prove unfaithful to her divine spouse, she suffered to be burned alive by her barbarous lover.

The holy virgin St. Susanna made a similar reply to the Emperor Diocletian, who offered her the title of Empress, on the condition that she would marry his son- in-law Maximin, whom he had created Cæsar. In punishment of her refusal she was rewarded with the crown of martyrdom.

Many other holy virgins have declined the nuptials of earthly mon- archs to become the spouses of Jesus Christ. Thus blessed Jane, the Infanta of Portugal, refused the hand of Louis XI. King of France; Blessed Agnes, that of the Emperor Ferdinand II; and Elizabeth, the daughter and heiress of the King of Hungary, rejected the proposal of marriage with Henry, the Archduke of Austria.

2. How much more Happy are Virgins than Married Women even in this Life.

Besides, the virgin that consecrates herself to Jesus Christ is devoted entirely to God, in body as well as in mind. The unmarried woman says St. Paul, and the virgin-thinketh on the things of the Lord; that she may be holy both in body and in spirit. But she that is married thinketh on the things of the world, how she may please her husband. Virgins consecrated to God think only of God, and desire only to be- long to him without reserve; but married persons, being of the world, can think of nothing but of the things of the world. Hence the Apostle adds: and this I speak for your profit; not to cast a snare upon you, but for that which is decent, and which may give you power to attend upon the Lord, without impediment? Thus poor worldlings meet with insur- mountable difficulties in the way of virtue; and the more exalted their rank, the greater the obstacles to their sanctification.

To become a saint in the world, it is necessary for the married woman to adopt the means of sanctification, to frequent the sacraments, to make long and frequent mental prayer, to practice many interior and exterior mortifications, to love contempt, humiliations, and poverty; in a word, to make every effort in her power to please God. She must, then, be perfectly detached from the world, and all its goods, and perfectly free from the control and tyranny of human ties. But how can a married person find the time, the opportunities, and helps necessary for recollection, and continual application to the things of God?

She that is married thinketh on the things of the world, how to please her husband. The married woman must provide for her family, educate her children, please her husband, his parents, brothers, and relatives, who are sometimes to her a constant source of trouble. Hence the Apostle says, her heart must be divided, and her affections fixed partly on her husband, partly on her children, and partly on God. What time can she have for continual prayer, for frequent Communion, when, with all her efforts, she is not able to attend to the wants of the house? The husband must be attended; if his directions be neglected, or his commands be not immediately executed, he breaks out into complaints and reproaches. The servants disturb the house, at one time by their clamor or their quarrels, at another by their importunate demands. The children, if small, are a perpetual source of annoyance, either by their cries and screams, or by the endless variety of their wants; if grown up, they are an occasion of still greater inquietude, fears and bitterness, by associating with bad companions, by the dangers to which they are exposed, or the infirmities with which they are afflicted. How, in the midst of so many difficulties and embarrassments, is it possible for the married woman to attend to prayer, or to preserve recollection? And, as to her Communions, they can scarcely be as frequent as once a week. She may indeed have strong desires of sanctification; but to pay great and constant attention to the affairs of her soul will be morally impossible. The very privation of the opportunities of attending to the things of God may be made a source of great merit by patient submission to the divine will, in the unhappy state in which she is placed. All this is indeed possible; but to practice patience and resignation, in the midst of so many troubles and distractions, without the aid of prayer, of spiritual reading, or of the sacraments, will be exceedingly difficult and almost impracticable.

But would to God that seculars were exposed to no other evils than the obstacles to their devotions, to constant prayer, and the frequent use of the sacraments. Their greatest misfortune is to be in continual danger of losing the grace of God and their own immortal souls. They must appear like their equals; they must employ servants, and support their rank. They must go abroad to visit their friends, and in these visits they must converse with a variety of characters. At home they must hold constant intercourse with their own families, with their relatives, and with the friends of their husband. Oh, how great on such occasions is the danger of losing God! This is not understood by young persons, but it is well known to those who are settled in the world, and who are daily exposed to such dangers.

Oh, how unhappy and miserable is the life of the generality of married persons! I have known the circumstances, the feelings and disposi-tions, of numberless married persons, from the highest to the lowest classes of society, and how few of them were content! The bad treat-ment of husbands, the disaffection of children, the wants of the fam-ily, the control of relatives, the pains of childbirth, which are always accompanied with danger of death, the scruples and anxiety of con-science regarding the flight of occasions, and the education of children, plunge poor seculars into endless troubles and agitation, and fill their souls with continual regret for not having been called to a happier and more holy state. God grant that, in the midst of such troubles and agi-tation, many of them may not lose their immortal souls, and that, along with passing through a hell in this life, they may not be condemned to an eternity of torments in the next. Such is the unhappy condition of many of those who have engaged in the married state.

But you will ask, Are there no saints among so many thousands of married persons? I answer, that there are some who sanctify them-selves in the world by suffering a continual martyrdom, by bearing, for God's sake, all crosses and troubles with patience and cheerful-ness, and by peacefully and lovingly offering themselves in all things to God. There are some who attain this high degree of perfection: but they are as rare as white flies. And you will find that such holy souls are always employed in works of penance, and that they continually aspire after the sanctity and disengagement of those who have consecrated their virginity to Jesus Christ, devoted their lives to the glory of God, and have embraced a state of constant happiness.

The state, then, of virgins consecrated to Jesus Christ, and who are entirely devoted to his divine love, is of all states the most happy and sublime. They are free from the dangers to which married persons are necessarily exposed. Their affections are not fixed on their families, nor on men of the world, nor on goods of the earth, nor on the dress and vanities of women. To appear like their equals, and to please their husbands, married persons must wear rich apparel and costly orna-ments; but a virgin consecrated to Jesus Christ only requires a garment which will cover her body. In her, vanity of dress or the decoration of her person would be a scandalous exhibition. Besides, consecrated virgins are not troubled with the cares of a house, a family, and a hus-band; their sole concern, the only desire of their hearts, is to please Je-sus Christ, to whom they have dedicated their souls and bodies, and all their affections. They are unshackled by worldly ties, by subjection to friends or to relatives, and are far removed from the noise and tumult of the world. Hence they have more time and better opportunities for prayer, spiritual reading, and frequent Communion. Their minds are more free to think on the affairs of their soul, and to practice recollec-tion and union with God.

"She that is a virgin," says Theodoret, "Has her mind free from use-less thoughts." A religious, then, has no other occupation than to hold constant and familial converse with God. Œcumenius, in his commen-tary on the words of St. Paul, that she may be holy both in body and in spirit, says, "That her body is sanctified by chastity and her spirit by familiarity with God." St. Anselm says that in the mere exemption from the cares of the world, to think on the things of the Lord, virgins receive an abundant compensation for all their temporal sacrifices. Hence the saint adds, that virgins consecrated to God not only shall receive great glory in heaven, but shall be also rewarded beforehand by the enjoyment of continual peace on earth.

3. Excellence of Virginity.

Virgins who aspire to perfection are the beloved of Jesus Christ, be-cause they have consecrated to him their bodies and their souls, and seek nothing in this life but to do his holy will. St. John, because he was a virgin, was called the beloved disciple of Jesus: "Whom Jesus loved." Hence in the divine office we read of him that he was chosen, a virgin, by the Lord, and of all the apostles was the most beloved.

Virgins are called the first-fruits of God. For, says St. John, they are virgins. These follow the Lamb whithersoever he goeth. These were purchased from among men, the first-fruits to God, and to the Lamb. But why are virgins called the first-fruits of God? Because, says Cardinal Hugo, in his commentary on the preceding passage, as first fruits are the most delicious, so virgins consecrated to God are most pleasing and dear to him.

The spouse in the canticles feedeth among the lilies. One of the sacred interpreters, explaining these words, says, that "As the devil revels in the uncleanness of lust, so Christ feeds on the lilies of chastity." Venerable Bede asserts that the hymn of the virgins is more agreeable to the Lamb than that of all the other saints.

So great is the excellence of virginity, that the Holy Ghost says, no price is worthy of a continent soul. Hence Cardinal Hugo teaches that, in the other vows, a dispensation is sometimes granted, but not in the vow of chastity; because such is the value of continence, that its loss cannot be compensated. The price of chastity may be estimated by the answer of Mary to the Archangel Gabriel: How shall this be done, because I know not man? By these words she showed her readiness to renounce the offered dignity of Mother of God rather than forfeit her virginal integrity.

St. Cyprian says that "Virginity is the queen of all virtues and the possession of every good." Speaking of virginity, St. Ephrem says, "If you have loved it, you will be favored by the Lord in all things." St. Bernardine of Sienna teaches that "Virginity prepares the soul to see her spouse Jesus by faith in this life, and by glory in the next." Oh, what an immense weight of glory is prepared for those who dedicate their virginity to Jesus Christ!

The Redeemer showed to that great servant of God, Lucretia Orsini, the sublime dignity to which consecrated virgins are raised in heaven. In the vision she exclaimed, "Oh, how dear are virgins to God and to Mary!" Theologians teach that virgins are honored in heaven with a special crown of glory and of joy. And no man, says St. John, could say the canticle, but those hundred and forty-four thousand who were purchased from the earth. St. Augustine, explaining this passage, says that the joys of the virgins are not given to the other saints of God.

4. Means to preserve Virginal Purity.

But to be the virginal spouse of Jesus Christ it is not sufficient to be a virgin; it is necessary to be a prudent virgin, and to carry a lamp always filled with oil, that is, a heart inflamed with the love of God. The foolish virgins were indeed virgins; but, because their lamps were extinguished, they were shut out from the marriage, and were told by the bridegroom that he knew them not. A virgin, then, who wishes to be a true spouse of the Redeemer, ought to desire and seek nothing but to love and please Jesus Christ. "If," says St. Bernard, "He become a spouse, he will change his language, and say: If I am a spouse, where is my love? God requires to be feared as a master, to be honored as a father, and to be loved as a spouse."

To be a faithful lover of Jesus Christ her spouse, and to preserve unsullied the lily of her purity, a virgin must adopt the necessary means. The principal means of acquiring an ardent love of Christ are mental prayer, Communion, mortification, retirement. Although each of these means is fully discussed in another part of this work, still a brief notice of them in this place will not be irrelevant.

The first means to love Jesus Christ is mental prayer. Mental prayer is that blessed furnace in which the soul is inflamed with divine love. And, says holy David, in my meditation a fire shall flame out. In temptations against purity, the immediate invocation of the divine aid is absolutely necessary. The Venerable Sister Cecilia Gastelli used to say, that without prayer, chastity cannot be preserved. As I knew, says Solomon, that I could not otherwise be continent, except God gave it, I went to the Lord and besought him with my whole heart.

The second means is the Holy Communion. This, says St. Bonaventure, is the cellar of wine into which the King of heaven brings his spouses "To set in order charity," in their hearts, teaching them to love God above all things, and their neighbors as themselves.

The third means is mortification. As the lily among the thorns, so is my love among the daughters. As the lily blooms among the thorns, so virginity is preserved only in the midst of mortification. St. Mary Magdalene de Pazzi used to say that, "Chastity flourishes only among thorns." To fulfill the obligations of the religious state, in the midst of amusements, worldly attachments, and conversations with seculars, in the midst of sensual gratifications, of indulgence of the palate, of the eyes, and of the ears, is utterly impossible. Religious purity can be preserved only among the thorns of mortification. "A virgin," says St. Basil, "Should be immaculate in all things—in the tongue, the ears, the eyes, the touch, and above all in the mind." To be faithful to her spouse, a virgin must be immaculate in her tongue by the delicacy of her language, and by abstinence as much as possible from conversations with men; she must be immaculate in the ears, by shunning, like death itself, all worldly discourses; immaculate in her eyes by the modesty of her looks, always restrained so as never to fix them on the face of a man; immaculate in the touch, always observing the greatest caution towards herself and others; but, above all, immaculate in her soul, rejecting every unchaste thought, as soon as it is presented to the mind, by invoking the assistance of Jesus and Mary. As a queen tempted by a vile slave contemptuously turns away without condescending to notice him, so the spouse of Jesus Christ should reject with disdain and horror every immodest thought which intrudes itself into the mind. To preserve her soul and body free from stain, she must also chastise her flesh, by fasting, abstinence, by disciplines and other penitential works. And if she has not health or strength to practice such mortifications, she ought at least to bear in peace her infirmities and pains, and to accept cheerfully the contempt and ill-treatment that she receives from others. The spouse follows the Lamb whithersoever he goeth. Jesus Christ has not walked before us in the way of pleasures and honors; no, he has chosen the rugged path of pains and opprobrium. Hence many holy virgins have loved sufferings and contempt, and have joyfully encountered torments and death.

The fourth means is retirement. Thy cheeks are beautiful as the turtle doves. The spouse in the canticle is compared to the turtle, because the turtle avoids the company of other birds, and delights in solitude. A religious appears beautiful in the eyes of Jesus Christ only in retirement and at a distance from the society of men. St. Mary Magdalene de Pazzi was accustomed to say that chastity is a plant that thrives only in inclosed gardens and in the midst of thorns. A religious should observe not only the enclosure of the convent, but also that of the senses; and therefore, unless compelled by duty or by obedience, she should never approach the door, the grate, or the windows. "Jesus," says St. Jerome, in his epistle to Eustochia, "Is a jealous spouse: he is unwilling that your face be seen by others." The Saviour, then, is greatly displeased with the conduct of those who seek to appear before seculars, and delight in their conversation. Virgins distinguished for sanctity always seek retirement; and whenever it is necessary to go into the company of men, they endeavor to deform their persons, so as to excite feelings of aversion, rather than sentiments of affection. Bollandus relates that St. Andregesma, a virgin, besought the Almighty to change her beauty into deformity. Her prayer was heard, and she was instantly covered with a leprosy which made her an object of horror to all who beheld her. James of Vibriaco says that St. Euphemia, to free herself from the attention of a person who was greatly attached to her, cut off her nose and lips, saying, "Vain beauty, you shall be no longer an occasion of sin to me." Baronius relates that St. Ebba, abbess of the convent of Collingamens, fearing an invasion of the barbarians, cut off her nose and upper lip, and that all the other nuns, amounting to thirty in number, followed her example. The barbarians came, and, seeing the religious so deformed, set fire to the convent and burned them alive. The Church has placed all these holy virgins in the catalogue of her martyrs. St. Antonine cites a similar incident as having happened in 1291 in Palestine, in a convent of the Clares. It would not be lawful for others to imitate the heroic conduct of these saints: they acted from an impulse of the Holy Ghost. But from their example religious may learn how much virgins inflamed with the love of Jesus Christ shun the company and despise the esteem and affections of men. A religious should conceal herself as much as possible from the view of men. At her espousals with Jesus Christ she renounced the world and all its vanities. Such is the compact which she made with him, when, in answer to the question, "Do you renounce this world and all its vanities?" she answered, "I renounce them." St. Jerome, in his eighth epistle to Demetria, says: "Now, since you have left the world, fulfill your solemn engagements, and do not conform to this world."

In a word, if you desire to possess the purity which becomes the spouse of Jesus, you must cut off all dangerous occasions: you must cherish a holy ignorance of all that is opposed to chastity, and abstain from reading whatever has the slightest tendency to sully the soul. If, at the grate, language unbecoming your state be ever uttered, you should instantly withdraw, or change the subject of conversation, otherwise you shall have much to suffer from the temptations by which you will be assailed. If fire does not always burn, it never fails to scorch. A look, an endearing expression, or a trifling gift often enkindles a spark which soon becomes an infernal, a consuming fire. In all that regards purity, too much caution cannot be observed. Trust not in your own strength; believe one who has known a thousand cases in which that sublime virtue was lost by exposure to danger. If you say, I will expose myself so far, and no farther, be assured that before you perceive your danger you will be plunged into the abyss. If in voluntary perils you have hitherto escaped ruin, thank God for your preservation, but tremble for the future. Saints have retired into the deserts to preserve the virtue of chastity; and will you rush into unnecessary danger? It is particularly difficult for those who are in the vigour of youth to practice immaculate purity while the converse with young men on worldly subjects, jesting with them, and smiling at expressions which ought to cover them with shame. Fly, fly from all such occasions. Explain to the confessor not only your temptations, but also the occasions of them, and ask his advice about the best means of removing them.

5. The Spouse of Jesus Christ should be entirely His.

The day on which a virgin is espoused to Jesus Christ is to him a day of great joy. Go forth, he says in the canticles, daughters of Sion, and see King Solomon in the diadem, wherewith his mother crowned him on the day of his espousals, and the day of the joy of his heart. Yes, the day on which a religious consecrates her virginity to Jesus Christ is to him a day of triumph and exultation, provided she dedicates her whole being to his love and glory, and prepares herself in a becoming manner for her espousals with the God of holiness. On such days the Redeemer calls on all Paradise to rejoice with him. Let us be glad and rejoice, and give glory to him: for the marriage of the Lamb is come, and his wife hath prepared herself.

The ornaments which the Lamb requires in his spouses are the virtues recommended in the Gospel, but particularly charity and purity. He will make thee chains of gold inlaid with silver? These chains of gold, inlaid with silver, signify the virtues of charity and chastity. These, as

21

we learn from St. Agnes, are the garments and jewels with which the Lamb decorates his spouse. He surrounded my right hand and my neck with precious stones. The Lord clothed me with a garment of golden texture, and adorned me with immense necklaces.

Seculars direct all their attention to the things of the world; but the spouses of Jesus Christ seek God, and God alone. Of religious it is written, This is the generation of them that seek him. These holy virgins, whom you see confined within their convent poor and humble, are the generation of blessed souls who seek nothing on this earth but God's glory. "You then, O consecrated virgins," says St. Thomas of Villanova, "Should contend with one another, not about the preeminence of your birth, the superiority of your talents, nor the amplitude of your fortunes; but for the first place in the esteem and affections of Christ Jesus, and for the highest claim to familiarity with him, to humility and obedience." St. Jerome, in one of his letters to Eustochia, who wished to consecrate her virginity to Jesus Christ, writes: "Since, my child, you come to the service of God, the Holy Ghost admonishes you to stand in justice, and to prepare your soul for temptation; to practice patience in humility: for gold is tried in the fire. No one can serve two masters. You will, therefore, despise the world, and, espoused to Christ, you will sing, The Lord is my portion forever." Religious on the day of profession change their names to show that on that day they die to the world, to live to Christ, who died for them. All Christians should, according to St. Paul, die to themselves, and live only to Jesus Christ. And Christ died for all: that they also, who live, may not now live to themselves, but unto him who died for them and rose again. But if all do not attend to the instructions of the Apostle, religious at least, who are the chosen spouses of the Redeemer, should fulfill them.

The Venerable Sister Francis Farnese regarded the remembrance of being the spouses of Jesus Christ as the most powerful means of exciting her religious to fervor and perfection. It is certain, she would say to them, that since you have been raised to the dignity of his spouses, God has chosen each one of you to be a saint. St. Augustine, addressing a religious, says: O happy virgin, if you know not your dignity, endeavor to estimate its excellence by the doctrine of the saints. You have the most beautiful of spouses, who, by selecting you from among thousands, and making you his spouse, has given you a pledge of affection, from which you may learn how ardent should be your love for him. And St. Bernard, in his fortieth sermon on the Canticle of Canticles, addressing consecrated virgins, says: "Have nothing to do with the world: forget all things: reserve yourself for the Lord, whom, from all things, you have chosen for your inheritance." Cease, O spouse of Jesus, to think of yourself or of the world: you belong no longer to yourself or to the world, but to that God to whom you are consecrated. Forget all things, and attend to him only who has chosen you for his spouse. "Your God," continues the saint, "Has chosen you; and how many have been cast away who could not obtain the grace which has been bestowed on you? Your Redeemer and your Spouse has preferred you before all these; not because you were more worthy, but because he loved you more than them." You have not chosen God, but God has first chosen you for his spouse. How many has he left in the world who could not obtain the dignity to which you have been raised. He has chosen you in preference to them; he has called you to his tabernacle, not because you had superior claims, but because his love for you was greater than his love for them. The saint then concludes: "Wherefore, saith the Lord: 'Behold, thy time is the time of lovers.' Reflecting, then, upon these things in your soul, place all your hope and affection in Jesus, your spouse, who has loved you with an everlasting love, and in mercy has drawn you to himself."

Whenever, then, O spouse of Jesus, the world solicits your affection, answer in the words of St. Agnes: "Depart from me, food of death; I am already espoused to another lover." All the affections of my heart shall be reserved for my God, who has loved me before I could love him. A religious, when she receives the veil on the day of profession, makes use of similar language. "He has placed," she says, "A seal on my forehead, that I admit no lover but him." My spouse has covered my face with this veil, that not seeing, and not being seen, I may have no lover but Jesus. St. Jerome exhorts religious to take a holy pride in this exalted dignity of spouses of the Redeemer. "Learn," he says, "O spouse of God, a holy pride. Know that you are raised above worldlings, and say: I have found him whom my soul sought: I will hold him, and will not let him go." Seculars glory in their nuptials with men of rank and fortune; but you, who are the spouse of the King of heaven, can boast of better espousals. Say, then, with pride and with joy: I have found the object of my affections; I will embrace him with love, and will not permit him to depart from me. It is love that unites the soul with God. But above all things, says St. Paul, have charity, which is the bond of perfection.

Sublime, indeed, is the dignity of virgins: each of them can glory, and say, "I am espoused to Him whom the angels serve." He to whom the celestial spirits ardently desire to minister is my spouse; with his own ring he has pledged me, and with a crown has adorned me as his own spouse. My Creator, the Sovereign of the universe, has espoused me, and, conferring upon me a crown, has raised me to the dignity of a queen. But, O sacred virgin, remember that, while you remain on earth this crown is not eternal, and that by your negligence it may be lost. Hold fast that which thou hast, that no man take thy crown. Hold fast your crown, that no one may be able to snatch it from you; disengage yourself from all affection to creatures; unite yourself more and more every day to Jesus Christ by love, by petitions, and by continual supplication that he may never suffer you to abandon him. "Jesus, my spouse, never permit me to be separated from thee." And, when creatures seek to take possession of your heart, and to banish the Son of God from your soul, trust in the divine aid, and say with the Apostle, Who shall separate us from the love of Christ? Neither life, nor death, nor any other creature shall be able to separate us from the love of God, which is in Christ Jesus our Lord.

O Jesus, my Saviour and my God, how have I merited this singular favor, that while Thou hast left in the world so many innocent souls, Thou shouldst have chosen me, a sinner, for Thy spouse, to live in Thy own house here on earth, that I might afterwards receive from Thee an eternal crown in heaven? O Lord, since Thou hast bestowed upon me so great a grace, grant me light to understand its value, and strength to be always grateful for it, and with my whole soul to correspond to the love which Thou hast borne me. Thou hast chosen me, in preference to many others: it is my duty to prefer Thee to all. Thou hast given Thyself entirely to me; it is but just that I present my whole being to Thee, and that Thou be the sole object of all my love, and of all my affections. Yes, my Jesus, I love Thee above all things: I desire to love Thee alone. Thou hast given Thyself to me without reserve: I offer myself entirely to Thee. I beseech Thee to accept this oblation, and not to refuse the affections of a heart that once loved creatures, and even preferred them before Thee, the sovereign good. Accept and preserve my soul and body. Without Thy assistance I can do nothing: without it I shall certainly betray Thee. Since Thou hast chosen me for Thy spouse, make me a faithful and grateful spouse. O sacred fire, burning in the heart of Jesus, inflame my soul, and destroy in my heart every affection which is not for him; make me live only to love this my amiable spouse, who has given his life to be loved by me.

O Mary, Mother of God, since I am the spouse of thy Son, thou art not only my queen, but my mother. And since it was by thy intercession that I have been detached from the world, conducted into this house of God, and made the spouse of thy Son, assist me now, and do not abandon me forever. Grant that my life and death may be worthy the spouse of Jesus Christ.

CHAPTER II.

THE ADVANTAGES OF THE RELIGIOUS STATE.

1. The Religious State is like the Promised Land; it is Paradise on Earth; it is a Great Grace.

WELL may the words of the Canticle of Moses and of the children of Israel, after their delivery from the tyranny of Pharaoh and the bondage of Egypt, be applied to religious: In thy mercy thou hast been a leader to the people which thou hast redeemed, and in thy strength thou hast carried them to thy holy habitation. As the Hebrews compared with the Egyptians were, in the Old Law, the beloved people of God; so religious, contrasted with seculars, are, in the New Law, the chosen spouses of the Saviour. As the Hebrews went forth from Egypt, a land of labor and of slavery, where God was not known, so religious retire from the world, which gives to its servants no other recompense than pains and bitterness, and in which God is but little known. Finally, as the Hebrews in the desert were guided by a pillar of fire to the land of promise, so the spouses of Jesus Christ are conducted, by the light of the Holy Ghost, into the sanctuary of religion—the bright image of the promised land of heaven.

In heaven there is no self-will; no thirst for earthly riches or for sensual pleasures; and from the cloister these pernicious desires, by means of the holy vows of obedience, poverty, and chastity, are effectually excluded. In heaven, to praise God is the constant occupation of the saints, and in religion every action of the Community is referred to the glory of his name. "You praise God," says St. Augustine, "By the discharge of every duty; you praise him when you eat or drink; you praise him when you rest or sleep." You, O sacred virgin, praise the Lord by regulating the affairs of the convent, by assisting in the sacristy, at the turn, or at the door; you praise the Lord when you go to table; you praise him when you retire to rest and sleep; you praise him in every action of your life. Lastly, in heaven the saints enjoy continual peace; because there they find in God the source of every good; and in religion, where God alone is sought, in him is found that peace which surpasses all understanding, and that content which the world cannot give.

Well, then, might St. Mary Magdalene de Pazzi say that the spouse of Jesus should have a high esteem and veneration for her holy state, since after baptism a vocation to religion is the greatest grace which God can bestow. You, then, who are religious should hold the religious state in higher estimation than all the dignities and kingdoms of the earth. In that holy state you are preserved from sins which you would commit in the world; there you are constantly occupied in holy exercises; there you meet every day with numberless opportunities of meriting an eternal crown. In this life religion makes you the spouse of a God, and in the next will raise you to the rank of queen in the eternal kingdom of his glory. How did you merit to be called to that holy state, in preference to so many others who had stronger claims than you? Black, indeed, must be your ingratitude if, for the benefit of your vocation, you do not thank God every day with all the affections of your soul.

2. Advantages of the Religious State according to St. Bernard.

The advantages of the religious state cannot be better described than in the words of St. Bernard: "Is not that a holy state in which a man lives more purely, falls more rarely, rises more speedily, walks more cautiously, is bedewed with the waters of grace more frequently, rests more securely, dies more confidently, is cleansed more quickly, and rewarded more abundantly?" Let us examine these advantages separately, and meditate on the great treasures which each of them contains. Vivit purius. —"A religious lives more purely."

Surely all the works of religious are in themselves most pure and acceptable before God. Purity of action consists principally in purity of intention, or in a pure motive of pleasing God. Hence our actions will be agreeable to God in proportion to their conformity to his holy will, and to their freedom from the corruption of self-will. The actions of a secular, however holy and fervent she may be, partake more of self-will than those of religious. Seculars pray, communicate, hear Mass, read, take the discipline, and recite the divine Office when they please. But a religious performs these duties at the time prescribed by obedience—that is, by the holy will of God. For in her Rule and in the commands of her Superior she hears his voice. Hence a religious, by obedience to her Rule and to her Superior, merits an eternal reward, not only by her prayers and by the performance of her spiritual duties, but also by her labors, her recreations, and attendance at the turn; by her meals, her amusements, her words, and her repose. For, since the performance of all these duties is dictated by obedience, and not by self-will, she does in each the holy will of God, and by each she earns an everlasting crown.

Oh, how often does self-will vitiate the most holy actions? Alas, to how many, on the day of judgment, when they shall ask, in the words of Isaias, the reward of their labors, Why have we fasted, and thou hast not regarded?—Have we humbled our souls, and thou hast not taken notice?—To how many, I say, will the Almighty Judge answer, Behold, in the day of your fast, your own will is found. What, he will say, do you demand a reward? Have you not, in doing your own will, already received the recompense of your toils? Have you not, in all your duties, in all your works of penance, sought the indulgence of your own inclinations, rather than the fulfillment of my will?

Abbot Gilbert says that the meanest work of a religious is more meritorious in the sight of God than the most heroic action of a secular. St. Bernard asserts that if a person in the world did the fourth part of what is ordinarily done by religious, she would be venerated as a saint. And has not experience shown that the virtues of many whose sanctity shone resplendent in the world faded away before the bright examples of the fervent souls whom, on entering religion, they found in the cloister? A religious, then, because in all her actions she does the will of God, can truly say that she belongs entirely to him. The Venerable Mother Mary of Jesus, foundress of the convent of Toulouse, used to say that for two reasons she entertained a high esteem for her vocation: first, because a religious enjoys the society of Jesus Christ, who, in the holy sacrament, dwells with her in the same habitation; secondly, because a religious having by the vow of obedience sacrificed her own will and her whole being to God, she belongs unreservedly to him.

Cadit rarius.—"A religious falls more rarely."

Religious are certainly less exposed to the danger of sin than seculars. Almighty God represented the world to St. Anthony, and before him to St. John the Evangelist, as a place full of snares. Hence, the holy Apostle said, that in the world there is nothing but the concupiscence of the flesh, or of carnal pleasures; the concupiscence of the eyes, or of

28

earthly riches; and the pride of life, or worldly honors, which swell the heart with petulance and pride. In religion, by means of the holy vows, these poisoned sources of sin are cut off. By the vow of chastity all the pleasures of sense are forever abandoned; by the vow of poverty the desire of riches is perfectly eradicated; and by the vow of obedience the ambition of empty honors is utterly extinguished.

It is, indeed, possible for a Christian to live in the world without any attachment to its goods; but it is difficult to dwell in the midst of pestilence and to escape contagion. The whole world, says St. John, is seated in wickedness. St. Ambrose, in his comment on this passage, says, that they who remain in the world live under the miserable and cruel despotism of sin. The atmosphere of the world is noxious and pestilential, whosoever breathes it, easily catches spiritual infection. Human respect, bad example, and evil conversations are powerful incitements to earthly attachments and to estrangement of the soul from God. Everyone knows that the damnation of numberless souls is attributable to the occasions of sin so common in the world. From these occasions religious who live in the retirement of the cloister are far removed. Hence St. Mary Magdalene de Pazzi was accustomed to embrace the walls of her convent, saying, "O blessed walls! O blessed walls, from how many dangers do you preserve me." Hence, also, Blessed Mary Magdalene of Orsini, whenever she saw a religious laugh, used to say: "Laugh and rejoice, dear Sister, for you have reason to be happy, being far away from the dangers of the world."

Surgit velocius. "A religious rises more speedily."

If a religious should be so unfortunate as to fall into sin, she has the most efficacious helps to rise again. Her Rule which obliges her to frequent the holy sacrament of penance; her meditations, in which she is reminded of the eternal truths; the good examples of her saintly companions, and the reproofs of her Superiors, are powerful helps to rise from her fallen state. Woe, says the Holy Ghost, to him that is alone; for when he falleth he hath none to lift him up. If a secular forsake the path of virtue, he seldom finds a friend to admonish and correct him, and is therefore exposed to great danger of persevering and dying in his sins. But in religion, if one fall he shall be supported by the other. If a religious commit a fault, her companions assist her to correct and repair it. "She," says St. Thomas, "Is assisted by her companions to rise again."

Incedit cautius,—"A religious walks more cautiously."

Religious enjoy far greater spiritual advantages than the first princes or monarchs of the earth. Kings, indeed, abound in riches, honors, and pleasures, but no one will dare to correct their faults, or to point out their duties. All abstain from mentioning to them their defects, through fear of incurring their displeasure; and to secure their esteem many even go so far as to applaud their vices. But if a religious go astray, her error will be instantly corrected; her Superiors and companions in religion will not fail to admonish her, and to point out her danger; and even the good example of her Sisters will remind her continually of the transgression into which she has fallen. Surely a Christian, who believes that eternal life is the one thing necessary, should set a higher value upon these helps for salvation than upon all the dignities and kingdoms of the earth.

As the world presents to seculars innumerable obstacles to virtue, so the cloister holds out to religious continual preventives of sin. In religion, the great care which is taken to prevent light faults is a strong bulwark against the commission of grievous transgressions. If a religious resist temptations to venial sin, she merits by that resistance additional strength to conquer temptations to mortal sin; but if, through frailty, she sometimes yields to them, all is not lost—the evil is easily repaired. Even then the enemy does not get possession of her soul; at most he only succeeds in taking some unimportant outpost, from which he may be easily driven; while by such defeats she is taught the necessity of greater vigilance and of stronger defenses against future attacks. She is convinced of her own weakness, and being humbled and rendered diffident of her own powers, she recurs more frequently, and with more confidence, to Jesus Christ and his holy Mother. Thus, from these falls, the religious sustains no serious injury; since, as soon as she is humbled before the Lord, he stretches forth his all-powerful arm to raise her up. When he shall fall he shall not be bruised, for the Lord putteth his hand under him. On the contrary, such victories over her weakness contribute to inspire greater diffidence in herself, and greater confidence in God. Blessed Egidius, of the Order of St. Francis, used to say that one degree of grace in religion is better than ten in the world; because in religion it is easy to profit by grace and hard to loose it; while in the world grace fructifies with difficulty and is lost with facility.

Irroratur frequentius.—"A religious is bedewed more frequently."

O God, with what internal illuminations, spiritual delights, and expressions of love does Jesus refresh his spouses at prayer, Communion, in presence of the holy sacrament, and in the cell before the crucifix! Christians in the world are like plants in a barren land, on which but little of the dew of heaven falls, and from that little the soil for want of proper cultivation seldom derives fertility Poor seculars! They desire to devote more time to prayer, to receive the holy Eucharist, and to hear the word of God more frequently; they long for greater solitude, for more recollection, and a more intimate union of their souls with God. But temporal affairs, human ties, visits of friends, and restraints of the world place these means of sanctification almost beyond their reach. But religious are like trees planted in a fruitful soil, which is continually and abundantly watered with the dews of heaven. In the cloister, the Lord continually comforts and animates his spouses by infusing interior lights and consolations during the time of meditation, sermons, and spiritual readings, and even by means of the good example of their Sisters. Well, then, might Mother Catharine of Jesus, of the holy Order of St. Teresa, say, when reminded of the labors she had endured in the foundation of a convent: "God has rewarded me abundantly, by permitting me to spend one hour in religion, in the house of his holy mother."

Quiescit securius.—"A religious rests more securely."

Worldly goods can never satisfy the cravings of the human soul. The brute creation, being destined only for this world, is content with the goods of the earth, but being made for God, man can never enjoy happiness except in the possession of the divinity. The experience of ages proves this truth; for if the goods of this life could content the heart of man, kings and princes, who abound in riches, honors, and carnal pleasures, should spend their days in pure unalloyed bliss and felicity. But history and experience attest that they are the most unhappy and discontented of men; and that riches and dignities are always the fertile sources of fears, of troubles, and of bitterness. The Emperor Theodosius entered one day, unknown, into the cell of a solitary monk, and

31

after some conversation said: "Father do you know who I am? I am the Emperor Theodosius." He then added: "Oh, how happy are you, who lead here on earth a life of contentment, free from the cares and woes of the world. I am a Sovereign of the earth, but be assured, Father, that I never dine in peace."

But how can the world, a place of treachery, of jealousies, of fears and commotions, give peace to man? In the world, indeed, there are certain wretched pleasures which perplex rather than content the soul; which delight the senses for a moment, but leave lasting anguish and remorse behind. Hence the more exalted and honourable the rank and station a man holds in the world, the greater is his uneasiness and the more racking his discontent; for earthly dignities, in proportion to their elevation, are accompanied with cares and contradictions. We may, then, conclude that the world, in which the heart-rending passions of ambition, avarice, and the love of pleasures, exercise a cruel tyranny over the human race, must be a place not of ease and happiness, but of inquietude and torture. Its goods can never be possessed in such a way that they may be had in the manner and at the time we desire their possession; and when enjoyed, instead of infusing content and peace into the soul, they drench it with the bitterness of gall. Hence, whosoever is satiated with earthly goods is saturated with wormwood and poison.

Happy, then, the religious who loves God, and knows how to estimate the favour which he bestowed upon her in calling her from the world and placing her in religion; where conquering, by holy mortification, her rebellious passions, and practicing continual self-denial, she enjoys that peace which, according to the Apostle, exceeds all the delights of sensual gratification: The peace of God, which surpasseth all understanding. Find me, if you can, among those seculars on whom fortune has lavished her choicest gifts, or even among the first princesses or queens of the earth, a soul more happy or content than a religious divested of every worldly affection, and intent only on pleasing God? She is not rendered unhappy by poverty, for she preferred it before all the riches of the earth; she has voluntarily chosen it, and rejoices in its privations; nor by the mortification of the senses, for she entered religion to die to the world and to herself; nor by the restraints of obedience, for she knows that the renunciation of self-will is the most acceptable sacrifice she could offer to God. She is not afflicted at her humiliations, because it was to be despised that she came into the house of God. I have chosen to be an abject in the house of my God, rather than dwell in the tabernacles of sinners. The enclosure is to her rather a source of consolation than of sorrow; because it frees her from the cares and dangers of the world. To serve the Community, to be treated with contempt, or to be afflicted with infirmities, does not trouble the tranquility of her soul, because she knows that all these make her more dear to Jesus Christ. Finally, the observance of her Rule does not interrupt the joy of a religious, because the labors and burdens which it imposes, however numerous and oppressive they may be, are but the wings of the dove which are necessary to fly towards God and be united with him. Oh, how happy and delightful is the state of a religious whose heart is not divided, and who can say with St. Francis: "My God and my all."

It is true that, even in the cloister, there are some discontented souls; for even in religion there are some who do not live as religious ought to live. To be a good religious and to be content are one and the same thing; for the happiness of a religious consists in a constant and perfect union of her will with the adorable will of God. Whosoever is not united with him cannot be happy; for God cannot infuse his consolations into a soul that resists his divine will. I have been accustomed to say, that a religious in her convent enjoys a foretaste of paradise or suffers an anticipation of hell. To endure the pains of hell is to be separated from God; to be forced against the inclinations of nature to do the will of others; to be distrusted, despised, reproved, and chastised by those with whom we live; to be shut up in a place of confinement, from which it is impossible to escape; in a word, it is to be in continual torture without a moment's peace. Such is the miserable condition of a bad religious; and therefore she suffers on earth an anticipation of the torments of hell. The happiness of paradise consists in an exemption from the cares and afflictions of the world, in the conversations of the saints, in a perfect union with God, and the enjoyment of continual peace in God. A perfect religious possesses all these blessings, and therefore receives in this life a foretaste of paradise.

The perfect spouses of Jesus have, indeed, their crosses to carry here below; for this life is a state of merit, and consequently of suffering. The inconveniences of living in Community are burdensome; the reproofs of Superiors, and the refusals of permission, galling; the mortification of the senses, painful; and the contradiction and contempt of companions, intolerable to self-love. But to a religious who desires to belong entirely to God all these occasions of suffering are so many sources of consolation and delight; for she knows that by embracing pain she offers a sweet odour to God. St. Bonaventure says that the love of God is like honey, which sweetens everything that is bitter. The Venerable Cæsar da Bustis addressed a nephew who had entered religion in the following words: "My dear nephew, when you look at the heavens, think of paradise; when you see the world, reflect on hell, where the damned endure eternal torments without a moments enjoyment; when you behold your convent, remember purgatory, where many just souls suffer in peace and with a certainty of eternal life." And what more delightful than to suffer (if suffering it can be called) with a tranquil conscience, than to suffer in favour with God, and with an assurance that every pain will one day become a gem in an everlasting crown? Ah, the brightest jewels in the diadems of the saints are the sufferings which they endured in this life with patience and resignation.

Our God is faithful to his promises, and grateful beyond measure. He knows how to remunerate his servants, even in this life, by interior sweetness, for the pains which they patiently suffer for his sake. Experience shows that religious who seek consolation and happiness from creatures are always discontented, while they who practice the greatest mortifications enjoy continual peace. Let us, then, be persuaded that neither pleasures of sense, nor honors, nor riches, nor the world with all its goods can make us happy. God alone can content the heart of man. Whoever finds him possesses all things. Hence St. Scholastica said, that if men knew the peace which religious enjoy in retirement, the entire world would become one great convent; and St. Mary Magdalene de Pazzi used to say that they would abandon the delights of the world and force their way into religion. Hence, also, St. Laurence Justinian says that, "God has designedly concealed the happiness of the religious state, because if it were known all would relinquish the world and fly to religion."

The very solitude, silence, and tranquility of the cloister give to a soul that loves God a foretaste of paradise. Father Charles of Lorraine, a Jesuit of royal extraction, used to say that the peace which he enjoyed during a single moment in his cell was an abundant remuneration for the sacrifice that he had made in quitting the world. Such was the happiness which he occasionally experienced in his cell that he would sometimes exult and dance with joy. Blessed Seraphino of Ascoli, a Capuchin, was in the habit of saying that he would not give one foot of his cord for all the kingdoms of the earth. Arnold, a Cistercian, comparing the riches and honors of the court which he had left with, the consolations which he found in religion, exclaimed: "How faithfully fulfilled, O Jesus, is the promise which Thou didst make of rendering a hundred-fold to him who leaves all things for Thy sake!" St. Bernard's monks, who led lives of great penance and austerities, received in their solitude such spiritual delights, that they were afraid they should obtain in this life the reward of their labors.

Let it be your care to unite yourself closely to God; to embrace with peace all the crosses that he sends you; to love what is most perfect; and, when necessary, to do violence to yourself. And that you may be able to accomplish all this, pray continually; pray in your meditations, in your Communions, in your visits to the Blessed Sacrament, and especially when you are tempted by the devil; and you will obtain a place in the number of those fervent souls who are more happy and content than all the princesses and queens and empresses of the earth.

Beg of God to give you the spirit of a perfect religious; that spirit which impels the soul to act, not according to the dictates of nature, but according to the motions of grace, or from the sole motive of pleasing God. Why wear the habit of a religious, if in heart and soul you are a secular, and live according to the maxims of the world? Whosoever profanes the garb of religion by a worldly spirit and a worldly life has an apostate heart. "To maintain," says St. Bernard, "A secular spirit under the habit of religion, is apostasy of heart." The spirit of a religious, then, implies an exact obedience to the rules and to the directions of the Superior, along with a great zeal for the interests of religion. Some religious wish to become saints, but only according to their own caprice; that is, by long silence, prayer, and spiritual reading, without being employed in any of the offices of the Community. Hence, if they are sent to the turn, to the door, or to other distracting occupations, they become impatient; they complain and sometimes obstinately refuse to obey, saying that such offices are to them occasions of sin. Oh, such is not the spirit of a religious. Surely what is conformable to the will of God cannot hurt the soul. The spirit of a religious requires a total detachment from commerce with the world; great love and affection for prayer, for silence, and for recollection; ardent zeal for exact observance; deep abhorrence for sensual indulgence; intense charity towards all men; and, finally, a love of God capable of subduing and of ruling all the passions. Such is the spirit of a perfect religious. Whosoever does not possess this spirit should at least desire it ardently, should do violence to herself, and earnestly beg God's assistance to obtain it. In a word, the spirit of a religious supposes a total disengagement of the heart from everything that is not God and a perfect consecration of the soul to him, and to him alone.

Moritur confidentius.—"A religious dies more confidently."

Some are deterred from entering religion by the apprehension that their abandonment of the world might be afterwards to them a source of regret. But in making choice of a state of life I would advise such persons to reflect not on the pleasures of this life, but on the hour of death, which will determine their happiness or misery for all eternity. And I would ask if, in the world, surrounded by seculars, disturbed by the fondness of children, from whom they are about to be separated forever, perplexed with the care of their worldly affairs, and disturbed by a thousand scruples of conscience, they can expect to die more contented than in the house of God, assisted by their holy companions, who continually speak of God; who pray for them, and console and encourage them in their passage to eternity? Imagine you see, on the one hand, a princess dying in a splendid palace, attended by a retinue of servants, surrounded by her husband, her children, and relatives, and represent to yourself, on the other, a religious expiring in her convent, in a poor cell, mortified, humble; far from her relatives, stripped of property and self-will; and tell me, which of the two, the rich princess or the poor nun, dies more contented? Ah, the enjoyment of riches, of honors, and pleasures in this life do not afford consolation at the hour of death, but rather beget grief and diffidence of salvation; while poverty, humiliations, penitential austerities, and detachment from the world render death sweet and amiable, and give to a Christian increased hopes of attaining that true felicity which shall never terminate.

Jesus Christ has promised that whosoever leaves his house and relatives for God's sake shall enjoy eternal life. And every one that hath left house or brethren, or sisters, or father, or mother, or lands for my sake shall receive a hundred-fold, and shall possess life everlasting. A certain religious, of the Society of Jesus, being observed to smile on his death-bed, some of his brethren who were present began to apprehend that he was not aware of his danger, and asked him why he smiled; he answered: "Why should I not smile, since I am sure of paradise? Has not the Lord himself promised to give eternal life to those who leave the world for his sake? I have long since abandoned all things for the love of him: he cannot violate his own promises. I smile, then, because I confidently expect eternal glory." The same sentiment was expressed long before by St. John Chrysostom, writing to a certain religious. "God," says the saint, "Cannot tell a lie; but he has promised eternal life to those who leave the goods of this world. You have left all these things; why, then, should you doubt the fulfillment of his promise?"

St. Bernard says that "It is very easy to pass from the cell to heaven; because a person who dies in the cell scarcely ever descends into hell, since it seldom happens that a religious perseveres in her cell till death, unless she be predestined to happiness." Hence St. Laurence Justinian says that religion is the gate of paradise; because living in religion, and partaking of its advantages is a great mark of election to glory. No wonder, then, that Gerard, the brother of St. Bernard, when dying in his monastery, began to sing with joy and gladness. God himself says: Blessed are the dead who die in the Lord. And surely religious who by the holy vows, and especially by the vow of obedience, or total renunciation of self-will, die to the world and to themselves must be ranked amongst the number of those who die in the Lord. Hence Father Suarez, remembering at the hour of death that all his actions in religion were performed through obedience, was filled with spiritual joy, and exclaimed that he could not imagine death could be so sweet and so full of consolation.

Purgatur citius.—"A religious is cleansed (in purgatory) more quickly."

St. Thomas teaches that the perfect consecration which a religious makes of herself to God by her solemn profession remits the guilt and punishment of all her past sins. "But," he says, "It may reasonably be said that a person by entering into religion obtains the remission of all sins. For, to make satisfaction for all sins, it is sufficient to dedicate one's self entirely to the service of God by entering religion, which dedication exceeds all manner of satisfaction. Hence," he concludes, "We read in the lives of the Fathers, that they who enter religion obtain the same grace as those who receive baptism." The faults committed after profession by a good religious are expiated in this world by her daily exercises of piety, by her meditations, Communions, and mortifications. But if a religious should not make full atonement in this life for all her sins, her purgatory will not be of long duration. The many sacrifices of the Mass which are offered for her after death, and the prayers of the Community, will soon release her from her suffering.

Remuneratur copiosius.—"A religious is more abundantly rewarded."

Worldlings are blind to the things of God; they do not comprehend the happiness of eternal glory, in comparison with which the pleasures of this world are but wretchedness and misery. If they had just notions, and a lively sense of the glory of paradise, they would assuredly abandon their possessions, even kings would abdicate their crowns,— and, quitting the world, in which it is exceedingly difficult to attend to the one thing necessary, they would retire into the cloister to secure their eternal salvation. Bless, then, dear Sister, and continually thank your God, who, by his own lights and graces, has delivered you from the bondage of Egypt, and brought you to his own house; prove your gratitude by fidelity in his service, and by a faithful correspondence to so great a grace. Compare all the goods of this world with the eternal felicity which God has prepared for those who leave all things for his sake, and you will find that there is a greater disparity between the transitory joys of this life and the eternal beatitude of the saints than there is between a grain of sand and the entire creation.

Jesus Christ has promised that whosoever shall leave all things for his sake shall receive a hundred-fold in this life, and eternal glory in the next. Can you doubt his words? Can you imagine that he will not be faithful to his promise? Is he not more liberal in rewarding virtue than in punishing vice? If they who give a cup of cold water in his name shall not be left without abundant remuneration, how great and incomprehensible must be the reward which a religious who aspires to perfection shall receive for the numberless works of piety which she performs every day?—For so many meditations, offices, and spiritual readings?—For so many acts of mortification and of divine love which she daily refers to God's honor? Do you not know that these good works which are performed through obedience, and in compliance with the religious vows, merit a far greater reward than the good works of seculars? Brother Lacci, of the Society of Jesus, appeared after death to a certain person, and said that he and King Philip II. were crowned with bliss, but that his own glory as far surpassed that of Philip as the exalted dignity of an earthly sovereign is raised above the lowly station of an humble religious.

The dignity of martyrdom is sublime; but the religious state appears to possess something still more excellent. The martyr suffers that he may not lose his soul; the religious, to render herself more acceptable to God. A martyr dies for the faith; a religious for perfection. Although the religious state has lost much of its primitive splendour, we may still say, with truth, that the souls who are most dear to God, who have attained the greatest perfection, and who edify the Church by the odour of their sanctity, are, for the most part, to be found in religion. How few are there in the world, even amongst the most fervent, who rise at mid night to pray and sing the praises of God? How few who spend five or six hours each day in these or similar works of piety? Who practice fasting, abstinence, and mortification? How few who observe silence, or accustom themselves to do the will of others rather than their own? And, surely, all these are performed by the religious of every Order, even in convents where the discipline is relaxed many are found, who, on the day of judgment, will condemn the others who aspire to perfection, observe the rules, and perform, in private, many works of supererogation. It is evident that the conduct of the generality of pious Christians in the world cannot be compared with that of good religious.

No wonder, then, that St. Cyprian called virgins consecrated to God the flower of the garden of the Church, and the noblest portion of the flock of Jesus Christ. St. Gregory Nazianzen says the religious "Are the first- fruits of the flock of the Lord, the pillars and crown of faith, and the pearls of the Church." I hold as certain that the greater number of the seraphic thrones vacated by the unhappy associates of Lucifer will be filled by religious. Out of the sixty who during the last century were enrolled in the catalogue of saints, or honoured with the appellation of Blessed, all, with the exception of five or six, belonged to the religious orders. Jesus Christ once said to St. Teresa: "Woe to the world, but for religious." Ruffinus says: "It cannot be doubted that the world is preserved from ruin by the merits of religious." When, then, the devil affrights you by representing the difficulty of observing your Rule, and practicing the self-denial, and the austerities necessary for salvation, raise your eyes to heaven, and the hope of eternal beatitude will give you strength and courage to suffer all things. The trials, mortifications, and all miseries of this life will soon be past, and to them will succeed the ineffable delights of paradise, which shall be enjoyed for eternity without fear of failure or of diminution.

Prayer.

O God of my soul, I know that Thou dost most earnestly desire to save me. By my sins I had incurred the sentence of eternal condemnation; but instead of casting me into hell, as I deserved, Thou hast stretched forth Thy loving hand, and not only delivered me from hell and sin, but Thou hast also drawn me, as it were by force, from amidst the dangers of the world, and placed me in Thy own house amongst Thy own spouses. I hope, O my Spouse, to be admitted one day to heaven, there to sing for eternity the great mercies Thou hast shown me. Oh! That I had never offended Thee. O Jesus, assist me, now that I desire to love Thee with my whole soul, and wish to do everything in my power to please Thee. Thou hast spared nothing in order to gain my love: it is but just that I devote my entire being to Thy service. Thou hast given thyself entirely to me: I give myself without reserve to Thee. Since my soul is immortal, I desire to be eternally united to Thee. And if it is love that unites the soul to Thee, I love Thee, O my Sovereign Good; I love Thee, my Redeemer; I love Thee, O my Spouse, my only treasure and object of my love: I love Thee! I love Thee, and hope that I shall love Thee for eternity. Thy merits, O my Redeemer, are the grounds of my hope. In Thy protection, also, O great Mother of God, my Mother Mary, do I place unbounded confidence. Thou didst obtain pardon for me when I was in the state of sin; now that I hope I am in the state of grace, and am a religious, wilt thou not obtain for me the grace to become a saint? Such is my ardent hope, my fervent desire. Amen.

CHAPTER III

THE RELIGIOUS SHOULD BELONG ENTIRELY TO GOD.

1.   She Should Renounce everything, and Love only God.

PLUTARCH relates that in Rome it was the duty of a woman, on her first arrival at the house of her husband, to address him in the following words: "Wherever you are, there also shall I be. Wheresoever your will leads you, there likewise my desires shall carry me." It is this perfect conformity of her will with his that Jesus Christ demands of every virgin who aspires to the dignity and glory of his spouse. My son, he says, give me thy heart. My child and my spouse, what I desire from you is, that you give me your heart, your affections, and your will. The Holy Ghost says that when God created our first parents, Adam and Eve, he set his eyes upon their hearts. He fixed his eyes not upon their hands, but upon their hearts; because external works are of no value before God, unless they proceed from the heart, and be accompanied by the affections of the soul. All the glory of the spouse of Christ consists in an entire and a perfect union of her heart with the heart of God. All the glory of the Kings daughter is within. This union of her interior makes a religious belong entirely to the Lord.

"God," says St. Bernard, "Requires to be feared as a Sovereign, to be honored as a Father, and to be loved as a Spouse." Hence in his virginal spouses the Redeemer bears more patiently with every imperfection than with a divided heart or a want of love. It was to show the necessity of a complete and unqualified dedication of themselves to his glory that he ordained by his Church that in receiving the sacred veil on the day of their profession his spouses should be reminded of their obligation to reject every other lover. "Receive," the bishop says, "The veil, that you may admit no lover but him." Receive this veil, that you may no longer have regard to creatures, and that you may banish from your heart every affection that is not for God. The Church commands religious at their profession to change their name, that they may forget the world, that they may esteem themselves dead to all earthly things, and that the dispositions of their souls may correspond to the words which they utter on that solemn occasion: "The empire of the world and all the grandeur of the earth I have despised for the love of my Lord Jesus Christ, whom I have seen, whom I have loved, in whom I have believed, towards whom my heart inclineth." I have despised the world and all its pomps, for the sake of Jesus, my Spouse, to whom, because he is most amiable and most worthy of my love, I have consecrated all the affections of my heart. Every religious should say to the world with St. Agnes: "Depart from me, food of death, for I am pledged to another lover." Whenever any earthly object steals into her heart, and claims a share in that love which had been entirely consecrated to her divine Spouse, she should exclaim: "Begone, pernicious affection, you seek to poison my heart: depart, therefore, for another lover, more noble, more faithful, and more acceptable than you, has loved me before I could love him, and has taken possession of my whole soul: you are a vile and miserable creature; but my Spouse is the Lord, the King of heaven and earth. I am espoused to Him whom the angels serve."

Without love the soul of man cannot exist. Her affections must be fixed on God or on creatures: if she love not creatures, she will certainly love God. Hence, the Holy Ghost exhorts us to guard our hearts with the utmost vigilance against all affections which have not God for their object: With all watchfulness keep thy heart, because life issueth out from it. While the heart loves God, the soul shall have life; but if the heart transfer its affections to creatures, spiritual death will be the inevitable consequence. In order, then, to become a saint, the spouse of the Lamb must expel from her soul whatsoever has not God for its end and object. When any one demanded admission into the Society of the Fathers of the Desert, they answered him by the following question: "Do you bring a vacant heart, that it may be filled by the Holy Ghost?" Justly did they require a soul detached from earthly goods; for a heart in which the world dwells cannot be replenished with the love of God. Whoever brings to the fountain a vessel replete with sand, will labor in vain to fill it with water unless it be first emptied of its contents. O my God, why do so many religious frequent the holy exercises of prayer and Communion, and draw from them so little increase of divine love? It is because their hearts are so full of the world, of self-esteem, of vanity, or of self-will, of affection to friends, attachment to creatures. Until the world is rooted out of their hearts, the love of God cannot take possession of their souls. Give me a religious who is detached from the world and the things of the world, and I pledge myself that divine love shall abound in her soul. To obtain this detachment from the earth, it is necessary to call continually on the Lord, in the language of holy David: Create in me a clean heart, O God Give me, O

Lord, a heart free from every affection which does not proceed from the love of Thee. Woe to them that are of a double heart. "Woe," says St. Augustine, in his comment on these words, "To them who divide their heart, giving it partly to God and partly to the devil." For, continues the saint, the anger of God is justly provoked against those who treat him and his sworn enemy with equal attention, and therefore he departs from them, and yields to the devil the undivided possession of their hearts. "God is angry, because in the affections of a double heart he is associated with the devil: he departs, and the devil possesses the whole." The holy Doctor then concludes, that because a soul loves God less in proportion as her affections are fixed on other objects, a religious cannot be entirely devoted to the love of her Spouse while she is attached to creatures. "He loves you less, who loves anything else with you."

In a word, every little attachment to created objects impedes the perfect consecration of the soul to God. St. Teresa, while she cherished a certain little inordinate though not an unchaste affection for a relative, was but imperfectly united to God; but when she afterwards disengaged her heart from all earthly attachments, and consecrated her whole soul to the love of Jesus, she merited to hear from him: "Teresa, now thou art all mine, and I am all thine." St. Joseph Calasanctius used to say that a religious who gives not to Jesus her whole heart gives him nothing. The assertion was most just; for it is impossible to divide a heart too small to love a God who deserves infinite love, and to give one part of it to him and another to creatures. No, says blessed Egidius, The soul, which is one, must be entirely given to Him who is one, who merits all our love, and who has done and suffered so much to extort our love. Surely, observes Father Nieremberg, it was not necessary for our redemption that Jesus Christ should have submitted to all the miseries and endured all the pains of his life and death. A single drop of his blood, a tear, a prayer, would have been sufficient to save the whole world, and an infinite number of worlds. But the Son of God has shed the last drop of his blood, and has given his life, not only to redeem us, but also to compel us to love him with our whole hearts. He could have sent an angel to deliver us from sin: "But," says Hugh of St. Victor, "Lest you should divide your love between the Creator and the redeeming angel, he who was your Creator has chosen to become your Redeemer."

The Lord commands all to love him with their whole heart. To each one he says: Thou shalt love the Lord thy God with thy whole heart. This precept of love is especially directed to the spouses of the Redeemer. A brother in religion said once to the Venerable Father John Joseph of Alcantara, that he had become a religious to save his soul. The Venerable Father replied: "My child, do not say that you have left the world to secure your salvation; say rather that you have entered religion to become a saint; for the object of a religious should be to love God in the highest degree." O my God, if a religious love not Jesus Christ with her whole soul, to whom will she give the preference in her heart? Oh, how many marks of predilection must he have shown to you in making you his spouse in religion? He must first have selected you for creation from among an infinite number of possible beings. Then to make you from your birth a child of the Church, by the holy sacrament of baptism, he must have chosen you from among so many millions who are born in infidelity and heresy. Lastly, in bringing you into religion by his lights, his invitations, and by his special graces, he must have preferred you before the numberless multitudes of seculars whom he has left in the world in the midst of so many dangers and occasions of losing their immortal souls. Now if you do not love your God with your whole heart and soul, if you do not consecrate your entire being to his service, to whom will you give your heart? This, says the Psalmist, is the generation of them that seek the Lord. Who can behold virgins of noble birth and splendid fortunes despising the pomp and pleasures of the world, which they might have enjoyed, and shutting themselves up in a convent, to live in poverty and abjection; who, I say, can behold these holy virgins without exclaiming, This is the generation of them that seek the Lord.

Since, then, God has called you to be his spouse, all your thoughts and affections must be fixed on him and on him alone. "Have no connection," says St. Bernard, "With the world; forget all things; reserve yourself for him alone whom you have chosen from among all." Now that you are consecrated to Jesus Christ, what have you to do with the world? Forget all things and endeavor to preserve your whole heart for that God who has chosen you for his spouse in preference to so many others. You must give him your whole heart; for Jesus Christ requires that his spouse be an enclosed garden, a sealed fountain. My spouse is a garden enclosed, a fountain sealed up. The spouse of Jesus must be an enclosed garden admitting into her heart no lover but Jesus. "An enclosed garden," says Gilbert, "Which admits none but her beloved." She must be a sealed-up fountain; for he is a jealous Spouse who will suffer no one to share in the affections of his beloved. Put me, he says, as a seal upon thy heart; as a seal upon thy arm: for love is strong as death. I desire to be placed as a seal upon your heart and upon your arm, that you may love none but me, and that my glory may be the sole object of all your actions. "The Beloved," says St. Gregory "Is put as a seal upon the heart and arm of his spouse; because, in a holy soul, the intensity of her love is shown by the affections of the will, and by the works of her hands." Oh, how love, when it is strong, banishes from the soul every affection which is not for God: For love is strong as death. As no created power can avert the stroke of death when the hour of dissolution arrives, so there is no obstacle which a soul filled with divine love will not overcome. If a man should give all the substance of his house for love, he shall despise it as nothing. A heart which loves God despises all that the world can give, and disregards all that is not God. "When," says St. Francis de Sales, "A house takes fire, the furniture is thrown out of the windows; and when a soul burns with divine love, she, without the aid of sermons, or spiritual reading, or the exhortations of directors, divests herself of all affection for creatures, to possess and to love her only Supreme Good—the God of Majesty and Sovereign of the universe."

Perhaps, dear Sister, so much love is not due to your Spouse, Jesus, who died upon the cross for your redemption; who has given you himself so often in the holy Communion, and has enriched your soul with so many special graces which have not been granted to others? Reflect, says St. John Chrysostom that he has given you himself entirely and without reserve. "He has given all to you: he has reserved nothing for himself." This consideration was one of the principal means by which St. Bernard enkindled in his soul the flame of divine love. "He," says the saint, "Was given to me entirely: he was wholly consumed for my benefit." My Saviour has given me his adorable divinity and his sacred humanity; he has become a whole-burnt offering for my sake: can I refuse to consecrate my entire being to his love? My beloved to me, and I to him. My beloved has given himself entirely to me: it is but just that I dedicate to him my soul, my body, my life, and all my possessions. St. Mary Magdalene de Pazzi used to say that a religious being called to be the spouse of a crucified God, should, in her whole life and in all her actions, have in view no other object than Jesus crucified; and should in her whole life have no other occupation than the continual meditation of the eternal love which her divine Spouse bore to her. When Jesus was about to accomplish the redemption of man, he said: Now shall the prince of this world be cast out. Perhaps by these words the Son of God meant that after his crucifixion the devil was to be banished from the earth? "No," says St. Augustine, "But from the hearts of the faithful." Now if Jesus Christ has died for all, he has suffered in a special manner for his virginal spouses. Since, then, a God has given himself entirely for your salvation, would it not be enormous ingratitude in you to refuse to him the sacrifice of your whole heart, or to love him only with reserve? Say, then, frequently to your Spouse: O my Jesus, Thou hast given Thyself to me without reserve; Thou hast given all Thy blood, all Thy labors, all Thy merits, for my sanctification. In a word, Thy favours were so abundant and magnificent that nothing more remained to be conferred upon me. I therefore give myself entirely to Thee; I offer to Thee all that I possess or shall ever possess upon earth; I consecrate to Thee all my pleasures, my body, my soul, my will, my liberty. I have nothing more to present to Thee: if I had Thou shouldst have it. I renounce all that the world can give, and declare that Thou alone canst satisfy the desires of my heart. "Oh!" said St. Teresa, "What a profitable exchange to give our hearts to God and in return to be made the objects of his love." "But," continues the saint, "Because we do not offer to him the undivided affections of our souls, he does not bestow upon us all the treasures of his love."

The spouse of Jesus should sing no other than that canticle of love recommended by holy David: Sing to the Lord a new canticle "What," says St. Augustine, "Is a new canticle, but new love?" The old canticles are those affections to creatures and to ourselves to which we have been subject from our birth, and which continually spring up from the inclinations to evil transmitted to us by our first parents. For, says the Holy Ghost, the imagination and thought of man's heart are prone to evil from his youth. But the new canticle is love, by which the soul is consecrated to God. "The voice," says St. Augustine, "Of this singer of canticles is the voice of holy love: let us love him for his own sake." The voice of the soul praising God is the fervour of charity which makes her love him, because he merits her love, and banishes from her affections whatever is not God. Jesus crucified, command his spouses to be crucified to all earthly things. Whenever, then, the world places before your eyes its pomps and delights, you should exclaim with St. Paulinus: "Let the rich enjoy their treasures, and kings their thrones; Christ is our kingdom and our glory." His love is more valuable to us than the sovereignty of the earth. The spouse of Jesus should desire nothing but love; should live but for love; should seek only to advance continually in love: she should incessantly languish with love, in the choir, in the cell, the dormitory, the garden, in all places. Such should be the ardor of her charity that the flames of her love would extend to all parts of the convent, and even beyond the boundaries of the enclosure. To this love the Apostle exhorts and invites her, by the example of her beloved Spouse. Happy the religious who can say with St. Francis, "My God and my all." My God, who hast shown to me such an excess of love, why should I seek earthly possessions? I have found Thee, the source of all happiness. My God and my all, I care not for honors, for riches, or for pleasures. Thou art my glory, my treasure, my delight, and my all. What have I in heaven, and besides thee, what do I desire upon earth? Thou art the God of my heart, and the God that is my portion forever. Can I, O my God, find any one in heaven or on earth who is so deserving of my affection, or who has done so much to gain my love? Thou alone shalt be the Lord of my heart; Thou shalt reign in its affections, and shalt rule its motions with sovereign sway. Thee alone shall my soul obey, seeking in all things Thy holy will. I found him whom my soul loveth; I held him and will not let him go? Yes, I have found the object of all my affections: I have found him who alone can make me happy. Though the world, with all its pleasures, and hell, with all its powers of darkness, should endeavor to separate me from Thee, I will not abandon Thee, O Jesus, my Spouse. "I held him, and will not let him go." I will hold Thee fast by my love, and will never suffer Thee to depart from me. I desire to live and to die always, and in all things, united to Thee.

2.   We must overcome ourselves and courageously Strive for Perfection—Means to be adopted for this Purpose.

To attain perfection, and to enjoy true peace of con science, it is necessary to die to the world and to self. Blessed are the dead who die in the Lord. As corporal death is necessarily accompanied with pain, so abandonment of the world and detachment from its pleasures is utterly impossible without trials and sufferings. The kingdom of heaven is represented to us in the Holy Scriptures under various images. It is sometimes compared to a treasure which can be obtained only by sell-

47

ing all our possessions; sometimes to a city which, because the gate is narrow, no one can enter without fatigue and industry; sometimes to a palace in which the stones (that is, the souls of which it is composed) must be polished with the utmost care; sometimes to a feast, to which no one is admitted unless he abandon all other concerns; sometimes to a prize which cannot be won without running to the end; and, finally, to a crown, for the acquisition of which it is necessary to fight and conquer. In a word, to die to the world, self-love must die in the soul.

St. Augustine says, that the love of God increases in proportion as self-love is diminished; and that the destruction of the latter is the perfection of the former. "The diminution of cupidity," says the holy Doctor, "Is the nutriment of charity; but its total absence is the perfection of charity." Charity is estimated, not by its tenderness, but by its strength. Ardent charity smooths every asperity and surmounts every obstacle. "There is nothing," says St. Augustine, "So difficult, which the fire of love does not conquer." In another place he says: "In what we love there is no labor; or if there be, we love the very labor itself."

In a soul that loves God, torments endured for his sake excite no pain; or if they do, these pains are to her a source of happiness and delight. In his confessions, the saint writes, that when he gave himself entirely to God, the very privation of sensual gratifications filled his soul with joy; and that though at first he dreaded their loss, he afterwards had reason to rejoice at their relinquishment. "How sweet, on a sudden, was it become to me to be without these joys, and what I was before so much afraid to lose, I now cast from me with joy." To a religious who has fixed her whole heart on God, the practice of poverty, of obedience, mortification, and of all virtues is easy and agreeable; but to her whose affections are divided between God and creatures, all the duties of religion are an intolerable burden.

It is true that whatever good we do, comes from God, and that without his grace we cannot, according to the Apostle, even pronounce the name of Jesus. But not withstanding our absolute dependence on divine grace, God commands us to perform our part, and to cooperate with him in the work of our salvation. Many desire to become saints, but wish that God would do all, and that he would bring them to eternal glory without labor or inconvenience to them. But this is impossible. The law of God is said to be a yoke borne by two, to show that the divine aid, on the one hand, and our cooperation on the other, are indispensably necessary for its observance. And sometimes, to carry this yoke, and merit everlasting happiness, we must do violence to the feelings of flesh and blood. The kingdom of heaven suffereth violence and the violent bear it away. And St. Paul says, that the crown of life shall be given to him only who shall combat till he overcomes the enemies of his salvation.

O spouse of Jesus, I say to you with the same apostle, hold fast that which thou hast, that no man takes thy crown. Since Jesus Christ has made you his spouse, do not allow your enemies to snatch from you the eternal dignity of queen which he has prepared for you in his kingdom; but, on the contrary, hold fast your crown, by assimilating yourself to your beloved, the predestined model of the elect: For, whom He foreknew, he also predestined to be made conformable to the image of his Son. He has gone before you, crowned with thorns, scourged at the pillar, loaded with the cross, and saturated with contempt and reproach; and in that pitiable condition he invites you to follow him, and to deny yourself: If any man will come after me, let him deny himself, and take up his cross and follow me. He has died for you, and it is your duty to sacrifice your life for him, and to say with the seraphic St. Francis: "O good Jesus, may I die for the loves of thee, who hast condescended to die for the love of me." Yes, it is but just that you should die to yourselves, and live only for that God who has died for your salvation. "That they also," says the Apostle, who live, may not now live to themselves, but unto him who died for them You indeed, are weak; but if you trust in the goodness of your Spouse, his grace and strength will prepare you to execute so arduous a task. When the devil molests you, and endeavors to cast you into despair, by representing to you the difficulties and miseries of a life of continual mortification, of incessant self-denial, and of perpetual abstinence from sensual pleasures, answer him in the words of the Apostle: I can do all things in him who strengtheneth me. Of myself I can do nothing; but the Lord, who has chosen me for his spouse, and called me to his love, will give me courage and strength to walk in the rugged path of his commandments. "If," says St. Teresa, "We be not in fault, God will assuredly, by his all-powerful aid, enable us to become saints." And, O my God, upon whom, if not upon your spouses, will the obligation of sanctity be imperative? O consecrated virgins, offer yourselves frequently to God, with a strong desire and determination to please him in all things, and implore continually the assistance of his holy grace. He has promised to grant whatsoever is asked of him with confidence. All things whatsoever you ask, when ye pray, believe that you shall receive; and they shall come unto you.

What then do you fear? Have courage; God has taken you from the world; he has delivered you from its snares; has called you to his love; and has, if you be faithful to him, prepared for you numberless helps and graces. You have already left the world; you have, as St. Teresa used to say to her spiritual children, taken the most difficult and important step; and to become a saint little now remains to be done. Resolve, then, at once to dissolve every worldly attachment. Perhaps, after having forsaken the world, and renounced all its goods, after having voluntarily relinquished your liberty, and bound yourself, by vow, to perpetual enclosure; perhaps, after all these sacrifices, you are disposed, for the miserable gratifications of sense or caprice, to risk your all—the everlasting possession of paradise and of God—and to prefer, before the exalted glory of spouse of the Most High, the unhappy slavery of Satan, who will render you unhappy in this life, and eternally miserable in the next. Resolve, then, I say again, to burst every earthly tie, and tremble lest the words which you now read should be the last invitation of your Spouse. Do not resist the voice of God any longer. If you neglect his call on this occasion, he may perhaps abandon you forever. Resolve, then, resolve! "The devil," says St. Teresa, "Is afraid of resolute souls." St. Bernard teaches that many souls are lost through want of fortitude. Take courage, then, and trust in the power and goodness of God: strong resolutions overcome all difficulties. Oh, happy, thrice happy soul, if, in obedience to the voice of God, you give yourself entirely to your Spouse, Jesus. When death approaches you can return thanks to him for his favours, and address him in the words of the glorious St. Agnes: "O Lord, who hast taken from me the love of the world, receive my soul." O my God, who hast disengaged my heart from creatures, that all its affections might be fixed on Thee, receive, now, my soul, that I may be admitted into the kingdom of Thy glory, to love Thee with all my strength, without fear of being ever separated from Thee—the Supreme and Infinite Good.

Oh, that all religious would imitate the example of the Venerable Frances Farnese! Her life at first was very imperfect; but happening one day to read the history of the Franciscans in Japan, she was suddenly seized with compunction, and exclaimed: "And what, my Sisters, will we do? We have forsaken our families and our goods, and shall we now draw down upon our souls the vengeance of God and the sentence of eternal death by attachment to the things of the world which we do not possess?" From that moment she resolved to give up the world, and to consecrate herself entirely to God. This resolution she afterwards fulfilled in the accomplishment of that wonderful reformation of the Order which was planned and executed by her directions.

"Men," says St. Jerome, "Always seek to advance in, the knowledge of their secular profession, but are satiated with the mere rudiments of the science of the saints. In all their worldly pursuits," says the saint, "Men are never satiated; but in virtue it is sufficient for them to have made a beginning." Every Christian is bound to tend to perfection. "When I speak of a Christian," says St. Ambrose, "I mean a perfect man." The precept by which all are commanded to love God with all their strength, imposes upon all the obligation of perfection. Besides, to discharge the duty of preserving sanctifying grace it is necessary to struggle always to perfect charity in the soul; for in the path of virtue he that does not advance, recedes, and exposes himself to the danger of sin. Now, if this is true with regard to all Christians, how much more so must it be with regard to religious, who are bound by a stricter obligation to seek perfection, not only because they receive more abundant graces and more powerful helps to sanctity, but also because they have promised to observe the vows and rules of religion!

But to fulfill the command by which you are obliged to aspire to perfection, an inefficacious and fruitless desire of sanctity is not sufficient. You must do violence to yourself, and adopt the means of attaining perfection. It will not be necessary for you to undertake very extraordinary things: it will be sufficient to perform your ordinary exercises with diligence and attention, to observe your Rule with exactness, and to practice with fidelity the Gospel virtues. However, a religious who desires to become a saint will not confine herself to the mere discharge of the duties prescribed by her Rule, which is accommodated to weak as well as to perfect souls; she must also perform supererogatory works of prayer, of charity, of mortification, and of the other virtues. St. Bernard says that "What is perfect must be singular." A religious, who barely discharges the ordinary duties of the Community, will never attain sublime sanctity. It is your duty, then, to do violence to

51

yourself, and courageously to adopt the means of arriving at perfection.

The principal means are:

1. A strong and ardent desire to become a saint.

2. Great confidence in Jesus Christ and in his holy Mother.

3. To avoid every deliberate sin or defect, and after a fault not to lose courage, but to make an act of contrition for it, and then resume your ordinary occupations.

4. To cut off all attachment to creatures, to self-will, and self-esteem.

5. To resist continually your own inclinations.

6. To observe with exactness the rules of religion, however unimportant they may appear.

7. To perform your ordinary duties with all possible perfection.

8. To communicate often—with the permission of your director; to make long and frequent meditations, and to perform all the mortifications which he will permit.

9. To prefer, on all occasions, those actions which are most agreeable to God, and most opposed to self-love.

10. To receive all crosses and contradictions with joy and gladness from the hands of God.

11. To love and serve those who persecute you.

12. To spend every moment of your time for God.

13. To offer to God all your actions in union with the merits of Jesus Christ.

14. To make a special oblation of yourself to God, that he may dispose

of you and of all you possess in whatever way he pleases.

15. To protest continually before God that his pleasure and love are the only objects of your wishes.

16. Lastly, and above all, to pray continually, and to recommend yourself, with unbounded confidence, to Jesus Christ and to his Virgin Mother, and to entertain a special affection and tenderness towards Mary.

I conclude with the words which the Venerable Father Anthony Torres, after an ecstasy of love, addressed to a religious who was one of his penitents: "My child, love, love your Spouse, who is the only object that merits your love."

Prayer.

O my God! O amiable love! O infinite lover, and worthy of infinite love, when shall I love Thee as Thou hast loved me? It is not in Thy power to give me stronger proofs of love than those Thou hast already given. Thou hast spared nothing; Thou hast expended Thy blood and Thy life to oblige me to love Thee; and shall I love Thee only with reserve? Pardon me, O my Jesus, if, in my past life, I have been so ungrateful as to prefer my accursed pleasures before the love which I owed to Thee. Ah, my Lord and my Spouse, discover to me always, more and more, Thy infinite loveliness that I may be daily more enamoured of Thy perfection, and that I may continually endeavor to please Thee as Thou dost deserve to be pleased. Thou dost command me to love Thee, and I desire nothing but Thy love. Speak, Lord, for thy servant heareth. Speak, O Lord: tell me what Thou desirest from me: my wish is to obey Thee in all things. I will no longer resist the graces and mercies Thou hast bestowed upon me. Thou hast given Thyself entirely to me: I offer myself without reserve to Thee. For Thy mercy's sake accept, and do not refuse this oblation. By my infidelities I have deserved to be cast away from Thy love: but the desire to be Thine which Thou hast infused into my soul assures me that Thou hast already accepted the offer. I love Thee, O God, who art infinitely amiable: I love Thee, O my Sovereign Good. Thou art, and shalt be forever, the only delight of my heart, and the sole object of my affections. And since Thou hast said, Ask, and you shall receive, and hast promised to grant whatsoever we ask, I beg, with St. Ignatius, that, "Thou wilt give me only Thy love along with Thy grace, and I shall be sufficiently rich." Give me Thy love and Thy grace; grant that I may love Thee, and be beloved by Thee, and I shall be content, and shall desire nothing else from Thee.

O Mary, who belonged always and entirely to God, by that love which our Lord bore thee through all eternity, obtain for us the grace henceforth to love God, and to love him alone.

CHAPTER IV.

THE DESIRE OF PERFECTION.

1.　　How Holy Desires are Useful, and even Necessary.

AN ardent desire of perfection is the first means that a religious should adopt in order to acquire sanctity and to consecrate her whole being to God. As the sports man, to hit a bird in flight, must take aim in advance of his prey, so a Christian, to make progress in virtue, should aspire to the highest degree of holiness which it is in his power to attain. Who, says holy David, will give me wings like a dove, and I will fly and be at rest. Who will give me the wings of the dove to fly to my God, and, divested of all earthly affection, to repose in the bosom of the divinity? Holy desires are the blessed wings with which the saints burst every worldly tie, and fly to the mountain of perfection, where they find that peace which the world cannot give.

But how do fervent desires make the soul fly to God? "They," says St. Laurence Justinian, "Supply strength, and render pains light and tolerable." On the one hand, good desires give strength and courage, and on the other they diminish the labor and fatigue of ascending the mountain of God. Whosoever, through diffidence of attaining sanctity, does not ardently desire to become a saint, will never arrive at perfection. A man who is desirous of obtaining a valuable treasure which he knows is to be found at the top of a lofty mountain, but who, through fear of fatigue and difficulty, has no desire of ascending, will never advance a single step towards the wished for object, but will remain below in careless indifference and inactivity. And he who, because the path of virtue appears to him narrow and rugged, and difficult to be trodden, does not desire to climb up the mountain of the Lord, and to gain the treasure of perfection, will always continue in a state of tepidity, and will never make the smallest progress in the way of God.

On the contrary, he that does not desire, and does not strenuously endeavor, always to advance in holiness, will, as we learn from experience and from all the masters of the spiritual life, go backward in the path of virtue, and will be exposed to great danger of eternal misery. The path of the just, says Solomon, as a shining light goeth forwards and increaseth even to perfect day. The way of the wicked is darksome: they know not when they fall. As light increases constantly from sunrise to full day, so the path of the saints always advances; but the way of sinners becomes continually more dark and gloomy, till they know not where they go, and at length walk into a precipice. "Not to advance," says St. Augustine, "Is to go back." St. Gregory beautifully explains this maxim of spiritual life by comparing a Christian who seeks to remain stationary in the path of virtue to a man who is in a boat on a rapid river, and striving to keep the boat always in the same position. If the boat be not continually propelled against the current, it will be carried away in an opposite direction, and consequently, without continual exertion, its station cannot be maintained. Since the fall of Adam man is naturally inclined to evil from his birth. For the imagination and thought of man's heart are prone to evil from his youth. If he do not push forward, if he do not endeavor, by incessant efforts, to improve in sanctity, the very current of passion will carry him back. "Since you do not wish to proceed," says St. Bernard, addressing a tepid soul, "You must fail." By no means, she replied; "I wish to live, and to remain in my present state. I will not consent to be worse; and I do not desire to be better." "You, then," rejoins the saint, "Wish what is impossible." Because, in the way of God, a Christian must either go forward and advance in virtue, or go backward and rush headlong into vice.

In seeking eternal salvation, we must, according to St. Paul, never rest, but must run continually in the way of perfection, that we may win the prize, and secure an incorruptible crown. So run that you may obtain. If we fail, the fault will be ours; for God wills that all be holy and perfect. This is the will of God—your sanctification. He even commands us to be perfect and holy. Be you therefore perfect, as also your Heavenly Father is perfect? Be holy because I am holy. He promises and gives, as the holy Council of Trent teaches, abundant strength, for the observance of all his commands, to those who ask it from him. "God does not command impossibilities; but by his precepts he admonishes you to do what you can, and to ask what you cannot do; and He assists you, that you may be able to do it." God does not command impossibilities; but by his precepts he admonishes us to do what we can by the aid of his ordinary grace; and when greater helps are necessary, he exhorts us to seek them by humble prayer. He will infallibly attend to our petitions, and enable us to observe all, even the most difficult, of his commandments. Take courage, then, and adopt the advice of the

Venerable Father Torres to a religious, who was one of his penitents: "Let us, my child, put on the wings of strong desires, that, quitting the earth, we may fly to our Spouse and our Beloved, who expects us in the blessed kingdom of eternity."

St. Augustine teaches, that the life of a good Christian is one continued longing after perfection. "The whole life," says the saint, "Of a good Christian is a holy desire." He that cherishes not in his heart the desire of sanctity may be a Christian; but he will not be a good one. If this be true of all the servants of God, how much more so must it be of religious, who, though it is not imperative on them to be actually perfect, are strictly obliged to aspire after perfection. "He that enters the religious state," says St. Thomas, "Is not commanded to have perfect charity; but he is bound to tend to it. It is not," continues the saint, "Obligatory on him to adopt all the means by which perfection may be attained; but it is his duty to perform the exercises prescribed by the Rule, which at his profession he promised to observe." Hence, a religious is bound not only to fulfill her vows, but also to assist at public prayer; to make the Communions, and to practice the mortifications ordained by the Rule; to observe the silence, and to discharge all the other duties of the Community.

You will, perhaps, say that your Rule does not bind under pain of sin. That may be; but theologians generally maintain, that to transgress without a sufficient cause even the rules which of themselves do not impose a moral obligation, is almost always a venial fault. Because the willful and unnecessary violation of rule generally proceeds from passion or from sloth, and consequently must be at least a venial offence. Hence, St. Francis de Sales, in his Entertainments, teaches that though the Rule of the Visitation did not oblige under the penalty of sin, still the infraction of it could not be excused from the guilt of a venial transgression. "Because," says the saint, "By disobedience to her Rule a religious dishonors the things of God, violates her profession, disturbs the Community, and dissipates the fruits of the good example which everyone should give." Whoever, then, breaks the Rule in the presence of others, will, according to the saint, incur the additional guilt of scandal. It should be observed that the breach of rule may be even a mortal sin, when it is so frequent as to do serious injury to regular observance in the Community. To violate the Rule, through contempt, is likewise a grievous transgression. And St. Thomas remarks, that the frequent infraction of rule practically disposes to the contempt of it. This is my answer to those tepid religious who excuse their own irregularities by saying that the Rule imposes no obligation. The fervent spouses of Jesus Christ do not inquire whether their rule has the force of a precept or not: it is enough for them to know that it is approved by God, and that he takes complacency in its observance.

As it is impossible to arrive at perfection in any art or science, without ardent desires of its attainment, so no one has ever yet become a saint, but by strong and fervent aspirations after sanctity. "God," observes St. Teresa, "Ordinarily confers his signal favours on those only who thirst after his love." Blessed, says the royal prophet, is the man whose help is from thee: in his heart he hath disposed to ascend by steps in the vale of tears. . . . They shall go from virtue to virtue. Happy the man who has resolved in his soul to mount the ladder of perfection: he shall receive abundant aid from God, and will ascend from virtue to virtue. Such has been the practice of the saints, and especially of St. Andrew Avellino, who even bound himself by vow "To advance continually in the way of Christian perfection." St. Teresa used to say that "God rewards, even in this life, every good desire." It was by good desires that the saints arrived in a short time at a sublime degree of sanctity. Being made perfect in a short space, He fulfilled a long time. It was thus that St. Aloysius, who lived but twenty-five years, acquired such perfection, that St. Mary Magdalene de Pazzi, who saw him in bliss, declared that his glory appeared equal to that of most of the saints. In the vision he said to her: My eminent sanctity was the fruit of an ardent desire, which I cherished during my life, of loving God as much as he deserved to be loved: and being unable to love him with that infinite love which he merits, I suffered on earth a continual martyrdom of love, for which I am now raised to that transcendent glory which I enjoy.

The works of St. Teresa contain, besides those that have been already adduced, many beautiful passages on this subject. "Our thoughts," says the saint, "Should be aspiring: from great desires all our good shall come." In another place she says: "We must not lower our desires, but should trust in God, that by continual exertion we shall, by his grace, arrive at sanctity and felicity of the saints." Again she says: "The divine Majesty takes complacency in generous souls who are diffident in themselves." This great saint asserted that in all her experience she never knew a timid Christian to attain as much virtue in many years

58

as certain courageous souls acquire in a few days. The reading of the Lives of the saints contributes greatly to infuse courage into the soul.

It will be particularly useful to read the Lives of those who, after being great sinners, became eminent saints; such as the Lives of St. Mary Magdalene, St. Augustine, St. Pelagia, St. Mary of Egypt, and especially of St. Margaret of Cortona, who was for many years in a state of damnation, but even then cherished a desire of sanctity; and who, after her conversion, flew to perfection with such rapidity, that she merited to learn by revelation, even in this life, not only that she was predestined to glory, but also that a place was prepared for her among the seraphim.

St. Teresa says that the devil seeks to persuade us that it would be pride in us to desire a high degree of perfection, or to wish to imitate the saints. She adds, that it is a great delusion to regard strong desires of sanctity as the offspring of pride; for it is not pride in a soul diffident of herself and trusting only in the power of God, to resolve to walk courageously in the way of perfection, saying with the Apostle: I can do all things in him who strengthened me. Of myself I can do nothing; but, by his aid I shall be able to do all things, and therefore I resolve, with his grace, to desire to love him as the saints have loved him.

It is very profitable frequently to aspire after the most exalted virtue, and to desire it; such as to love God more than all the saints; to suffer for the love of him more than all the martyrs; to bear and to pardon all injuries; to embrace every sort of fatigue and suffering, for the sake of saving a single soul; and to perform similar acts of perfect charity. Because these holy aspirations and desires, though their object shall never be attained, are, in the first place, very meritorious in the sight of God, who glories in men of good will, as he abominates a perverse heart and evil inclinations. Secondly, because the habit of aspiring to heroic sanctity animates and encourages the soul to perform acts of ordinary and easy virtue. Hence it is of great importance to propose in the morning to labor as much as possible for God during the day; to resolve to bear patiently all crosses and contradictions; to observe constant recollection; and to make continual acts of the love of God. Such was the practice of the seraphic St. Francis. "He proposed," says St. Bonaventure, "With the grace of Jesus Christ, to do great things."

59

St. Teresa asserts that "The Lord is as well pleased with good desires as with their fulfillment." Oh, how much better is it to serve God than to serve the world. To acquire goods of the earth, to procure wealth, honors, and applause of men, it is not enough to pant after them with ardor; no, to desire and not to obtain them only renders their absence more painful. But to merit the riches and the favour of God, it is sufficient to desire his grace and love. St. Augustine relates that in a convent of hermits there were two officers of the emperor's court, one of whom began to read the life of St Anthony. "He read," says the holy Doctor, "And his heart was stripped of the world." Turning to his companion, he said: "What do we seek? Can we expect from the emperor anything better than his friendship? Through how many dangers are we to reach still greater perils, and how long shall this last? Fools that we have been, shall we still continue to serve the emperor in the midst of so many labors, fears, and troubles? We can hope for nothing better than his favour; and should we obtain it, we would only increase the danger of our eternal reprobation. It is only with difficulty that we shall ever procure the patronage of Cæsar, but if I will it, behold I am in a moment the friend of God. Because who ever wishes, with a true and resolute desire for the friendship of God, instantly obtains it.

I say with a true and resolute desire, for little profit is derived from the fruitless desires of slothful souls, who always desire to be saints, but never advance a single step in the way of God. Of them Solomon says: The sluggard willeth and willeth not. And again: Desires kill the slothful. The tepid religious desires perfection, but never resolves to adopt the means of its acquirement. Contemplating its advantages, she desires it; but reflecting on the fatigue necessary for its attainment, she desires it not. Thus, "She willeth and willeth not." Her desires of sanctity are not efficacious; they have for their object means of salvation incompatible with her state. Oh, she exclaims, were I in the desert, all my time should be employed in prayer and in works of penance, were I in another convent, I would shut myself up in a cell to think only of God, if my health were good, I would practice continual mortifications. I would wish, I would wish, she cries, to do all this; and still the miserable soul does not fulfill the obligations of her state. She makes but little mental prayer, and is even absent from the common meditations; she neglects Communion; is seldom in the choir, and frequently at the grate and on the terrace; she practices but little patience or resignation in her infirmities; in a word, she daily commits willful and deliberate faults, but never labors to correct them. What, then, will it profit her to desire what is inconsistent with the duties of her present state, while she violates strict obligations? Desires kill the slothful. Such useless desires expose the soul to great danger of everlasting perdition; because wasting her time, and taking complacency in them, she will neglect the means necessary for the perfection of her state, and for the attainment of eternal life.

"I do not," says St. Francis de Sales, "Approve of the conduct of those who, while bound by an obligation, or placed in any state, spend their time in wishing for another manner of life, inconsistent with their duties; or for exercises incompatible with their present state. For these desires dissipate the heart, and make it languish in the necessary exercises." It is, then, the duty of a religious to aspire only after that perfection which is suitable to her present state and to her actual obligations; and whether a Superior, or a subject, whether in sickness or in health, the vigour of youth or the imbecility of old age, to adopt, resolutely, the means of sanctity suitable to her condition in life. "The devil," says St. Teresa, "Sometimes persuades us that we have acquired the virtue, for example, of patience; because we determine to suffer a great deal for God. We feel really convinced that we are ready to accept any cross, however great, for his sake; and this conviction makes us quite content, for the devil assists us to believe that we are willing to bear all things for God. I advise you not to trust much to such virtue, nor to think that you even know it, except in name, until you see it tried. It will probably happen that on the first occasion of contradiction all this patience will fall to the ground."

2.   Means for Acquiring Perfection.

Let us now come to what is most important—the means to be adopted for acquiring perfection.

The first means is mental prayer, and particularly the meditation of the claims which God has to our love, and of the love which he has borne us, especially in the great work of redemption. To redeem us, a God has even sacrificed his life in a sea of sorrows and contempt; and to obtain our love, he has gone so far as to make himself our food. To inflame the soul with the fire of divine love, these truths must be frequently meditated. In my meditation, says David, a fire shall flame out.

When I contemplate the goodness of my God, the flames of charity fill my whole heart. St. Aloysius used to say, that to attain eminent sanctity it is first necessary to arrive at a high degree of mental prayer.

We should frequently renew our resolution of advancing in divine love. In this renewal you will be greatly assisted by considering, each day, that it is only then you begin to walk in the path of virtue. This was the practice of holy David: And I said, now have I begun. And this was the dying advice of St. Anthony to his monks: "My dear children, figure to yourselves that each day is the day on which you begin to serve God."

We should search out continually and scrupulously the defects of the soul. "Brethren," says St. Augustine, "Examine yourselves with rigor; be always displeased with what you are, if you desire to become what you are not." To arrive at that perfection which you have not attained, you must never be satisfied with the virtue you possess; "For," continues the saint, "Where you have been pleased with yourself, there you have remained." Wherever you are content with the degree of sanctity which you have acquired, there you will rest, and, taking complacency in yourself, you will lose the desire of further perfection. Hence the holy Doctor adds, what should terrify every tepid soul, who, content with her present virtue, has but little desire of spiritual advancement; "But if you have said it is sufficient, you have perished." If you have said that you have already attained sufficient perfection, you are lost; for not to advance in the way of God is to retrograde. And, as St. Bernard says, "Not to wish to go forward, is certainly to fail." Hence St. John Chrysostom exhorts us to think continually on the virtues which we do not possess, and never to reflect on the little good which we have done; for the thought of our good works "Generates indolence and inspires arrogance," and serves only to engender sloth in the way of the Lord, and to swell the heart with vain-glory, which exposes the soul to the danger of losing the virtues she has acquired. "He that runs," continues the saint, "Does not compute the progress he has made, but the distance he has to travel." He that aspires after perfection does not stop to calculate the proficiency he has made, but directs all his attention to the virtue he has still to acquire. Fervent Christians, as they that dig a treasure, advance in virtue as they approach the end of life. As St. Gregory says, in his comment on this passage of Job, that the man who seeks a treasure, the deeper he has dug the more he exerts himself in the hope of finding it; so the soul that pants after holiness multiplies its efforts to attain it in proportion to the advancement it has made.

IV. The fourth means is that which St. Bernard employed to excite his fervor. "He had," says Surius, "This always in his heart, and frequently in his mouth: 'Bernard, for what purpose hast thou come?'" Every religious should continually ask herself the same question: I have left the world and all its riches and pleasures, to live in the cloister, and to become a saint; what progress do I make? I do not advance in sanctity; no, but by my tepidity I expose myself to the danger of eternal perdition. It will be useful to introduce, in this place, the example of the Venerable Sister Hyacinth Mariscotti, who at first led a very tepid life, in the convent of St. Bernardine, in Viterbo. She confessed to Father Bianchetti, a Franciscan, who came to the convent as extraordinary confessor. That holy man thus addressed her: "Are you a nun? Are you not aware that paradise is not prepared for vain and proud religious?" "Then," she replied, "Have I left the world to cast myself into hell?" "Yes," rejoined the Father, "That is the place which is destined for religious who live like seculars." Reflecting on these words of the holy man, Sister Hyacinth was struck with remorse; and, bewailing her past life, she made her confession with tearful eyes, and began from that moment to walk resolutely in the way of perfection. Oh, how salutary is the thought of having abandoned the world to become a saint! It awakens the tepidity of the religious, and encourages her to advance continually in holiness, and to surmount every obstacle to her ascent up to the mountain of God. Whenever, then, O spouse of Jesus, you meet with difficulties in the practice of obedience, say in your heart: I have not entered religion to do my own will; if I wished to follow my own inclinations, I should have remained in the world; but I have come here to do the will of God, by obedience to my Superiors, and this I desire to do in spite of all difficulties. Whenever you experience the inconveniences of poverty, say: I have not left the world and retired into the cloister for the enjoyment of ease and riches, but to practice poverty for the love of my Jesus, who for my sake became poorer than I am. When you are rebuked or treated with contempt, say: I have become a religious only to receive, and bear with patience, the humiliations due to my sins, and thus render myself dear to my divine Spouse, who was so much despised on earth. By this means you will live to God and die to the world. In conclusion, I recommend you frequently

63

to ask yourself this question: What will it profit me to have abandoned the world, to have confined myself in the cloister, to have given up my liberty, if I do not become a saint; but if, on the contrary, I expose my soul to everlasting misery by a careless and tepid and negligent life?

V. The fifth means for a religious to attain sanctity is frequently to call to mind and to renew the sentiments of fervor and the desires of perfection which she felt when she first entered religion. The Abbot Agatho being once asked by a monk for a rule of conduct in religion, replied: "See what you were on the day you left the world, and persevere in the dispositions you then entertained." Remember, O consecrated virgin, the resolutions which you made on the day you retired from the world, to seek nothing but God; to have no will but his, and to suffer all manner of contempt and hardship for the love of Jesus Christ. This thought, as we learn from the Lives of the Fathers, brought back to his first fervor a young monk who had fallen into tepidity. When he first determined to retire into a monastery, his mother strongly opposed his design, and endeavored by various reasons to show that it was his bounden duty not to abandon her. To all her arguments he replied: "I am resolved to save my soul." And in spite of her opposition he entered religion; but after sometime his ardor cooled, and tepidity stole into his heart. His mother died, and a little after her death he was seized with a dangerous malady. In his sickness he thought he saw himself before the judgment-seat of God, and his mother reproaching him with the violation of his first resolution: My son, said she, you have forgotten the words, "I am resolved to save my soul," by which you replied to all my entreaties. You have become a religious, and is it thus you live? He recovered from his infirmity, and, reflecting on his first fervor, he began a life of holiness, and practiced such mortifications that his companions advised him to moderate his austerities. To their admonitions he answered: "If I have not been able to bear the rebuke of my mother, how shall I, if I abuse his graces, support the reproaches of Jesus Christ in judgment?" The reading of the Lives of the saints is very profitable to us; their examples humble us, and make us know and feel our own miseries. The poor understand their poverty only when they see the treasures of the rich.

VI. The sixth means is, not to lose courage when you perceive that you have not as yet arrived at the perfection to which you aspire. To be discouraged by the imperfections which you desire to correct, would be to yield to a great illusion of the devil. St. Philip Neri used to say, that to become a saint is not the work of a day. It is related in the Lives of the Fathers, that a certain monk, after having begun his religious career with great fervor, relaxed his zeal, and remained for some time in a state of tepidity; but reflecting on his unhappy condition, he began to sigh after his former piety, and became greatly afflicted because he knew not how to recover it. In this disposition of mind he sought advice from an aged Father. The good Father consoled and encouraged him by relating the conduct of a parent who commanded his son to clear a certain portion of land from thorns and briars. Disheartened by the difficulty of the task, and despairing of success, the son neglected altogether the duty imposed upon him, and excused himself to his father, saying that he had not courage to undertake such labor. In answer the father said to him: My son, I only ask you to cleanse, every day, as much land as will be the size of your body. The son began to work, and by degrees he removed every useless and noxious plant. This example is well adapted to encourage and stimulate us in our progress to perfection. He that always cherishes an ardent desire of advancement, and strives continually to go forward, will, with the divine assistance, obtain the perfection after which he aspires. St. Bernard says that to make constant exertions to advance in virtue is the perfection that can be attained in this life. "Continual efforts for perfection," says the saint, "Are reputed perfection." You must be careful never to omit your usual exercises, your meditations, Communions, or mortifications. This rule must be particularly observed in the time of aridity. It is then that God tries his faithful servants, and that they prove their fidelity to him, by discharging, in spite of their darkness, pains, and difficulties, the duties which, amid the abundance of his celestial consolations, they were accustomed to perform.

VII. The last and most efficacious means of perfection is, to have continually before your eyes the examples of the Sisters who are most distinguished for sanctity, in order to imitate the virtues which they practice. St. Anthony says, as the bee gathers honey from every flower, so a religious should draw lessons of perfection from the good examples of all her companions. She should emulate the modesty of one, the charity and affection for prayer of another, the frequent Communion of a third, and all the other virtues practiced by the rest of the Community. Such is the holy zeal with which a good religious should endeavor to rival, and even to excel, all the Sisters in all virtues. Worldlings seek to surpass one another in riches, honors, and earthly pleasures; but a religious ought to struggle for the superiority in humility, patience, meekness, charity, love of contempt, poverty, purity, and obedience. To outstrip one another in loving and pleasing God should be the object of their emulation. To succeed in this holy contest, a religious must perform all her ordinary actions with an intention of pleasing God, and of edifying her companions that thus she may sanctify herself, and give greater glory to the Lord. So let your light shine before men, that they may see your works, and glorify your Father who is in heaven. Hence, they who admit to the religious profession a novice whose conduct has disedified her Sisters, incur a great responsibility; for as good example stimulates to virtue, so the loose and irregular lives of the tepid scandalize the Community, and lead many of its members into the faults which they witness every day.

Prayer.

O divine Heart of my Jesus! Heart enamoured of men! Heart created to love them, how is it possible that thou hast been so much dishonored and despised by them? Unhappy me! I, too, have been one of those ungrateful souls; I, too, have lived so many years in the world and have not loved thee. Pardon me, O my Jesus, the great fault of not having loved Thee, who art so amiable, and who hast loved me so much, that Thou couldst not have done more than Thou hast done to oblige me to love Thee. In punishment of having so long despised Thy love, I would deserve to be condemned to that miserable state in which I could never love Thee. But no, my Spouse; I cheerfully accept every chastisement except the eternal privation of Thy love. Grant me the grace to love Thee, and then dispose of me as Thou pleasest. But how can I fear such a chastisement when Thou dost continue still to command me to love Thee, my Lord and my God. Thou shall, thou sayest, love the Lord thy God with thy whole heart. It is Thy will that I love Thee with my whole soul, and I desire nothing but to love Thee with all my strength. O loving Heart of my Jesus, light up in my soul that blessed fire which Thou earnest on earth to enkindle. Destroy all the earthly attachments that still live in my heart, and prevent me from belonging entirely to Thee. O my beloved Saviour, do not reject the love of a heart which has hitherto so much afflicted Thee. Ah, since Thou hast loved me so much, do not permit me to live for a single moment without Thy love. O love of my Jesus, Thou art my love. I hope that

I shall always love Thee, and that Thou wilt always love me; and that this mutual love shall never be dissolved.

O Mary, mother of fair love; O thou who dost desire to see thy Son loved, bind and unite me to Jesus, so that I may become entirely his, as he desires me to be.

CHAPTER V.

THE DANGER TO WHICH AN IMPERFECT RELIGIOUS, WHO IS BUT LITTLE AFRAID OF THE CONSEQUENCES OF HER IMPERFECTIONS, EXPOSES HER SALVATION.

1. One can and should avoid all venial sins plainly voluntary.

THE first step to be taken in the formation of a garden is to root out all useless and noxious weeds, and to put in their place fruitful and salutary plants. It was in this way the Almighty commanded Jeremiah to proceed when he imposed upon him the arduous task of cultivating the Church. Go, I have set thee this day over the nations and over kingdoms, to root up, and to pull down, and to waste, and to destroy, to build, and to plant. To become a saint, then, a religious must, in the first place, endeavor to eradicate from her soul all imperfections, and to plant in their stead the virtues of the Gospel.

"The first devotion," says St. Teresa, "Is to take away all sins."

I do not speak of grievous sins, from which I suppose the religious who reads this book to be exempt. I hope that she has never lost the grace of God infused by baptism, or at least that she has recovered it, and that she is resolved to suffer a thousand deaths rather than forfeit it again. To prevent the danger of relapse, I entreat her to keep always in mind the alarming doctrine so strongly inculcated in the Holy Scriptures, and taught by St. Basil, St. Jerome, St. Augustine, and other Fathers, that God has fixed for each person the number of sins which he will pardon. Being ignorant of this number, we should tremble, lest, adding another to our past sins, we complete the measure of our iniquities, be abandoned by God, and lost forever. This thought has powerful efficacy in dispelling the illusion by which the devil so often induces Christians to relapse into sin. Holding out the hope of pardon to them, he says: You may indulge your passions for this time; you will afterwards confess it, and obtain forgiveness. Oh, if Christians were penetrated with the salutary fear that any new sin should never be forgiven, would they not be struck with horror at the very idea of relapse? But through a false hope of pardon, innumerable souls return to their former crimes, until the measure of their iniquities is filled up, and they are thus irremediably lost.

Nor do I speak of venial faults of imperfect advertence, or of human frailty, when I say that a religious should cleanse her soul from all sins. From such imperfections no one is exempt: For, says St. James, In many things we all offend. Even the saints have fallen into the sins of frailty. If, says St. John, we say we have no sin, we deceive ourselves, and the truth is not in us. Our corrupt nature is so strongly inclined to evil, that it is impossible for us, without a most special grace (which has been given only to the Mother of God), to avoid, during our whole lives, all venial sins—even those that are but imperfectly deliberate. God permits such defects even in souls dedicated to his love, to keep them humble, and to make them feel that, as they fall into light transgressions, in spite of all their resolutions and promises, so but for his divine support they should likewise be precipitated into grievous crimes. When we are guilty of a venial fault we must humble our souls, and, confessing our weakness, must endeavor to multiply prayer, and to implore the aid of the protecting arm of God against more grievous offences. Here, then, I mean to speak only of deliberate and fully voluntary venial sins. All these may be avoided, and are seldom or never committed by holy souls, who live with the firm and constant resolution rather to suffer death than, with full advertence, to be guilty of a venial violation of God's holy law. St. Catharine of Genoa used to say that to a soul inflamed with the pure love of God the smallest fault is more intolerable than hell itself. Hence she frequently protested that, rather than willfully commit a venial sin, she would suffer to be cast into an ocean of fire. It is no wonder that the saints had such a horror of the smallest sin: for, illuminated by the light of God, they saw and felt that the least offence against his infinite Majesty is a much greater evil than the death and destruction of all men and angels. "What sin," says St. Anselm, "Will the sinner dare to call small? For when can it be a slight fault to dishonour God?" Who shall ever be daring enough to assert that such a sin, because it is venial, is not a great evil? Can it be ever said that an indignity to the Lord is but of little moment? If a subject said to his sovereign, In other things I will obey you, but not in this, because it is unimportant,—what censure and chastisement would he not deserve?

Hence St. Teresa used to say: "Would to God we had a horror not of the devils, but of every venial sin from which we may suffer far greater injury than from all the devils in hell." She would frequently say to her spiritual children, "From all deliberate sins, however small, may God deliver you." Religious should take particular care to avoid the least offence of God. Of them St. Gregory Nazianzen says: "Do you know that in you a wrinkle is a greater deformity than the greatest wounds are in seculars?" If a servant, whose occupation renders cleanliness impossible, appear in soiled clothes before the king, he treats her with compassion rather than with severity. But if he sees a stain on the garments of his spouse, the queen, he is indignant, and bursts out into expressions of complaint and reproach. Jesus Christ is likewise indulgent to the sins of seculars, but bitterly complains of the faults of his spouses. Unhappy the religious who is regardless of light defects! She shall never become a saint, and shall never enjoy peace. St. Teresa, while she led an imperfect life, made no progress in virtue, and enjoying neither spiritual consolation nor sensual pleasure, lived in a state of continual misery. It is because they are heedless of their imperfections that so many nuns are always unhappy. They are, on the one hand, far removed from the pleasures of the world, and, on the other, never experience the joy and tranquility of a good conscience. For, since they are not generous to God, he is justly sparing in his favours to them. Let us offer our whole being to God, and he will give himself entirely to us. I to my beloved and his turning is towards me.

But you will say, venial sins however great, though they may prevent me from being a saint, will never deprive me of the grace of God, nor of eternal life; and for me it is enough to obtain salvation. Whosoever speaks thus should reflect on the words of St. Augustine: "Where you have said it is sufficient, you have perished." Do you then say that for you it is sufficient? If you do, you are lost. To understand this truth, and to see the danger of venial sins, particularly when they are deliberate and habitual, it is necessary to consider that the habit of light faults inclines the soul to grievous transgressions. Thus the habit of slight aversions disposes the will to mortal hatred, the habit of small thefts to gross rapine, and the habit of sensual attachments to impure affections. St. Gregory says that, "The soul never remains where it falls;" no, she always sinks still lower. As mortal diseases frequently proceed from slight indisposition, so grievous transgressions often have their origin in habitual venial sins. "Trivial detractions," says Father Alvarez, "Slight aversions, culpable curiosity, acts of impatience and intemperance, do not kill the soul; but they render her so weak, that when assailed by any grievous temptation she has not strength to resist it, and falls."

Venial sins do not indeed separate the soul from God, but they estrange her affections from him, and thus expose her to great danger of losing his grace. When Jesus was taken in the garden, St. Peter did not wish to abandon his Master, but followed him afar off. Many, though unwilling to be separated from Jesus Christ by mortal sins, will follow him only at a distance, and will make no effort to abstain from venial faults. But how many of that class of Christians have imitated the conduct of St. Peter, who three times denied that he was a disciple of the Redeemer, and to his denial added the guilt of perjury? St. Isidore says, that in punishment of their indifference, and the tepidity of their love to him, God justly permits those who disregard venial faults to fall into mortal sins. He that contemneth small things shall fall by little and little.

Do not then, therefore, says St. Dorotheas, say that the habit of venial sins is only a small evil; but reflect on its consequences. A bad habit is an ulcer which infects the soul; and as it diminishes her strength to avoid light faults, so it gradually renders her unable to resist grievous temptations. "Do not," says St. Augustine, "Contemn them because they are numerous: ruin is to be apprehended from their multitude, though not from their magnitude." Despise not your faults because they are venial, but tremble because they are many: for the greatness of their number may bring upon you that destruction which the heinousness of their malice does not deserve. You, says the saint in another place, carefully fly from the danger of being crushed by a rock; but I caution you to shun the risk of suffocation by a heap of sand. By a collection of sand the Holy Father means frequent habitual venial transgressions, which, when committed with deliberation and without efforts of amendment, destroy in the soul the fear of committing mortal sins. And whoever fears them but little, will easily fall into them. Hence St. John Chrysostom has gone so far as to assert that we should, in a certain manner have a greater dread of habitual venial sins than of mortal sin. Because the latter naturally excites horror; but as the habit of the former generates negligence and contempt for small faults, so likewise it induces a disregard for grievous transgressions. Hence the Holy Ghost says: Catch us the little foxes that destroy the vines. He does not tell us to catch the lions, or the leopards, but the little foxes. We tremble at the approach of the lion or of other fierce animals, and therefore we take care to guard against their attacks; but we fear not little foxes, and therefore through our negligence they by their excavations dry up the root and destroy the vine. In like manner, frequent and voluntary faults, though small, dry up the good desires of the soul, which are the roots of spiritual life, and thus produce decay and ruin.

Habitual and voluntary venial sins expose the soul to the danger of perdition: first, because, as we have already seen, they incline the will to mortal sin, and diminish its strength to resist temptations. Let us consider besides how they deprive her of numberless helps from God, which he had prepared for her.

To incline the will to good, the understanding must be continually illuminated by the light of God; and to become pliant and obedient to the motions of grace, the will requires the constant assistance of God. Besides, to resist the powers of hell, we stand in need of the continual protection of the Lord. Without it, we should all yield to the temptations of the devil, which of ourselves we are utterly unable to overcome. It is God that either enables us to conquer all the powers of darkness, or prevents the devil from suggesting temptations to which we would yield. Hence Jesus Christ has taught us the prayer, and lead us not into temptation; that is, preserve us from those temptations to which we would consent. Now, what are the effects of venial sins? They diminish the lights, the helps, and the protection of God; so that the soul, being darkened, weak, and dry, will lose all affection for the things of God, will become attached to the things of the world, and thus exposed to great danger of renouncing the grace of God for the sake of earthly goods. Besides, in punishment of venial sins Almighty God permits the soul to be assailed with more violent temptations. Whosoever is ungenerous to God does not deserve liberality from him. He who soweth sparingly shall also reap sparingly. Blessed Henry Suso, in the vision of the rocks, described in his life, seeing a great many on the first rock, asked who they were. Jesus Christ answered: "These are the tepid who only seek to avoid mortal sin." The holy man then asked whether they should be saved. "If," replied the Redeemer, "They die in the state of grace, they shall be saved; but their danger is much greater than they imagine. They think they can serve God and the senses; but this is scarcely possible; for it is exceedingly difficult to persevere in the grace of God and at the same time to indulge in sensual pleasures."

Be not without fear about sins forgiven. Why does the Holy Ghost admonish us to be afraid of sin which has been already pardoned? Because after the guilt is remitted the temporal penalties of sin still remain; and among them we must reckon the withdrawal of God's graces. Hence the saints never ceased to weep for their faults, though only venial, and even after they had been forgiven; for they always trembled lest their past transgressions should be punished by the subtraction of the graces necessary to obtain eternal life. A favorite who has offended his sovereign will not be raised to his former rank and dignity immediately after he has obtained pardon, nor until he has given strong proofs of a determination to atone by subsequent services for his past misconduct. And when Christians insult the Majesty of their God he justly withdraws his protecting arm and his former familiarity, until by tears of sorrow and other good works they have expiated their guilt. The more frequently the soul displeases God, the more will he retire from her. By repeated faults her weakness and her inclination to evil are increased, while the graces of God are diminished, and then she will easily fall into eternal ruin.

2.   Venial Sins injure, above all, the Religious, who are most especially called to Perfection.

Every Christian who, because he desires to do only what is necessary for salvation, commits habitually deliberate venial sins, is, as we have seen, exposed to the danger of being lost. How much more perilous must be the state of a religious who, with full knowledge, and without any thought or effort of amendment, commits light faults, saying, For me it is sufficient to be saved. The spouse of Jesus being called to religion, is called not only to be saved, but also to be a saint. Now St. Gregory says that he who is called to sublime sanctity will not be saved without it. Jesus Christ said one day to Blessed Angela of Foligno: "They who, after being enlightened by me to walk in the way of perfection, will only tread in the ordinary path, shall be abandoned by me." It is certain that every religious is called and commanded to walk in the way of perfection. It is to enable her to become a saint that God has bestowed upon her so many special lights and graces. Now if she lead a life of habitual negligence and continual defects, without ever seeking to correct them, she will justly forfeit all claim to the helps necessary for the fulfillment of her obligations, and thus she will neither become a saint nor be saved. St. Augustine says that God ordinarily abandons tepid souls who, reckless of the consequences, willfully neglect their duties and disregard their defects. "God is accustomed to desert the negligent."

"If," says Jesus to St. Peter, I wash thee not, thou shall have no part with me. Jesus Christ spoke in this place not of the physical washing of the feet, but of the spiritual cleansing of the soul from venial sins, which, unless corrected and expiated, will make those who are called to perfection liable to great danger of perdition. St. Gertrude saw the devil gathering all the little tufts of wool which she allowed to be destroyed; as if her negligence in not preserving them were a fault against holy poverty. To another religious who, contrary to Rule, permitted the fragments of bread which remained after meals to fall off the table, he showed at the hour of death a large mass of these fragments which he had collected, and by this representation endeavoured to lead the religious into despair. The enemy of our souls is well aware that God will demand a much stricter account from religious than from seculars.

And here it may be remarked, that, according to the common opinion of theologians, many violations of rule which in subjects are but light faults will be grievous sins in the Superior if, when they are frequent and apt to produce general relaxation of discipline, she do not correct them according to the best of her ability, and insist on the reparation necessary to preserve exact observance. To this class belong the faults regarding silence, poverty, fasts, the grate, and all similar transgressions. And Superiors are strictly obliged not only to correct such defects, but also to examine carefully whether they have been committed.

Let us now return to the obligation of a religious to aim at perfection, and to avoid even venial sins. In the time of St. Ignatius there was one of the lay-brothers very negligent in the service of God. One day the saint said to him: "Tell me, Brother, for what purpose have you entered religion?" "I have come," replied the Brother, "To serve God." "O Brother," rejoined the saint, "What have you said? If you answered that you had come to attend a Cardinal or an earthly prince, your conduct would be more excusable: but you say you have come to serve the Lord; and is it thus you serve him?" To become a saint, the religious stands in need of particular and abundant graces. Now how can God be expected to bestow his favours in abundance on the religious, who after having retired into the cloister to serve the Lord, dishonors rather than glorifies his name? For by her negligence and continual defects she insinuates that God does not merit to be served with greater fervour. By her imperfect life she declares that his service does not content the soul or impart that felicity which is represented in the Holy Scriptures as the portion of God's servants on earth; in a word, she proclaims that his divine Majesty does not deserve to be loved in preference to the indulgence of all caprice or sensuality.

"It is true," says Father Alvarez, "That even souls devoted to the love of God are not free from all imperfections. But they seek continually to amend their lives by diminishing the number of their defects." But how will the tepid religious, who commits habitual faults, and continues to commit them without remorse or desire of amendment—how, I say, will she be ever able to purify her soul from them, or to escape the danger of falling into mortal sin? The Venerable Louis de Pont used to say: "I have been guilty of many faults; but never without scruple and uneasiness of conscience." Woe to the religious who sins, even venially, with full knowledge and tranquility of soul. As long, says St. Bernard, as the soul detests her imperfections we may hope for amendment; but when she commits faults without fear or remorse, then she will always go from bad to worse. Dying flies, says the Wise man, spoil the sweetness of the ointment. "These dying flies," says Denis the Carthusian, "Are the defects which remain in the soul, and are not detested; such as habitual feelings of dislike, inordinate affections, vanity, indulgence of the appetite, want of modesty in looks and of delicacy in words. These defects spoil the sweetness of the ointment; they diminish devotion at Communion, at meditation, and in the visits to the Blessed Sacrament. Thus the soul loses all the spiritual unction and consolations of religion."

These habitual faults, like a foul incrustation, take away the beauty of the soul, render it an object of disgust, and unworthy the embraces of the Holy Ghost. "They are," says St. Augustine, "As it were an eruption, and destroy our comeliness so as to remove us from the embraces of the Spouse." Hence, feeling no more consolation in her exercises of devotion, the soul will soon omit and abandon them; and neglecting the means of salvation, she will probably be lost. If the tepid religious should continue her Communions, meditations, and visits to the Blessed Sacrament, she will draw but little fruit from them. In her will be verified the words of the Holy Ghost: You have sowed much, and brought in little. . . . And he that hath earned wages, put them into a bag with holes. Such, precisely, is the tepid and imperfect religious. All her spiritual exercises are laid up in a bag with holes: for them no reward remains. Being performed with so much tepidity, they render her always more and more deserving of chastisement, and deprive her of those abundant helps which God had prepared for her, had she corresponded to his holy inspirations. For he that hath, to him shall be given, and he shall abound; but he that hath not, from him shall be taken away that also which he hath. Whoever by his cooperation treasures up the fruit of the graces received from God shall obtain an increase of grace and glory; but from the man who buries his talent, thus rendering it unprofitable, that which he hath shall be taken, and the graces prepared for him shall be withheld.

Prayer.

Behold, O Lord, I am one of those unhappy souls who deserved to be left by Thee in the miserable state of tepidity, in which, deprived of Thy light and abandoned by Thy grace, I lived for so many years. But I now see the light which Thou givest me; and I hear Thy voice calling me again to Thy love. These graces are so many proofs that Thou hast not as yet abandoned me. And since Thou hast not cast me away in punishment of so much ingratitude, I desire never more to be ungrateful to Thee. Thou art ready to pardon me, if I repent of the offences that I have committed against Thee. Pardon me, O Jesus, for I detest and abhor my sins above all things. Would that I had died before I ever offended Thee. Thou dost wish for my love: I desire nothing more but to love Thee. I love Thee, O my Sovereign Good: I love Thee, O my God, who art worthy of infinite love. Increase, O Lord, in my soul Thy own light, and the desire Thou givest me to belong entirely to Thee. Thou art omnipotent: Thou canst easily change my heart, and make a rebel to Thy graces become an ardent lover of Thy goodness. Such I desire and hope to be, with the assistance of Thy grace. Thou hast promised to hear all who pray to Thee. I now ask Thee to make me belong entirely to Thee, and love nothing but Thee alone. Ah! Jesus, my Spouse, through the merits of Thy blood, make me love Thee as a sinner ought to love, whom Thou hast loved so much, and whose ingratitude Thou hast borne with so much patience, and for so many years. Trusting, then, in Thy infinite mercy, I hope with a firm confidence to love Thee with my whole heart in this life, and in the next to praise for all eternity Thy mercies to me. The mercies of the Lord I will sing forever.

O Mary, my Mother, I acknowledge that these graces, this light, these desires, and this good-will, which God now gives to me, are the fruits of thy intercession. Continue, O Mary, continue to intercede for me, and do not cease to pray for my sanctification, until my whole being shall be, as thou dost desire, consecrated without reserve to Jesus Christ. Such, O Mary, my firm hope: may it soon be realized. Amen.

CHAPTER VI.

CONTINUATION OF THE SAME SUBJECT.

1.   A Religious has especially to fear being lost when she sins by Attachment to some Passion, or when she lives in Tepidity.

THE religious whose faults spring from attachment to any passion is exposed in a particular manner to the danger of being lost. O God, how many religious are there who, because they do not disengage their hearts from certain earthly attachments, never become saints, and endanger their eternal salvation. To conquer her passions, to expel from her soul all worldly affections, and to remove every obstacle to her progress in perfection, should be the end and object of a religious, in all her spiritual exercises, in her Communions, meditations, spiritual readings, and in all similar duties. To this end she should direct all her devotions and all her prayers, begging continually of the Almighty a perfect detachment from every creature, and a complete victory over all her corrupt inclinations. To gain this victory she ought, in the first place, to direct her attention to the practice of exterior mortification, and particularly to the mortification of the eyes, of the appetite, and of the tongue. Secondly, she should endeavor to mortify and to eradicate all the irregular affections of the heart, such as attachment to self-esteem, to the things of the world, or to any other object in which she takes delight. Thirdly, she must strive to destroy self-will, by acting continually in opposition to her own inclinations. Lastly, she should seek to do all this with ease and with cheerfulness; for in this great contest with the corruption of nature she shall always have some passion to moderate or some virtue to improve.

There are some who continue their Communions and meditations, but in them they only seek spiritual refreshment and sensible devotion. Hence they remain always bound down to the earth by worldly attachments, which continually impede their advancement in holiness, and make them recede more and more every day from their first fervor. It frequently happens that such persons in the end lose the grace of God.

It is necessary to impress deeply on your mind that the artifice by which the devil seeks to draw spiritual souls from the service of God is, not to tempt them at first to any mortal sin. In the beginning he is, as St. Francis says, satisfied to hold them in bondage by a single hair; for if he attempted to bind them at once in the bonds of servitude they would fly from him with horror. But fearing not the trammels of a single hair, they are easily led into the snares prepared for their destruction. At first they are caught by a single hair; then they are bound by a slender thread; next by a strong cord; and finally they are chained in the fetters of hell and the slavery of Satan. For example, a religious, after a dispute with some of her Sisters, will at first retain feelings of dislike, and thus is held by a single hair. After a little time she will neither speak to them nor salute them: she is now bound by a slender thread. Next she will begin to injure them by words and deeds, and is fettered by a strong cord: then on the first occasion of provocation she conceives a mortal hatred towards them, and thus puts on the chains of hell and the slavery of the devil. Again, another religious will at first entertain a human affection towards a friend; she then cherishes this affection under the pretext of gratitude: mutual presents follow; they are succeeded by words of endearment; and by the first assault of passion the miserable soul is bound in the chains of death. In fine, as gamblers by the loss of many small sums are induced to risk and to lose their whole property, so the tepid soul by frequent venial faults is rendered reckless of God's grace, and too weak to resist the temptations of the enemy. Thus she loses her God and her all. To find us addicted to any passion, is to the devil a powerful stimulus to exert himself for our destruction. "It is," says St. Ambrose, "Principally when he sees any passions generated in us that the adversary lays his snares: it is then that he excites concupiscence, and prepares his nets." The enemy endeavors to discover the evil inclinations which predominate in our hearts, and presenting to us opportunities of indulging these corrupt tendencies, foments our passions, and prepares a snare for our destruction.

"When," says Cassian, "We hear of the fall of a soul consecrated to God, we are not to imagine that she fell at once into mortal sin. No: we must suppose that she began by light faults, and by them was led into grievous transgressions." St. John Chrysostom asserts that he knew many persons who appeared to be adorned with all virtues, and who, because they disregarded venial sins, were precipitated into an abyss of crime. The Venerable Sister Anne of the Incarnation saw in hell a soul reputed by her and by all to be a saint. On her countenance appeared a multitude of small animals, representing the first faults which she disregarded. Of these animals some were heard to say to the un-happy soul, "With us you began;" others, "By us you continued;" and the rest, "By us you were lost." Hence, Mother Mary Victoria Strada used to say: "The devil, when he cannot have much, is content with a little; and with that little he afterwards acquires a great deal." At first the serpent tempted Eve not to eat, but only to behold the forbidden fruit; he then raised doubts about the fulfillment of the divine threats; and in the end induced her to violate the command of God. St. Teresa observes that the enemy is satisfied when a soul begins to open to him the gate of her heart: he will afterwards obtain full possession of it. This is likewise the doctrine of St. Jerome. "The devil," says the holy Doctor, "Does not contend at once against any one by temptations to great vices, but only to small faults that he may by some means enter and govern the heart of man, and that he may afterwards impel him to more heinous crimes." He does not immediately tempt any one to mortal sin; but commences by suggesting light defects, that, gaining admission into the soul, and beginning his rule, he may afterwards draw her into grievous transgressions. "No one," says St. Bernard, "Is plunged at once into the depths of turpitude: they who fall into the greatest enormities begin by the smallest faults." An insignificant spark will set fire to a whole forest. Behold, says St. James, how small a fire—what a great wood it kindleth! A single unmortified passion will precipitate the soul into ruin.

And here it is necessary to remark most particularly, that whenever a religious is guilty of mortal sin, her fall will expose her to great danger of being abandoned by God: for being committed amid the lights and graces of God, imparted to her by means of so many sermons, Com-munions, meditations, good example of companions, admonitions of spiritual directors and of Superiors, her trangression will not be like that of seculars, who sin in the midst of the darkness of the world, but will be a sin of malice. After having received so many lights, and having in her hands so many means of obtaining strength against the enemy of her salvation, she cannot allege ignorance or weakness in extenuation of her guilt. According to the doctrine of St. Thomas, a sin of malice is that which is committed with a full knowledge of its enormity. Hence, because the darkness arising from sin is proportional to the lights bestowed on its author, the sin of malice produces great misery in the soul.

Besides, the angelic Doctor teaches that the grievousness of sin increases in proportion to the ingratitude of the sinner. Now the graces and favors which a religious has received from God are innumerable. He has taken her from the midst of the dangers of the world, and because every convent is the house of God, has given her a place in his own habitation. From a vast multitude of his servants he has selected her for his spouse; and to make her a saint, and fit to be a spouse of God, he has enriched her with so many lights and so many external and internal helps to sanctity. He has frequently given himself to her in the Holy Eucharist; and in her meditations, visits, and spiritual readings has often spoken to her with the familiarity of a friend. In a word, he has raised her up from the depth of lowliness and placed her among the princes of his people. And after all these favors she by sin turns her back upon him, and deliberately determines to become his enemy. Unhappy soul, her fall will be her destruction. He that falls on level ground seldom sustains serious injury; but he that tumbles from a lofty eminence is said not to fall, but to be dashed to ruin. "A fall from on high," says St. Ambrose, "Is accompanied with great destruction." And the prophet Ezechiel says: And I set thee in the holy mountain of God. . . . And thou hast sinned: and I cast thee out from the mountain of God and destroyed thee ungrateful soul, the Almighty will say to the religious, I have placed you on my holy mountain, and from its summit you have voluntarily fallen into sin. In punishment, then, of your ingratitude, remain in perdition, for I have banished you forever from my face. "God," says Sister Mary Strozzi, "Wishes religious to be the mirror of the entire world. Hence, because they are called to extraordinary perfection they dishonour him greatly by an imperfect life. The sin of a religious excites the horror of paradise, and obliges the Almighty to turn away from her; for he repudiates faithless spouses who violate the contract made at their profession, and therefore he abandons them to their irregular passions." Oh how difficult is the conversion of a soul who, after having once tasted the sweetness of God, becomes a rebel to his love!

A religious, then, should tremble at the thought of being bound to the service of Satan by any passion, or by any, even the smallest sin. She should, I say, tremble, because every little attachment may be the cause of her damnation. St. Teresa used to say that "Whoever approaches ruin will be lost." This observation is most just. For although she had never been guilty of a mortal sin, Almighty God showed her the place

81

prepared for her in hell if she had not relinquished an irregular though not an unchaste affection which she entertained towards a relative. A bird unshackled flies with ease, but when tied even by a slender thread it remains on the earth, and, like the toad, will continue to crawl in the mire. So a religious free from all earthly attachments flies and will continually fly to God. But while any affection to creatures dwells in her heart she will never rise above the earth, but will fall continually into greater defects, till at length all is lost. In fine, you must be persuaded that the salvation of a religious depends on the correction of light faults, particularly when frequent and habitual: for so many little streams will form a river in which she will be overwhelmed. Habitual faults disregarded and not corrected will by degrees draw her into the state of tepidity—that miserable state of which the Redeemer said to the Bishop of Laodicea: I know thy works, that thou art neither cold nor hot. Behold the state of a tepid religious. She is not daring enough to abandon God altogether, but she despises light faults. She commits a great many of them every day, by impatience, lies, murmuring, greediness, and imprecations; by aversions, and by attachments to worldly goods, to the grate, to curiosity, to self-esteem, and to self-will. And these imperfections she neither regrets nor endeavors to correct. I would, continues the Lord, thou were cold or hot; but because thou art lukewarm, and neither hot nor cold, I will begin to vomit thee out of my mouth. I would, he says, thou were cold: that is, it were better for you to be altogether deprived of my grace; for then there would be stronger hopes of your repentance. But, remaining in a state of tepidity, you will stand in greater danger of damnation; because you will easily fall from that state into mortal sin, and then there will be but little reason to hope for your resuscitation.

Speaking of a sinner not as yet converted, St. Gregory holds out hopes of repentance; but, speaking of a tepid soul who is not afraid of her imperfections, he despairs of her amendment. "Warmth which has failed from fervor is in despair." The Son of God says: Because thou art lukewarm, I will begin to vomit thee out of my mouth. A draught, when cold or hot, may be taken without repugnance; but when tepid it is nauseous. The lukewarm Christian stands in great danger of being vomited forth by Almighty God; that is, of being forsaken by his grace. By the words, I will begin to vomit thee out of my mouth, the Redeemer signified that he was ready to abandon the tepid soul; for what is vomited is taken back only with horror.

But how does God begin to vomit the tepid religious out of his mouth? He ceases to give her the vivid lights of faith, the spiritual consolations, the holy desires, and the loving calls which he was accustomed to bestow upon her. Bereft of these blessings, she begins to neglect her meditations, Communions, and visits to the Blessed Sacrament, or to discharge these duties with repugnance, disgust, and distraction. She will perform all her exercises with reluctance, dissipation, with inquietude, and without devotion. Behold, how the Lord begins to vomit her out of his mouth. Thus the miserable soul finding only pain and trouble, and no comfort in any of her exercises of piety, she finally abandons them all, and falls into grievous sins.

In a word, tepidity is a moral fever which is scarcely felt, but irremediably leads to death. The tepid soul never thinks of correcting her faults. She becomes so insensible to the stings of conscience, that without perceiving her fall she will be one day precipitated into eternal misery.

2.   Means to extricate One's Self from Tepidity.

Then, the tepid religious will say, for me there is no hope of salvation. Because, she will add, it is almost impossible for me to arise from my miserable state. But let her attend to the answer of Jesus Christ: The things that are impossible with men are possible with God. What is impossible to man is not impossible to God. Whoever prays and adopts the necessary means obtains all graces. What are the necessary means?

First, as to Faults committed through Frailty.

If your faults are sins of inadvertence, or of frailty, they do but little injury to the soul as long as you detest them with humility. And here it is necessary to remark, that two sorts of humility arise from our defects—the one holy, and the gift of God; the other pernicious, and the offspring of the devil. The former is that by which the soul sees her imperfections, and is covered with confusion before God, and filled with a sense of her own nothingness. She is sorry for her faults: she detests them, but without being disturbed; and at the sight of her misery she is not discouraged or agitated; but, trusting in God, she resolves to atone for her imperfections by greater attention to her duties, and by greater fervor in works of piety. The other species of humility is that which fills the soul with agitation, with inquietude, and with diffidence; thus making her weak and almost incapable of doing any good. "True humility," says St Teresa, "Though it makes the soul feel her own sinfulness, does not disturb her peace, but, on the contrary, infuses consolation. It fills, indeed, the heart with grief and affliction for having offended God, but at the same time inspires strong hopes of mercy. By such humility the soul is enlightened to see her own misery, and to praise God for having so long borne with her. But false humility instilled by the devil brings with it no light to make the soul do good, but represents God as a tyrant who will destroy all by fire and sword. Of all the deceitful inventions of the devil which I have known this is the most subtle."

In the imperfections, then, which human weakness cannot avoid, as negligence is censurable, so excessive fear is reprehensible. "In such almost inevitable faults," says St. Bernard, "Immoderate fear, as well as negligence, is culpable." We should be sorry, but not lose courage, when we commit such faults; for God readily grants pardon when the soul detests them. For the just man falls seven times, and shall rise again. He that sins through frailty easily rises. "He falls and will rise again." St. Francis de Sales says that as daily defects are in deliberately committed, so they are in deliberately taken away. St. Thomas teaches that such faults are cancelled "When the soul is fervently moved towards God," that is, by acts of divine love, of resignation, of oblation, and by similar works which spiritual souls are accustomed to perform. The angelic Doctor adds, "That the sacramentals—such as to recite the Pater Noster, the Confiteor; to strike the breast; to receive the blessing of the bishop; to sprinkle one's self with holy water; and to pray in a consecrated Church—produce the remission of such venial defects." The sacraments, but especially the Holy Eucharist, have particular efficacy to remit venial sin. "The mind," says St. Bernardine of Sienna, "May be so absorbed in devotion, by receiving Holy Communion, that the soul will be purified from all venial sins."

Secondly, as to Deliberate though not Habitual Venial Sins.

If a religious should have the misfortune to commit sometimes, but not often, a deliberate venial sin, she should not even then lose courage, or permit the peace of her soul to be disturbed. Let her endeavor immediately to repair her fault by repentance, and by a strong determination not to be guilty of it again. Whenever she relapses her sorrow and resolution should be renewed, and all her confidence placed in God, who, if she continue to act in this way after every fault, will finally deliver her from such deliberate sins. St. Philip Neri used to say that to become a saint is not the business of a day. Whoever leaves not the road of perfection in which he began to walk ought not to despond, for he will ultimately arrive at sanctity. To convince us of our weakness, to show us that without his aid and protection we should fall into the greatest crimes, God sometimes permits us to commit deliberate venial sins. Such faults, then, though voluntary, provided they be unfrequent, do not seriously injure the soul, or at least they do not bring her to ruin.

Thirdly, as to Deliberate Venial and Habitual Sins.

But light sins which are deliberate and habitual easily lead the soul into perdition, particularly when they are committed through attachment to any passion, and without sorrow or efforts of amendment; for they show that the soul has fallen into a state of tepidity from which, as we have already seen, it is very difficult to recover. But if a religious should be so unfortunate as to fall into such a state, let her attend to the following means of emerging from it:

1. The first means is a true desire of being delivered from her miserable condition. If she feel not that desire, she ought at least to beg it of God, trusting in his promises to give us whatsoever we ask. Ask, and you shall receive.

2. She should endeavor to search out her defects, particularly her predominant failing. If, for example, she is full of self-esteem; if she frequently speaks in the language and tone of authority; if she is addicted to self-praise; if she is disturbed by every humiliation and inattention from others—then she may conclude that pride is her ruling passion. Self-love will predominate in some who are afflicted at every little infirmity, who are annoyed at every inconvenience, and who always seek to gratify their palate, and cannot bear any food that is not agreeable to their taste. In others anger is the prevailing fault: they are provoked by every contradiction, and complain of the conduct of all who thwart their inclinations. Others, for every trivial cause, neglect mental prayer, Communion, the choir, and other similar duties: in them sloth holds the ascendancy.

3. As soon as she has discovered her predominant passion, a religious should make a strong resolution to free herself from it, and to contend with it till it is completely vanquished. Thou shalt, says the Lord, utterly destroy them." "God," says St. Teresa, "Requires of us only strong resolutions; he himself will do the rest." In another place she asserts that the devil is afraid of resolute souls; but he fears not those who, though they desire perfection, never desire to become saints. Again the saint says that God cheerfully lends his aid to all, however great their sinfulness may be, who with a firm resolution consecrate themselves entirely to his love. The meditations of a religious should always be concluded by strong resolutions. "Short prayer," says St. Teresa, "Which produces great effects, is better than prayer continued for many years, but devoid of holy resolutions." And of what use, I ask, is the meditation in which we are content with certain devout affections, and certain general petitions made through habit, but in which we never resolve to correct the faults we know to be an obstacle to our spiritual advancement?

4. One of the most necessary resolutions is to remove as much as possible the occasions of our defects. The devil laughs at all our resolutions and promises of amendment as long as we expose ourselves to the occasions of sin. He once said that of all instructions that which treated on avoiding the occasions of sin was the most displeasing to him. A religious, then, should endeavor to discover the causes of her defects; she ought to examine if they arise from familiarity with any person within or without the monastery; from remaining in such a place; from keeping up a correspondence by letters or by presents, or from similar causes. St. Teresa says that if a soul does not relinquish worldly diversion she will soon begin to fall back in the way of the Lord; and that if all sinful occasions be taken away she will advance rapidly in the love of God. This great saint also says that a religious should communicate her temptations only to those who love perfection. If she disclose them to imperfect souls she will do injury to herself and to others.

5. A religious ought to be particularly exact in performing acts of the virtues opposed to the evil inclinations which are most troublesome to her, and which most frequently lead her into defects. For example, if she is prone to pride, she should take particular care to humble herself before all, and to bear patiently all the humiliations that she receives

from others. If she is addicted to greediness, she ought to abstain as much as possible from the indulgence of her appetite. They that are inclined to other defects should adopt similar means of conquering them. It will also, as Cassian observes, be very useful to represent to ourselves, in the time of mental prayer, the occasions which may occur; as, for example, any insult or injury that we are likely to receive, and then to resolve to humble ourselves, and to be resigned to the divine will. Such previous resolutions (except with regard to temptations against chastity) prepare the soul for sudden and unforeseen contradictions. It was by this means that the saints were always prepared to bear with peace and joy all the derision, injuries, stripes, and injustices that they received.

6. It is also very useful to make the particular examination on the predominant passion, and to perform some penance as often as we yield to it. We must never cease to combat this passion until it is completely conquered; we must trust in the divine aid, and say with holy David: I will pursue after my enemies, and overtake them; and I will not turn again till they are consumed. I will persecute my enemies; I will beat them down, and will not cease to combat them till they are utterly destroyed. Remember that however great your progress in virtue may be, it would be a fatal delusion to imagine that your passions are dead, for, although they may be extinguished for a time, they will again spring up as long as you remain in the body. "How much so ever," says St. Bernard, "You have advanced here below, you err if you think your vices are not only suppressed, but dead." Hence Cassian observes that to prevent the passions that you have subdued from resuming their sway, it is necessary to watch continually; for if you slacken your exertions they will return, and will rule your soul with still greater despotism.

7. To overcome any defect whatever, it is necessary, above all, to distrust altogether our own strength and exertions, and to place entire confidence in God, saying with David: For I will not trust in my bow; neither shall my sword save me. If we confide in our own resolutions and exertions our labor will be lost. We must therefore pray without ceasing for the divine assistance, continually crying out, Have mercy on me, O Lord; assist me O my God. Jesus Christ has promised that he who asks shall receive, and that he who seeks shall find; but to obtain God's gifts we must pray continually, and never cease to pray. We

ought, says the Redeemer, always to pray and not to faint. Whenever we give up prayer we shall be defeated; but if we persevere in prayer, with a true desire of receiving the graces of God, though as yet we have not been conquerors, the victory shall, nevertheless, ultimately belong to us.

Prayer.

O my Jesus, look not on my ingratitude to Thee, after all Thy mercies, but turn Thy eyes to Thy own merits, and to the pains that Thou hast suffered for me, from the crib of Bethlehem to the cross of Calvary. I repent, with my whole soul, of all the offences that I have offered to Thee. From this moment I consecrate to Thee my life, which I desire to spend in doing all that I can to obey and to love Thee. I love Thee, O my Redeemer, but I love Thee too little; for Thy mercy's sake, increase in my soul Thy love. Hear my prayer O Jesus, and make me, by Thy grace, continue to repeat this prayer. O love of my soul, O that my heart may burn continually with Thy love. I have offended Thee grievously; but for the future I desire to love Thee intensely. I desire to love Thee alone, because Thou alone deservest to be loved above all things; and I desire to love Thee for no other reason than because Thou art worthy of all love.

O Mary, my mother and my hope, assist me.

CHAPTER VII.

INTERIOR MORTIFICATION, OR ABNEGATION OF SELF-LOVE.— OBEDIENCE.

I.

Necessity of combating Self-love.—Practical Rules.

THERE are two sorts of self-love: the one good, the other pernicious. The former is that which makes us seek eternal life—the end of our creation; the latter inclines us to pursue earthly goods, and to prefer them to our everlasting welfare, and to the holy will of God. "The celestial Jerusalem," says St. Augustine, "Is built up by loving God so as to condemn one's self; but the earthly city is raised by loving self so as to despise Almighty God." Hence, Jesus Christ has said: If any man will come after me, let him deny himself: Christian perfection, then, consists in self-abnegation. Whoever denies not himself, cannot be a follower of Jesus Christ. "The augmentation of charity," says St. Augustine, "Is the diminution of cupidity: the perfection of charity is its destruction." The less, then, a Christian desires to indulge passion, the more he will love God; and if he seeks nothing but God, he will then possess perfect charity. But in the present state of corrupt nature it is not possible to be altogether exempt from the molestation of self-love. Jesus alone among men, and Mary alone among women, have been free from its suggestions. All the other saints had to combat their irregular passions. The principal and the only care of a religious should be, to restrain the inordinate inclinations of self-love. "To regulate the motions of the soul is," as St. Augustine says, "The office of interior mortification."

Unhappy the soul that suffers itself to be ruled by its own inclinations. "A domestic enemy," says St. Bernard, "Is the worst of foes." The devil and the world continually seek our destruction, but self-love is a still more dangerous enemy. "Self-love," says St. Mary Magdalene de Pazzi, "Is like a worm which corrodes the roots of a plant, deprives us not only of fruit, but of life." In another place she says, "Self-love is the most deceitful of all enemies: like Judas, it betrays us with the kiss of peace. Whoever overcomes it conquers all. He that cannot cut it off by a single stroke should at least endeavor to destroy it by degrees."

We must pray continually, in the language of Solomon: Give me not over to a shameless and foolish mind. O my God, do not abandon me to my foolish passions, that seek to destroy in my soul Thy holy fear, and even to deprive me of the use of my reason.

Our whole life must be one continued contest. The life of a man upon earth, says Job, is a warfare. Now he that is placed in the front of battle must be always prepared for an attack: as soon as he ceases to defend himself he is conquered. And here it is necessary to remark, that the soul should never cease to combat her passions, however great her victories over them may have been; for human passions, though conquered a thousand times, never die. "Believe me," says St. Bernard, "That after being cut off they bud forth again; and after being put to flight they return." Hence by struggling with concupiscence we can only render its attacks less frequent, less violent, and more easy to be subdued. A certain monk complained to the Abbot Theodore that he had contended for eight years with his passions, and that still they were not extinguished. "Brother," replied the abbot, "You complain of this warfare of eight years, and I have spent seventy years in solitude, and during all that time I have not been for a single day free from assaults of passion." We shall be subject during our mortal lives to the molestation of our passions. "But," as St. Gregory says, "It is one thing to look at these monsters, and another to shelter them in our hearts." It is one thing to hear their roar, and another to admit them into our souls, and suffer them to devour us.

The human soul is a garden in which useless and noxious herbs constantly spring up: we must, therefore, by the practice of holy mortification continually hold the mattock in our hands to root them up and banish them from our hearts; otherwise our souls will become a wild, uncultivated waste, covered with briers and thorns. "Conquer yourself," was an expression always on the lips of St. Ignatius of Loyola, and the text of his familiar discourses to his religious. Conquer self-love and break down your own will. Few (he would say) of those who practice mental prayer become saints, because few of them endeavor to overcome themselves. "Of a hundred persons," says the saint, "Devoted to prayer, more than ninety are self-willed." Hence he preferred a single act of mortification of self-will to long prayer, accompanied with many spiritual consolations. "What does it avail," says Gilbert, "To close the gates, if famine—the internal enemy—produce general affliction." What does it profit us to mortify the exterior senses and to perform exercises of devotion while at the same time we cherish in our hearts rancor, ambition, attachment to self-will and to self-esteem, or any other passion which brings ruin on the soul?

St. Francis Borgia says that prayer introduces the love of God into the soul, but mortification prepares a place for it, by banishing from the heart earthly affections—the most powerful obstacles to charity. Whoever goes for water to the fountain must cleanse the vessel of the earth which it may contain; otherwise he will bring back mire instead of water. "Prayer without mortification," says Father Balthasar Alvarez, "Is either an illusion, or lasts but for a short time." And St. Ignatius asserts that a mortified Christian acquires a more perfect union with God in a quarter of an hour's prayer, than an unmortified soul does by praying for several hours. Hence, whenever he heard that any one spent a great deal of time in mental prayer, he said: "It is a sign that he practices great mortification."

There are some religious who perform a great many exercises of devotion, who practice frequent Communion, long meditations, fasting, and other corporal austerities, but make no effort to overcome certain little passions—for example, certain resentments, aversions, curiosity, and certain dangerous affections. They will not submit to any contradiction; they will not give up attachment to certain persons, nor subject their will to the commands of their Superiors, or to the holy will of God. What progress can they make in perfection? Unhappy souls, they will be always imperfect: always out of the way of sanctity. "They," says St. Augustine, "Run well, but out of the way." They imagine that they run well because they practice the works of piety which their own self-will suggests; but they shall be forever out of the way of perfection, which consists in conquering self. "Thou shalt advance," says the devout Thomas a Kempis, "In proportion to the violence thou shalt have offered to thyself." I do not mean to censure vocal prayer, or acts of penance, or the other spiritual works. But, because all exercises of devotion are but the means of practising virtue, the soul should seek in them only the conquest of its passions. Hence, in our Communions, meditations, visits to the Blessed Sacrament, and other similar exercises, we ought always to beseech Almighty God to give us strength to practice humility, mortification, obedience, and conformity to his holy will. In every Christian it is a defect to act from a motive of self-satisfaction. But in a religious who makes a particular profession of perfection and mortification it is a much greater fault. "God," says Lactantius, "Calls to life by labor; the devil, to death by delights." The Lord brings his servants to eternal life by mortification; but the devil leads sinners to everlasting death by pleasure and self-indulgence.

Even works of piety must be always undertaken with a spirit of detachment; so that whenever our efforts are unsuccessful we shall not be disturbed, and when our exercises of devotion are prohibited by the Superior we shall give them up with cheerfulness. Self-attachment of every kind hinders a perfect union with God. We must therefore seriously and firmly resolve to mortify our passions, and not to submit to be their slaves. External as well as interior mortification is necessary for perfection: but with this difference, that the former should be practiced with discretion; the latter without discretion, and with fervor. What does it profit us to mortify the body while the passions of the heart are indulged? "Of what use is it," says St. Jerome, "To reduce the body by abstinence, if the soul is swelled with pride?—Or to abstain from wine, and to be inebriated with hatred?" It is useless to chastise the body by fasting while pride inflates the heart to such a degree that we cannot bear a word of contempt or the refusal of a request. In vain do we abstain from wine while the soul is intoxicated with anger against all who thwart our designs or oppose our inclinations. No wonder, then, that St. Bernard deplored the miserable state of religious who wear the external garb of humility, and at the same time inwardly cherish their passions. "They," says the saint, "Are not divested of their vices: they only cover them by the outward sign of penance."

By attention to the mortification of self-love we shall become saints in a short time, and without the risk of injury to health; for since God is the only witness of interior acts, they will not expose us to the danger of being puffed up with pride. Oh, what treasures of virtue and of merits are laid up by stifling in their very birth those little inordinate desires and affections, those bickering, those suggestions of curiosity, those bursts of wit and humor, and all similar effects of self-love! When you are contradicted, give up your opinion with cheerfulness, unless the glory of God requires that you maintain it. When feelings of self-esteem spring up in your heart, make a sacrifice of them to Jesus Christ. If you receive a letter, restrain your curiosity, and abstain from opening it for some time. If you desire to read the termination of an interesting narrative, lay aside the book, and defer the reading of it to another time. When you feel inclined to mirth, to pull a flower, or to look at any object, suppress these inclinations for the love of Jesus Christ, and deprive yourself for his sake of the pleasure of indulging them. A thousand acts of this kind may be performed in the day. Father Leonard of Port Maurice relates that a servant of God performed eight acts of mortification in eating an egg, and that it was afterwards revealed to her that as the reward of her self-denial eight degrees of grace and as many degrees of glory were bestowed upon her. It is also narrated of St. Dositheus, that by similar mortifications of the interior he arrived in a short time at a high degree of perfection. Though unable, in consequence of bodily infirmities, to fast or to discharge the other duties of the Community, he attained so perfect an union with God, that the other monks, struck with wonder at his sublime sanctity, asked him what exercises of virtue he performed. "The exercise," replied the saint, "To which I have principally attended is the mortification of all self-will."

Blessed Joseph Calasanctius used to say that, "The day which is spent without mortification is lost." To convince us of the necessity of mortification, the Redeemer has chosen a life of self-denial, full of pains and ignominy, and destitute of all sensible pleasure. Hence he is called by Isaias a man of sorrows. He might have saved the world, amid the enjoyment of honors and delights; but he preferred to redeem it by sorrows and contempt. Who having joy set before him, endured the cross. To give us an example, he renounced the joy which was set before him, and embraced the cross. "Reflect again and again," says St. Bernard, "On the life of Jesus, and you will find him always on the cross." The Redeemer revealed to St. Catharine of Bologna that the sorrows of his passion began in his mother's womb. For his birth he selected the season, the place, and the hour most adapted to excite pain. During life he chose to be poor, unknown, despised; and, dying, he preferred the most painful, the most ignominious, and the most desolate of all sorts of death which human nature could suffer. St. Catharine of Sienna used to say, that as a mother takes the bitterest medicine to restore the health of the infant she suckles, so Jesus Christ has assumed all the pains of life to heal the infirmities of his children.

Thus he invites all his followers to accompany him to the mountain of myrrh; that is, of bitterness and of sorrows. I will go to the mountain of myrrh. Behold, he invites us to follow him if we wish for his company. "Do you come," says St. Peter Damian, "To Jesus crucified? If you do, you must come already crucified, or to be crucified." If, O sacred spouse, you come to embrace your crucified Saviour, you must bring with you a heart already crucified, or to be crucified. Speaking especially of his virginal spouses, Jesus Christ said to blessed Baptist Varani: The crucified Bridegroom desires a crucified spouse. Hence, to be the true spouses of Jesus, religious must lead lives of continual mortification and self-denial. Always bearing about in our body the mortification of Jesus. They must never seek their own satisfaction, in any action or desire, but the pleasure of Jesus Christ, crucifying for his sake all their inclinations. They that are Christ's have crucified their flesh, with the vices and concupiscences. Religious, if they expect to be recognized as the spouses of the Redeemer, must transfix all their passions.

Let us now see what are the means by which the spirit of interior mortification may be acquired.

I. The first means is, to discover the passion which predominates in our heart, and which most frequently leads us into sin; and then to endeavor to conquer it. St. Gregory says, that to overcome the devil we must avail ourselves of the artifices by which he seeks our destruction. He labors continually to increase in us the violence of the passion to which we are most subject; and we must direct our attention principally to the extirpation of that passion. Whoever subdues his predominant passion will easily conquer all other evil inclinations; but he that is under its sway can make no progress in perfection. "Of what advantage," says St. Ephrem, "Are wings to the eagle when his foot is chained?" Oh, how many religious are there who, like the royal eagle, are capable of lofty flights in the way of God, and who, because they are bound by earthly attachments, never fly, and never advance in holiness. St. John of the Cross says that a slender thread is sufficient to fetter a soul that flies not with eagerness to its God. Besides, he that submits to the tyranny of any passion, not only does not go forward in the way of virtue, but is exposed to great danger of being lost. If a religious neglects to subdue her ruling passion, other mortifications will be unprofitable to her. Some despise worldly riches, but are full of self-esteem. If they do not endeavor to bear the humiliations which they receive, their contempt of mammon will profit them but little. Others, on the contrary, are patient and humble, but enslaved to the love of money. If they do not mortify the desire of wealth, their patience and humility in bearing with contempt will be of little use to them.

O sacred virgin, resolve then, with a resolute will, to subdue the evil inclination which is most predominant in your heart. A resolute will, aided by the grace of God (which is never wanting), conquers all difficulties. St. Francis de Sales was very prone to anger; but by continual violence to himself he became a model of meekness and of sweetness. We read in his life that he bore without murmur or complaint the injuries and calumnies which, to try his patience, were by the divine permission heaped upon him. As soon as one passion is subdued we must endeavor to overcome the others; for a single unmortified passion will be sufficient to lead the soul to destruction. St. Joseph Calasanctius asserts that while a single passion reigns in a heart, though all the others should have been extirpated, the soul shall never enjoy tranquility. "A ship," says St. Cyril, "However strong and perfect it may be, will be unsafe while the smallest hole remains in the bottom." And St. Augustine says: "Trample under foot passions already subdued, and combat those that still offer resistance." If you wish to be a saint, I advise you to entreat the Superior and director to point out the way in which you ought to walk. Tell them not to spare you, but to contradict your inclinations as often as they shall judge it useful to you. "Be of an upright and perfect will," says that great servant of God, Cardinal Petrucci. St. Teresa relates that she derived more advantage from one of her confessors, who sought on all occasions to oppose her desires, than from all the others. She adds, that she was frequently tempted to leave him; and that, as often as she yielded to the suggestion of the devil, God rebuked her severely. "Every time," says the saint, "I resolved to leave him, I felt within me a rebuke more painful than the conduct of my confessor towards me."

II. The second means to obtain the spirit of interior mortification is, to resist the passions, and to beat them down before they acquire strength. If one of them become strong by habitual indulgence, the subjugation of it will be exceedingly difficult. "Lest cupidity," says St. Augustine, "Should gain strength, strike it to the ground whilst it is weak." Sometimes it will happen that a religious will feel inclined to make use of an angry expression, or to entertain an affection for a certain person. If she do not resist these desires in the beginning, the slight wound, inflicted by her consent to them, shall soon become incurable. "Unless," says St. Ephrem, "You quickly take away the passions, they produce an ulcer." One of the ancient monks, as we learn from St. Dorotheus, has beautifully illustrated this doctrine. He commanded one of his disciples to pluck up a young cypress. The disciple executed the command without difficulty. The Superior then told him to pull up another tree of greater growth: to perform this task all the strength of the young monk was necessary. Lastly, the venerable Father commanded the disciple to tear up a tree which had taken deep root. In obedience to this precept the young religious exerted all his strength; but his efforts were fruitless—the tree was immovable. Behold, said the old man, how easily our passions are eradicated in the beginning, and how difficult it is to conquer them after they have acquired strength and vigour by evil habits. This truth is confirmed by daily experience. A religious when she receives an insult feels within a motion of resentment; if in the beginning she stifles the spark, and silently offers to God the sacrifice of her feelings, the fire is extinguished, she escapes unhurt, and even acquires merit before the Lord. But if she yield to the impulse of passion, if she pause to reflect on the insult she has received, and manifest externally the feelings of her soul—that spark of resentment will soon be kindled into a flame of hatred. Another religious entertains a certain little attachment towards a certain person; if in the beginning she avoid the company of that person, the affection will vanish; but if she encourage the attachment, it will in a short time become sinful and mortal. We must therefore abstain with the greatest care from nourishing our passions—the monsters that would devour us.

III. The third means is, as Cassian says, to endeavor to change the object of our passions, that thus the pernicious and vicious desires of the heart may become salutary and holy. Some are inclined to an inordinate love of all from whom they receive a favour. They should seek to change the object of this propensity, and to turn their affections to God, who is infinitely amiable, and who has bestowed the most inestimable blessings upon them. Others are prone to anger against those who are opposed to them: they ought to direct their resentment against their own sins, which have done them more injury than all the devils in hell could inflict upon them. Others pant after honors and temporal goods: they should aspire to the goods and honors of God's eternal kingdom.

But to practice successfully this means of conquering our passions, frequent meditation on the truths of faith, frequent spiritual readings, and frequent reflections on the eternal maxims are indispensably necessary. And, above all, it is necessary to impress deeply on the mind certain fundamental spiritual maxims, such as: "God alone deserves to be loved. Sin is the only evil which we ought to hate. Whatever God wills is good. All worldly goods shall have an end. The most insignificant action, performed for God's sake, is more profitable than the conversion of the whole world affected from any other motive than the love of God. It is necessary to do what at the hour of death we would wish to have done. We ought to live on this earth as if there were nothing in existence but ourselves and God." He whose mind is continually filled with holy maxims suffers little molestation from earthly objects, and is always strong enough to resist his corrupt inclinations. The saints have kept their souls always occupied with the truths of eternity, and thus in the time of temptation have been almost insensible to the goods or the evils of this life. To conquer self-love, and to shake off the tyranny of passion, we must above all things pray without ceasing, and continually ask of God the assistance of his grace. He that prays obtains all God's gifts: For every one that asketh receiveth. We ought especially to beg the gift of divine love; for to him who loves God, nothing is difficult. Consideration and reflection assist us greatly in the practice of virtue; but in the observance of the divine commands a single spark of the love of God affords more help than a thousand reflections and considerations. Acts of virtue which proceed from reflection are accompanied with labor and violence; but he that loves is not fatigued by doing what pleases his beloved. "He that loves, labors not," says St. Augustine.

Prayer.

O my God, after so many graces, so many Communions, and so many good examples of companions; after so many interior lights and loving invitations— my whole soul should at this moment be one flame of divine love. But notwithstanding all Thy favors I am still as imperfect and miserable as ever. Nothing has been wanting on Thy part; the fault is entirely mine, and is to be ascribed to the obstacles which I have opposed to Thy grace by obeying my passions. I see, O my Jesus, that my life has not given glory to Thee, but has rather brought dishonour on Thy name, by exhibiting to others one of Thy spouses so attached to the world and to herself. Thou hast taken me from the world, and I have loved it more than even seculars. O Lord, have mercy upon me; do not abandon me, for I desire to amend. I repent with my whole heart of all the insults which for the indulgence of my pleasures, I have offered to Thee. I desire to begin to love Thee from this moment. I have abused Thy patience too long, but now I love Thee with my whole soul. From this day forward Thou shalt be the only object of my affections. I desire to leave all, and to do everything in my power to please Thee. Show me Thy will and assist me to execute it, I am ready to please Thee in all things. Do not permit me to be any longer insensible to the excessive love by which Thou hast obliged me to love Thee. I am willing to be deprived of every earthly consolation, and to suffer every cross which Thou wilt please to send me. Dispose of me as Thou pleasest. I desire and hope to belong to Thee entirely and forever. I desire Thee alone, and nothing more.

Mary, my mother, beg of thy Son to hear me; for he denies thee nothing.

II.

Detachment from Self-will.

Nothing is more injurious to religious who have consecrated their will to Jesus Christ than to be guided by the dictates of their own will and inclinations. Hence, to guard against this enemy of the spirit—self-will—the vow of obedience has been prescribed in every religious Order. Nothing but self-will can separate us from God. Neither all the men upon earth nor all the devils in hell can deprive us of his grace. "Let self-will cease," says St. Bernard, "And there will be no hell." Let men give up their own will, and for them there shall be no hell. It is self-will that destroys all virtues. St. Peter Damian calls it "The great destroyer of all virtues;" and St. Anselm says that "The will of God is the fountain of all good, and the will of man the source of all evil." And what fruit can be expected from the disciple who chooses a master destitute of reason, that is, his own will? "Whoever," says St. Bernard, "Constitutes himself his own master, becomes the disciple of a fool." St. Anthony used to say that self-love is that wine which inebriates man so as to render him incapable of comprehending the value of virtue or the evil of sin.

St. Augustine asserts that "The devil has been made a devil by self-will." It is principally by self-will that Satan seeks to effect the perdition of religious. Cassian relates that the Abbot Achilles, being asked by his disciples with what arms the devil fights against religious, answered, that he employs pride against the great, avarice against merchants, intemperance against youth, but that his principal weapon against religious are their own will: that with this he attacks and frequently defeats them. The Abbot Pastor says that "The demons do not contend with us when we do our own will, for then our wills become devils." When we do our own will, the enemy ceases to combat us; because then our wills are devils, and more injurious to us than all the devils in hell. St. John Climacus (quoted by Gerson) says that he who, despising the authority of his Superior, wishes to direct himself, does not require a devil to tempt him, because he is become a devil to himself.

Go not, says the Holy Ghost, after thy lusts, but turn from thy own will. Do not follow your own desires, but fly from the indulgence of self-will. This admonition is directed in a particular manner to religious who have sacrificed their will to God by promising obedience to their Rule and to their Superior. As God should be the only object of their love, so obedience is the only means by which they can obtain his love. To be the fruit of obedience is the highest perfection which the actions of religious can attain. The Venerable Catharine of Cardona, having left the Spanish court, retired into a desert, where she lived for many years in the practice of penitential austerities, the very recital of which would fill the mind with horror. In her life it is related that seeing one day a discalced Carmelite carrying through obedience a bundle of wood, and knowing by inspiration that he murmured interiorly against the command of his Superior, she thus addressed him: "Brother, carry, carry with alacrity these fagots; and be assured that by this act of obedience you will merit a greater reward than I have deserved by all my penances." But as the works of religious derive from obedience the highest degree of perfection, so by self-will they are rendered most imperfect and defective. Hence, Tritemius says that nothing is more hateful to the devil than the practice of obedience. "The devil detests nothing more than obedience." Speaking of obedience, St. Teresa says that "Satan knows that it is the remedy of the soul, and therefore he labors hard to prevent its attainment." When St. Francis de Sales was devising the Rule for the nuns of the Visitation a certain person said that they ought to be barefooted. "You," replied the saint, "Wish to begin with the feet, but I wish to begin with the head." St. Philip Neri continually impressed on his penitent that sanctity consists in the mortification of self-will. "You will," says St. Jerome, "Advance in proportion as you deny your own will." Your progress in virtue will be proportional to your denial of self-will. It was because they knew that they could not offer to God a more agreeable sacrifice than that of their own will, by the vow of obedience, that so many parish priests and bishops, who led exemplary lives in the world, retired into the cloister to live under obedience.

Oh, how happy the religious who, at the hour of death, can say, with the Abbot John, I have never done my own will. St. Mary Magdalene de Pazzi used to say that the only means of dying a happy death is to submit with simplicity to the direction of a Superior. "To crucify all her desires is," says Cassian, "The end of a religious." The religious, then, who does not attend to the mortification of self-will cannot be called a religious, but a sacrilegious violator of her profession. What greater sacrilege than to take back the will that has been once consecrated to God? "There is not," says St. Bernard, "A more heinous sacrilege than to resume power over a will once offered to God." The Holy Ghost has declared by the mouth of Samuel, that to violate obedience and to follow self-will in contempt of authority is a species of idolatry. It is like the sin of witchcraft, to rebel; and like the crime of idolatry, to refuse to obey. St. Gregory applies this passage in a particular manner to the disobedience of religious. "It is," says the saint, "Like the sin of witchcraft to rebel, because they believe the proud inventions of their own hearts, and resist the counsels of their prelates." The sin of religious who despise the commands of Superiors, and follow the dictates of self-love, is like the crime of idolatry; because they in a manner adore self-will as their God. Hence, St. Basil ordained that monks who were attached to their own will should, like lepers, be separated from the rest of the Community, lest others might be infected by their bad example.

Blessed Charlotte used to say that mortification of self-will is more meritorious than the renunciation of all the riches of the world. And here it is right to observe, that sanctity depends on the abnegation of self-will, not only in what is imperfect or indifferent, but also in the exercises which have the appearance of virtue; as, for example, prayer,

100

alms-deeds, acts of penance, and other works of piety. Cassian remarks that acts of virtue performed through self-will and disobedience are productive of the worst consequences; because sinful actions which wear the appearance of holiness are corrected only with the greatest difficulty. "Vices," he says, "Which appear to be virtues are the most irremediable." Religious who desire to attain sanctity by following self-will are precisely the souls who, according to Isaias, will say to Jesus Christ on the Day of Judgment: Why have we fasted and thou hast not regarded? To them the Judge will answer, that their works were performed to please themselves rather than to do the will of God, and that therefore they deserve no reward. Behold, he will say, in the day of your fast your own will is found Oh, how great, then, is the evil of self-will, which vitiates and destroys the most perfect actions! "Great," says St. Bernard, "Is the evil of self-will, which renders your good works unprofitable to you." But, on the other hand, to be the result of obedience, is an infallible sign that an action is pleasing to God. Nicephorus relates that when the Superiors of St. Simon Stylites wished to ascertain whether the extraordinary and singular life which he led, remaining on a pillar in the open air, night and day, were pleasing to God, they commanded him to come down from his pillar and to live with the other monks. On hearing the command, the saint instantly stretched out his foot to descend, but was told by his Superiors to persevere in his austerities, which he proved by his obedience to be acceptable before God. It is necessary, then, to seek even holy things without attachment to self-will. St. Francis de Sales used to say: "I desire but few things, and for these I am not solicitous." He wished for them, not through self-love, but to please God; and was therefore prepared to give them up as soon as he knew they were not conformable to the holy will of God.

Oh, how great is the peace of a religious whose desires are the dictates of obedience! St. Dositheus, having consecrated his whole will to obedience, enjoyed continual peace. Fearing that in this peace there was some delusion of the enemy, he one day said to his Superior, St. Dorotheus: "Father, tell me why it is that I experience such tranquility as to be free from every other desire?" "My son," replied the Father, "This peace is altogether the fruit of obedience." And what can give more content to religious that love God, than to know with certainty that in all their actions they do the will of God? They can say with the prophet: We are happy, O Israel, because the things that are pleasing to God are made known to us. We enjoy constant happiness; because being obedient in all things we are certain of doing in all the will of our Spouse. "Oh, what sweetness," says Mary Magdalene de Pazzi, "Is contained in this expression— the will of God?" St. Laurence Justinian says that "He who has rejected his own will has thrown off a most grievous burden." "What tyrant," says St. Peter Damian, "More cruel than self-will?" A religious cannot be subject to a more galling tyranny than the domination of her own will; for her inclinations will lead her to seek after things that cannot be had in the cloister. Fruitless desires will keep her in perpetual misery and agitation of mind, and she shall frequently suffer within herself a little hell. "Of what use," says St. Eucherius, "Are the silence and repose of a habitation, if the inhabitants be disturbed by the struggling of passions? Of what use is external serenity, if the tempest rage within?" What will it profit a religious to live in the retirement of the cloister, if her heart be agitated by the conflicts of her passions? Without, indeed, there will be a calm, but within a storm.

And from what source arise all our troubles? Do they not spring from attachment to our own inclinations? "Whence," says St. Bernard, "Is disturbance of mind, if not from following self-will?" Cassian relates that the ancient Fathers were accustomed to say that the religious who does not conquer self-will cannot persevere in religion: certainly she cannot persevere with profit and with peace. Attachment to self-will is the only reason why many religious lead an unhappy life. One is unhappy because she cannot have the confessor or Superior of her choice: another, because she desires an office, and it is not given to her. She is so discontented, that the Superiors, to put an end to her complaints, accede to her wishes; and still she is not content. How can she expect to enjoy peace, when, instead of practicing obedience, she obliges her Superiors to submit to her desires? Others are disturbed because an occupation opposed to their inclinations is assigned to them; others, because they are forbidden to keep up a certain communication or correspondence with their friends. Others, because some disagreeable precept is imposed upon them; they are displeased, and endeavor to excite against the Superior the aversion of their relatives, and even of the Community, and thus produce endless scandal and disorder.

Their crime, as is related by Surius, would merit the chastisement of two monks, who refused to receive as their abbot a holy man named

Philibert: one of them was struck with lightning, the other suddenly attacked with a mortal disease. "Have peace with your prelates," says St. Bernard: "Do not detract, nor willfully listen to others detracting them: for God punishes inferiors in a special manner for this vice, and even in the present life." And St. Gregory says that "The works of Superiors, though they may appear reprehensible, are not to be struck with the sword of the tongue." Thou shall not, says the Lord, speak ill of the gods, You shall not censure the conduct of your Superiors, who hold the place of God in your regard.

Attend to what Mary M. de Pazzi, while in an ecstasy, said of the evil done to religious by self-love: "I see," says that great saint, "A multitude of souls, among whom there is one who, at the time of uniting herself to you, O divine Word, is wholly recollected; but before the lapse of an hour something occurs that is opposed to her inclinations, and she is thrown into confusion and agitation. I see another who, during the holy Mass, burns with divine love; but when reminded of a fault she will not acknowledge it; in her, pride and self-love reign. Another appears to rival St. Anthony by the rigor of her austerities; but if her penances be prohibited, she is pertinacious, and will not obey. Another is reserved and mortified in the refectory; but she takes complacency in her mortifications, and desires to be esteemed more holy than her companions. To her, discretion appears excess; but she imputes to immoderate zeal the want of anything that she desires. Another will appear in the parlour to surpass St. Augustine by her wisdom; and to manifest her own perfection, will exhibit in her conversation an extraordinary degree of prudence. Others are ready to forego in the exercises of charity every personal advantage, but wish to be thanked for their services, and to be praised by all their companions." Of such religious the Lord once said to the same saint: "They desire my spirit, but they desire it in a manner and at a time pleasing to themselves, and thus they render themselves unfit to receive it."

But let us return to ourselves. If you, dear Sister, wish to become a saint, and to enjoy continual peace, seek to overcome as much as possible your own will; adopt the rule of religious who love perfection; never do anything for your own satisfaction, but do all to please God: by this means you cut off all vain desires and all evil inclinations. Worldlings continually seek the gratification of their own wishes; but the saints constantly endeavor to mortify self-will, and to find occasions of self-denial. St. Andrew Avellini, as we read in his Office, bound himself by an express vow to resist continually his own will. You should at least prescribe to yourself to deny your own will a certain number of times in the day. Repeat often the words by which St. Bernard was accustomed to excite his fervor in God's service: "Bernard, for what purpose have you come here?" Say to yourself: have I entered religion to do my own will? If I wish to live according to my own inclinations, I should have remained in the world. At my profession I consecrated my will to God by the vow of obedience: why should I now seek to indulge it? Why am I disturbed when not permitted to follow my own will? Be not troubled, then, when your requests are refused, and when a duty painful to self-love is imposed upon you; but remember that by your obedience you will merit a greater reward, and will make greater progress in virtue than you would by many spontaneous acts of penance and devotion. A great servant of God used to say, that to perform a single act of abnegation of self-will is more profitable than to build a thousand hospitals. Have continually before your eyes the words of the Venerable Father Anthony Torres to a religious who was one of his penitents: A soul entirely consecrated to God loves nothing, wants nothing, seeks nothing, "Desires nothing."

I will conclude this chapter by an extract from a letter of the same Father Torres to a religious whom he wished to detach from herself and from all created objects, in order to love nothing but God: "Since the Lord gives you so many occasions of suffering and of desolation, endeavor to improve in charity, which is said to be as strong as death. Study to strengthen divine love in your soul, so that it may disengage your heart from all creatures, from all human respect, from all that is prized by the world, from your own desires, and from all self-love; that there may be nothing in you to prevent your thoughts, your desires, and your affections from being entirely directed to your beloved. Let the heart sigh after the beloved; let the will rest only on him; let the thoughts be wholly fixed on him. Let every motion of the body, let every act of your life, be for and with the beloved. To attain the love of your beloved, I advise you to renounce every day before the crucifix every object of your affections, all honors, interests, consolations, and relatives, and to protest that you desire no other glory than his ignominies; no riches but his charity, no other convenience than the cross: that you desire him only, your dear and beloved Spouse. When you walk in the garden, or look up to the heavens, invite frequently and with your whole heart all creatures to the love of your beloved. Avoid all conversation; give up every employment which is not pleasing to him; omit every action which will not redound to the glory of your Spouse."

Prayer.

Ah, my God, my Lord, and my Spouse! Thou hast loved me so much, and hast given me a will to love Thee, and I have so often employed this will in offending and insulting Thee. If I were not convinced that Thou art a God of infinite mercy, I should lose all hope of recovering Thy grace, which I have unfortunately lost. By my ingratitude I deserved to have been long since abandoned by Thee. But I see that Thy light still assists me, and I know that Thou dost still call me to Thy love. Behold, O Lord, I do not wish to continue any longer in my ingratitude, or to resist any longer Thy invitation. I offer to Thee my whole being: receive an unfaithful soul who for so many years has despised Thy love, but who now desires to love Thee and to belong entirely to Thee. Assist me, O my Jesus; give me a sorrow for my sins which will fill my soul with pain and anguish for having outraged so good and so amiable a God. Unhappy me, if, after the lights which Thou now givest me, I betray Thee again. How canst Thou bear with me any longer? The fear of again offending Thee afflicts my soul. Ah, Lord, do not permit me to be evermore separated from Thee. Chastise me as Thou pleasest, but not by permitting me to lose Thy grace. If Thou seest that I shall ever turn my back upon Thee, take me out of life, at this moment, in which I hope to enjoy Thy friendship. Of what use will life be to me if by living I continue to offend Thee?

O Mary, my hope, obtain for me the grace of perseverance, or of instant death.

III.

The Merit of Obedience.

"Since," as St. Bonaventure says, "All the perfection of religious consists in the destruction of self-will," obedience should, of all virtues, be the most dear to a religious. Obedience to rule and to the commands of Superiors is the greatest sacrifice that a Christian can offer to God; because, as St. Thomas says, "Nothing is more amiable in the eyes of man than the liberty of his own will." Hence we cannot present to God a more acceptable gift than the consecration of our wills to his service. "For," says the Holy Ghost, obedience is better than sacrifices. Obedience is more pleasing to God than all the sacrifices that we can offer to him. They who give to the Lord their worldly goods by alms-deeds, their honor by embracing contempt, and their body by mortification, by fasts, and by works of penance, make only a partial consecration of themselves to him. But he that offers to God the sacrifice of his own will by the practice of obedience consecrates all that he possesses to God's glory, and can say: Lord, after having given to Thee my will, I have nothing more to present to Thee. Besides, as St. Gregory says, "By the other virtues we give to God what belongs to us, but by obedience we dedicate ourselves to him." The same Father says in another place that "Obedience is a virtue that infuses the other virtues into the mind and preserves them in the soul." St. Teresa asserts that, "From a soul resolved to love God he requires nothing but obedience;" and again, that "The devil knows well that obedience is the remedy of the soul, and therefore he labors hard to prevents its attainment."

The Venerable Father Sertorio Caputo used to say that obedience merits even the reward of martyrdom; because as by martyrdom a Christian submits, for God's sake, to the loss of life, so by obedience he offers to the Lord the sacrifice of self-will, which is, as it were, the head of the soul. Hence the wise man says that he who practices obedience shall conquer every enemy. An obedient man shall speak of victory. Yes, says St. Gregory, the obedient shall overcome all the temptations of hell, because by obedience they subject their will to men, and thus become superior to the devils who fell through disobedience. "They who obey," says the saint, "Are conquerors, because when they submit their will to others, they triumph over the angels who sinned by disobedience." Cassian observes that since all vices proceed from self-will when the latter is destroyed the former die in the soul. "By mortification of the will all vices wither and decay. God promises those who renounce their own will that he will raise them above the earth, and give them a celestial spirit. If, says the Lord, thou turn away from doing thy own wills I will lift thee up above the high places of the earth, and will feed thee with the inheritance of Jacob. St. Laurence Justinian teaches that all who sacrifice their own will to God become so dear to him that they shall obtain whatever they ask. "He that has consecrated himself to God by the immolation of self-will will receive all that he shall demand."

St. Augustine says that after Adam had by his disobedience entailed misery on himself and the whole human race, the Son of God became man, principally to teach us obedience by his own example. Jesus from his infancy began to obey Mary and Joseph: he continued to obey them during his life; and by his obedience was in the end brought to the ignominious death of the cross. He humbled himself, becoming obedient unto death—even to the death of the cross." St. Bernard says that "The disobedient seek to be exempted from obedience. Jesus Christ did not do so: he, indeed, gave his life lest he should violate obedience." The mother of God once revealed to one of her servants that our Redeemer died with a special affection for obedient souls.

The Venerable Father de Leonardis, founder of the Order of the Mother of God, being importuned by his disciples to give them a rule, wrote this single word— obedience. He wished by this act to signify what Father Sertorio Caputo used to say, that in religion, obedience and sanctity are identical; that to be obedient and to be a saint are one and the same thing. St. Thomas teaches that it is principally by the vow of obedience a Christian is made a religious; and, according to St. Teresa, a religious who is not obedient cannot be called a religious. Of what use is a disobedient nun? Many are versed in the belles-lettres, in poetry, foreign languages, and in history, but are unacquainted with obedience. A religious who knows not how to obey, knows nothing.

St. Teresa used to say that obedience is the short road to perfection. It is related in the Lives of the Fathers, that one of them saw in a vision two orders of saints: the first consisted of those who had left the world and retired into the desert to practice continual prayer and penance; the second, of those who for the love of Jesus Christ lived in obedience and subjection to the will of others. He also saw that the latter enjoyed greater glory than the former: for although the solitaries had pleased God in all their exercises, still they had always done their own will; but they who lived under obedience had given their will to God, and thus offered to him the most acceptable of all sacrifices. St. Dorotheus relates that his disciple St. Dositheus, being weak in health, could not practice the exercises performed by the other monks, but cast off self-will and consecrated himself entirely to obedience. He died in the space of five years. After his death the Lord revealed to the abbot that this young man obtained the same reward as St. Paul, the first hermit, and as St. Anthony, the abbot. The monks were amazed, and could not conceive how Dositheus, who did not perform the ordinary duties of his state, could merit so exalted a glory. Almighty God told them that the glory of the young saint was the reward of the obedience which he had practiced. St. Gregory says that "A repast of precept deserves a greater reward than fasting voluntarily undertaken." To eat through obedience is more meritorious in the sight of God than to fast through self-will. The same truth was revealed by the Blessed Virgin to St. Bridget. Being prohibited by her confessor to practice her accustomed penances, the saint began to apprehend a diminution of her fervor; but the mother of God encouraged her to obey without fear, by saying to her that, "They who do penance deserve but one reward, while he that omits through obedience one act of mortification, receives a twofold remuneration—one for the penance which he wished to perform, another for his obedience in omitting it."

St. Joseph Calasanctius used to say that an obedient religious is the precious gem of the convent. Oh, if all nuns were obedient, every convent would be a paradise. Besides, a nun faithful to obedience lays up in every action an immense treasure of merit; because in every exercise she does the will of God; and in doing his will all merit consists. To enable us to acquire eternal treasures, by whatsoever we do through obedience, is the principal advantage of the religious state. Even duties agreeable to our own feelings, when performed through a motive of obedience, merit a great reward. St. Aloysius used to say that religion is a ship, in which even he that labors not makes the voyage! Yes; for a religious merits not only when she fasts or meditates, or recites the Office, but also when through obedience she takes repose or abstains from labor, when she eats or indulges in recreation. Oh, how profitable and meritorious is every act performed in obedience to the will of Superiors!

If, then, dear Sister, you desire soon to become a saint, consecrate yourself entirely to obedience; divest yourself of all self-will; and endeavor with all your might to obey your Rule and your Superior in the external exercises, and your spiritual Father in whatever regards the interior. It is by obedience and by the absence of self-will that perfect religious are distinguished from the imperfect. The latter do nothing cheerfully, but what pleases self-love and self-will. They, indeed, desire to be entrusted with some of the offices of the Community; because to be without office they deem to be dishonorable. But they wish for those employments that tend to their own ease and convenience, and in everything else they seek their own will. In a word, they desire to become saints, but only according to their own will, and according to the dictates of self-love. But St. Joseph Calasanctius used to say that "He who in serving God seeks his own convenience, serves himself, and not God." But religious who love perfection do not act in this manner: they never omit what obedience commands, and -desire only what obedience prescribes. Imitate their example, and you will soon become a saint. Endeavor to perform all your actions from a motive of obedience, and you will always walk securely to salvation. To secure their profits, merchants obtain an insurance of their property. Let it be your care to make sure your eternal gain by procuring for every work the insurance of obedience—the approbation of your Superiors: otherwise your works may prove injurious, or at least unprofitable, to you. When St. Anselm was made Archbishop of Canterbury he became unhappy in consequence of being so free from the yoke of obedience, and at his own solicitation the Pope appointed for the saint a Superior whom he might obey. The saint regulated his conduct by the advice of the Superior, and undertook nothing without his consent. How much more should you who by your profession have consecrated your will to obedience how much more, I say, should you seek occasions of practicing that sublime virtue!

Prayer.

Ah, my Jesus, to save me Thou hast been obedient unto death—even the death of the Cross; and I, for a vile and wretched gratification, have been so often disrespectful and disobedient to Thee. Wait, O Lord; do not abandon me yet. I repent with my whole soul of all the offences I have offered Thee. I now see that I have abused Thy mercy too much, and that therefore I am undeserving of Thy pity. But I also see that Thou hast borne with me till now, that, entering one day into myself, I might consecrate my whole being to Thee. I hope the day has arrived when I shall dedicate myself entirely to Thy love. I hear Thy voice calling me to Thy love. I shall no longer resist Thy invitation. Behold! I offer myself to thee; refuse not, O Lord, my oblation. Tell me what Thou dost require of me: I am ready to do all in my power to please Thee. I promise Thee that henceforth I shall never violate the obedience due to my Superiors. I love Thee, my Jesus; and because I love Thee, I desire to do all that I can to please Thee. Assist me, O Lord; draw and unite me more and more every day to Thy love. Eternal Father, I offer to Thee the Passion of Thy Son, and through his merits I beseech Thee to give me all the graces necessary to make me a saint, such as Thou dost wish me to be.

O Mary, my mother and my hope, beg of thy Son that I may be no longer mine, but that I may belong to him entirely and forever.

IV.

The Obedience Due to the Superiors.

The principal and most efficacious means of practising the obedience due to the Superiors, and of rendering it meritorious before God, is to consider that in obeying them we obey God himself; and that by despising their commands we despise the authority of our divine Master, who has said of Superiors: He that heareth you, heareth me; and he that despiseth you, despiseth me. Hence St. Paul addressed to his disciples the following words: Not serving to the eye, as it were pleasing men, but as the servants of Christ, doing the will of God from the heart. When, then, a religious receives a precept from her prelate, Superior, or confessor, she should immediately execute it, not only to please men, but principally to please God, whose will is made known to her by their command. In obeying their directions she is more certain of doing the will of God than if an angel came down from heaven to manifest his will to her. Hence St. Paul says, in his epistle to the Galatians, that though an angel from heaven preach a gospel to you, besides that which the apostles preach, he should not be believed. No, says the apostle, let him be anathema.

St. Bernard says that "God deigns to make prelates his own equals. He takes to himself the reverence or contempt manifested to them." Obedience shown to Superiors is shown to God; for he has said: He that heareth you, heareth me; and he that despiseth you, despiseth me. Bear, then, always in mind, dear Sister, that the obedience which you practice towards your Superiors is paid to God himself. Now if Jesus Christ himself came down from heaven, and imposed any duty upon you, or gave you any particular charge, would you attempt to decline it, or would you dare to disobey his commands? "But," continues St. Bernard, "Whether God, or a creature who is his representative, impose a precept, they are both to be obeyed with equal exactness." If, then, you receive a command from one that holds the place of God, you should observe it with the same diligence as if it came from God himself. St. John Climacus relates that in a certain monastery the Superior, to set an example to the Community, commanded in their presence an old man of eighty years to stand in the refectory for two hours without interruption. The aged monk being asked how he had been able to bear this mortification, replied: "I imagined that I stood before Jesus Christ, and that he imposed on me that humiliation; and this thought made me obey without difficulty or repugnance."

For our greater merit the Lord wishes to lead us to salvation by means of faith, and therefore does not speak to us himself, but manifests his will by the commands of our Superiors. When Jesus Christ appeared to St. Paul, and transformed him into a new man, he might in person have directed the apostle what to do, but Jesus only said to him: Go into the city, and there it will be told to thee what thou must do. Go into the city, and Ananias will make known my will to you. Hence blessed Egidius used to say that it is more meritorious to obey man for the love of God, than to obey God himself.

It may be added, that there is more certainty of doing the will of God by obedience to Superiors, than by obedience to Jesus Christ should he appear in person and give his commands. Because should Jesus Christ appear to a religious she would not be certain whether it was he that spoke or an evil spirit, who under the appearance of the Redeemer wished to deceive her. But when her Superiors speak, she knows for certain, from the words of Jesus Christ, that in obeying them she obeys him. He says our Lord that heareth you heareth me. Even when it is doubtful whether the object of a precept is conformable to the law of God, the generality of theologians and masters of spiritual life teach that a religious is bound to obey; and that in obeying she is certain of not sinning, and of even pleasing God. Attend to the doctrine of St. Bernard, which he has taken from the Rule of St. Benedict: "Whatever a man holding the place of God commands, unless it be certain that it is displeasing to God, is to be received as if commanded by God himself."

111

Thus, on the day of judgment, religious will be charged with every act of disobedience; but, as St. Philip Neri used to say, they shall be most certain of not having to render an account of the actions performed through obedience. For these the Superiors only, who commanded them, shall be held accountable. Speaking particularly of nuns, the Lord once said to St. Catharine of Sienna: "Religious will not be obliged to render an account to me of what they do through obedience; for that, I will demand an account from the Superiors." Obey, says the Apostle, your prelates, and be subject to them; for they watch, as being to render an account of your souls: that they may do this with joy, and not with grief. And, O blessed spouse of the Lord, if you practice obedience, when after death you shall be asked by Jesus Christ why you have not done greater penance, why you have not made more mental prayer, or why you have performed such an action, you can answer with confidence, that in all this you only fulfilled his commands by obeying your Superiors, whom he commanded you to obey as you would obey himself; and that if you have done wrong, the blame is imputable to your Superiors, whose authority you obeyed.

Attend to the words of St. Paul: That they (your prelates) may do this with joy, and not with grief. From this passage it clearly appears that it is the duty of a religious to obey promptly, without reply, and without thwarting her Superiors or disturbing their peace. Oh, how miserable is the condition of a Superior whose subjects violate obedience by excuses, by colored pretexts, by complaints, and even by murmurings. The situation of abbesses at the approach of the time for distributing the offices of the Community is truly deserving of pity. They are, on the one hand, troubled by scruples arising from the apprehension that through human respect or through the fear of displeasing a sister they will intrust her with a charge for which she is unfit; and on the other, they are afflicted to find that after the distribution one declines her office, another complains, a third murmurs, and others refuse to accept the duties assigned to them. This state of things sometimes compels the Superior to dispense the offices, not according to the rules of reason and for the good of the Community, but according to human prudence. In acting according to the dictates of human wisdom to prevent greater evils, the Superior may be blameless; but whoever accepts or discharges her duties not in the spirit of obedience, but through caprice, will certainly be inexcusable. The Apostle commands you to obey, and to be subject to your Superiors, that they may discharge their duty with joy, and not with grief. For, says St. Paul, this is not expedient for you. No, it is not expedient for you that the Superiors be resisted and thwarted; but if they be supported and consoled in the government of the Community, good order and your spiritual progress will be promoted.

What a scandal is it to see certain religious decline certain offices assigned to them, and thus extort obedience from their Superiors! St. Bernard, in his comment on the words of the Redeemer to the blind man, What wilt thou that I do to thee says: "He was truly blind, otherwise he would have exclaimed: 'Far be it from me, O Lord, to ask Thee to do what I will; tell me rather what Thou wilt have me do for Thee." Let us apply to ourselves this passage of St. Bernard. There are some nuns whom the abbess must ask what office they wish to have. Perfect religious do not require to be consulted about the office they wish for: should the Superior ask them what charge would be most agreeable to them, they answer that it is not for them to say what employment they desire, but that it belongs to her to tell them what she will have them do.

If, then, dear sister, you wish to be truly obedient and truly religious, bear continually in mind:

I. That your Superiors hold in your regard the place of Jesus Christ; and endeavor to show them all the veneration and love that are due to his representatives not through a feeling of self-interest, not to be esteemed by them or to avoid their censure, but from the sole motive of pleasing God. And this obedience is due not only to the prelate and abbess, but to all that hold office in the convent: such as the Infirmarian, the Sacristan, and the sister who is charged with the care of the refectory. In obeying the abbess, a religious may be easily influenced by human respect; but in obeying sisters entrusted with the inferior offices, she shows that she possesses the true spirit of obedience. St. Francis of Assisi thanked God in a particular manner for having given him the grace to be always ready to obey the least of the novices in all things in which they might be appointed his Superiors. The saint was accustomed to say that the less the authority of a Superior and the more humble his station and qualifications, the greater is the merit of obedience; because then it proceeds from the sole motive of pleasing God.

II. Do not seek the society of imperfect sisters, who have little affection for obedience.

III. Receive correction with humility; beg of the Superior to reprimand you as often as reproof may be necessary for you. Be not of the number of those who resent even the slightest rebuke, to whom the Superior cannot give even the necessary admonitions without great caution; whose correction, lest they should be wanting in respect to her, and should disturb the Community she is, perhaps, compelled to defer for several months, till a seasonable opportunity occurs. But woe to the religious who cannot be admonished without such caution, she must be very imperfect indeed.

IV. When corrected receive the admonition with humility, and without excusing your fault; and should the Superior charge you with a defect which you had not committed, do not speak of her mistake, unless she commands you to state your guilt or innocence. But I shall hereafter treat this subject more at large.

V. Banish from your mind all thoughts and suspicions against the Superior, with the same promptness as if they were thoughts opposed to chastity, and when you hear any one attribute to her a fault which cannot be denied, seek to excuse her as much as you can. But should the fault of the Superior be evident and inexcusable,—for example, were she impatient with all the sisters,—persuade yourself that God permits this defect in her, not for your injury, but for your profit. St. Gertrude once besought the Lord to deliver the abbess from the fault of frequent impatience. In answer, she was told that he permitted this defect in the abbess, as well for her own advantage as for the good of the religious: for her good, that she might be kept humble; for the good of the religious, that by bearing with her impatience their merit might be increased. "The more," says St. Bernard, "You are oppressed, the more you gain." The greater the burden you bear the greater the merit you acquire. St. Gregory teaches that "The commands of Superiors should be respected, though their life be not deserving of praise." And speaking of the Scribes and Pharisees, who blasphemed his works, Jesus Christ says: All things whatsoever they shall say to you, observe and do; but according to their works, do ye not.

With regard to the offices of the convent, observe the excellent rule of

St. Francis de Sales: "Never to seek and never to refuse any of them." Prefer always that which is least honorable, and least suited to your convenience. Few nuns merit the full reward of obedience by fulfilling the duties of their office, because few accept and discharge them in the true spirit of obedience, and with a pure intention of pleasing God. Imperfect religious look only to the advantages and disadvantages of office; but the perfect regard only the will of God, and therefore seek not their own ease or convenience, but cheerfully embrace pains and labors. Endeavor to belong to the number of the perfect. Do not imagine that the refusal of office, through fear of committing faults in the discharge of its duties, will be excusable before God; but be persuaded that by becoming a religious you bound yourself to serve the convent. Could the fear of committing faults justify you in declining a charge, the same fear would exempt all the sisters from the obligation of accepting office. Should they give way to such fears, who would serve the monastery or support the Community? Have a pure intention of pleasing God: fear not; he will assist you.

Accept, in the spirit of obedience, the office intrusted to you; and in accepting it, regard not the power of domination; look not to self-ease nor self-esteem, but solely to the obligations of obedience. Accept it with a holy confidence, and listen not to the devil, who will perhaps suggest to you that the duties of such an office are above your strength. If you be obedient, the Lord will give you that strength which you do not possess. Do not imagine that, because the duties of your charge are of a distracting nature they will destroy in your soul the spirit of fervor and recollection. Be assured that if you comply with your duties God will bestow upon you more graces in a quarter of an hour spent in prayer, than, without performing them, you would receive in a retreat of ten days. In the fulfillment of your office endeavor as much as possible to set apart some little time to recollect yourself in prayer. Do not say that your office requires every moment of your time. Perfect religious who have an affection for prayer can find abundant time for the discharge of their duties and for recollection. Do not imitate the conduct of some who burden themselves with such a multiplicity of occupations that they cannot find a moment's time to recollect themselves before God. In discharging the duties of office be careful not to be partial to your friends. Be still more careful not to abuse your office by employing it as a means of procuring for yourself advantages which the other sisters do not enjoy.

Lastly, remember that neither obedience nor even the perfection of obedience forbids a religious to make known to her Superiors all secret disqualifications for the duty imposed upon her. She may, for example, without any violation of obedience, make known to them any bodily infirmity, or whatever would render her unfit for the office assigned to her; because her Superiors are not angels, but human beings, who require to be made acquainted with what of themselves they do not know. But in stating your disqualifications for any charge, you must take care, in the first place, not to speak of those which the Superior already knows; for these she must be supposed to have already taken into consideration. Secondly, after explaining your difficulties, you must cheerfully acquiesce in the judgment of the Superior; and your acquiescence must be manifested externally, as well for her peace and satisfaction as for the edification of the Community. Hence, before they represent to the Superior their unfitness for office, religious would do well to figure to themselves that, notwithstanding their supposed difficulties, she insists on the acceptance of the charge intrusted to them. By this means they will be better disposed to receive, without reply, the decision of the Superior.

It is necessary to remark in this place, that a discreet attention to the preservation of health, with a view to be better able to serve God, is not a defect, but an act of virtue. But a superfluous solicitude about health is a fault; and, aided by self-love, makes many unnecessary indulgences appear indispensable. St. Bernard says that some are fitter to be the disciples of Hippocrates and Galenus than of Jesus Christ. "Consider," says the saint, "That you are a monk and not a physician." And he continues: "Consult for your own repose." As if he said, Seek to promote your own peace by living like the rest of the Community, and by avoiding all singular and superfluous indulgence. "Spare the labor of those who serve the Community." Spare the labor of the attendant in the refectory, and of the cook; and seek not after delicacies withheld from others. "Spare the burden of the house." Abstain from putting the Community to any superfluous expense.

St. Basil exhorted religious to accustom themselves as much as possible to the common fare. Oh, how much better is it for a religious to eat and drink like her companions, than to fast, to take discipline, or wear hair-shirts, and afterwards practice singularity in her food! In singularity has originated the relaxation of many religious orders. Be not afraid

116

that by using the common food you will be wanting in the care of your health; for although it is not lawful directly to shorten life with the intention of accelerating death, still, according to the common opinion of theologians, it is allowable to abstain from some indulgences, particularly those that are singular, which might prolong life for some time. Such abstinence is even an act of virtue, when practiced with the intention of promoting our own spiritual advancement, and the edification of our neighbour. When the celebrated Chapter of Matts was held, St. Francis of Assisi saw that the demons convened a Chapter, in which they agreed that, to introduce a relaxation of discipline into his Order, in which the spirit of fervor then flourished, the most effectual means would be to induce the religious to receive a great number of novices of noble extraction and of delicate health, because such subjects would be treated with less rigor; thus by degrees discipline would be relaxed, and the spirit of fervor banished from the Order. This reasoning was most just. Beware, then, lest by immoderate care of your health you put your salvation in peril, or at least lose the crown of a saint. Remember that, had the Saints, like you, been unnecessarily solicitous about the preservation of health, they should never have become saints.

Prayer.

O my beloved Lord, Thou art beauty itself, goodness itself, and love itself: how can I love anything but Thee! Fool that I have been! In my past life I have offered numberless insults to Thee. I have violated Thy law, but I am sorry above all things for my sins, and desire to die of grief for having offended Thee. O my Jesus, have mercy upon me. I desire to cry out continually: My Jesus, mercy; O my Jesus, mercy. But if for the past I have despised Thy love, I now prefer it to all the goods of the earth. Thou, O my Jesus, art, and shalt be forever, the only object of all my affections. My love, I leave all things and desire nothing but Thee. I now say and desire to repeat every moment of my life, that I desire Thee only, O my God, and nothing more. Assist me, O Lord, to be faithful to Thee. Look not on my sins, but on the love that Thou didst bear to me when Thou wast nailed to the Cross for my salvation. In the merits of Thy Passion I place all my hopes. I love Thee, O infinite Good! O my supreme Good, and ask nothing of Thee but the grace to love Thee; to love Thee intensely, and henceforward to love no other object but Thee, my treasure and my all. My Jesus, I give Thee my will: purify its affections. I give Thee my body: preserve it unsullied. I give Thee my soul: make it belong entirely to Thee. Burn with Thy own consuming fire every affection that is opposed to the pure love of Thy divinity.

O Mary, my great advocate, I hope first in the merits of thy Son, and afterwards in thy intercession.

V.

The Obedience due to the Rule.

St. Francis de Sales has asserted that "The predestination of religious is connected with the observance of their rules." And St. Mary Magdalene de Pazzi used to say, that the observance of Rule is the shortest way to eternal life and to sanctity. In a word, the only way by which a religious can become a saint and be saved, is to observe her Rule. For her there is no other way that leads to salvation. Hence, no matter how great her austerities, how frequent her prayers, and how numerous her other spiritual works, a religious who habitually violates any, even the most unimportant, rule, will never advance a single step towards perfection. She will labor, but without fruit, verifying in herself the words of the Holy Ghost: He that rejecteth wisdom and discipline is unhappy; and their fruit is vain, and their labors without fruit, and their works unprofitable. They who despise discipline, that is, their Rule, are miserable, and trust in vain in their works; for their labors are without fruit. "We," says St. Teresa, "Do not fulfill certain easy duties prescribed by rule, such as silence, which gives no pain; and still we go in search of works of penance; but afterwards we neglect the former and omit the latter." Not to advance in perfection is but a small part of the evils that arise from the infraction of light rules. According to St. Bernard, the worst consequence of such transgressions is that the habit of them renders very difficult the observance of the most important rules, and even of the vows.

Oh, what a scandal to see certain religious, so well instructed during their novitiate in the observance of the rule, and after their profession, disregard regular discipline, as if their solemn consecration to Jesus Christ exempted them from all the obligations of the religious state! A learned author says: "It is better to be a finger united to the body, than to be an eye separated from it." An eye torn from the body is but rottenness; and an action that wears the appearance of virtue, but is not conformable to rule, will never please God; instead of promoting, it will impede the perfection of a religious. For, as St. Augustine says, acts of devotion opposed to rule are but so many steps out of the way, and so many stumbling-blocks to the soul.

But you, dear sister, have left the world to become a saint; and do you not see, that not to conquer yourself in small things will not only prevent you from being a saint, but will also expose you to the danger of perdition? "We had," says St. Eucherius of Lyons, "Abundant strength to relinquish the dearest affections, and we are not strong enough to overcome negligence." We had the courage to renounce all attachments to relatives, to property, and to the pleasures of the world; and now we are too weak to conquer our tendency to violate rule. Cassian relates that to a certain monk who had abandoned the dignity of senator to enter religion, but afterwards did not observe his rule, St. Basil said, in a tone of commiseration: "You have lost the rank of senator, and have not become a monk." Unhappy man, what have you done? To become a monk, you have forfeited the honourable station of senator, and have not attained the sanctity of a religious. Tertullian says: "If you deem the liberty of the world to be true liberty, you have returned to servitude, and have lost the liberty of Christ." As if he said: O spouse of Jesus, you have gone forth from the slavery of the world, and have taken possession of the liberty of Christ, by putting off all earthly affections—the unhappy chains which hold so many poor souls in bondage; and will you still esteem the liberty of the world to be true liberty? If you do, you have miserably returned to the slavery of the world, and have lost the freedom of the children of God, which Jesus Christ purchased for you.

FIRST EXCUSE.

Some religious excuse their negligence by saying that the rules which they violate are of no importance.

To them I answer, in the first place, that no Rule of religion can be deemed unimportant or undeserving of attention. All the rules of religion should be respected, because they are all ordained by Almighty God, and approved by the Church, as means of attaining the perfection

119

"To which every religious consecrated to God should continually aspire; and because the neglect of even trifling rules injures regular discipline, and disturbs the whole Community. It is certain that the spirit of fervor flourishes in the convent where attention is paid to the smallest rules; but where they are neglected, there piety is either lost or begins to decay Father St. Jure relates that Father Oviedo, the Superior of the college of the Jesuits in Naples, insisted on the punctual observance of even the smallest rules. He was opposed by Father Bobadilla, who asserted that it was not right to oblige subjects to observe such trifles. By this opposition the rigor of discipline was relaxed; the event showed the evil consequences of the neglect of rule. By the habitual violation of order, a contempt for the most important as well as for the smallest rules was engendered in some, who afterwards abandoned religion. Being informed of the relaxation which had taken place, St. Ignatius ordained that the rules should be observed with the utmost exactness, and thus discipline was re-established.

Tepid and negligent religious disregard trifles, but, the devil sets great value on the smallest violation of rules; he carefully marks all our transactions to charge us with them one day before the tribunal of Jesus Christ. St. Richard, a religious, having once got his hair cut before the usual time, saw the devil gathering and numbering the hairs that were scattered over the floor. In like manner, St. Gertrude saw the enemy collecting all the little tufts of wool which, for want of the perfect spirit of poverty, she had allowed to be wasted; and all the syllables of the Office that had been omitted because it was recited with too much rapidity. Blessed Denis the Carthusian relates that Satan appeared once to a religious with a needle and a silk thread in his hand, which she had used without permission. Thus the enemy of mankind keeps an account of every word uttered in the place or time of silence, of every look of curiosity, and of every transgression of rule into which negligent religious fall.

It is because they are heedless of small faults that these miserable souls experience nothing but aridity and irksomeness in their meditations, Communions, and in all their exercises of devotion. In punishment of one look of curiosity, contrary to the inspiration of the Holy Ghost not to indulge her eyes, St. Gertrude was visited with spiritual dryness for eleven days. It is but just that whoever sows little should gather but little fruit. He who soweth sparingly shall also reap sparingly. How can the Lord be liberal of his graces and consolations to a religious who serves him with reserve and with negligence? Had she faithfully observed such a rule God would perhaps have bestowed upon her great graces; but in punishment of her negligence he has justly withheld them from her. Blessed Egidius used to say, "By a small neglect a great grace may be lost."

"Many," says St. Bonaventure, "Desire to die for Christ, and are at the same time unwilling to bear light crosses for his sake." Many pant after the crown of martyrdom, and will violate a small rule rather than submit to a trifling inconvenience. If, says the Saint, you received a command hard to be observed, and in its fulfillment attended with serious disadvantages, there might perhaps be some apology for its violation; but for the infraction of rules of easy observance there cannot be the shadow of an excuse. The more unimportant a rule, and the more easy it is to be observed, the more imperfect the religious who transgresses it, because the greater is her attachment to self-will. But God grant, as has been said above, that the disregard of small rules may not lead her one day to the violation of her vow, and to eternal perdition. He that breaketh a hedge, says the Holy Ghost, a serpent shall bite him. Whoever breaks down the fence of the Rule stands in great danger of being one day bitten by the infernal serpent. When you see a religious of exemplary conduct fall into the pit of sin, do not imagine that the devil, by the first attack, succeeded in effecting her ruin. No, he first induced her to neglect her Rule and to despise small things, and then drew her into grievous transgressions.

SECOND EXCUSE.

Others excuse themselves by saying that the Rule does not bind under pain of sin.

It has been already said (Chap. IV.) that to violate without sufficient necessity even the Rules that are not obligatory under the penalty of moral guilt, is, according to the common opinion of theologians, at least a venial transgression. Speaking of the Rule of his Order, which has not the force of a strict precept, St. Thomas, after stating that the violation of the vows is a mortal sin, says that "The transgression of the other Rules is only a venial fault." I have said that to break any Rule without sufficient cause is at least a venial sin. For when the violation of Rule is productive of serious injury or of great scandal in the convent, it may be a mortal sin. For example, to disturb habitually the general silence, to enter the cells of your companions, to break without leave the fasts prescribed by the Rule, and similar irregularities, sometimes rob the soul of sanctifying grace. But that the violation of Rule is at least a venial sin, cannot be doubted: 1. Because a religious by transgressing her Rule neglects the means of attaining the perfection to which she is bound to aspire; 2. Because she is unfaithful to the promise which at her profession she made to observe the Rules of the Community; 3. Because by her bad example in transgressing the Rule she disturbs the good order of the Community; 4. And lastly (and this is the strongest reason): Because every infraction of the Rule proceeds from self-love, and is a departure from the will of God. Unnecessary transgressions of rule are certainly not acts of virtue; neither can they be said to be indifferent. For how can we call an action indifferent that is performed through self-will that gives bad example, and destroys the order of regular discipline? If, then, the violation of the Rule cannot be good or indifferent, it must be sinful. Some perhaps will say: It is enough for me that the violation of the Rule is not a mortal sin. To such persons I would answer, that they are in a very dangerous state. If they are not dead, they are in the last agony. Their unhappy souls are infected with a slow fever which will soon bring on death. Let them read what is said in Chapter V.

THIRD EXCUSE.

In extenuation of their neglect of the Rule others say that they are advanced in years, and that they cannot bear the rigors practiced by young persons.

In answer to them I say, that a religious, whether young or old, does injury to herself and the Community by the transgression of the Rule. St. Peter Chrysologus says that "By its shade a barren tree is pernicious not only to itself, but also to the fertile plants by which it is surrounded." Yes, every religious who gives bad example by inattention to the Rule does an injury to her own soul and to her fervent companions.

Besides, religious advanced in years are more strictly bound to perfect observance than those who are young in religion. First, because they have been longer in the cloister: and as the more time a person

122

has devoted to study, the more extensive should be his learning; so the longer a religious is engaged in the meditation of Jesus crucified, the greater should be her progress in the science of the saints and in Christian perfection. Secondly, because the example of the more advanced is most efficacious in inducing the juniors to observe or to violate the Rule. Religious of long standing are the torches that enlighten the Community; they are the pillars that sustain regular observance; and by their example they engage the young in the support of order. But if discipline be disregarded by the oldest members of the Community, the Rule will be despised by the novices in religion. Generally speaking, all the irregularities that creep into convents are to be ascribed not so much to the young as to the advanced religious, who by their bad example lead the others to seek a relaxation of the rigor of the Rule. As long as their works contradict their words, all their exhortations and entreaties to the juniors to observe the Rule will be unprofitable. "The eyes," says St. Ambrose, "Persuade sooner than the ears." Example is far more persuasive than admonition. And how is it possible to induce novices to observe the Rule when the conduct of Superiors is subversive of regular observance? "Nothing," says Tertullian, "Can be built up by the same means as that by which it is pulled down."

When Eleazar was tempted by the wicked Antiochus to transgress the divine command, which forbade the Hebrews to eat swine's flesh, his friends through compassion for his old age besought him, in order to escape death, at least to pretend to comply with the tyrants order. But the venerable old man wisely replied, that he would rather be sent into the other world: for it doth not become our age to dissemble. He would rather sacrifice his life than pretend, at such an advanced age, to break the divine precept, and thus teach his young countrymen to transgress the law.

"The look of a just man," says St. Ambrose, "Is an admonition." Oh, what an affecting admonition to novices, and how far superior to the most eloquent exhortation, to see an aged religious observing with punctuality all the Rules, great and small! All the zeal and exertions of religious who love perfection should be directed to the support of discipline in all its rigor. When Jesus Christ, by stretching forth his right hand, showed St. Teresa that he was espoused to her, he said: "Henceforth, as my true spouse, you shall be zealous for my honor." Every spouse, then, of Jesus should ardently seek his glory. But it is for the

123

observance of the Rules, which are the principal support of perfection in the Community, that religious should display all their zeal. And this zeal should be cherished not only by Superiors, but by all, and especially by those whose office or age gives them authority over the other Sisters. Whenever St. Andrew Avellini saw the rules transgressed, he admonished with great fervor not only his companions in religion, but also his Superiors. It is related in the life of Father Torres that one of his penitents, Sister M. Teresa Spinelli, a religious of great zeal and piety, in the convent of the Most Holy Trinity at Naples, seeing certain abuses introduced into the Community, opposed them vehemently without regard to any person, however great his dignity. She had in view only God's honor; and to uphold it by resisting the introduction of irregularity into religion, she endured many troubles and contradictions. When manifest abuses and relaxation of discipline steal into a convent, it is not pride or temerity, but an act of virtue and zeal, to exclaim against them, and even to oppose the Superiors themselves, should such opposition be necessary for the correction of abuses.

FOURTH EXCUSE.

Through a pretended fear of being troublesome to the Superior, some abstain from asking permission to do what they are forbidden by rule to do without her leave.

This, too, is a vain excuse; for Superiors, instead of being annoyed, are edified by the religious who ask permissions as often as they may be required. Besides, how can a Superior complain of the sisters for asking leave to do what their Rule forbids them to do, without her permission? Be careful, then, never to abstain from asking any permission which your Rule commands you to ask. And when, to support the observance of the Rule, your Superior refuses your request, be not disturbed, but thank her for the refusal, and keep your soul in peace. All the passengers in a ship rejoice, and even feel grateful to the pilot, when they see that he compels all the sailors, without exception, to attend to their duty; for should even one of them neglect his post the vessel might be lost.

The rules are burdensome, but they are only the burden of the wings with which we fly to the Lord. "The burden of Christ," says St. Augustine, "Has wings." Yes, it has wings which assist us to rise on high.

The rules are fetters; but they are bonds of love which unite us to the Supreme Good. When bound by rule, we should say with holy David: The lines are fallen unto me in goodly places. To me these cords are not a badge of dishonour, but of nobility; they are the object of my love because they deliver me from the chains of hell. And when we feel pain or sorrow in consequence of being deprived by our Rule of any gratification which self-love prompts us to desire, let us rejoice, and say with the Apostle I, a prisoner in the Lord. As if he said: I see that I am a prisoner, but I exult in those chains which bind me to my God and merit for me an eternal crown. "He would not," says St. Augustine, "Put a golden necklace on you if he had not first chained you in iron fetters." The Lord would not give you the golden necklace of eternal glory without having first bound you with the chains of rule.

Should a sister, then, ask you to do what without permission you are forbidden to do, tell her without hesitation that you cannot accede to her request. You ought not to be ashamed to refuse when there is question of avoiding a fault, and especially the violation of the Rule. No: should the others be negligent, it is your duty to be singular in regular observance. Be not afraid that your regularity will be an occasion of vainglory. That your example may shine forth, and serve as an incentive to others to observe the Rule and thus give glory to God, it is certainly his will that, if the rest of the Community be careless, you should be singular in attending even to the smallest rules. So let your light shine before men, that they may see your good works, and glorify your Father who is in heaven. If you are not able to do great things for God, to perform rigorous penances, or to devote much time to prayer, strive at least to observe your Rule with exactness; and be assured that by its sole observance you will in a short time make rapid progress in perfection. A great servant of God used to say that the punctual observance of the Rule is the short way to sanctity. "The best perfection," says St. Bonaventure, "Is to fulfill all things whatsoever that are prescribed." God will be liberal to a religious in proportion to her fidelity to him. "A religious," says St. Teresa, "Faithful to the minutest of the rules does not walk, but flies to perfection without either wings or feathers."

St. Augustine justly calls the Rule the mirror of religious; for by its observance the character of a religious may be known. Yes, says Hugo of Victor, commenting on St. Augustine, the Rule is the best test by which we may discover "Whether religious are just or unjust, whether they advance, whether they are pleasing or displeasing to God." By seeing religious attentive to the Rule, or careless about its observance, we ascertain at once whether they love or do not love perfection; whether they go forward or recede; whether they please or displease God. Be assured that a religious will become a saint not by doing a multiplicity of works, but by the faithful observance of the Rule. At the times set apart by the Rule for labor or for recreation a religious should not go to prayer, to the choir, nor take the discipline. These unseasonable devotions are, says Father Alvarez, sacrifices of rapine, which God does not accept.

A certain Capuchin was accustomed to absent himself from the common labors for the purpose of attending to his private devotions. On the bed of sickness Jesus Christ, in quality of his judge, appeared to him, and ordered all the vocal prayers and other devotions performed during the time of the common exercises to be taken from him and to be distributed among those who had labored for the Community. By the mercy of God his life was prolonged, his health was restored, and ever after the good brother assisted most punctually at all the common duties.

St. Mary Magdalene de Pazzi used to say that the best means to acquire great merit is to be present at every assembly of the Community. It is true that in certain circumstances, as when you labor under infirmity or are engaged in some very important duty of office, it is not a fault to break some small rule. But it is likewise true that transgressions committed under pretence of sickness or necessity frequently proceed from sloth, and from a want of affection for the Rule. For others who are perhaps more infirm, and not less occupied in the offices of the convent, never violate the rules that you so often transgress. They who love discipline find the means of observing the Rule, and also of discharging the duties of office. St. Teresa used to say that "Sometimes the evil is small, and therefore we imagine that we are not bound to avoid it."

To read your Rule frequently for the purpose of seeing what faults you commit and what you have to correct will contribute greatly to infuse into your soul an affection for exact observance. The reading of the rules is one of the best spiritual readings that you can make. It will also be very profitable to make your particular examination on the rules that you transgress most frequently. Whenever you violate the Rule be not ashamed to acknowledge your fault to the Superior, and to ask penance for it. The devil once said to St. Dominic, that in the chapter at which religious confess their defects, and receive penance and admonition for them, he lost all that he had gained in the refectory, in the parlour, and in the other places of the monastery. Before you confess your fault, dispose your heart to accept whatever reproof or penance may be given to you, lest you should be like the religious who, to show that they are humble and exact in the observance of the Rule, acknowledge their defects, but are at the same time unwilling to be reproved for their transgressions.

But to be profitable, the observance of the Rule, as St. Ignatius has remarked, must above all be accompanied with "The spirit of love, and not the perturbation of fear." You should observe the rules not to escape the rebukes of the Superior, nor to win the admiration of the sisters, but through the spirit of love and to please Jesus Christ. Hence the same saint has declared, that in not annexing the penalty of sin to the violation of the Rule of the Society of Jesus, his object was "To make love take the place of the fear of offending God." Count, says St. Eucherius of Lyons, "Among the days of your life that day only on which you have denied self-will, and which you have spent without any violation of the Rule." St. Mary Magdalene de Pazzi has recommended three very efficacious means of observing the Rule: "1. Prize the Rule as you esteem God himself. 2. Act as if you only were obliged to observe the Rule. 3. If the others fail in regular observance, endeavor to supply their deficiency."

In a word, I say again, you must be persuaded that the perfection of a religious does not consist in great and manifold works, but in performing all her actions well. Great indeed was the praise of the multitude to Jesus Christ when they said: He hath done all things well. To achieve what is difficult and extraordinary is not given to all; nor can extraordinary works be performed at all times. But ordinary actions—such as the common prayer, the examination of conscience, Communion, the hearing of Mass, the recitation of the divine Office, the fulfillment of the duties annexed to the offices of the Community, and the other obligations imposed by the Rule—are duties that may be discharged every day, and by all the members of the convent. Be assured that though in the fulfillment of ordinary duties you should be employed in the meanest occupations, the faithful discharge of them will certainly make you a saint. It is not enough to do what God wills: it is moreover necessary to do it in the manner he wishes. It is related in the Chronicles of the Cistercians, that St. Bernard saw many angels noting what the monks were doing in the choir. The works of one were written in gold, of another in silver, of a third in ink, and of a fourth in water, to denote the perfection or imperfection with which each attended to prayer. Consider then how easily, if you will, you can arrive at perfection: by the discharge of your ordinary duties you may become a saint. The Lord does not require of you lofty flights of contemplation, nor formidable penances: all that he demands is, that you perform all your actions well.

Many religious, on days of devotion,—for example, during the novena of the Nativity, of the Holy Ghost, and of the Blessed Virgin,—practice many exercises of piety, fasts, disciplines, vocal prayers, and similar works of penance. All these are very good; but the best devotion for a religious on such occasions is to perform her ordinary duties with extraordinary perfection. The perfection of an action consists, first, in that it is done through the sole motive of pleasing God; for it is not the external act, but purity of intention, that constitutes perfection. All the glory of the king's daughter is within. The perfection of an action consists, secondly, in doing it well; that is, with promptness, attention, and exactness. The following are the means of performing our actions well:

1. The first means is to preserve during the discharge of your duties a lively sense of the presence of God, that thus every act may be worthy of his divine eyes.

2. The second means is, to perform every work as if it were the only duty you had to fulfill. When at prayer, let your sole care be to pray well; when you say the divine Office, direct all your attention to the devout recitation of it; when engaged in any employment enjoined by obedience, your sole concern should be to discharge it well. Think of nothing but the duty in which you are occupied. To examine, during the time of prayer, how you will execute a certain command, or how you will direct a certain work, or to reflect on the means of performing any other duty, is a temptation of the enemy. "When," says Father M. Avila, "Any unseasonable thought enters your mind, say: God does

not will that I think at this moment on such a subject; and therefore it is not useful for me to reflect upon it: when he commands me, I shall attend to it."

3. The third means is, to perform every action as if it were the last of your life. St. Anthony frequently recommended this means to his disciples. "In every work," says St. Bernard, "Let each one say to himself: If I were about to die, would I do this?" Would I do it in this manner? Were this the last Mass that I should hear, with what devotion would I be present at it? Were this the last Office that I should recite, with what attention would I say it! Were this my last Communion or my last meditation, with what fervor would I perform it! When, says St. Basil, you discharge the duties of the morning, imagine that you shall not live till evening; when night approaches, think that you shall not see the morning. It is related of a certain Dominican, who was accustomed to go to confession every morning before he offered the Holy Sacrifice of the Mass, that, being seized with a serious malady, his Superior commanded him to prepare for death by a good confession. The good religious raised his hands to heaven, and exclaimed: Blessed be God, I have confessed every day for the last thirty years, as if I were to die suddenly. Blessed, says the Redeemer, is that servant, whom, when His Lord shall come, he shall find so doing: And happy the religious whom, should death come suddenly upon her, Jesus Christ, her judge, shall find performing the duty in which she may be engaged, as if she knew it to be the last of her life.

4. To think each day only on the labors of the day, is another means which greatly assists weak souls to discharge their duties with fervor. The apprehension of the pains to be endured, in living till death with so much exactness, and in continually resisting self-love, is one of the causes which make many lose courage in the way of God. The best means of conquering this temptation is, to imagine each morning that you have but one day to live. Whoever represents to himself that only one day of life remains, will certainly perform all the actions of that day with great perfection. This means is very profitable to weak souls; but strong and perfect Christians do not require to conceal from themselves the labors necessary for the attainment of sanctity; they rejoice in suffering, and pant for opportunities of pleasing God.

5. To religious beginning to walk in the way of perfection it will be

very useful means to consider that what is in itself difficult and painful will by habit soon become easy and agreeable. I will, says the Holy Ghost, lead thee by the paths of equity; which, when thou shalt have entered, thy steps shall not be straitened; and when thou run-nest, thou shalt not meet a stumbling-block. I will, says the Lord, first conduct you into the narrow paths of virtue; but you shall soon walk through a broad and pleasing way, and there you shall run without difficulties or obstacles. "At first," says St. Bernard, writing to Pope Eugenius, "Some duty will seem intolerable; if you accustom yourself to it, in process of time it will not appear so difficult: afterwards you shall not feel it; and in the end you will delight in it." Behold with your eyes, says Ecclesiasticus, how I have labored a little, and have found much rest to myself.

Prayer.

O my God! I am that unhappy soul that has long since merited the curse of the barren fig-tree. Since I have produced no fruit, why should I occupy a place in religion? I have deserved to be cut down and cast into the fire. Unhappy me! I have been for so many years in religion, and favoured with so many helps to sanctity, and what fruit have I brought forth? But Thou dost not wish that I despair, or doubt in Thy mercy. Thou hast said: Ask, and you shall receive. Since Thou dost desire me to ask for Thy graces, the first favour I seek is the pardon of all the displeasure that I have given to Thee. I have repaid Thy love and Thy benefits by so many insults; but I repent, my God, with my whole soul. The second grace I ask of Thee is the gift of Thy love, that henceforth I may love Thee, not with tepidity, as in my past life, but with my whole soul, and that I may never more give Thee the least displeasure, but that I may always do whatever I know to be pleasing to Thee. The third grace I ask is holy perseverance in Thy love. I now esteem Thy love more than all the kingdoms of the earth. Thou wishest me to be entirely Thine, and I desire to belong to Thee without reserve. On the Cross and in the Blessed Sacrament Thou hast given Thyself entirely to me; I offer my whole being to Thee. I thank Thee for enabling me by Thy grace to make this oblation. Since Thou hast inspired, I hope thou hast accepted it. O my Jesus, I am Thine, and I trust that Thou wilt be mine for all eternity. I desire not that my inclinations, but Thy holy will, may live henceforth in me. And I promise from this day forward to observe all, even the smallest, of the rules of religion; because

I know that all of them are approved by Thee. O my Love, my Love! I will say with St. Catharine of Genoa, no more sins. I beseech Thee to make me always love Thee, or to take me out of life. Either love or death, O my God!

Mary, my mother, speak to thy Son, and obtain for me the grace to love him or to die.

VI.

The Four Degrees of Perfect Obedience.

To be perfect in obedience, a religious must obey with promptness, exactness, cheerfulness, and simplicity. These are the degrees of perfect obedience.

THE FIRST DEGREE.

The first degree, then, is to obey with promptness, executing immediately and without reply every injunction imposed by obedience. There are some who obey only after many entreaties of the Superior, and after many attempts to elude her commands. Religious that are truly obedient do not act in this manner. "A Christian faithful to obedience," says St. Bernard, "Knows not delays, but prepares his ears for hearing, and his hands and his feet for labor." A religious truly obedient is never slow to obey, but instantly applies her ears to hear every precept, and her hands and feet to execute every command. She does not indulge in slothful slumbers after the morning bell, but obeying its sound as the call of God himself, she instantly rises. On receiving a precept, she makes no reply, offers no excuses, manifests no repugnance, as some do, by a silence which often afflicts the Superior, but instantly and with external joy shows her readiness to obey, and immediately fulfils the command. She is not like those who are with difficulty made to submit to authority, and who by their reluctance to obey lose the greater part of the merit of obedience. No; to insure her compliance with every duty, neither entreaties, nor arguments, nor repeated commands are necessary. She fulfils at once, and without reply, every obligation of obedience.

Oh, how meritorious in the sight of God is prompt obedience. He has several times shown, even by supernatural prodigies, how acceptable it is in his sight. St. Mark, a monk, while engaged in writing, was called by his Superior, the Abbot Silvan; the saint left unfinished a word which he had just begun, and instantly obeyed. On his return he found the remainder of the word written in letters of gold. Blosius relates that a nun to whom the infant Jesus appeared, being summoned at the moment of his appearance to a certain duty, instantly obeyed the call. On her return she found him grown up to the age of manhood, and was addressed by him in the following words: "My child, your ready obedience has made me grow thus in your heart." Jesus appeared to another religious, who on hearing the bell for Vespers left him, and went to the choir. When she returned to her cell, he appeared to her again and said: "Because you left me, you have found me again; had you not obeyed the call of duty, I should have departed from you." To try the obedience of some of his monks who were confined to bed by sickness, St. Columban commanded them to rise, and go to the barn to thrash corn. As many as were filled with the true spirit of obedience instantly arose, and were suddenly restored to health. The others, because they were weak in spirit as well as in body, remained in bed and continued in their infirmities.

God has also sometimes shown how much he dislikes tardy obedience. Blessed Juniper, while employed in planting a tree in the garden, was called by St. Francis. The brother did not obey the call immediately, but waited till he had finished the work in which he was engaged. The saint, to show him the fault he had committed by the tardiness of his obedience, cursed the tree, and on the part of God, commanded it to grow no larger. The tree obeyed, and never increased in size. The narrator of this fact states, that when he wrote his annals the tree was preserved in the convent of the city of Carinula; that It remained green, but was as small as when it was planted. How scandalous is it to see certain religious slow to obey, for no other reason than because they are commanded to obey! Were the duty of obedience not of precept, they should perhaps discharge it without delay, because it would be agreeable to self-will. Some will obey only after having frequently said to the Superior: I cannot perform this duty. They would speak with more truth if they said: I do not wish to do what you command. St. Joseph Calasanctius used to say that he who instead of saying "I will not," says "I cannot," deceives himself, and not the Superior.

THE SECOND DEGREE.

The second degree of obedience is to obey with exactness; that is, with punctuality, and without interpretation.

PUNCTUALLY.—You should obey with punctuality, and not rob God of any part of your sacrifice by a mutilation of the victim you offer to him. You should carefully fulfill the whole duty imposed upon you, and employ in its discharge all the time prescribed by obedience. Some are punctual in the presence of the Superior, but in her absence they comply so imperfectly with the obligations of obedience, that it would be difficult to determine whether the fulfillment of their duties is a source of merit or demerit. St. Mary Magdalene de Pazzi used to say, that "Religious have consecrated their will not to men, but to God; that they have given it to him, not in part, but entirely and without reserve."

WITHOUT INTERPRETATIONS.—It is also necessary to obey without interpreting in your own favour the commands that you receive. A lay-brother, from another convent, came one day to the house of the Dominicans in Bologna. Being obliged to go out in haste on pressing and important business, he obtained permission from the Superior to take for his companion the brother whom he should first meet. Meeting, by chance, St. Thomas, he asked the saint in the name of the Superior to accompany him. The saint instantly obeyed, but being corpulent, walked slowly; the lay-brother, because his business was urgent, entreated the saint to quicken his pace. When the brother knew who his companion was, he frequently begged pardon of St. Thomas for having treated him so disrespectfully; but the holy Doctor bore all without the least sign of impatience. St. Thomas might have interpreted the command of the Prior, and have reasonably inferred that it did not extend to him; but no: he wished to obey without reply and without interpretation, and when he was told that he might have excused himself, he answered that the sole concern of a religious should be, to fulfill with exactness the obligations of obedience.

Cassian relates that two young religious being sent by the Abbot John with a basket of figs, as a present to an aged monk who lived at a distance, missed their way and wandered through a desert for many days without food. In such necessity they might, without violating obedience, have interpreted in their own favour the command of the Superior, and have eaten of the figs sent to the monk; but rather than depart from even the letter of the precept, they submitted to a painful death. They were afterwards found dead, and the figs untouched.

I do not mean to say that it is never lawful to transgress the letter of a precept; or that it is wrong to interpret the will of Superiors, when circumstances justify or render necessary an interpretation of their command. But I assert that certain forced and sophistical interpretations differ but little from formal acts of disobedience. Subjects should always comply even with the letter of a precept, unless they be certain that the Superior does not intend to oblige them to fulfill it. Some religious, though fully acquainted with the will of the Superior, follow the dictates of their own caprice, saying that what they do is not forbidden. But Albert Magnus says that, "A truly obedient man never waits for a command, but performs, as if commanded, whatever he knows or judges to be the will of his Superior." It is in the prompt fulfillment of the will of the Superior that perfect obedience consists. St. Thomas teaches that the will of the Superior, in whatever way it is known, should be regarded as a tacit precept by the religious who aspires to perfect obedience.

THE THIRD DEGREE.

The third degree of obedience is to obey with JOY. To obey with reluctance, and murmuring against Superiors, is a defect rather than an act of virtue. "If," says St. Bernard, "Murmuring in your heart, you begin to judge the Superior, though you externally comply with the precept, your compliance is not a virtue, but a covering of malice." If you murmur interiorly against the Superior, the fulfillment of her commands is but a cloak thrown over your malice. For your obedience is only external, and in your heart you disregard her authority and violate the divine law. Oh, what a misery to see certain religious who discharge with cheerfulness only the duties which they themselves have asked, or which they have been requested and entreated to perform, and who accept without reluctance only the offices by which their own self-love is gratified?

How can a person who importunes the Superior for a charge agreeable to her inclinations, who is willing to accept such a charge and no other—how, I say, can she be called an obedient religious? St. Ignatius

134

used to say, that to regard as an act of obedience the fulfillment of a command extorted from a Superior is an illusion; and in confirmation of his assertion he adduced the following words of St. Bernard: "Whosoever, either openly or secretly, labors to obtain from his spiritual Father a precept agreeable to self-will, deceives and vainly flatters himself by imagining that he practices obedience; for in this he does not obey his Superior, but the Superior rather obeys him." Tritemius goes so far as to call the religious who obeys with reluctance a monster of the devil; for he too obeys, but his obedience is forced. A religious who obeys only by constraint is in a certain sense worse than the demons; because she has promised obedience to God by her solemn vow, but they have not. In what, I ask, does the obedience of such a religious consist? Is it not in doing with cheerfulness what pleases her own caprice, and in performing what is painful to self-love with reluctance, and with external signs of discontent? "What room is there for obedience," says St. Bernard, "Where the bitterness of sadness is perceived?"

God loveth a cheerful giver says the Apostle. The Lord loves the man who performs with cheerfulness whatever he does for the love of God. Religious filled with the true spirit of obedience execute with the greatest joy the commands that are most opposed to their inclinations; because it is in the fulfillment of such commands that they are most certain of not doing their own will, and of doing the will of God. And what can give greater happiness to a Christian than in the performance of every duty to be able to say: By this action I please God? If you, dear sister, desire to give great pleasure to Jesus Christ, beg of the Superior to impose upon you whatever precepts she pleases without any regard to your inclinations; for thus she will be more free in prescribing to you the necessary duties, and you shall have greater merit in executing her orders. You shall then be certain of deserving as great a reward by works agreeable to self-love as by the exercises opposed to the feelings of flesh and blood. Never depart from the excellent rule of St. Francis de Sales—neither to ask nor to refuse any duty.

"Obedience," says St. John Climacus, "Is the sepulchre of self-will." Some call obedience the death of self-will; but it is more properly denominated its sepulchre. For the dead, as long as they are unburied, may be seen; but after their interment they are no longer visible. Some destroy self-will by the practice of obedience, but still allow it

135

to appear in their exterior. In the perfect, self-will is not only dead, but buried; so that in their actions it can never be perceived.

In St. Mary Magdalene de Pazzi self-will was so completely extinguished that her Superiors could never know what was agreeable or disagreeable to her. Endeavor to imitate her conduct, and to receive with perfect indifference all the duties, offices, and employments that may be assigned to you; and to fulfill them with cheerfulness and alacrity. If you desire to discharge your obligations with true joy, you must perform them from the pure intention of pleasing God. If you comply with them to obtain the friendship of the Superior, to induce her to grant your requests, to escape her displeasure, or the charge of disobedience, or through any other motive of self-interest, you may indeed satisfy the Superior, but you will not please God, and therefore you shall suffer all the fatigue and pains of obedience without enjoying the tranquility of an obedient religious. Moreover, if to please God be the sole end of your obedience, you will cheerfully obey, not only when the tone and manner of the Superior are sweet and agreeable, but also when her directions are given in severe and commanding language: in this merit consists.

Father Rodriguez relates that St. Gertrude besought the Lord to deliver the abbess from her roughness of manner and impatience towards the sisters, but in answer Almighty God told her that he permitted these defects in the abbess to keep her humble, and for the greater trial and merit of the religious.

THE FOURTH DEGREE.

The fourth and last degree of perfect obedience is to obey with SIMPLICITY. Servants, says the Apostle, be obedient . . . in the simplicity of your hearts. To be simple of heart you must subject your own judgment to that of the Superior, and esteem as just and reasonable whatever she commands. Behold how the Holy Ghost teaches his spouse the duty of perfect obedience: If thou knowest not thyself, O fairest among women, go forth, and follow after the steps of thy flocks. O fairest of women, if you know not how to make yourself the object of my love, come and I will teach you; go forth from thyself, and follow after the steps of thy flocks, which, when sent to pasture, ask not where or when or why they go? They obey their pastor without reply: so should a religious obey without demanding the reasons why she should obey.

That great servant of God, Father Pavone, of the Society of Jesus, used to say that obedience, to be perfect, should captivate the intellect as well as the will. The obedience of a religious whose will only obeys, and whose understanding condemns what the Superior commands, is lame and imperfect. St. Mary Magdalene de Pazzi says that "Perfect obedience requires a soul without a will, and a will without an intellect." Hence to acquire the perfect spirit of obedience the saint was accustomed, first to captivate her judgment, and then to perform the duty imposed upon her. He who does not practice obedience of the intellect will hardly obey with cheerfulness; his submission will be that of a slave—the result of force, not the obedience of a child, and the fruit of love. Hence the Apostle says: With a good will serving as to the Lord, and not to men. Obey with a good will, serving God rather than men. Your obedience will never be cheerful unless it proceed from a motive of pleasing God, who can never err in his precepts, and who commands only what will be profitable to us.

St. Thomas teaches that though the commands of a Superior may appear impossible, a religious should make an effort to fulfill them. Because subjects have no right to decide on the possibility or impossibility of a precept imposed upon them. "Perfect obedience," says St. Bernard, "Is indiscreet." In subjects perfect obedience does not require discretion. And in another place the saint says: "It is impossible for a prudent novice to persevere in religion." A novice who regulates her obedience by her own prudence cannot persevere in the religious state. Because, continues the saint, to assume the office of Superior is, in a novice, insufferable pride. "To decide belongs to the Superior; and to obey is the duty of the subject." To decide what is to be done is the prerogative of the Superior, and to fulfill her commands the bounden duty of subjects. St. Ignatius once said that should the Pope command him to undertake a voyage by sea in a ship without a mast, without oars or sails, he would blindly obey the precept. And when he was told that it would be imprudent to expose his life to danger, he answered that prudence is necessary in Superiors; but in subjects the perfection of prudence is to obey without prudence.

This doctrine is conformable to Holy Scripture: Behold, says the Lord, as clay is in the potter's hands. Religious must leave themselves in the hands of the Superior to be moulded as she wills. Shall the clay say to him that fashioneth it: What art thou making? If clay should dare to say to the potter, Why hast thou formed me thus?—The potter ought to answer: Be silent: it is not your business to inquire what I do, but to obey and to receive whatever form I please to give you. Such the answer merited by religious who seek to know why a precept, an office, or a duty is imposed upon them. St. Jerome, in an epistle to Rusticus, a monk, says: "It is your duty to obey: judge not of the decision of your Superiors." In the lives of the monks of La Trappe we read that a good religious called Arsenius judged to be superfluous the expense incurred by the Superior in making the church more commodious. But afterwards, reflecting that his judgment was in opposition to that of his Superior, he went immediately and with tears accused himself of his fault as if it were a great crime. The abbot told him that his fault was not so grievous as he imagined; but Arsenius could not restrain the torrent of tears which flowed from his eyes.

To regard as good whatever Superiors command, is the blind obedience so much praised by the saints; and is the duty of every religious, and this for four reasons: 1. Because, according to the proverb, no one is fit to be a judge in his own cause. When there is question of their own interest, self-love renders it difficult for all men to distinguish truth from falsehood; and therefore no one should be the judge of what regards himself. 2. Because a Superior is acquainted with a great many circumstances of which subjects are ignorant; and therefore her opinion should be preferred to theirs. 3. Because subjects only regard their own interests; but the Superior looks to the good of the Community. 4. Because Superiors are assisted, in a particular manner, by Almighty God to govern the Community; and therefore are favoured with lights not given to subjects.

Of St. Paul it is written, that after his conversion, when his eyes were opened, he saw nothing. But they leading him by the hand, brought him to Damascus. Some religious are unwilling to obey without examining whether the duty imposed upon them will be profitable or unprofitable to them. Should it appear not suited to them, they either refuse to obey, or obey only with reluctance, and sometimes go so far as to charge the Superior with imprudence, indiscretion, or partiality. All this arises from a want of the spirit of blind obedience, and from a desire to demand from the Superior the reason why she imposes certain duties. "To seek for reasons is," according to St. Bernard, "A sign of an imperfect heart." Whoever demands the reason of a precept shows a very imperfect will. It was by asking the reasons of the divine command that the devil tempted Eve to eat the forbidden apple, and succeeded in making her prevaricate. Why, said the serpent, hath God commanded you, that you should not cat of every tree in paradise. Had Eve answered: It belongs not to us to seek the reason of the precept: it is our duty to obey;—she should not have fallen. But because she began to examine the reason of the command, she replied, We can eat of the fruits of paradise. There is but one tree which we are forbidden to touch, lest perhaps we die. Perceiving that she began to doubt the threatened punishment of death, he rejoined, Be not afraid, you shall not die, and thus he persuaded her to transgress the command of God.

Religious that are truly obedient seek not for reasons; but, like St. Paul, with open eyes, they see not, and reduce a haughty intellect to the subjection of obedience, by submitting their judgment to that of their Superior. St. John Climacus says that a religious should banish thoughts opposed to obedience, as she would reject thoughts against chastity, that is, immediately, and without reply; and that, instead of questioning the reasonableness of the precepts of her Superior, she should always seek for reasons to defend their expediency. Almighty God has several times shown, in a miraculous manner, how much he delights in the blind obedience of religious. Sulpitius Severus relates, that to try the obedience of a young man who applied for admission into a certain monastery, the abbot commanded him to walk into a furnace filled with burning coals. The young man instantly plunged into the fire, but received no injury; his clothes were not even touched. St. Gregory relates that St. Benedict commanded St. Maurus to follow the young St. Placidus, who had fallen into a river. St. Maurus obeyed, walked on the waters, and saved the life of the boy. These examples are not to be imitated. The precepts given by these holy men, and their fulfillment, proceeded from extraordinary impulses of the Holy Ghost, who assured the Superiors that by their commands, and the subjects that by their obedience, they were accomplishing the divine will. But at the same time they show how much God is pleased by blind unhesitating obedience.

To try the obedience of their subjects, Superiors sometimes impose commands that are inexpedient, and even absurd. St. Francis commanded his disciples to plant cabbages with their roots uppermost. He obliged Brother Matthew to continue turning round till he fell to the ground. St. Teresa made similar trials of her children. But you will ask, Of what use are such precepts? In answer I ask, Why are untrained horses made sometimes to run, sometimes to stop, and sometimes to go back? All these contribute to make them obedient to the bridle; and to exercise religious in what appears extravagant and useless accustoms them to subdue the stubbornness of their own will, and to subject their own judgments to that of their Superiors.

St. Joseph Calasanctius used to say, that "To follow one's own judgment in the practice of obedience, is not obedience." In every act of your life, be careful, dear sister, never to prefer your opinion to that of your Superiors. St. Philip Neri has remarked, that nothing is more dangerous than to be directed by one's own counsel. Peter of Blois says that "To trust one's self-alone, is the greatest of evils." Cassian asserts that "It is impossible for him who confides in his own judgment to escape the deceits and illusions of the devil." Hence St. John Chrysostom teaches that "Nothing is so destructive of the Church as a separation of disciples from their masters." There is nothing which does greater injury to the Church of God than the opposition of disciples to the opinion of their masters; and there is nothing more ruinous to a religious Community than the disregard of the sisters for the judgment of their Superiors.

Prayer.

O my Jesus, Thou dost never abandon a soul that seeks Thee. Thou hast not forsaken them that love thee. I have left the world to find Thee in this holy place: but I have only sought myself and my own pleasures, and thus I have greatly offended Thee. Forget, O Lord, the past, and pardon the offences which I have committed against Thee, and which I now abhor with my whole soul. I feel a strong desire to become a saint, and to please Thee in all things. I know that this desire is Thy gift. Ah, my Spouse, what has induced Thee to visit with so much love a soul so ungrateful, and to bestow upon me so many graces, after all the insults I have offered to Thee? With a humble and a contrite heart I thank Thee for all Thy favors: be a thousand times blessed for them. Thou dost invite me to Thy love; and I desire to obey Thy call. I know the value of this grace, and am resolved never more to be unmindful of Thy benefits, as I have hitherto been. I love Thee, O my Sovereign Good! I love Thee, O my God! Thou art my only treasure, and the only object of my love. Give me strength to correspond, by my affections, to the love which Thou dost bear me. Grant that I may love Thee always; that I may love Thee intensely: I ask nothing more.

O my mother, Mary, thank thy Son for me, and obtain for me the grace to be faithful to him during the remainder of my life. O Mother of God, in thee I trust.

CHAPTER VIII.

EXTERIOR MORTIFICATION.

I.

It's Necessity and Advantages.

THERE is no alternative: we poor children of Adam must till death live in continual warfare; For, says the Apostle, the flesh lusteth against the spirit. The flesh desires what the spirit dislikes; and the spirit pants for what the flesh abhors. Now, since it is peculiar to irrational creatures to place all their happiness in sensual enjoyment, and to the angels to seek only the accomplishment of God's will, surely if we attend to the observance of the divine commands, we shall, as a learned author justly says, he transformed into angels; but if we fix our affections on the gratifications of sense, we shall sink to the level of the brute creation.

If the soul do not subdue the body, the flesh will conquer the spirit. To maintain his seat on a furious steed, and to escape danger, the horseman must hold a tight rein; and to avoid the corruption of the flesh, we must keep the body in perpetual restraint. We must treat it as a physician treats a patient, to whom he prescribes nauseous medicine, and to whom he refuses palatable food. Cruel indeed must be the physician who gives to a sick man noxious draughts because they are pleasing to the taste, and who does not administer useful remedies, because they are bitter and disgusting. And great is the cruelty of the sensual, when to escape some trifling corporal pain in this life they expose their souls and bodies to eternal torments in the next. "Such charity," says St. Bernard, "Is destructive of charity: such mercy is full of cruelty; because it serves the body so as to destroy the soul." The false love of the flesh destroys the true charity which we owe to ourselves: inordinate compassion towards the body is full of cruelty, because by indulging the flesh it kills the soul. Speaking of sensualists who deride the mortifications of the saints, the same Father says: "If we are cruel in crucifying the flesh, you by sparing it are far more cruel." Yes, for by the pleasures of the body in this life you shall merit for soul and body inexpressible torments forever in the next. Father Rodriguez tells us of a solitary who had emaciated his body by very rigorous austerities. Being asked why he treated his body so badly, he replied: "I only chastise what chastises me." I torment the enemy who persecutes my soul, and who seeks my destruction. The Abbot Moses being once censured for his severity towards his body replied: "Let the passion cease and I will also cease to mortify my flesh." When the flesh ceases to molest me, I shall cease to crucify its appetites.

If, then, we wish to be saved, and to please God, we must take pleasure in what the flesh refuses, and must reject what the flesh demands. Our Lord once said to St. Francis of Assisi: "If you desire my love, accept the things that are bitter as if they were sweet, and the things that are sweet as if they were bitter."

Some will say that perfection does not consist in the mortification of the body, but in the abnegation of the will. To them I answer with Father Pinamonti, that the fruit of the vineyard does not consist in the surrounding hedge; but still if the hedge be taken away, you will seek in vain for the produce of the vine. Where there is no hedge, says the Holy Ghost, the possession shall be spoiled. So ardent was the desire of St. Aloysius to crucify his flesh, that, although weak in health, he sought nothing but mortifications and penitential rigors; and, to a person who once said that sanctity does not consist in corporal works of penance, but in the denial of self-will, he wisely answered in the words of the Redeemer: These things you ought to have done, and not to have those undone. He meant to say that, to keep the flesh in subjection to reason, the mortification of the body is necessary, as well as the denial of the will. I chastise my body, says St. Paul, and bring it into subjection. The flesh, when indulged, will be brought with difficulty to obey the divine law. Hence St. John of the Cross, speaking of certain spiritual directors who despise and discourage external penance, says that "He who inculcates loose doctrine regarding the mortification of the flesh, should not be believed though he confirmed his preaching by miracles."

The world and the devil are very powerful enemies of our eternal salvation; but our own body, because it is a domestic enemy, is a still more dangerous antagonist. "A domestic enemy," says St. Bernard, "Is the worst of foes." A town that is besieged has more to apprehend from the enemies that are within than from those that are without the walls; because it is far more difficult to ward off the attacks of the former than those of the latter. St. Joseph Calasanctius used to say that "We should pay no more attention to the body than to the vilest rag." Such indeed has been the practice of the saints. As the indulgence of the body by sensual pleasures is the sole and constant study of world-lings, so the continual mortification of the flesh is to the saints the only object of their care and of their desires. St. Peter of Alcantara was accustomed to say to his body: O my body, keep your peace; I shall give you no rest here below; pains and torments shall be your portion in this life; when we shall be in paradise, you will then enjoy that repose which shall never end. Similar was the practice of St. Mary Magdalene de Pazzi, who, on the bed of death, stated that she did not remember to have ever taken pleasure in any other object than in God alone. If we read the lives of the saints and see the works of penance that they performed, we shall be ashamed of the delicacy and of the reserve with which we chastise the flesh. In the lives of the ancient Fathers we read of a large Community of nuns who never tasted fruit or wine. Some of them took food only once every day; others never ate a meal, except after two or three days of rigorous abstinence: all were clothed and even slept in haircloth. I do not require such austerities from religious of the present day: but is it too much for them to take the discipline several times in the week,—to wear a chain round some part of the body till the hour of dinner,— not to approach the fire in winter on some day in each week, and during novenas of devotion,—to abstain from fruit and sweet meats,—and, in honor of the Mother of God, to fast every Saturday on bread and water, or at least to be content with one dish?

But you will say: I am weak, and my director forbids me to practice any corporal austerity. Obey your confessor, but take care to embrace with peace all the troubles of your infirmities, and all the inconveniences arising from the heat or cold of the seasons. If you cannot chastise your body by positive rigors, abstain at least from some lawful pleasures. St. Francis Borgia, when amusing himself in hawk-hunting, used to cast down his eyes when he saw the hawk about to spring upon its prey. St. Aloysius always turned away his eyes from the objects of curiosity exhibited at the festivities at which he was present. Why cannot you practice similar mortifications? If denied lawful pleasures, the body will not dare to seek forbidden indulgence; but if continually gratified by every innocent enjoyment, it will soon draw the soul into sinful gratifications. Besides, that great servant of God, Father Vincent

Carafa, of the Society of Jesus, used to say that the Almighty has given us the goods of the earth, not only that we may enjoy them, but also that we may have the means of pleasing him by offering to him his own gifts, and by voluntarily renouncing them in order to show our love for him. It is true, indeed, that certain innocent pleasures assist our weakness, and prepare us for spiritual exercises; but it is likewise true that sensual pleasures poison the soul, by attaching her to creatures. Hence, like poison, they must be used sparingly. Poisons, when properly prepared and taken with moderation, are sometimes conducive to health; and sensual delights, because they are poisonous remedies, must be taken with great caution and reserve, without attachment to them, only through necessity, and to be better able to serve God.

Besides, for the recovery of bodily health you must take care never to impair the strength of the soul, which will be always weak as long as the flesh is not mortified. "I compassionate," says St. Bernard, "The infirmities of the body; but the infirmity of the soul should be an object of greater alarm." I pity the infirmities of the body, but feel greater commiseration for the more formidable and dangerous maladies of the soul. Oh, how often is bodily weakness made the pretext for unnecessary indulgence. "We leave the choir," says St. Teresa, "Today, because the headaches; on tomorrow, because it has ached; and on the day after, lest it should ache." Hence on another occasion she thus addresses her dear children: "You have entered religion not to indulge the flesh but to die for Jesus Christ. If we do not resolve to disregard the want of health, we shall do nothing. What injury will death do us? How often have our bodies molested us? Shall not we torment them in return?" St. Joseph Calasanctius says: "Woe to the religious who loves health more than sanctity."

St. Bernard considered it indecent in a religious to take costly medicine; for them, he said, decoctions of herbs should be sufficient. I do not require this of you; but I say that small indeed must be the spiritual progress of the religious who is continually seeking physicians and remedies; who is sometimes not content with the prescription of the ordinary physician; and who, by her discontent, disturbs the whole Community. "Men," says Salvian, "Devoted to Christ are weak, and wish to be so: if they were robust, they could with difficulty be saints." All, and particularly nuns who have consecrated themselves to the love of Jesus Christ, are weak in body, and desire to continue in their infirmities: were they strong and vigorous, it would be difficult for them to attain sanctity. The truth of this observation appears from the lives of St. Teresa, St. Rose, St. Mary Magdalene de Pazzi, and other saints. The Venerable Beatrix of the Incarnation, the first spiritual daughter of St. Teresa, though afflicted with pains and infirmities, was accustomed to say that she would not exchange her condition for that of the happiest princess on earth. Such was her patience, that in the greatest sufferings she never uttered a word of complaint. Hence a sister once said to her: "You are like one of those wretched paupers who languish for want of food, but continue to endure the pains of hunger rather than submit to the shame of manifesting their poverty."

If bodily weakness renders us unable to practice corporal austerities, let us at least learn from her example to embrace with joy the infirmities with which Almighty God visits us. If borne with patience, they will conduct us to perfection better than voluntary works of penance. St. Syncletica used to say, that "As corporal maladies are cured by medicine, so the diseases of the soul are healed by the infirmities of the body."

Oh, how profitable to the spirit are the mortifications of the flesh. They detach the heart from sensual pleasures, which wound the soul, and frequently deprive her of life. "The wounds of charity," says Origen, "Make us in sensible to the wounds of the flesh."

Moreover, by mortifications we atone in this life for the pains due to our sins. He that has offended God, though the offence may be pardoned, must either by expiatory works in this life, or by the pains of purgatory in the next, make satisfaction for the temporal punishment due to sin after remission of its guilt. His sufferings in purgatory will be infinitely greater than any torments that he could endure on earth. They shall be in very great tribulation, unless they do penance from their deeds. They who have not expiated their sins shall suffer the sharpest torments in the other world. St. Antoninus relates that an angel proposed to a sick man the choice of being confined to purgatory for three days, or of being condemned to a continuation of his infirmities for two years. The sick man chose the three days in purgatory; but scarcely had an hour elapsed in that place of torments when he began to complain of the angel for having condemned him to a purgation not of three days, but of several years. "What!" replied the angel, "Your body is still warm on the bed of death, and you speak of having spent years in purgatory." If, dear Sister, you wish to suffer in peace, imagine that you have still to live fifteen or twenty years, and say, This is my purgatory: it is the spirit rather than the body that I must conquer.

Mortifications raise the soul to God. St. Francis de Sales used to say that a soul cannot ascend to the throne of God unless the flesh is mortified and depressed. There are many beautiful remarks on this subject in the works of St. Teresa: "It would be folly," says this great saint, "To think that God admits to his familiar friendship those who seek their own ease. Sensuality and prayer are incompatible. Souls who truly love God cannot desire repose."

Mortifications merit great glory in heaven. If "Everyone who striveth for the mastery," abstains from whatever is likely to diminish his strength, and thus endanger the conquest of a miserable earthly crown, how much more should we deny the flesh for the attainment of an eternal kingdom? And they, indeed, says St. Paul, that they may receive a corruptible crown; but we an incorruptible one.
St. John saw all the saints with palms in their hands. From this passage we learn that all the elect must be martyrs, either by the sword of the tyrant or by the voluntary crucifixion of the flesh. But while we meditate on the necessity of works of penance, we should at the same time remember that the pains of this life bear no proportion to the eternal glory that awaits us in paradise. The sufferings of this life, says St. Paul, are not worthy to be compared with the glory to come, that shall be revealed in us. The few transitory mortifications which we practice here below will produce complete and everlasting felicity. For, says the Apostle, that which is at present momentary and light of our tribulation, worketh for us above measure exceedingly an exceeding weight of glory.

Let us then animate our faith. Our pilgrimage on earth will not be of long duration: our home is eternity, where he who has practiced the greatest mortifications during life shall enjoy the greatest glory. St. Peter says the saints are the living stones of which the celestial Jerusalem is built. But before they are translated to the city which is above, they must be polished by the salutary chisel of penance.

Scalpri salubris ictibus   Many a blow the biting sculpture

147

Et tunsione plurima	Polished well those stones elect,
Fabri polita malleo,	In their places now compacted
	By the heavenly Architect,
	Who therewith hath willed forever
Hanc saxa molem construunt.	That his palace should be decked.

Let us consider each act of self-denial as a work that will prepare us for paradise. This thought will sweeten all our pains and all our toils. How pleasing is the fatigue of a journey to him who is assured that he shall obtain possession of all the territory through which he travels? It is related in the Lives of the Fathers, that a certain monk was anxious to exchange his cell for another nearer to the fountain from which he was accustomed to draw water, but as he was one day going to the fountain, he heard his steps counted by a person behind him. Turning round he saw a young man, who said: "I am an angel: I count your steps, that none of them may be without a reward." The monk immediately abandoned the intention of changing his cell; and even wished it to be more distant from the water, that he might be able to acquire greater merit.

Mortified religious enjoy peace and content in this life, as well as in the next. What greater happiness can a soul possess than to know that by her mortifications she pleases God? The very privation of carnal pleasures, and even the pains of penance, are so many spiritual delights to a loving soul. Love cannot be at rest. He that loves God cannot live without giving continual proofs of his affection. Now a soul cannot give a stronger proof of its love for God than the voluntary renunciation of earthly pleasures for his sake, and the oblation of its pains to him. A Christian enamoured of Jesus Christ feels no pain in his penitential works. "He that loves," says St. Augustine, "Labors not." "Who," says St. Teresa, "Can behold his God covered with wounds and harassed by persecutions, without embracing and even desiring a portion of his Saviours sufferings?" Hence St. Paul exclaimed, that he wished for no other delight or glory than the Cross of the Redeemer. God forbid that I should glory, save in the cross of our Lord Jesus Christ. Again he says that the crucifixion of the flesh is the test by which the true lovers of Jesus Christ may be known. They that are Christ's have crucified their flesh, with the vices and concupiscences.

Worldlings go in search of sensual gratifications, but the followers of Christ seek only corporal austerities.

In conclusion, dear Sister, imagine that death is at hand, and that as yet you have done but little for paradise. Strive from this day forward to mortify yourself as much as possible, at least by abstinence from the pleasures that self-love seeks. Endeavor to profit by every opportunity of mortification. Let not the part of a good gift overpass you. Consider every occasion of self-denial as a gift which God bestows upon you that you may be able to merit greater glory in another life; and remember that what can be done today cannot be performed tomorrow, for time that is past never returns.

To animate your fervor in the practice of mortification, I shall here place before your eyes, in his own words, what St. John Climacus saw in a monastery called the Prison of Penitents. "I saw," says the saint, "Some of them standing the whole night in the open air, to overcome sleep. I saw others with their eyes fixed on heaven, and with tears begging mercy from God. Others stood with their hands bound behind their shoulders, and their heads bowed down, as if they were unworthy to raise their eyes to heaven. Others remained on ashes, with their heads between their knees, and beat the ground with their foreheads. Others deluged the floor with their tears. Others stood in the burning rays of the sun. Others, parched with thirst, were content with taking a few drops of water to prevent death. Others took a mouthful of bread, and then threw it out, saying that he who has been guilty of beastly actions is unworthy of the food of men. Some had their cheeks furrowed by continual streams of tears; and others had their eyes sunken. Others struck their breast with such violence, that they began to spit blood. And I saw all with faces so pallid and emaciated, that they appeared to be so many corpses." The saint then concludes by saying, that notwithstanding their fall, he considered them, on account of their penitential rigors, more happy than those who had never sinned and never done penance. What shall be said of them who have fallen and have never atoned for their crime by expiatory works?

Prayer.

O my Spouse, assist me and give me strength, that for the future I may serve Thee better than I have done for the past. Hitherto I have sought

149

the gratification of my senses and of self-love, but have been regard-less of offending Thee. But for the future I desire only to please Thee, who art so deserving of all my love. For the love of me Thou hast cho-sen a life of continual pains and sorrows; Thou hast spared nothing to draw me to Thy love, and shall I continue to be as ungrateful as I have been for so many years? No, my Jesus, it shall not be so: I have sinned enough in my past life. Pardon me all my transgressions; I am sorry for them, and repent with all my whole heart of all the displeasure I have given Thee by my irregular life. I now love Thee with my whole soul, and desire to do all that I can to please Thee in all things, and with-out reserve. Through my director, make known to me Thy will. I now purpose, and hope with the assistance of Thy grace, to fulfill Thy will in all things. My beloved Redeemer, replenish my memory with holy thoughts, that I may always remember the sorrows which Thou hast endured for my sake. Inflame my will with holy affections, that I may seek only what pleases Thee, and may desire only the accomplishment of Thy will, and to belong entirely to Thee. Grant, O Lord, that I may love Thee, and that I may love Thee ardently. For if I love Thee, all pains will be sweet and agreeable to me.

Holy Virgin Mary, my mother, assist me to please God during the re-mainder of my life. In thee I place all my hope.

II.

The Mortification of the Eyes, and Modesty in General.

1.   MORTIFICATION OF THE EYES.

Almost all our rebellious passions spring from unguarded looks; for, generally speaking, it is by the sight that all inordinate affections and desires are excited. Hence, holy Job made a covenant with his eyes, that he would not so much as think upon a virgin. Why did he say that he would not so much as think upon a virgin. Should he not have said that he made a covenant with his eyes not to look at a virgin? No; he very properly said that he would not think upon a virgin; because thoughts are so connected with looks, that the former cannot be sepa-rated from the latter, and therefore, to escape the molestation of evil imaginations, he resolved never to fix his eyes on a woman.

St. Augustine says: "The thought follows the look; delight comes after the thought; and consent after delight." From the look proceeds the thought; from the thought the desire; for, as St. Francis de Sales says, what is not seen is not desired, and to the desire succeeds the consent. If Eve had not looked at the forbidden apple, she should not have fallen; but because she saw that it was good to eat, and fair to the eyes, and beautiful to behold, she took of the fruit thereof, and did eat. The devil first tempts us to look, then to desire, and afterwards to consent.

St. Jerome says that Satan requires "Only a beginning on our part." If we begin, he will complete our destruction. A deliberate glance at a person of a different sex often .enkindles an infernal spark, which consumes the soul. "Through the eyes," says St. Bernard, "The deadly arrows of love enters." The first dart that wounds and frequently robs chaste souls of life finds admission through the eyes. By them David, the beloved of God, fell. By them was Solomon, once the inspired of the Holy Ghost, drawn into the greatest abominations. Oh, how many are lost by indulging their sight!

The eyes must be carefully guarded by all who expect not to be obliged to join in the lamentation of Jeremiah: My eye hath wasted my soul. By the introduction of sinful affections my eyes have destroyed my soul. Hence St. Gregory says, that "The eyes, because they draw us to sin, must be depressed." If not restrained, they will become instruments of hell, to force the soul to sin almost against its will. "He that looks at a dangerous object," continues the saint, "Begins to will what he wills not." It was this the inspired writer intended to express when he said of Holofernes, that the beauty of Judith made his soul captive.

Seneca says that "Blindness is a part of innocence." And Tertullian relates that a certain pagan philosopher, to free himself from impurity, plucked out his eyes. Such an act would be unlawful in us: but he that desires to preserve chastity must avoid the sight of objects that are apt to excite unchaste thoughts. Gaze not about, says the Holy Ghost, upon another's beauty; . . . hereby lust is enkindled as a fire. Gaze not upon another's beauty; for from looks arise evil imaginations, by which an impure fire is lighted up. Hence St. Francis de Sales used to say, that "They who wish to exclude an enemy from the city must keep the gates locked."

151

Hence, to avoid the sight of dangerous objects, the saints were accustomed to keep their eyes almost continually fixed on the earth, and to abstain even from looking at innocent objects. After being a novice for a year, St. Bernard could not tell whether his cell was vaulted. In consequence of never raising his eyes from the ground, he never knew that there were but three windows to the church of the monastery, in which he spent his novitiate. He once, without perceiving a lake, walked along its banks for nearly an entire day; and hearing his companions speak about it, he asked when they had seen it. St. Peter of Alcantara kept his eyes constantly cast down, so that he did not know the brothers with whom he conversed. It was by the voice, and not by the countenance, that he was able to recognize them.

The saints were particularly cautious not to look at persons of a different sex. St. Hugh, bishop, when compelled to speak with women, never looked at them in the face. St. Clare would never fix her eyes on the face of a man. She was greatly afflicted because, when raising her eyes at the elevation to see the consecrated host, she once involuntarily saw the countenance of the priest. St. Aloysius never looked at his own mother in the face. It is related of St. Arsenius, that a noble lady went to visit him in the desert, to beg of him to recommend her to God. When the saint perceived that his visitor was a woman, he turned away from her. She then said to him: "Arsenius, since you will neither see nor hear me, at least remember me in your prayers." "No," replied the saint, "But will beg of God to make me forget you, and never more to think of you."

From these examples may be seen the folly and temerity of some religious who, though they have not the sanctity of a St. Clare, still gaze around from the terrace, in the parlour, and in the church, upon every object that presents itself, even on persons of a different sex. And notwithstanding their unguarded looks, they expect to be free from temptations and from the danger of sin. For having once looked deliberately at a woman who was gathering ears of corn, the Abbot Pastor was tormented for forty years by temptations against chastity. St. Gregory states that the temptation, to conquer which St. Benedict rolled himself in thorns, arose from one incautious glance at a woman. St. Jerome, though living in a cave at Bethlehem, in continual prayer and macerations of the flesh, was terribly molested by the remembrance of ladies whom he had long before seen in Rome. Why should not similar molestations be the lot of the religious who willfully and without reserve fixes her eyes on persons of a different sex?

"It is not," says St. Francis de Sales, "The seeing of objects so much as the fixing of our eyes upon them that proves most pernicious." "If," says St. Augustine, "Our eyes should by chance fall upon others, let us take care never to fix them upon any one." Father Manareo, when taking leave of St. Ignatius for a distant place, looked steadfastly in his face: for this look he was corrected by the saint. From the conduct of St. Ignatius on this occasion, we learn that it was not becoming in religious to fix their eyes on the countenance of a person even of the same sex, particularly if the person is young. But I do not see how looks at young persons of a different sex can be excused from the guilt of a venial fault, or even from mortal sin, when there is proximate danger of criminal consent. "It is not lawful," says St. Gregory, "To behold what it is not lawful to covet." The evil thought that proceeds from looks, though it should be rejected, never fails to leave a stain upon the soul. Brother Roger, a Franciscan of singular purity, being once asked why he was so reserved in his intercourse with women, replied, that when men avoid the occasions of sin, God preserves them; but when they expose themselves to danger, they are justly abandoned by the Lord, and easily fall into some grievous transgressions.

The indulgence of the eyes, if not productive of any other evil, at least destroys recollection during the time of prayer. For, the images and impressions caused by the objects seen before, or by the wandering of the eyes, during prayer, will occasion a thousand distractions, and banish all recollection from the soul. It is certain that without recollection a religious can pay but little attention to the practice of humility, patience, mortification, or of the other virtues. Hence it is her duty to abstain from all looks of curiosity, which distract her mind from holy thoughts. Let her eyes be directed only to objects which raise the soul to God. St. Bernard used to say, that to fix the eyes upon the earth contributes to keep the heart in heaven. "Where," says St. Gregory, "Christ is, there modesty is found." Wherever Jesus Christ dwells by love, there modesty is practiced. However, I do not mean to say that the eyes should never be raised or never fixed on any object. No; but they ought to be directed only to what inspires devotion, to sacred images, and to the beauty of creation, which elevate the soul to the contemplation of the divinity. Except in looking at such objects, a religious should in

153

general keep the eyes cast down, and particularly in places where they may fall upon dangerous objects. In conversing with men, she should never roll the eyes about to look at them, and much less to look at them a second time.

To practice modesty of the eyes is the duty of a religious, not only because it is necessary for her own improvement in virtue, but also because it is necessary for the edification of others. God only knows the human heart: man sees only the exterior actions, and by them he is edified or scandalized. A man, says the Holy Ghost, is known by his look. By the countenance the interior is known. Hence, like St. John the Baptist, a religious should be a burning and shining light. She ought to be a torch burning with charity, and shining resplendent by her modesty, to all who behold her. To religious the following words of the Apostle are particularly applicable: "We are made a spectacle to the world, and to angels, and to men." And again: Let your modesty be known to all men: the Lord is nigh. Religious are attentively observed by the angels and by men; and therefore their modesty should be made manifest before all; if they do not practice modesty, terrible shall be the account which they must render to God on the day of judgment. Oh, what devotion does a modest religious inspire, what edification does she give, by keeping her eyes always cast down! St. Francis of Assisi once said to his companion that he was going out to preach. After walking through the town, with his eyes fixed on the ground, he returned to the convent. His companion asked him when he would preach the sermon. We have, replied the saint, by the modesty of our looks, given an excellent instruction to all who saw us. It is related of St. Aloysius, that when he walked through Rome the students would stand in the streets to observe and admire his great modesty.

St. Ambrose says, that to men of the world the modesty of the saints is a powerful exhortation to amendment of life. "The look of a just man is an admonition to many." The saint adds: "How delightful it is to do good to others by your appearance!" It is related of St. Bernardine of Sienna, that even when a secular, his presence was sufficient to restrain the licentiousness of his young companions, who, as soon as they saw him, were accustomed to give to one another notice that he was coming. On his arrival they became silent or changed the subject of their conversation. It is also related of St. Gregory of Nyssa, and of St. Ephrem, that their very appearance inspired piety, and that the sanctity and modesty of their exterior edified and improved all that beheld them. When Innocent II, visited St. Bernard at Clairvaux, such was the exterior modesty of the saint and of his monks, that the Pope and his cardinals were moved to tears of devotion. Surius relates a very extraordinary fact of St. Lucian, a monk and martyr. By his modesty he induced so many pagans to embrace the faith, that the Emperor Maximian fearing that he should be converted to Christianity by the appearance of the saint, would not allow the holy man to be brought within his view, but spoke to him from behind a screen.

That our Redeemer was the first who taught, by his example, modesty of the eyes, may, as a learned author remarks, be inferred from the holy evangelists, who say that on some occasion he raised his eyes. And he, lifting up his eyes on his disciples. When Jesus therefore had lifted up his eyes. From these passages we may conclude that the Redeemer ordinarily kept his eyes cast down. Hence the Apostle, praising the modesty of the Saviour, says: I beseech you, by the mildness and modesty of Christ.

I shall conclude this subject with what St. Basil said to his monks: If, my children, we desire to raise the soul towards heaven, let us direct the eyes towards the earth. From the moment we awake in the morning, let us pray continually in the words of holy David: Turn away my eyes, that they may not behold vanity.

2.   MODESTY IN GENERAL.

We must practice modesty, not only in our looks, but also in our whole deportment, and particularly in our dress, our walk, our conversation, and all similar actions:

I. Modesty of dress is not incompatible with neatness or cleanliness. But how disedifying is the conduct of the religious who attends too much to the neatness of her person and to the fineness or richness of her apparel, who wears superfluous ornaments, whose dress is made in a manner apt to attract notice, and whose whole appearance exhibits worldly vanity! Speaking of seculars, St. Cyprian says that "Women decorated with gold, necklaces, and precious stones lose the ornaments of the soul." What would the saint have thought of the religious who imitates worldlings in the vanity of her dress? "The ornaments of a woman are," says St. Gregory Nazianzen, "To be conspicuous for probity; to converse with the divine oracles; to seek wool and take hold of the spindle; and to keep a restraint on her eyes and on her lips." Yes, the ornaments of holy women are probity of life; continual conversation with God by prayer; constant labor; and a perpetual guard over the eyes and tongue, by modesty and by silence.

II. A religious should be modest in her walk. "Let your gait," says St. Basil, "Be neither slow nor vehement." Your walk, to be modest, must be grave, neither too quick nor too slow.

III. A religious must practice modesty in sitting. She must avoid every slothful posture; she must abstain from crossing her feet, and from putting one limb on the other.

IV. She must be modest at meals, by taking her food without avidity, and without rolling her eyes around in all directions, as if to observe how and what the others eat.

V. Above all, a religious must be modest in her conversation, by abstaining from all the words unbecoming the religious state. She must be persuaded that all words that savour of the world are indecorous in a religious. "If," says St. Basil, "A worldling make use of scurrilous expressions, he is not noticed. But if a man who professes to lead a perfect life appear to depart in the slightest degree from his duty, he is instantly remarked by all." In a secular, no one observes indecent words, because they are common in the world; but if religious who profess to aspire to sanctity be guilty of the smallest impropriety, universal attention is immediately directed to their conduct.

To observe modesty in words at the common recreations, you must attend to the following rules:

1. You must abstain from all murmurings, even against manifest abuses.

2. You must never interrupt the person that is speaking. And, says the Holy Ghost, interrupt not others in the midst of their discourse. How scandalous is it to see a religious engrossing to herself the whole conversation,—to see her ready to stop the sisters in the middle of

a word, or of a sentence, and thus show her pride by pretending to know everything, and constituting herself mistress of all! Such conduct is a source of great annoyance to all that join in the conversation. However, every religious should speak occasionally during the hours of recreation, and particularly when the others are silent; for, should all abstain from speaking, the end of the rule which prescribes recreation would be frustrated. But modesty requires, particularly from the young, that, after speaking as much as will be necessary for the ends of the recreation, they show a stronger inclination to listen than to speak. The best rule, then, is to speak when others are silent, and to be silent when others are speaking.

3. You must abstain from certain jests and jocose remarks on the real and known defects of others; for such jokes offend the persons to whom they are applied.

4. You must never utter a word of self-praise; when you are praised by others, you must raise your heart to God, and change the subject of conversation; and when you are contradicted or ridiculed, you must not be angry. Whenever the companions of St. John Francis Regis made him the subject of their jests at recreation, he endeavoured with great good-humor to keep up the conversation, that, by being the object of their laughter, he might contribute to their amusement.

5. You must speak always in a low tone, and never in such a manner as to offend the ears of others. "Let no one," says St. Ambrose, "Offend by too loud a voice."

6. You must observe modesty and moderation in laughter. St. Gregory relates, that the Mother of God appeared once to a devout virgin called Musa, and told her that, if she wished to please her, she must restrain immoderate laughter. "They who seek after piety," says St. Basil, "Must take care not to pour forth their souls in laughter." All that aspire to perfection should avoid excessive laughter. Moderate laughter, which shows the serenity of the soul, is neither a violation of decorum nor opposed to devotion. A religious should always present an appearance of modesty and devotion, but not of sadness and melancholy. By appearing sad and afflicted she dishonors religion, and gives all who behold her to understand that sanctity, instead of infusing peace and joy, fills the soul with sorrow and melancholy. But by a cheerful coun-

tenance she encourages others to the practice of piety. Two courtiers of a certain monarch, having witnessed the joy with which an aged monk remained in solitude, renounced the world, and remained in his retreat.

7. Lastly, you must not speak of things of the world; such as marriages, feasts, comedies, or of splendid dresses: you must not speak of eating, nor praise or censure the dishes that are brought to table. St. Francis de Sales used to say that "Well-behaved persons never think of the table but when they sit at it." When religious hear unseemly discourses, they should, like St. Aloysius, propose some useful question, or take occasion from what is said to introduce some pious subject of conversation. To be able to converse with his companions on spiritual subjects during recreation, he was accustomed to spend, each day, half an hour in reading the life of a saint, or some other book of devotion. When among the juniors, he was the first to introduce a religious subject. When with priests, or with his seniors, he proposed a case of conscience, as if for his own information, and thus succeeded in making the conversation turn upon holy things. In a short time his companions knew that he did not relish any but pious conversation, and therefore they sought on every occasion to gratify his wishes. When they happened to be discoursing on any other subject, when he came among them, they would immediately begin to speak of God. Everyone is inclined to speak continually of what he tenderly loves. St. Ignatius of Loyola appeared not to know how to speak of anything but God, and was therefore called the "Father who speaks always of God."

Prayer.

My Jesus, pardon me, for Thy mercy's sake, the numberless faults which I have committed for want of sufficient modesty, and of which I now repent with my whole heart. All my defects have arisen from my little love of Thee. I acknowledge that I do not deserve mercy; but Thy wounds and Thy death encourage and oblige me to hope. O my God, how often have I insulted Thee? And with what tenderness hast Thou pardoned all my sins? I have promised to be faithful to Thee, and still I have returned to my sins! Shall I wait till Thou abandon me to my tepidity, and thus to eternal misery? I desire, O Lord, to amend; and I place all my confidence in Thee, and purpose to seek continually Thy assistance to be faithful to Thee. Hitherto I have trusted in my own resolutions, and have neglected to recommend myself to Thee. This self-confidence and neglect of prayer have been the cause of my past sins. Eternal Father, through the merits of Jesus Christ, have mercy upon me and assist me; give me grace to recommend myself to Thee in all my wants. I love Thee, O my Sovereign Good, and desire to love Thee with all my strength; but without Thee I can do nothing. Give me Thy love: give me holy perseverance. I hope for all things from Thy infinite goodness.

O Mary, Mother of God, thou knowest how much I confide in thee; assist me; have pity on me.

III.

The Mortification of the Appetite.

St. Andrew Avellini used to say that he who wishes to advance in perfection should begin zealously to mortify the appetite. "It is impossible," says St. Gregory, "To engage in the spiritual conflict, without the previous subjugation of the appetite." Father Roggacci, in his "Treatise on the one thing necessary," asserts that the principal part of external mortification consists in the mortification of the palate. Since the mortification of the taste consists in abstinence from food, must we then abstain altogether from eating? No; it is our duty to preserve the life of the body that we may be able to serve God as long as he wills us to remain on earth. But, as Father Vincent Carafa used to say, we should attend to the body with the same feelings of disgust as a powerful monarch would perform by compulsion the meanest work of a servant.

"We must," says St. Francis de Sales, "Eat, in order to live; but we should not live as if for the purpose of eating." Some, like beasts, appear to live only for the gratification of the palate. "A man," says St. Bernard, "Becomes a beast by loving what beasts love." Who ever, like brute animals, fixes his heart on the indulgence of the appetite, falls from the dignity of a spiritual and rational creature, and sinks to the level of senseless beasts. Unhappy Adam, for the pleasure of eating an apple, is "Compared to senseless beasts, and is become like to them." In another place, St. Bernard says that, on seeing Adam forget his God and his eternal salvation, for the momentary gratification of his palate, the beasts of the fields, if they could speak, would exclaim:

"Behold Adam is become one of us." Hence, St. Catharine of Sienna used to say, that "Without mortifying the taste, it is impossible to preserve innocence, since it was by the indulgence of his appetite that Adam fell." Ah, how miserable is the condition of those whose God is their belly!

How many have lost their souls by intemperance! In his Dialogues, St. Gregory relates, that in a monastery of Sienna there was a monk who led a very exemplary life. When he was at the point of death, the religious, expecting to be edified by his last moments, gathered around him. "Brethren," said the dying man, "When you fasted, I ate in private, and therefore I have been already delivered over to Satan, who now deprives me of life, and carries away my soul." After these words he expired. The same saint relates in another place, that a certain nun, seeing in the garden a very fine lettuce, pulled and ate it, in opposition to her Rule. She was instantly possessed by a devil, who tormented her grievously. Her companions called to her aid the holy Abbot Equitius, at whose arrival the demon exclaimed: "What evil have I done? I sat upon the lettuce; she came and ate it." The holy man, by his commands, compelled the evil spirit to depart. In the Cistercian records we read that St. Bernard, once visiting his novices, called aside a brother whose name was Acardo, and said that a certain novice, to whom he pointed, would on that day fly from the monastery. The saint begged of Acardo to watch the novice, and to prevent his escape. On the following night, Acardo saw a demon approach the novice, and by the savoury smell of a roasted fowl tempt him to desire forbidden food. The unhappy young man awoke, and, yielding to the temptation, took his clothes and prepared to leave the monastery. Acardo endeavoured in vain to convince him of the dangers to which he would be exposed in the world. Overcome by gluttony, the unhappy man obstinately resolved to return to the world: there, the narrator adds, he died miserably.

Let us then take care not to be conquered by this brutal vice. St. Augustine says, that food is necessary for the support of life; but, like medicine, it should be taken only through necessity. Intemperance is very injurious to the body as well as to the soul. It is certain that excess in eating is the cause of almost all the diseases of the body. Apoplexy, diarrhea, headaches, complaints of the stomach and bowels, and innumerable other maladies, spring from the immoderate use of food.

But the diseases of the body are only a small part of the evils that flow from intemperance; its effects on the soul are far more disastrous.

This vice, according to St. Thomas, in the first place, darkens the soul, and renders it unfit for spiritual exercises, but particularly for mental prayer. As fasting prepares the mind for the contemplation of God and of eternal goods, so intemperance diverts it from holy thoughts. St. John Chrysostom says that the glutton, like an overloaded ship, moves with difficulty, and that in the first tempest of temptation he is in danger of being lost. "Take," says St. Bernard, "Even bread with moderation, lest a loaded stomach should make you weary of prayer." And again he says: "If you compel a person who takes a heavy meal to watch, you will extort from him wailing rather than singing." Hence it is the duty of religious to eat sparingly, and particularly at supper: for in the evening a false appetite is frequently created by the acid that is produced by the food taken at dinner. Whoever satisfies his appetite in the evening is exposed to great danger of excess; and in consequence of indigestion will frequently feel his stomach overburdened in the morning, and his head so stupid and confused that he will not be able to say a "Hail Mary." Do not imagine that the Almighty will, at the time of prayer, infuse his consolations into the souls of those who, like senseless beasts, seek delight in the indulgence of the appetite. "Divine consolation," says St. Bernard, "Is not given to those that admit any other delight." Celestial consolations are not bestowed on those that go in search of earthly pleasures.

Besides, he that gratifies the taste will readily indulge the other senses; for, having lost the spirit of recollection, he will easily commit faults, by indecent words and by unbecoming gestures. But the greatest evil of intemperance is, that it exposes chastity to great danger. "Repletion of the stomach," says St. Jerome, "Is the hotbed of lust." Excess in eating is a powerful incentive to incontinence. Hence, Cassian says that "It is impossible for him who satiates his appetite not to experience conflicts." The intemperate cannot expect to be free from temptations against purity. To preserve chastity, the saints practiced the most rigorous mortifications of the appetite. "The devil," says St. Thomas, "Vanquished by temperance, does not tempt to lust." When his temptations to indulge the palate are conquered he ceases to provoke incontinence.

He that attends to the abnegation of the appetite makes continual progress in virtue. That the mortification of the palate will facilitate the conquest of the other senses, and enable us to employ them in acts of virtue, may be inferred from the following prayer of the Church: "O God, who by this bodily fast extinguishest our vices, elevatest our understanding, bestowest on us virtue and its reward, etc." By fasting, the Lord enables the soul to subdue her vices, to raise her affections above the earth, to practice virtue, and to acquire merits for eternity.

Worldlings say: God has created the goods of this earth for our use and pleasure. Such is not the language of the saints. The Venerable Vincent Carafa, of the Society of Jesus, used to say, that God has given us the goods of the earth, not only that we may enjoy them, but also that we may have the means of thanking him, and showing him our love by the voluntary renunciation of his gifts, and by the oblation of them to his glory. To abandon, for God's sake, all worldly enjoyments, has always been the practice of holy souls.

The ancient monks, as St. Jerome relates, thought it a great defect to make use of food dressed with fire. Their daily sustenance consisted of a pound of bread St Aloysius, though always sickly, fasted three times in the week on bread and water. St. Francis Xavier during his missions was satisfied each day with a few grains of toasted rice. St. John Francis Regis, in the great fatigues of his missions took no other food than a little flour steeped in water. The daily support of St. Peter of Alcantara was but a small quantity of broth. We read in the life of the Venerable Brother John Joseph of the Cross, who lived in our own days, and with whom I was intimately acquainted, that for twenty-four years he fasted very often on bread and water, and never ate anything but bread and a little herbs or fruit. When commanded, on account of his infirmities, to use warm food, he took only bread dipped in broth. When the physician ordered him to take a little wine, he mixed it with his broth to increase the insipidity of his scanty repast.

I do not mean to say, that to attain sanctity it is necessary for nuns to imitate these examples; but I assert that whoever is attached to the pleasures of the table, or does not seriously attend to the mortification of the appetite, will never make any considerable progress in perfection. In religious Communities there are generally several meals in the day: hence, they who neglect the mortification of the taste will daily commit a thousand faults.

Let us now come to the practice of denying the appetite. In what is it to be mortified? St. Bonaventure answers: "In the quantity, the quality, and the manner"

I. In the quality, adds the saint, by seeking not what is delicate, but what is simple. The saint says, in another place, that small is the progress of the religious who is not content with what is offered to her, but requires that it be prepared in a different manner, or seeks more palatable food. A mortified religious is satisfied with what is placed before her; and instead of seeking after delicacies, she selects among all the dishes that may be presented to her, the least palatable, provided it be not prejudicial to health. Such was the practice of St. Aloysius, who always chose what was most disagreeable to the taste.

"Wine and flesh," says Clement of Alexandria, "Give strength indeed to the body, but they render the soul languid." From the sacred Canons we learn that formerly monks were not permitted even to taste flesh. "To a monk, the privilege of either taking or of tasting flesh is not granted." Speaking of himself, St. Bernard says: "I abstain from flesh, lest I should cherish the vices of the flesh." Give not wine to kings, says the Wise Man. By kings, in this place, we are to understand, not the monarchs of the earth, but the servants of God, who rule their wicked passions and subject them to reason. In another place Solomon says: Who hath woe? . . . Surely they that pass their time in wine, and study to drink off their cups. Since, then, the word woe, in the Sacred Scriptures, according to St. Gregory, signifies everlasting misery, woe, eternal woe, shall be the lot of all who are addicted to wine! Because wine is a luxurious thing and incites to incontinence. "My first advice," says St. Jerome, in one of his epistles to the virgin Eustochia, "Is, that the spouse of Christ fly from wine as from poison. Wine and youth are a twofold incentive to pleasure." If you desire to preserve the chastity which becomes the spouse of Jesus, avoid wine as poison: wine and youth are a double fire, which kindle the desire of unlawful pleasures. From the words of the holy Doctor we may infer that he who has not enough of courage or of bodily strength to abstain altogether from flesh and from wine, should at least use them with great moderation: otherwise he must be prepared for continual molestation from temptations against purity.

A mortified religious would also do well to abstain from superfluous seasonings which serve only to gratify the palate. The seasonings used by the saints were ashes, aloes, and wormwood. I do not require such mortifications of you; nor do I recommend very extraordinary fasts. On the contrary, it is, according to Cassian, the duty of all that are not solitaries, and that live in Community, to avoid, as a source of much vain glory, whatever is not conformable to the common usages of the monastery. "Where," says St. Philip Neri, "There is a common table, all should eat of what is served up." Hence he frequently exhorted his disciples to "Avoid all singularity as the origin of spiritual pride." A courageous religious finds opportunities of practising mortification without allowing it to appear to others. St. John Climacus partook of whatever was placed before him; but his refection consisted in tasting rather in eating what was offered to him; and thus, by his abstemious-ness, he practiced continual mortification of the appetite without the danger of vanity. St. Bernard used to say that he that lives in Commu-nity will take more pleasure in fasting once, while his companions at table take their ordinary repast, than in fasting seven times with them.

However, religious may, without the danger of vain glory, occasion-ally perform very rigorous mortifications. For example, by living on bread and water on days of devotion, on Fridays and Saturdays, on the vigils of the Blessed Virgin, and on similar occasions; for such fasts are ordinarily practiced by fervent religious. If, on account of bodily infirmity, or through want of fervor you do not practice rigid fasts, you should at least not complain of the common fare; and should be content with whatever is brought to table. St. Thomas never asked for particular food, but was always satisfied with what was placed before him, and ate of it with great moderation. Of St. Ignatius we read that he never refused any dish, and never complained that the food was not well dressed or well seasoned. It is the duty of the Superior to provide the Community with wholesome food, but a religious should never complain when what is laid before her is rare or overdone; when it is scanty, smoked, insipid, or too highly seasoned with salt. The poor, provided they receive what is necessary for the support of life, take what is offered to them without conditions or complaints; and a reli-gious should, in like manner, accept whatever is laid before her as an alms from Almighty God.

II. With regard to the quantity, St. Bonaventure says that "Food ought not to be taken too often, or in excess, but in such a quantity that it may be a reflection and not a burden to the body." Hence the rule of all who seek perfection is never to eat to satiety. "Let your repast be moderate," says St. Jerome, "So that the stomach will never be replete." Some religious fast one day and eat to excess on the next. St. Jerome says that it is better to take always a reasonable quantity of food than to fast sometimes, and afterwards to commit excess. The same holy Doctor remarks that satiety is to be avoided in the use, not only of delicacies, but also of the coarsest food. If a nun commit excess, it matters not whether she eat of partridges or of vegetables: the bad effects of her intemperance are the same in both cases. St. Jerome's rule for determining the quantity of food is that a person should always rise from the table in such a state that he may be able to apply immediately to prayer or to study. "When," says the holy Doctor, "You eat, think that it will be your duty to pray or to read immediately after."

An ancient Father wisely said, that "He who eats a great deal, and is still hungry, will receive a greater re ward than the man who eats little and is satiated." Cassian relates that to comply with the duty of hospitality a certain monk was one day obliged to sit at table many times with strangers, and to partake of the refreshment prepared for them, and that after all he arose the last time with an appetite. This is the best and most difficult sort of mortification; for it is easier to abstain altogether from certain meats than, after having tasted them, to eat but little.

He who desires to practice moderation in eating would do well to diminish his meals gradually till, by experience, he ascertains the quantity of food necessary to support the body. It was in this manner that St. Dorothy trained his disciple, St. Dositheus, to the just practice of mortification. But the most secure means of removing all doubts and scruples with regard to fasts and abstinence is to follow the advice of your director. St. Benedict and after him St. Bernard say that mortifications that are performed without the permission of one's confessor are not meritorious, because they are the fruit of a criminal presumption: "What is done without the permission of the spiritual Father will be regarded as presumption, and shall not be rewarded." All, but particularly nuns, as we have said above, should make it a general rule to eat sparingly at supper, even when there is some apparent necessity for a plentiful meal; for in the evening all are subject to a false appetite, and therefore a slight excess will occasion, on the following morning, headaches, fullness of the stomach, and by consequence a repugnance and incapacity for all spiritual exercises.

Abstinence from drink, except at meals, may be safely observed by all, unless when, in particular circumstances, such as in the heats of summer, the want of liquid might be prejudicial to health. However, St. Laurence Justinian, even in the burning heats of summer, never drank out of meal-time; and to those who asked how he could bear the thirst, he replied: "How shall I be able to bear the burning thirst of purgatory if I cannot now abstain from drink?" On fasting days the ancient Christians abstained from drink till the hour of their repast, which was always taken in the evening. Such is the practice of the Turks at the present day during their fasts of Lent. We should at least observe the rule that is universally prescribed by physicians, not to take any drink for four or five hours after dinner.

III. With regard to the MANNER of eating, St. Bonaventure says that "Food should not be taken unseasonably nor inordinately, but religiously."

1. Food should not be taken unseasonably; that is, before the hours prescribed for the Community. To a penitent who could not abstain from eating till the hour of meals, St. Philip Neri said: "Child, if you do not correct this defect you will never advance in virtue." Blessed, says the Holy Ghost, is the land whose princes eat in due season. And happy the monastery whose members never eat out of the hours of meals. When St. Teresa heard that some of her nuns had asked permission from the Provincial to keep eatables in their cells, she reproved them very severely: "Your request," said the saint, "If granted, would lead to the destruction of the monastery."

2. To avoid the fault of taking your food inordinately, you must be careful not to eat with avidity, with eagerness, or with haste. Be not greedy in your feasting, says the Holy Ghost. Your object in eating must be to support the strength of the body, and to be able to serve the Lord. To eat through mere pleasure cannot be excused from the guilt of venial sin; for Innocent XI has condemned the proposition which asserts that it is not a sin to eat or to drink from the sole motive of satisfying the palate. However, it is not a fault to feel pleasure in eating; for it is, generally speaking, impossible to eat without experiencing

the delight which food naturally produces. But it is a defect to eat like beasts through the sole motive of sensual gratification, and without proposing any reasonable end. Hence the most delicious meats may be eaten without sin if the motive be good and worthy of a rational creature; and in taking the coarsest food through attachment to pleasure there may be a fault. In the Lives of the Fathers it is related that though the same food was served to all the monks of a certain monastery, a holy bishop saw some of them feasting on honey, others on bread, and others on mire. By this vision he was given to understand that the first ate with a holy fear of violating temperance, and were accustomed at meals to raise their souls to God by holy aspirations; that the second felt some delight in eating, but still returned thanks to God for his benefits; and that the third ate for the mere gratification of the taste.

To practice temperance in the manner of eating, you must not perform indiscreet fasts, which would render you unable to serve the Community, or to observe your Rule. Transported with a certain fervor, by which the Almighty animates their zeal for virtue, beginners are often very indiscreet in their fasts and other works of penance. Their rigors sometimes bring on infirmities, which disqualify them for the duties of the Community, and sometimes make them give up all exercises of piety. Discretion is necessary in all things. A master who intrust a servant with the care of a horse will be equally displeased whether the animal be rendered unfit for use by an excess or by a want of food. St. Francis de Sales used to say to his nuns of the Visitation that "Continual moderation is better than fits of violent abstinence interspersed with occasional excesses. Besides, such abstinences make us esteem ourselves more holy than others who do not practice them." It is certainly the duty of all to avoid indiscretion, but it has been justly remarked by a great spiritual master (and the remark deserves attention), that the spirit seldom deceives us by suggesting excessive mortifications; while the flesh, under false pretences, frequently claims commiseration, and procures an exemption from what is displeasing to its propensities.

The following are some of the mortifications that are very useful:

1. To abstain from delicacies agreeable to the taste, and in some measure injurious to health.

2. To refrain from the fruits that come first in season.

3. To deprive yourself throughout the year from some particular fruit, determined by lot.

4. To abstain once or twice in the week from all fruit, and every day from a portion of what is laid before you.

5. To deny yourself some delicacy, or merely to taste it, and say with St. Mary Magdalene de Pazzi, that it is not useful for you.

6. To leave, every day, according to the advice of St. Bernard, a part of what is most pleasing to the palate. "Let everyone," says the saint, "Offer at table something to God."

7. To check for some time the desire of drinking or of eating what is before you; and to abstain from wine, spirits, and spices. Such abstinence is particularly useful for young persons.

The preceding mortifications may be practiced without pride, or injury to health. It is not necessary to perform all of them. Let each person observe the abstinences that her Superior or director permits. It is certainly better to practice small and frequent works of penance, than to perform rare and extraordinary fasts, and afterwards lead an unmortified life.

Prayer.

My dear Redeemer, I am so tepid and full of defects, that I am ashamed to appear before Thee. Had I corresponded to Thy graces, I should now be a seraph by the ardor of my love. But I am more imperfect than ever. How often have I promised to become a saint, and to consecrate myself entirely to Thee? But my promises have been so many treasons. I console myself with the reflection that I have to deal with infinite Goodness. Do not abandon me, O Lord, but continue to strengthen me, for I desired to amend, by the assistance of Thy grace. I do not wish to resist the love that Thou bearest me; I see that Thou dost wish me to become a saint; and to please Thee, I desire to sanctify my soul. I promise to mortify my senses, particularly by abstaining from certain pleasures. (Name them). Ah, my Jesus, I know that to gain my heart Thou hast done too much. Great, indeed, should be my ingratitude if I denied Thee anything, or loved Thee but little. I do not wish to be any longer ungrateful. Thou hast been infinitely good to me; I shall not be ungenerous to Thee as I have hitherto been. I love Thee, O my Spouse; I am sorry for all the displeasure that I have given Thee. Pardon me, and assist me to be faithful to Thee.

O Mary, thou hast always been faithful to God, obtain for me the gift of fidelity to his graces during the remainder of my life.

IV.

The Mortification of the Sense of Hearing, of Smell, and of Touch.

I. The sense of HEARING must be mortified by not listening to indecent words, to detraction, or to worldly conversations, which fill the mind with a thousand thoughts and images, that afterwards distract and disturb the soul in prayer, and in the other exercises of devotion. Should you ever happen to be present at such discourses, endeavor to cut them short by proposing some useful question. If that be not sufficient, you ought either to retire or remain silent, and cast down your eyes, to show how much you dislike such language.

II. To mortify the SMELL, you must abstain from the use of perfumes and of scented waters: such delicacies are unbecoming even in worldlings. Animated by the spirit of charity and mortification, the saints felt as much delight in the offensive odours that surround the sick and the infected, as they would in a garden of the most fragrant flowers. Let it be your study to imitate their example, and to bear patiently the disagreeable smell that you may experience in the rooms of the sick.

III. With regard to the TOUCH, you must take the greatest care to avoid all, even the smallest, defects. For every fault committed by the indulgence of that sense exposes the soul to the danger of eternal death. I cannot explain myself fully on this subject: I shall only say, that to preserve the precious jewel of purity, religious should observe all possible modesty and caution, not only towards others, but also towards themselves. Even in his last agony St. Peter of Alcantara would not allow any of his brethren to touch any part of his body. Feeling himself touched by one of them, he exclaimed: "Withdraw, touch me not; I am still alive, and may still offend God." This sense of touch must be kept under the greatest restraint by external mortifications, of which I shall now speak. These mortifications are reduced to four heads—to fasts, haircloths, disciplines, and watchings.

1. In the preceding section enough has been said of fasting.

2. Haircloths are of various kinds: some are made of strong or coarse hair; the others are bands or chains of brass or iron wire. The former may be injurious to persons of a delicate constitution: for, as Father Scaramelli justly remarks, they inflame the flesh, and weaken the stomach by drawing its natural heat to the external surface of the body. The latter may be worn on the arms, thighs, or shoulders without injury to the health, but not on the breast or round the body. These are the ordinary species of haircloths, and may be safely used by all. Far different from them were the hair cloths worn by the saints. D. Sancia Carriglio, the celebrated penitent of Father M. Avila, wore a shirt of coarse hair which reached from the neck to the knees. St. Rose of Lima used a long hair-shirt interwoven with needles, and carried a broad iron chain round her loins. St. Peter of Alcantara wore on his shoulders a large plate of iron, which was so rough, and covered with sharp projections, that it kept the flesh in a state of continual laceration. Would it then be too much for you to wear a small band of iron from morning till the hour of dinner?

3. Disciplines or flagellations are a species of mortification strongly recommended by St. Francis de Sales, and universally adopted in religious Communities of both sexes. All the modern saints, without a single exception, have continually practiced this sort of penance. It is related of St. Aloysius that he often scourged himself unto blood three times in the day. And at the point of death, not having sufficient strength to use the lash, he besought the Provincial to have him disciplined from head to foot. Surely, then, it would not be too much for you to take the discipline once in the day, or at least three or four times in the week. However, the practice of this penance should be regulated by the confessor.

4. Lastly, vigils or watchings consist in the retrenchment of sleep. It is related of St. Rose, that to prevent sleep, and thus be able to spend the night in prayer, she tied her hair to a nail fastened in the wall. When she was overcome by sleep the inclination of the head caused pain sufficient to awake her. Of St. Peter of Alcantara we read that for

forty years he slept but an hour, or at the most an hour and a half, each night; and that he might not be overcome by sleep, he lay with his head on a piece of wood fixed in the wall of his cell. Such austerities cannot be practiced by all, nor without a special grace. Indeed, watching is a species of penance in which great moderation and discretion should be observed. Severe watchings generally render us unfit for the exercise of the mental faculties, for the recitation of the office, for prayer, and spiritual reading. St. Charles Borromeo, in consequence of watching during the night, was sometimes overcome by sleep even during public functions, and was therefore obliged to prolong the time for rest. However, they that pretend to virtue should not, like brute animals, give to their body all the repose that the flesh desires. It is necessary to take as much rest as is requisite, and no more. Generally speaking, women require less sleep than men. In general, five, or at the most six hours sleep is sufficient for women. At least, dear sister, be careful to rise at the first sound of the morning bell, and not to remain, like the sluggard, turning about in bed after having heard the signal for rising. St. Teresa used to say that a religious should leap out of bed the instant she hears the bell.

The saints have not only curtailed the time for sleep, but have also practiced various mortifications in the manner of taking repose. St. Aloysius was accustomed to scatter fragments of wood and of stones over his bed. St. Rose of Lima lay on the trunks of trees, the space between which was filled with broken earthenware. The Venerable Sister Mary Crucified, of Sicily, used a pillow of thorns. These austerities are extraordinary, and are not adapted to all persons. But a religious should not seek a bed of down; if a straw bed be not injurious to her health, why should she require a mattress of hair?—Or, if a single mattress be sufficient for her, why does she make use of two?

To bear with patience the excessive heat or cold of the seasons is a very useful mortification of the sense of touch. St. Peter of Alcantara went barefooted and bareheaded throughout the winter, and never wore more than a single coat, which was generally torn. You cannot practice such rigors; but would it be too much for you to refrain from approaching the fire during the winter? St. Aloysius, even when he lived in Lombardy, where the cold is very intense, never approached the fire. You can, at least on one day of the week, bear with patience, and accept as a penance from the hands of God, the cold and heat of

171

the seasons. St. Francis Borgia, on arriving one night at a college in the country, found the gates locked, and was therefore obliged to remain all night exposed to the cold and the snow, which fell heavily. In the morning the religious expressed great regret at what had happened. Be assured, replied the saint that though I suffered much in the body I was greatly consoled in spirit by the reflection that God rejoiced at my pains. It appeared to me that God himself sent to me from heaven the flakes of snow that fell upon me.

Prayer.

My beloved Redeemer, I blush to appear before Thee with so many attachments to earthly pleasures. During life Thou hast thought of nothing but of suffering for me. But, forgetful of Thy pains, and of Thy love for me, I have hitherto attended only to my own gratification. In my past life I have had nothing of the character of a religious, and of Thy spouse, except the habit and the name. I would deserve to be banished from this holy place, where Thou hast favored me with so many lights and graces, which I have always repaid with ingratitude. I have certainly made many good purposes; and though I have frequently promised, I have not fulfilled them. O my Jesus, give me strength: I desire to do something for Thee before I die. If I were now to die, how unhappy should I be? Thou dost prolong my life that I may become a saint. I desire to be perfect: I love Thee, O my God and my Spouse; and I desire to love Thee as becomes Thy spouse. I wish to think only of pleasing Thee. Pardon me all the offences that I have hitherto offered to Thee: I detest them with my whole heart. O God of my soul, to gratify myself I have insulted Thee, my treasure and my life, who hast loved me so much. Assist me to give myself entirely to Thee from this day forward.

Holy Virgin Mary, my hope, come to my aid, and obtain for me the grace to do something for God before the hour of my death.

CHAPTER IX.

RELIGIOUS POVERTY.

I.

The Vow of Poverty, the Perfection of Poverty, and Community Life.

ALL the views of the world are opposed to the laws of God: in the estimation of the world riches are the basis of greatness; but in the eyes of God poverty is the foundation of sanctity. It is not certain that the rich are damned; but the Redeemer has declared that it is easier for a camel to pass through the eye of a needle than for a rich man to enter the kingdom of heaven. Hence the founders of every religious order have endeavoured to establish in all the Communities of their Institute a perfect spirit of poverty as the basis of the common good. St. Ignatius of Loyola called religious poverty the fortification by which the spirit of fervor is preserved. The truth of this observation is demonstrated by daily experience; for in the Communities in which poverty is maintained fervor flourishes, and in which poverty is violated irregularities soon prevail. Hence the powers of hell labor so hard to introduce a relaxation of poverty into the observant Orders. Speaking of her own religious, St. Teresa once said from heaven: "Let them endeavor to have a great esteem for poverty; for while it lasts fervor will be maintained." Poverty is justly styled by the holy Fathers the guardian of virtues, since in religious it preserves mortification, humility, detachment from creatures, and, above all, interior recollection.

In treating of religious poverty it is necessary to distinguish between the perfection of poverty and that which is the object of the religious vow.

The vow implies that a religious has no dominion over worldly goods, and that her use of them is dependent on the will of her Superior. But, alas, this is a rock on which many religious are lost. St. Mary Magdalene de Pazzi saw many nuns in hell for the transgression of the vow of poverty. In the Chronicles of the Capuchins it is related that the devil once took away from among his brethren and in their presence a religious, from whose sleeve, at the moment when he was carried off, a breviary fell, which the unhappy man had, in violation of the vow of

173

poverty, appropriated to his own use. The fact related by St. Cyril to St. Augustine is still more alarming. In Thebais there was a convent containing two hundred nuns who did not live according to the rules of holy poverty. St. Jerome appeared to one of them, who was more exact than the rest, and commanded her to admonish the abbess and the other nuns that, if they did not amend, a frightful chastisement should be inflicted upon them. The good religious executed the command, but her advice was received with derision. While at prayer she was again commanded to repeat the admonition, and, should it be fruitless, to depart immediately from the convent. She obeyed a second time; but the abbess, instead of profiting by the advice, threatened to expel the sister from the monastery if she said any more on the subject. "You shall not," replied the nun, "Expel me; for I will depart instantly, that I may not be involved in the common ruin." Scarcely had she gone out when the monastery fell, and crushed to death all the religious.

Woe to those that introduce into religion a relaxation of holy poverty. Examine, dear sister, whether you keep money or any other kind of property without leave. And remember that the permission of the Superior is invalid, whenever its object is not just; for she cannot permit you to retain what cannot be lawfully kept. All the money, furniture, clothes, and whatever species of property you possess, all that you receive from your relatives, or for the fruits of your industry, belong not to you, but to the monastery. You have only the use of what the Superior gives you. Hence, if you dispose of anything without her leave, you are guilty of theft, and of a sacrilegious theft, by violating the vow of poverty. Be persuaded that the Lord will demand a very rigorous account. Hence, zealous Superiors are always most exact and severe in chastising every fault against that virtue. Cassian relates that among the ancient Fathers, the procurator, in consequence of allowing a few lentils to be wasted through negligence, was deprived of the benefit of common prayers, and was excluded from the holy Communion till he had done public penance. It is related of Rinald, the prior of the Dominican convent at Bologna, that he chastised very severely a lay-brother for having taken without permission a shred of cloth to mend his habit, and that he caused the cloth to be burned at Chapter, in presence of the whole Community.

What has been just said regards the vow of poverty; but the perfection of holy poverty requires that a religious be divested of every affection

174

for the goods of the earth, and that she make use of them only as far as is necessary for the preservation of life. It was this that the Redeemer wished to signify to the young man, who asked what he should do in order to attain perfection. If, says Jesus, thou wilt be perfect, go sell what thou hast, and give it to the poor. The Saviour told him that he should renounce all his possessions without a single exception. For when, as St. Bonaventure says, the spirit is encumbered with the weight of any temporality, the soul cannot rise to union with God. "Burdened with the load of temporal things, the spirit cannot ascend to God." "The love of terrestrial objects," according to St. Augustine, "Is the birdlime of the spiritual wings," which impedes the flight of the soul to God. And again the holy Doctor says: "By the great wing of poverty a Christian quickly flies to heaven." Hence, St. Laurence Justinian exclaimed: "O blessed voluntary poverty, possessing nothing, fearing nothing; always cheerful, always abounding, because it turns to advantage every inconvenience."

It was for our edification and instruction that Jesus Christ wished to live in continual poverty on earth. Hence, St. Mary Magdalene de Pazzi called poverty the spouse of Jesus. "Poverty," says St. Bernard, "Was not found in heaven—it abounded on earth; but man did not know its value: therefore the Son of God, longing after it, came down from heaven to choose it for himself, and to make it precious to us." Being rich, says St. Paul, he became poor for your sakes, that through his poverty you might be rich. Our Redeemer was the Lord of all the riches in heaven and on earth, but he wished to be miserably poor in this life, in order to enrich us, and to excite us by his example to the love of poverty, which, by withdrawing our affections from temporal goods, procures for us eternal riches. He wished to be poor during his whole life. Poor in his birth—he was born not in a palace, but in a cold stable, having only a manger for his cradle and straw for his bed. Poor in his life and poor in all things, he dwelt in a miserable hut containing but a single room; which served for all the purposes of life. Poor in his garments and in his food. St. John Chrysostom says that the Redeemer and his disciples ate nothing but barley-bread; and this may be inferred from the Gospel. Poor, in fine, in his death: leaving nothing behind him but his miserable garments; and these, even before his death, were divided among the soldiers. Thus for his winding-sheet and sepulchre he depended on the bounty of the charitable.

Hence, Jesus once said to Blessed Angela of Foligno: "If poverty were not a great blessing, I should not have chosen it for myself, nor should I have left it as an inheritance to my elect." It was because they saw Jesus poor that the saints loved poverty so much. Father Granada and Father M. Avila discussed one day the reason why St. Francis of Assisi had such affection for poverty. Father Louis of Granada maintained that it was because the saint wished to be freed from every impediment to a perfect union with God. But Father Avila asserted with more truth, that the ardent love of St. Francis for holy poverty arose from his ardent love of Jesus Christ. And surely a soul that loves Jesus Christ intensely cannot but exclaim with the Apostle: I count all things as dung that I may gain Christ. I esteem all the goods of the earth as dung, and therefore I despise them all, that I may gain Jesus Christ. Hence, St. Francis de Sales used to say, that when a house is on fire the furniture is thrown out of the windows; and long before, the Holy Ghost said: If a man should give all the substance of his house for lore, he shall despise it as nothing. The ardent lover cheerfully despises all things through the love which he bears to God.

From the Sacred Scriptures we learn that the reward of poverty is most certain, and great beyond measure. It is most certain; because Jesus Christ has said: Blessed are the poor in spirit, for theirs is the kingdom of heaven. To the other beatitudes, heaven is promised only as a future reward. Blessed are the meek, for they shall possess the land. Blessed are the clean of heart, for they shall see God. But to the poor in spirit God's kingdom is promised as a present recompense: for theirs is the kingdom of heaven. Because, to those that are truly poor in spirit the Lord gives very great helps, even in this life. Hence, Cornelius à Lapide says, that since, by the decree of God, the kingdom of heaven belongs to the poor, they have a full right to it. The reward of poverty is very secure, and great beyond conception. "The less we have here," says St. Teresa, "The more we shall enjoy in God's kingdom, in which the mansion of each is proportioned to the love with which he shall have imitated the life of Jesus Christ." "O happy commerce," exclaims St. Peter Damian, "Where clay is given away and gold received." O happy traffic, in which we renounce the goods of the earth, which are but mire, and receive in exchange the graces of God and eternal rewards; which are more precious than the purest gold.

The poor in spirit shall also have the honor of sitting with Jesus Christ as the judges of the world. Behold, says St. Peter to Jesus, we have left all things and have followed thee: what, therefore, shall we have? And Jesus said to them: Amen, I say to you, that you who have followed me in the regeneration, when the Son of Man shall sit on the seat of his Majesty, you shall also sit on twelve seats, judging the twelve tribes of Israel. God has promised eternal glory here after, and a hundredfold in this life, to all who abandon earthly goods for his sake. And every one that hath left house or lands for my name's sake, shall receive a hundredfold, and shall possess life everlasting. This promise is fulfilled in all the poor in spirit who, because they desire nothing on earth, possess all riches: As having nothing and possessing all things. The Redeemer has justly compared riches to thorns, for in proportion to their abundance, riches torment the soul by cares, by fears, and by the desires of increased possessions. Hence, St. Bernard says, that while the avaricious, because their desire of riches is never satiated, like mendicants, thirst after the goods of this world; the poor in spirit, because they wish for nothing upon earth, despise mammon. "The avaricious man, like a mendicant, hungers after earthly things; the poor man, like a lord, contemns them." Oh, how great is the happiness of a religious, who desires and possesses nothing upon earth. She enjoys true peace— a blessing more valuable than all worldly goods, which can never content a soul destined to be made happy only by the possession of God.

Thus the poor in spirit receive a great reward in this as well as in the next life. But where shall we find a religious truly poor in spirit? Let us examine in what true poverty of spirit consists.

It consists, first, not only in the absence of all property, but also in the destruction of every desire which has not God for its object. "A pauper meets me, says St. Augustine," and still I seek a man who is poor. Yes, in the world the number of the indigent is countless, but few of them are poor in spirit and desire. St. Teresa used to say, that the religious who appears to be bereft of all property, but at the same time is not poor in spirit, deceives the world and herself. What will her actual poverty profit her? The poor that desire the possession of riches suffer indeed the pains of want, but do not practice the virtue of poverty. "He that desires the goods of the earth," says St. Philip Neri, "Will never become a saint." You, dear sister, have abandoned the world; you have left all things, and will you, after so many sacrifices, expose yourself to the danger of being lost, or at least of not being a saint? Ah,

177

be content with humble food and raiment; seek to become a saint, and do not, for miserable trifles, risk your eternal inheritance. But, says the Apostle, having food and wherewith to be covered, with these we are content. For they that will become rich fall into temptation, and into the snare of the devil, and into many unprofitable and hurtful desires, which draw men into destruction and perdition. Whoever covets worldly riches shall fall into the snares of the enemy, and into numberless desires, which lead to death and to eternal misery.

Poverty of spirit consists, secondly, in keeping the heart detached, not only from what is valuable, but also from what is trifling. The adhesion of the smallest portion of earth prevents the free ascent of a feather in the air; and the possession of a particle of worldly goods, in opposition to the perfection of poverty, impedes the perfect union of a religious with God, and the enjoyment of true peace. Thorns (or riches), however small, torment the traveler, and diminish the expedition of his journey. To be perfect, it is not necessary for a religious to abandon large possessions; no, it is sufficient to leave in effect and in affection the little that it is in her power to relinquish. St. Peter gave up little; but because, in affection, he left all that he possessed (Behold, we have left all things), he merited to hear from Jesus Christ that he was chosen for one of the Redeemer's assessors at the general judgment. You shall sit on twelve seats, judging the twelve tribes of Israel. There are some religious who have an affection, not for precious stones, nor for vessels of gold, but for certain miserable trifles, such as some article of furniture, a book, or the like. They have not renounced all attachments to the goods of the earth, but have transferred their affections from things of value to trifles, and their solicitude about these trifles occasions as many imperfections and as much inquietude as the care of large possessions.

If seculars are lost, they are lost for the attainment of something great in the eyes of the world; but what a pity, says Cassian, to see a nun, after having left the world, and after having renounced her inheritance and liberty, lose the crown of a saint for trifles that are vile and miserable even in the estimation of worldlings. "The adversary," says St. Eucherius, "Exults when he sees us, who contemned the most valuable goods, overcome in matters of the smallest importance." What a source of triumph to the devil to find a person who has left considerable possessions shamefully conquered by the love of trifles. "Some," says Cassian, "Who despise the most magnificent property, we see disturbed for a needle or a pen, and thus fall into the occasions of death." St. Eucherius asserts what appears very extraordinary, that "The love of property, unless it be perfectly eradicated, is most ardent in small things." Most ardent, and therefore most criminal; for by attachment to trifles a religious shows a greater avidity for earthly goods than by an affection for what is valuable. Hence Jesus Christ has said, So likewise, every one of you that doth not renounce all that he possesseth, cannot be my disciple.

Thirdly, poverty of spirit consists not only in being poor, but in loving poverty. "For," says St. Bernard, "It is not poverty, but the love of poverty, that is reputed virtue." It is not the poor man, but the lover of poverty, that is esteemed virtuous. And to love poverty is to love the effects of poverty, that is, hunger, cold, and, above all, the contempt attendant upon want. For St. Thomas teaches that the honor of judging the world shall be given to the poor in spirit, as the reward of the humiliations occasioned by their indigence. Many religious, says St. Vincent Ferrer, glory in the name of poverty, but shun the sufferings and opprobrium that are its constant companions. "They glory in the name, but fly from the associates of poverty." St. Joseph Calasanctius used to say, that he who feels not the inconveniences of want, is not poor. And Blessed Salome, a religious of the Order of St. Clare, used to say, that "Angels and men shall laugh at the religious who desires to be poor, and at the same time wishes to enjoy the advantages of wealth, or complains whenever she is deprived of them." But, my God, what is to be said of the poverty of the religious who, should her food be scanty or not well seasoned, breaks out into complaints,—who, should she not be supplied with a new habit before the old one is torn, disturbs the whole Community by her murmuring against the Superior, and against those who hold office in the convent? What shall I say of the poverty of the nun who seeks finer cloth and linen than become her state, who is disquieted if her dress be not made in a neat and graceful form, so as to give her a genteel appearance? "They indeed," says St. Bernard, "Wish to be poor, but only on the condition that nothing may be wanting to them."

But you will, perhaps, say that the Community life not being observed in your convent, you must think of everything, of food, of clothing, of medicines, and that you must go to the grate to sell your work and to receive a price for it in order to procure for yourself the things that you need. I answer: Although your Institute, or the present usage of your convent, permits this to you, yet you should not show yourself like a secular who sells her wares by directly treating with outside persons without the modesty and gentleness that suit your state. This kind of traffic is often the effect, not of necessity, but of cupidity that induces certain religious to work much at night, to neglect the duties of their office, the choir mental prayer, the sacraments, and even sometimes to use without permission what belongs to the Community. Ah, when the true love of God enters the heart of a nun, she easily finds the means of practising perfect poverty, even though Community life no longer exists in the convent. Blessed Hyacinth Mariscotti, when she had laid aside her tepidity and given herself up entirely to God, immediately set to work to strip her cell of all that was superfluous, and to give it to the Superior; and she even gave up her habit to take another that was torn and patched, that had covered the body of a deceased nun.

Since mention has been made of the Community life, I must make a few reflections on this point. It is certain that all the cares and disquietudes of nuns, all the annoyances that they frequently experience, and all the obstacles that hinder them from advancing in perfection, usually arise from the possession of personal property, and from the desire of preserving and increasing it. The necessity of providing for their own maintenance in regard to food, clothing, furniture, medicines, is indeed a source of care and embarrassment for the poor nuns, and the cause of distractions in their prayers and Communions. It is true the vow of poverty does not forbid them to keep or use things with the requisite permission; but this must be done with such indifference regarding these things that one is always ready to deprive one's self of these should the Superior so ordain. Unfortunately this total indifference is not found in all nuns. There are some who are willing to deposit the money with the Superior; but if the latter should wish to use it for the benefit of the convent they would excite a great commotion. I therefore say that this depositing of money is a mere sham, is a fiction, and I should say it is an attempt to deceive the Superiors and God at the same time, since such nuns are in fact real owners. All those who live a private life are exposed to this danger. Now community life delivers and preserves the nuns from all these inconveniences. Hence St. John Climacus says: "This is community life in which true spiritual poverty is preserved: it frees us from worldly cares; it is a smooth road that enables us, without any obstacle, to unite ourselves to God; it removes all sadness and all disquietude."

It is certain that all the holy founders of religious Orders had in view the establishment of community life; and as long as community life has been maintained, fervor has reigned in the communities. We must here remark, that, according to the common opinion of theologians, such as Suarez, Navarro, Lessius, and others, the vow of poverty obliges the religious always to be interiorly disposed to enter community life when the Superiors, after having examined the circumstances, judge it opportune. This being the case, we must conclude that a religious would be in a bad state as to her conscience if the Superiors wishing to re-establish community life, she would refuse to accept it, even though it did not exist when she entered the convent. We should not be afraid that in community life we shall not find the means of living; for our Lord one day said to St. Catharine of Sienna: "While the religious Order observed poverty, they did not surfer; but now, when they are living by themselves, they suffer." Oh, how happy you would be if you would cooperate in the introduction into your convent of this great good—the community life!

If, however, the community life does not exist in your house, and if under present circumstances it cannot be established, I do not wish to force you observe it. It is therefore permitted to you to take a moderate care of what concerns food, medicines, and other things of which you may be in need. You may also, with the requisite permissions, sell your work, procure for yourself what is required for your sustenance, and retain the money necessary for your daily wants, depositing the rest in the common fund and leaving it at the disposal of the Superior in case she should think fit to use it. You may also receive permission to spend or receive money up to a certain amount. In acting in this manner you may still merit the reward promised to the poor in spirit.

Prayer.

My Jesus, if hitherto my heart has been attached to the goods of the earth, Thou shalt henceforth be my only treasure. O God of my soul! Thou art a good infinitely greater than any other, Thou dost merit infinite love; I esteem and love Thee above all things, and even more than myself; Thou art the only object of all my affections. I desire nothing in this world. If I had any desires, it would be to possess all the treasures and kingdoms of the earth, for the purpose of renouncing them all, and depriving myself of them for the love of Thee. Come, O my love, come and consume in me every affection that is not for Thee. Grant that, in future, I may regard nothing but Thee, think only of Thee, and sigh only after Thee. The love that made Thee die on the cross for me, makes me die to all my inclinations—makes me love only Thy infinite goodness, and desire only Thy grace and Thy love. My dear Redeemer, when shall I be entirely Thine, as Thou art all mine? I am not able even to give myself to Thee as I ought. Oh, take me and make me live only for Thy glory.

Trusting in the merits of Thy blood, O Jesus, and in Thy intercession, O my mother Mary, I hope for all things.

II.

The Degrees and the Practice of Perfect Poverty.

FIRST DEGREE.

The first degree of perfect religious poverty is not to possess anything as one's own. Hence a religious should regard but as a loan whatever she possesses, and should be ready to give it up at the first intimation of the Superior's will. She ought to be like a statue, which when dressed is not elated, and when stripped is not dejected. A sister who is afflicted at being deprived of anything by the Superior shows that she did not retain it with the true spirit of poverty, or at least that she had some attachment to it. A religious should remember that what she is permitted to receive or retain, belongs not to her, but is the property of the monastery. She should, therefore, hold it as a deposit, and ought not to expend it on vanity, or in superfluous presents. Neither should she complain when the Superior applies it to the use of the Community, or of any of the religious. What then are we to think of the nun who throws the whole convent into confusion whenever the sisters, with the permission of the Superior, use what she possesses. Search, then, dear sister, your heart, and see if it is detached from all you possess.

Examine how you would feel if the Superior refused to permit you to incur a certain expense, to retain a certain sum of money or a certain

piece of furniture. And if you feel an attachment to anything whatsoever, resolve, in imitation of that great servant of God, Sister Mary of
the Cross, either to deprive yourself of it, or to bring it to the Superior
and leave it at her disposal. In a word, you must preserve the heart
free from all affection, even for those things that you are permitted to
retain.

SECOND DEGREE.

The second degree of poverty is, to deprive yourself of whatever is
superfluous: for the smallest superfluity will prevent a perfect union of
the soul with God. St. Mary Magdalene de Pazzi went so far as to strip
her little altar of all its ornaments except the crucifix. St. Teresa relates
of herself that, knowing God to be most jealous of religious poverty,
she could not recollect herself in prayer as long as she retained anything that she thought to be superfluous. If in your convent there is
not a perfect community of property, endeavor at least to imitate the
poverty practiced by the most exemplary and exact among your companions, as well in dress as in food and furniture.

But you will perhaps say that whatever you possess is retained with the
leave of the Superior. Permission to keep superfluities may save you
from the punishments inflicted on proprietors but will not secure to
you the merit of perfect poverty.

Again, you will perhaps say that you have no attachment to what you
keep. But whether you have an attachment to it or not, the possession
of what is not necessary will always prevent you from attaining the
perfection of poverty.

You may imagine that a certain sum of money or a certain portion of
property will enable you to relieve the poor or to assist your companions. But I repeat that it is the nun that has nothing to give, and not
the religious that has the means of distributing alms, who edifies the
Church. St. Thomas says that "It is good to give your goods to the
needy, but it is better to be poor with Christ." It is meritorious to dis-
tribute your property to the poor, but it is better to be like Jesus Christ,
without the means of giving alms. Besides, as the Venerable Sister
Amadea, a Visitation nun, used to say, a good religious should desire
to dispense only the goods that she receives from God, that is, good

183

example, prayers, salutary advice, and the helps to spiritual life.

If, dear sister, you desire to please your Spouse, you must renounce whatsoever you know to be superfluous. Should you be unable to ascertain what is absolutely necessary for your use, beg of the abbess to examine your cell and to remove whatever is not indispensable. If you truly desire to be with Jesus Christ, I advise you not indeed to be singular, but not to allow any of your companions to surpass you in poverty. And that you may be among the poorest of your companions, you must endeavor to be poor in all things, in your dress, in your furniture, and in your food.

I. With regard to clothes, be careful to practice the highest degree of poverty compatible with the usage of the Community. Let your clothes be such as necessity requires, and not what vanity would suggest. Of what use are fine clothes to religious except to gratify vanity, and to attract the notice and esteem of all that behold them? "For," says St. Gregory, "No one desires to be clothed in precious garments, when he cannot be seen by others." But the Holy Ghost has declared that beauty does not consist in external decoration, but in interior comeliness. All the glory of the king's daughter is within. On the contrary, "The exterior signs betray what is concealed within the soul." Thus, every vain ornament of dress shows that he who wears it is puffed up with vanity. Hence St. John Chrysostom says that a religious who attends to the decoration of her person manifests the deformity of her soul. "Attention to the ornaments of the body indicates internal deformity." St. Jerome observes that "The soul is defiled in proportion as the body is adorned." St. Mary Magdalene de Pazzi saw many nuns in hell for violating poverty, and especially by vanity in dress.

I do not require of you to wear a torn or sordid dress: a torn garment is not decent in a religious; but a patched habit is suited to all that have made a vow of poverty: a sordid veil is not becoming, but an affected whiteness sought after by some is not proper. What edification is to be expected from the nun that wears wristbands of fine linen, fastened with silver buttons; that carries a costly ring on her finger, and beads of great value by her side; that uses only fine veils, and casts them aside as soon as the smallest break appears in them? She may be assured that her contempt of poverty is highly displeasing to God. To the Venerable Sister Constantia of the Conception, a Carmelite nun, Jesus once appeared, and, because she threw away a torn veil, said to her: "Is it thus you despise the badge of spouse which I gave you?"

Religious that love Jesus Christ do not thus disregard holy poverty. When the Venerable Sister Margaret of the Cross, a daughter of Maximilian II and a barefooted Clare, appeared before her brother Albert, the Archduke, in a patched habit, he was struck with astonishment, and expressed his surprise at seeing her dressed in such a manner. "Brother," replied the good religious, "I am more happy in these rags than all the monarchs of the earth are in their purple." What the world contemns is highly prized and rewarded by Almighty God. Violante Palombara, a noble lady, used only a garment of coarse linen, the poorest bedclothes, and beads of plain wood. At the hour of death she exclaimed: "Oh, what do I see? My dress resplendent with rays,—my covering made of gold,—and my beads of diamonds!"

II. You must also take care to practice poverty in the furniture of your cell. In the chronicles of St. Jerome we read that when Superiors found curiosities in the convent they immediately cast them into the fire, calling them idols of religious. The great servant of God, Sister Mary Magdalene Carafa, who had been duchess of Andria, and afterwards a religious in the Sapienza of Naples, would not keep in her cell paintings, or presents, or even many books. "For reading," she would say, "A single book is sufficient, and contains more than we can put in practice." Her conduct should cover with confusion certain religious who keep in their cells a great number of spiritual books, but do not practice the lessons that they read in any of them.

St. Teresa examined every day whether there was any superfluity in her cell; if she found any, she immediately removed it. What profit do religious draw from paintings that are not sacred, from gilded cornices, or splendid chests? Ornaments of silver and crystals are better suited to a lady in the world than to a nun in the cloister. Remember that what now pleases the eyes shall at the hour of death torture the soul, and in another life shall be severely punished—at least in purgatory. The learned Palafox relates that a Superior once appeared to a religious and told him that, with regard to the vow of poverty, God demands a most rigorous account of certain things that are not attended to in this life. He also said that he himself suffered severely in purgatory for having kept in his cell a walnut desk.

III. Some religious must have in their cells a supply of fruits, spices, and other eatables. When the physician prescribed for the Venerable Mother Mary John of the Annunciation a conserve of roses, she refused to keep any of it in the cell, but made a sister bring her every evening as much as was necessary for the night.

IV. Above all, seek to be poor in money. St. Paul compares avarice to idolatry. No covetous person (which is a serving of idols,) hath inheritance in the kingdom of Christ. The comparison is most just; for the avaricious man desires money as his last end, and thus makes it his God. Hence St. John Chrysostom said, "Let us contemn money, lest we be contemned by Christ." If we wish not to be despised by Jesus Christ, we must despise riches. Hence the first Christians, after having sold their goods, placed the price at the feet of the apostles, thus showing, as St. Jerome says, that money should not find a place in the heart of man, but should be trampled under his feet. Some religious, under the pretext of providing for their necessities, desire the possession of riches. St. Catharine of Sienna used to say: "We desire to abound in temporal goods, because, as long as we do not possess them in abundance, we imagine that we stand in need of them."

But, religious who love perfection seek not after riches; they desire only what is absolutely indispensable, and therefore they look for scarcely as much as is necessary for their support. By enabling them to indulge every whim and caprice, a superfluous income serves only to make religious more proud, more at ease, more vain, and less mortified. What a shame, says St. Catharine of Sienna, in one of her letters, to see some religious, who should be mirrors of poverty, enjoy more pleasures in the cloister than they would had they remained in the world! Surely it is a scandalous irregularity in a nun to seek more indulgence in religion than she should obtain in the world.

If you wish not to offend against poverty, you must observe great caution in your whole expenditure. There are some, and particularly in our own time, since the expenses of religious have become extravagant, who boast of their splendour and generosity, saying, While we have the means we must spend. Such language might be expected from a worldling, but should never be uttered by a religious. Nor is it any justification to say that the expenses are incurred for God's honor, on the solemn festivals of the monastery. Clement V. prohibited to religious all superfluous expenditure, even on the divine worship. Hence, St. Charles Borromeo ordained that on the festivals of nuns the decorations should be decent, but not sumptuous. What think you, says St. Bernard, "Is it penance, compunction, or the admiration of the bystanders that is sought in these things?" Do you think that a religious, in the sumptuous celebration of a feast, seeks the honor of God by inspiring others with devotion, or rather the indulgence of her own vanity, by exciting admiration of her generosity and splendor? But you will perhaps say that bishops incur great expenses in the celebration of festivals. In the words of St. Bernard, who has proposed and answered this objection, I reply that the condition of bishops is different from that of religious. We, says the saint, "Have left all that is precious in the world, and by this means we intended to excite devotion." The circumstances of bishops, and of religious who make a profession of poverty, are very different: the latter have left the world; even in their festivals they should appear poor, and by their exterior poverty should endeavor to excite devotion in others. Oh, how many faults are committed by religious in celebrating their feasts. They are not content with a great abundance of lights and of ornaments, or with the expense of music: no; they must also display their vanity by regaling all who are invited to the solemnity.

But you will say, What am I to do? Others act in this manner: shall I not be like them? If you must be like others, you ought at least not to endeavor to surpass them, nor increase the excesses that have been already introduced. If you indulge in any excess, the sister who will have to celebrate the next feast will strive to equal you in pomp and splendor. The abuses that already exist are more than sufficient. Do not, then, I repeat, introduce any new one; if you do, you shall have to render a frightful account to God. For it is by repeated acts of extravagance that the habit of lavish expenditure is established. One exceeds her companions in magnificence and liberality; she is surpassed by another, and thus a great degree of extravagance is gradually introduced. It is in this manner that many Communities have lost the spirit of fervor, and have fallen away from the habit of regular observance. How many nuns are there who, on account of their extravagant expenditure, lead a life of continual distraction and inquietude, without recollection or devotion, and full of faults and vanities! The Sovereign Pontiffs and the Sacred Congregations have frequently endeavoured to correct this evil; but their exertions have in a great measure proved abortive. On this subject I have nothing more to say, except to exclaim: Woe to the nun who introduces abuses and vanities into religion!

A few important remarks must here be made:

1. The sister who is charged with the management of the affairs of the convent should be careful not to expend extravagant sums for her own convenience. By her prodigality she might be guilty of a grievous transgression of the vow of poverty.

2. Let all remember that permissions to lay out money are not to be obtained from the confessor, but from the Superior. For in temporal all the religious are bound to obey her.
3. To lay out money on any object, different from that on which you obtained permission to expend it, is a violation of poverty.

4. Let it also be remembered that to make presents, without just reason, and only through caprice or vanity, to persons who do not stand in need of them, is also an offence against poverty. "It is a sacrilege," says St. Jerome, "To give the property of the poor to those that are not poor." It is a sacrilegious violation of poverty to give the goods of the poor—that is, of religious, who have nothing of their own—to those that are not in want.

5. The decrees of the Sovereign Pontiffs forbid confessors to receive presents from nuns: such presents, when mutual, are particularly prohibited. "Holy love," says St. Jerome, "Does not make frequent little presents, nor indulge in affectionate letters." But we shall treat of this subject in the next chapter.

THIRD DEGREE.

The third degree of poverty requires that you do not complain when you are in want even of necessaries. The Mother of God once said to one of her devout servants, a Franciscan nun: My child, as long as all your wants are supplied, you are not poor; true poverty consists in having less than is necessary. "To complain of poverty," says St. Jane Frances Chantal, "Is displeasing to God and to men. I never feel so happy as when I bear some of the marks of poverty." That great servant of God, Baptista Vernazza, a canoness regular, used to say that she experienced great pleasure in reflecting that she had no provision for any future necessity. St. Mary Magdalene de Pazzi was afflicted at seeing her wants supplied by the abbess. She once felt so much complacency, in not having bread at table, that she afterwards accused herself of having entertained too much pleasure in the privation. Sometimes she exclaimed: "Oh, how happy should I be, if I went to table and found no food, if I went to sleep and found no bed, if I went to dress and had no clothes! Oh that all things were wanting to me!"

Tell me, dear sister, do you practice such perfect poverty? Although you may have renounced all affection for the world, and for vain and superfluous possessions, you are perhaps still attached to what you regard as necessary, and still anxious to be furnished with decent and comfortable clothes, food, and bed. It is this solicitude about them that disturbs you whenever they are wanting to you. But in what way do you wish to be poor? Do you expect to enjoy the reward of poverty, and at the same time to want nothing? Would you not be in want of many necessaries had you remained in the world? And do you seek to be supplied with all necessaries in religion, which you embraced for the purpose of suffering, and in which you had made a solemn vow of poverty? "To desire to be poor," says St. Francis de Sales, "And not to feel any of the inconveniences of want, is to wish for the honor of poverty and the advantages of riches."

But you will say, Had I good health, I would cheerfully suffer all things; but I am weak and infirm, and therefore I cannot bear to see the Superior as forgetful of me as if I were in good health. You complain that others are unmindful of you, and you yourself forget that you have entered religion for the purpose of suffering. A nun should embrace sufferings in sickness as well as in health. In the Constitutions of the Teresians the following admonition is given: "Our sick brethren, if anything be wanting to them, should remember that they have embraced the poverty of Jesus Christ, and therefore, neither in sickness nor in health, should desire to be treated like the rich." St. Mary Magdalene de Pazzi gives a very excellent advice on this subject. "However great your infirmities," says the saint, "Never take and never seek what savors not of poverty." Hence, St. Bernard says that it is not becoming in poor religious to make use of costly remedies; and therefore he recommended his monks not to take any other medicine than decoctions of herbs. Had you remained in the world, you should

189

not, perhaps, be able to procure the medicine and the attendance of physicians, with which you are provided in religion; and still you seek for other remedies. Ah, be content, not only to live but to die in poverty; and rejoice that death, when it comes to take you out of this life will find you treated as a pauper. On every occasion in which you have to suffer from want have before your eyes the beautiful sentiment of St. Jane Frances Chantal, who was accustomed to say, that as the opportunities of practising poverty are so rare, we should, whenever they occur, accept them with gladness.

FOURTH DEGREE.

The fourth and last degree of poverty requires not only that a religious be content with what is poor, but also that she prefer and select what is poorest— the poorest cell, the poorest bed, the poorest clothes, and the poorest food. St. Mary Magdalene de Pazzi rejoiced in eating what was left by the other sisters. Her habit was so threadbare that the Superior obliged her to change it. St. Jane Frances Chantal used to say that for the perfection of poverty it is advisable not to use silver when tin is sufficient, nor tin when lead answers the purpose. The nun who wishes to be a saint observes a similar rule in all other things.

It will be useful to insert in this place the beautiful instruction of Father Anthony Torres to a nun who was one of his penitents: "Since your Spouse esteemed poverty so highly, you should love it as a treasure; you should practice it in all things, and glory in it more than in the most splendid ornaments. Do not allow any nun or lay-sister in the convent to be poorer than you. You should wear no ornaments, and no more clothes than are absolutely necessary; you must practice poverty even in your veil, which should be coarse and patched, and even in the beads that hang by your side. You should delight in wearing a poor patched habit, and should not cast it aside until it is no longer fit for use. Abstain as much as possible from keeping two habits, or more linen than the humblest of the lay-sisters. Do not possess or seek anything, however necessary it may appear, without first looking at your naked Spouse on the cross, and asking his permission. Neither give nor receive any presents, however small, without the Superiors leave. In your cell you should have only a poor bed, the coarsest bed-clothes, two chairs of straw, a crucifix, four unframed pictures, the few books that your director will prescribe for your use, and whatever else is indispensably necessary. You should frequently examine before the crucifix your conduct with regard to the virtue of poverty; and if you find that you possess any superfluity you should take it immediately to the Superior. Never ask from your relatives anything for your own use; you may ask something from them for the Community, but never reserve anything whatsoever for yourself."

Ah, dear sister, after having renounced the world and all its goods, do not, I pray you, prefer emptiness and nothingness to the Lord. When, to induce St. Clement, Bishop of Ancyra, to deny Jesus Christ, the Emperor Diocletian offered him silver, gold, and precious stones, the saint heaved a deep sigh of sorrow at seeing his God compared with dross. And when, on condition of renouncing Christianity, the dignity of first pontiff and head of the priesthood was offered by the tribune to St. Basil, Martyr, on the part of the Emperor Licinius, the saint replied: "Tell the emperor that though he made me master of all his dominions he could not give me as much as he would take from me by robbing me of my God to make me a slave of the devil." And, dearest sister, since you have left all things for God, do not, for the sake of any miserable earthly good, expose your soul to the danger of eternal perdition. Imagine that God places before you himself on the one hand and creatures on the other, and that he speaks to you in the language that he once addressed to the Venerable Mary Crucified: "Choose between me and creatures whichsoever will make you happy." A religious should have no treasure but God. I conclude in the words of St. Mary Magdalene de Pazzi: "O happy the religious who, detached from all things by means of holy poverty, can say, The Lord is the portion of my inheritance." God only is the portion that I desire in time as well as in eternity. Hence the saint was heard to exclaim: "Nothing, nothing but God; I desire to possess him only for his own sake."

Prayer.

My Jesus, in Thee I find all things: out of Thee I desire nothing. Ah, draw me entirely to Thee; enkindle in my heart Thy holy love, by which I desire to see myself entirely consumed. My dear Redeemer, I know that Thou hast been near to me for so many years, because thou dost wish me to belong entirely to Thee. Since, then, Thou dost so ardently desire my welfare, grant that henceforth I may seek only Thy love, and the fulfillment of Thy holy will. Ah! Lord, deliver me from all affections that remove me from Thee. Grant that my thoughts may be wholly employed in endeavoring to avoid every offence against Thy majesty, and in seeking to please Thee to the best of my power. O incarnate Word! Thou art come upon earth to kindle the flames of love in the hearts of men. Oh, take possession of my heart; fill it with Thy love; enlighten it, and make it ready and willing to execute all Thy holy desires. In a word, unite my soul perfectly to Thy divinity, and possess it entirely and forever. Unite Thyself to me, and me to Thee, by a perfect love that shall never be dissolved. Grant that I may be no longer mine own, but that I may be Thine entirely and forever, my treasure, my love, and my only good.

Mary, my mother, in thy intercession, my hopes are placed.

CHAPTER X.

DETACHMENT FROM RELATIVES AND OTHER PERSONS.

I.

Detachment from Relatives.

IF attachment to relatives were not productive of great mischief Jesus Christ would not have so strenuously exhorted us to estrangement from them. If, he says, any man come to me and hate not his father and mother . . . and brethren and sisters, he cannot be my disciple. And again: I came to set a man at variance against his father, and the daughter against her mother. But why does the Redeemer insist so strongly on alienation from relatives? Why does he take so much pains to separate us from them? He himself assigns the reason: it is because a man's enemies shall be they of his own household. Relatives are the worst enemies of the sanctification of Christians and particularly of religious; because they are, according to St. Thomas, the greatest obstacle to advancement in virtue. "Frequently," says the holy Doctor, "Carnal friends oppose the progress of the spirit; for in the affair of salvation the nearest akin are not friends, but enemies." The truth of this assertion is fully established by experience. Even St. Charles Borromeo, notwithstanding his great reserve and perfect detachment from relatives, acknowledged that after returning from among them he felt his soul tepid, and detached from the things of God. Hence, according to all the masters of the spiritual life, he that desires to walk in the way of perfection must fly from relatives, must abstain from taking part in their affairs, and when they are at a distance must not even inquire about them.

What progress can be expected from the religious that wishes to have her relatives near the convent, who, if she does not see them, is constantly sending letters and messages to request a visit from them; and who, if they yield not to her entreaties, is disturbed, and complains by frequent letters of their absence and neglect? It is impossible for a nun of this description ever to attain a close union with God. "Whoever," says St. Gregory, "Wishes to be truly united to the Father of all must be separated from relatives." Whoever aspires to a union with God, the common Father of all men, must fly altogether from his kindred. When the Blessed Virgin lost the infant Jesus she sought him in vain for three days among her kinsfolk. "Yes," says St. Bernard, "Jesus is not found among kinsfolk." Peter of Blois asserts that the love of flesh and blood soon robs the soul of the love of God. "Carnal love will soon remove you from the love of God."

Religious should regard the dying words of Moses as peculiarly applicable to themselves: Who hath said to his father and to his mother, I do not know you; and to his brethren, I know you not. These have kept thy word and observed thy covenant. The religious who tells her parents and her brothers and her sisters that she knows them not, is the true spouse of Jesus. She is the king's daughter who obeys the call of God, and fulfils the covenant made with him at her profession, when he spoke to her in the language that he addresses to every soul consecrated to his love: Hearken, O daughter, and see, and incline thy ear, and forget thy people and thy father's house. And the king shall greatly desire thy beauty. Hear my voice, O daughter, and learn to understand the great blessings that you will receive if you observe my commandments. Open, then, your ear to my words: forget your kindred and your father's house, and I, your King and Spouse, shall love your beauty. "It is," says St. Jerome, "A great advantage to forget your parents; for then the King shall greatly desire your beauty." Great shall be your reward: you shall become dear to the Lord, who will make you happy here and hereafter. Such is the recompense promised by the Redeemer when he said: And every one that hath left house or brethren, or sisters, or father, or mother . . . for my name's sake, shall receive an hundred fold, and shall possess life everlasting. The nun that leaves her relatives in effect and in affection shall obtain eternal beatitude in heaven and a hundredfold on earth; she will leave a few and shall find many sisters in religion; she will abandon a father and a mother, and in return shall have God for her father and Mary for her mother; and from them she shall experience the kindness and affection of the fondest parent.

Hence, convinced that detachment from kindred is highly pleasing to God, the saints have sought to be wholly removed from their relatives. St. Francis Xavier, when about to set out on the Indian mission, refused to visit his mother or relatives, though they repeatedly requested a visit from him, although he passed near their place of residence, and although he knew that he should never see them again. When his sister came to see St. Pachomius he sent her the following message: "It is enough for you to have learned that I am alive; go, then, in peace." Some of the saints have gone so far as to abstain from reading the letters of their dearest friends. St. John Climacus relates that St. Anthony, after having spent several years in the desert, on receiving some letters from his relatives, said to himself: What can I expect from the perusal of these letters, but disturbance of mind, and the loss of the peace that I enjoy? The holy man then cast them into the fire, saying: Begone from me, all thoughts of my country that I may not return to the things that I have already left. To the flames, ye letters, that I may not be one day burned by you.

"For my part," says St. Teresa, "I cannot conceive what consolation a nun can find in her relatives. By attachment to them she displeases God, and without being able to enjoy their amusements she shares in all their troubles." How applicable to you, dear Sister, is this reflection of the saint? When your parents and friends come to the grate, they certainly cannot make you a partaker of their worldly amusements, for you cannot go beyond the limits of the enclosure. In their visits, then, they only recount their misfortunes, their infirmities, and their wants. Surely such narratives only serve to fill your head and heart with so much inquietude, with so many distractions and defects, that after each visit you will be for several days disturbed and distracted in your meditations and Communions by the remembrances of what you have heard.

How is it possible that you who have left the world can so ardently desire the frequent visits of your relatives? Is it that they may frequently rob you of your peace and of the progress you have made? Oh, what an excess of folly to imagine that you cannot be happy without frequently seeing your friends. Ah, if you keep aloof from them, what torrents of consolation and happiness would your Spouse, Jesus, infuse into your soul! St. Mary Magdalene de Pazzi used to say that an abhorrence of the grate should be the principal fruit of the Communions of religious. And as an evil spirit once said to the Venerable Sister Mary Villani, there is certainly no place where the devil does so much injury to religious as in the parlour. Hence, St. Mary Magdalene de Pazzi would not even enter the parlour; and such was her hatred of it, that she could not bear to hear it mentioned. Whenever she was obliged to go to the parlour, she would begin to weep, and would say to her novices: "My dear children, pray to God for me; for I am called to the grate." When leaving them, she would beg of them soon to call her away from the grate under some pretext.

But you will say, What am I to do? Am I never to see my friends? When they visit me, must I send them away, and refuse to go to the grate? I do not require so much from you; but if you refuse to see them, would you do wrong,—would you do what would be inconvenient, or what is never done by religious? Several nuns have resolved never to see their relatives, and have fulfilled their resolution. In the life of Father Torres, it is related of Georama Snakelike, a religious in the convent of St. Alvina, that so great was her attachment to her relatives that her thoughts were continually upon them, that she desired frequent visits from them, and sent every day to inquire about her father. Her sister, Mary Antonia, who lived in the same convent, was so fervent, that she be sought the Lord to make her suffer a great deal in this life. Her prayer was heard, and she was afflicted with an ulcer, which ate away her flesh, and produced the very pangs of death. In her agony she would exclaim: "More suffering, O my Spouse, more suffering." When dying she said to Gerolama, that she hoped to obtain eternal glory, and that as soon as she should enter into bliss she would beg of God to transform her tepid sister into a saint. She died: Gerolama changed her life, and adopted and observed for forty years the resolution never more to see her relatives. It once happened that two of her nephews came to visit her, but she refused to see them; and having sent them away, she went to the grate of the church to pray before the Blessed Sacrament. The young men entered the church, expecting to see her at a distance; but she instantly retired behind the curtain, and such was the effort which she made on that occasion to stifle the feelings of flesh and blood that she fainted away. Whoever does not offer violence to herself will never become a saint. Sister Gerolama made rapid progress in divine love, and afterwards lived and died a saint. After death her body was opened and a cross of flesh was found on her heart, as a token of the great love that she had borne to Jesus crucified. Why cannot you imitate her example, and free yourself forever from the distractions that are caused by going to the grate?

But you will say that the abbess or the confessor will not permit you to observe such a resolution. On what grounds can they refuse you permission? Is not such a resolution the fruit of a divine inspiration, and if practiced, would it not be a source of great edification to the other sisters? Would it not, at least, make them see the impropriety and the dangers of attachments to their relatives and to the grate? But should the Superior command you to see your parents or relatives, I tell you to obey; but at the same time I entreat you to imitate the example of Blessed Theodore, who, when commanded to converse with his mother, who had come to see him, said to the abbot: "Father, you command me to speak with my mother, but do you assure me that from the conversation I shall suffer no spiritual injury?" Afraid of the consequence, the abbot released the brother from the obligation that he had imposed upon him. It may be useful to remind abbesses and confessors, that if, without just cause, and only through caprice, or unreasonable human respect, or self-interest, or to avoid trouble, they hinder the greater progress of a religious, who seeks to run to God, they will certainly have to render to the Lord an account of their conduct. As to you, dear Sister, when they oblige you to see your relatives, obey; again I say, that I do not require of you never more to see your friends; but whenever necessity compels you to speak with them, I exhort you to observe the following rules:

1. Before you go to the grate, recommend yourself to Jesus in the Blessed Sacrament or on the cross, and beg that he may assist you and preserve you from every fault in your conversation.

2. Take care not to imitate the religious who go to the parlour to amuse themselves, or to learn what passes in the world, and afterwards tell it to the whole Community.

3. Be careful not to make known to externs the internal affairs of the convent, and particularly what might tend to the discredit of the Superior or the sisters.

4. Should externs begin to speak on useless or worldly matters, such as marriages, balls, or fond attachments, break off, break off at once the conversation, and introduce some Christian maxim, or some fact from which you can draw a spiritual sentiment. You are not to learn the language of seculars, hut should teach them the language of religious, whose conversation should be always on the things of God. Time spent at the grate is not profitable to the soul; it is all lost, and for it you shall one day have to render an account to God.

5. Never seek a visit from your relatives. When they come, endeavor to withdraw from them as soon as possible; excuse your withdrawal by saying that you must attend to the duties of your office; that you must assist a person who is sick; or make some similar apology. Whoever wishes, easily finds very just reasons for taking leave of visitors. If you act in this manner, they will soon feel that their conversation is not very pleasing to you, and will come less frequently to disturb you. And be assured that the shorter their visits, the fewer will be your faults; and that the less frequently you see them, the more you will be recollected, and the greater will be the consolations that you will receive from Jesus Christ. The Venerable Sister Catharine, a Cistercian, because she became a nun against the consent of her parents, was altogether abandoned by them; but such was the joy that her Spouse poured into her soul, that she was accustomed to say: "I do not envy my sisters who are visited very frequently in the year by their parents, because as often as I wish, I go to my true father, Jesus, and to my dear mother, Mary, and they fill me with consolations."

6. Lastly, take care, above all things, not to implicate yourself in the temporal concerns of your relatives; such as marriages, contracts, expenses, or any similar affairs. If you do, you will lose all peace and recollection, and perhaps your immortal soul. "How many monks," says St. Jerome, "By compassion towards their father and mother have lost their own-souls?" How many religious by compassion for their relatives have been lost? In another place the saint says, that the more tender the affection of a religious for her kindred, the greater her impiety towards God. "Great piety towards relatives is impiety towards God." And what greater impiety than that a nun should, for the service of her family, give up the service of God, neglect mental prayer, the sacraments, and expose herself to all the distractions that necessarily arise from the care of worldly affairs. St. Bernard exhorts his religious "To fly from such cares, as being diabolical." St. Ignatius of Loyola refused to interfere in the marriage of one of his nieces, though she was the heiress of the family. St. Francis Borgia would not ask the Pope for a dispensation (which he would have easily obtained) to have his son married to a relative, although the acquisition of a large estate depended upon the marriage. No man, said the Redeemer, pulling his hand to the plough, and looking back, is fit for the kingdom of God.

Let us tremble, for God himself has declared that he who has begun to serve the Lord, and looks back to the things of the world, is unfit for paradise. When, then, relatives seek to implicate you in worldly affairs, withdraw at once from them. Attend to the advice of the Redeemer to the young man who, when asked to follow Jesus, answered, that he wished first to bury his father: Let the dead, says Jesus, bury the dead. Leave, then, dear sister, worldlings (who are said to be dead) to attend to their worldly business, and let it be your sole care and concern to love God and to become a saint. Tell your parents that worldly business is not fit for you, nor suited to your state. When his mother said to Jesus: Son, why hast thou done so to us, behold, thy father and I have sought thee sorrowing, he replied: Did you not know that I must be about my Father's business. Did you not know that I should attend only to the interests of my Fathers glory? Should your relatives complain of your unwillingness to serve them, should they even charge you with disaffection, with ingratitude, and even call you the enemy of your family, answer them with firmness that you are dead to the world, and that it is your duty to attend only to the service of God and of the monastery. I conclude this chapter with the words of St. Joseph Calasanctius: "A religious who is attached to her relatives has not yet left the world."

Prayer.

O my God and my Spouse, Thee alone I desire to serve and to love henceforth and forever. I desire to serve creatures only, when I know that Thou dost wish me to serve them. Ah! Lord, make Thy will known to me; I wish to do it in all things. Ah, inflame my whole soul with Thy holy love, that for the future I may seek only Thy will. Grant that nothing may please me but what pleases Thee. Grant that I may always say with sincerity: "My God and my Spouse, I desire Thee only, and nothing more." O my King and my Spouse, Jesus, reign alone in my whole soul; possess it without reserve; let Thy love command and point out what I am to do, what I am to avoid, and what I am to desire; and let my soul obey only Thy will. Ah, my dear Redeemer, through the merits of Thy Passion hear my prayer.

O Queen of heaven, in thee I trust; assist me by thy intercession.

II.

Detachment from Seculars, and even from the Sisters.

St. Augustine says that whoever does not shun dangerous conversations will soon fall into a precipice: "He that will not avoid suspected familiarity soon falls into ruin." The example of the unhappy Solomon should make us all tremble. At first he was most clear to God, and even the inspired of the Holy Ghost, but by the love of strange women he was in his old age led into idolatry. Nor should his fall be a subject of wonder; for, as St. Cyprian says, to stand in the midst of flames and not to burn is impossible.

Be assured, O blessed spouse of the Lord that for religious the atmosphere of the parlour, where conversations are held with seculars, is pestiferous. As in the choir religious breathe the salubrious air of paradise, so in the parlour they may inhale the pestilential vapours of hell. A religious, were she in her father's house, would certainly not dare to spend an hour or two in conversation with persons of every age and of both sexes, and will she not scruple to do so in God's own dwelling? Is the house of the Lord to be treated with less respect than the house of a secular?

But you will say: By the grace of God such conversations are harmless. Let those that speak thus remember, that all friendships founded on a sensible affection for external objects, if not productive of other evils, are at least great obstacles to perfection. They certainly destroy the spirit of prayer and recollection; and the nun that entertains such friendships will be in the church in body, but her thoughts will be fixed on her friends. Such friendships serve to weaken her affection for the sacraments and to conceal from herself and others the source of her tepidity; and thus she daily becomes more imperfect. She loses her peace; for should anything be said against those for whom she has conceived a regard, or whose conversation she seeks to enjoy, she is at once disturbed, and censures the person by whose language she is offended. She loses obedience; for when admonished by the Superior to break off such friendships, she excuses herself by various pretences, but does not obey. In fine, she loses the love of God, who desires to possess her whole heart, who will not suffer any affection that is not for him; and therefore seeing her soul attached to others, he withdraws himself, and deprives her of his special assistance. The Venerable

Sister Frances Farnese used to say to the religious under her care: "We are shut up in this monastery that we may neither see nor be seen, but that we preserve our souls spotless before God." The more we hide ourselves from seculars, the more God will manifest himself to us by his grace in this life, and by his glory in the next.

Affections that arise from certain external qualifications, possessed by persons of a different sex, not only deprive the soul of great advantages, but also expose her to very great danger. In the beginning they appear indifferent, but by degrees they become sinful, and finally lead the soul into some mortal transgression. St. Jerome says: "Man and woman are like fire and straw, and the devil does not cease to blow so that there may be a blaze." Persons of different sexes, as soon as there exists too much familiarity among them, are inflamed as easily as when straw is held near the fire; for the devil is there trying his best to produce a conflagration. St. Teresa was once shown the place prepared for her in hell had she not renounced a certain inordinate, though not impure, affection for a relative.

If, dear reader, you ever feel an attachment of this kind, your only remedy is a resolute and total retreat from the object of your affection. If you seek to withdraw by degrees, believe me your efforts will be fruitless: such chains, because they are strong, are burst only with difficulty—without a sudden and violent effort their bondage shall never be dissolved. You will perhaps say that no impropriety can occur. Remember that the devil never begins by suggesting the worst of evils, but by degrees he leads negligent souls to the brink of ruin, and then by an easy effort casts them over the precipice. It is a common maxim of masters of the spiritual life, that the only remedy is flight and the removal of occasions. St. Philip Neri used to say that in this warfare only cowards, that is, they that fly from the occasions of defeat, shall be conquerors. St. Thomas has said before: "Whoever can resist the other vices cannot resist this except by flight."

Although you have been free from such affections, you must still guard yourself against them with all possible care; for you too are exposed to the danger of being caught in the snare into which, through their own negligence, others have fallen. To preserve your soul free from every dangerous attachment, I advise you, in the language of St. Teresa, first, to prize yourself more for the plainness than for the elegance of your manners, the agreeableness of your conversation, or the facility of paying compliments to seculars. "With externs," says St. Catharine of Sienna in a letter to her niece, "You should be modest; your head should be bowed down, and your manner and conversation simple and unaffected." At the grate be careful to abstain from unguarded looks and indecent laughter, and never appear in a habit affectedly neat. It would be a still greater fault to go to the grate with any badge of worldly pomp or vanity.

In a word, if you expect to escape every danger, remove yourself as much as possible from all conversation with seculars. "Sit solitary," says St. Bernard, "As the turtle: have nothing to do with crowds." Remain in solitude; love the choir and the cell, and shun the parlour as the abode of pestilence. To consecrate your whole being to God, you have left the world; what, then, have you to do with seculars? "If," says the Venerable Sister Jane of St. Stephen, of the Order of St. Francis, "You are the spouse of the King of kings, turn not your eyes toward slaves." It is a crime in a slave to fix his eyes on the king's spouse, and should the queen take complacency in his attention to her, she would be guilty of a similar transgression. Speaking of nuns, St. Catharine of Sienna says: "We shall not be spouses but sacrilegious violators of our engagements, if we seek for happiness in the gratification of self-love; if we hate the cell, and love the society of seculars." Should you, in conversation, ever feel a disorderly affection, stifle it at once before it acquires the strength of a giant. "While," says St. Jerome, "The enemy is small, destroy him." To kill a lion when young is an easy task; but to conquer him when he has attained full growth is a work of extreme and insuperable difficulty.

It would be still more criminal and disgraceful to permit any secular to indulge in indecent jests; I do not speak of improper familiarities, not wishing to suppose such an excess. Should any worldling carry his sacrilegious insolence so far as to utter such jests in your presence, imagine not that because you only listen you are blameless By not retiring at once you cooperate with him and render yourself a partaker of his guilt. Besides, should you not instantly withdraw from such infernal conversation you will soon become more criminal than its author; and from the dignity of the spouse of Jesus you will fall to the degraded condition of the slave of Satan. Besides, you might easily be the cause of ruin to your convent; for such a religious that keeps up so unhallowed a relationship is sufficient by her bad example to seduce others into doing the same thing.

Be specially on your guard if your brother or another of your relatives in visiting you brings with him one of his friends who has taken a fancy to you; they may perhaps call in your aunt to be present, but you will after all be the principal person in the scene. Should you ever perceive that such a snare has been laid, cast down your eyes at once, keep silence, and show yourself very grave; but the best thing for you to do would be to go away immediately. If later on you are again called to the parlour, knowing that the same person is there, send word that you are busy and that you cannot go. Be careful not to act otherwise, for if you again allow that person to have an interview with you, I shall look upon you as lost.

Likewise, if you receive from any one a letter in which you notice tender and affectionate words, tear up the letter at once, throw it into the fire, and do not answer it. If, however, on account of some matter of importance, an answer should be necessary, answer it briefly and seriously, without showing that you have taken the least pleasure in the sentiments that have been expressed to you, or that you have paid any attention to them. And if afterwards the same person calls you to the grate, refuse absolutely to go there; for if after his letter you consent to speak to him, it will be all over with you. You must know, besides, that you will be an accomplice of the same disorder if you have less fear to displease God than to displease one of your sisters by daring to encourage her in her unlawful attachment. In this case you would have to expect an exemplary chastisement, such as was inflicted upon a religious who was sacristan. To please one of her sisters she took upon herself the care of having a letter forwarded to a person with whom her companion kept up an improper correspondence. But when she gave the letter to the porter, the latter, being in a hurry, closed the revolving turn of the sacristy with such violence that her hand was caught and entirely torn off. She died a few days after, in consequence of this accident.

With religious and ecclesiastics who visit you, not for the purpose of speaking of God, nor for your spiritual good, but for the pleasure of your society, you should be reserved. I would recommend you to speak with your confessor only in the tribunal of penance. I advise you to abstain as much as possible from all correspondence with him by little presents, or by any similar means; and if you have to speak to him, do so at the turn and not at the grate. It is of importance that you use great reserve in regard to your directors, because the confidence that you have to repose in them by revealing to them the secrets of your conscience is always accompanied by a certain sympathy, which, if it is not moderated, may degenerate into a fire of hell. This is the reason why I counsel you to abstain as much as possible from having any worldly business with your confessor; do not make him presents; do not undertake the care of his secular affairs, of providing him with meals, of taking care of his linen, and other similar things. "Oh!" says St. Teresa, "What obstacles does such worldly correspondence present to the spiritual progress of religious." Should there be an ancient custom in your convent of making presents to the confessor, it will be enough for you to send him two or three times a year some trifle as a mark of attention. Be always most watchful over your words so that nothing may ever escape you that would express the least affection or tenderness.

Do not pretend that there is no danger because that priest is a saint. "Nor," says St. Thomas, "Are they to be less avoided because they are more holy: for the greater their sanctity the more they excite sentiments of affection." The Venerable Father Sertorio Caputo of the Society of Jesus says that the devil first makes us love a man's virtue, then his person, and at length draws us over the precipice. St. Thomas teaches that the devil at first kindles an attachment which only slightly wounds the soul: but what appeared to be pure angelic love soon degenerates into the human affection of beings clothed with flesh. Looks and words of tenderness follow; these are succeeded by a desire of each other's society: thus by degrees a holy attachment will be converted into a natural affection. Such is the doctrine of St. Thomas.

St. Bonaventure gives five marks by which we may ascertain whether a mutual attachment between two friends is pure or otherwise, 1. It is not pure when it leads to long and useless discourses; and when conversations are very long they are always useless. 2. When each delights in looking at each other and in praising each other. 3. When either excuses the other's defects. 4. When they manifest certain little jealousies. 5. When either feels unhappy at being separated from the other. The attachment is not pure when personal beauty or gracefulness is a source of pleasure; when either desires to be esteemed by the other, or when either is unwilling that his friend should receive attention from others; when one does not wish that others should observe, hear, or speak of what is passing.

Father Peter Consolini of the Oratory has justly remarked that we should treat with holy persons of a different sex as with the souls in purgatory that is, at a distance, and without looking at them. Some religious have a strong desire of conversing with their spiritual Father because they imagine that his instructions will stimulate their fervor. But what need is there of such conversations, of such long and familiar discourses? Have they not an abundant supply of spiritual books? Have they not spiritual reading at table and at prayer? Have they not the benefit of sermons in the church? Without any of these the reading and observance of their Rules and Constitutions ought to be sufficient to make them saints.

What has been said refers to outside persons; but it is necessary to remark that even among the religious themselves inordinate attachments may be found, especially among those who are young. "Young man," says St. Basil, "Avoid familiarity with your equals: how many young persons has the devil, through their companions, drawn into hell to be burned with eternal fire." Many of them, continues the saint, were, in the beginning enticed into a certain attachment that appeared to be charity, but that afterwards led them to the loss of peace and of the perfection of their state. "Love," says Blessed Angela of Foligno, "Includes every evil as well as every good. I do not speak of criminal love, which everyone knows should be avoided, but of the love that one friend entertains for another; and that may degenerate into an irregular affection. Frequent conversations along with the manifestation of mutual regard produce too close a union of their hearts, render their friendship noxious; and by strengthening their attachment, obscure the light of reason. Each yields to the will of the other, and thus both are led into the neglect of duty."

It is, moreover, to be remarked, that if the friendships with outside persons cause more scandal, the friendships that exist at home among the religious themselves are more dangerous, either because they are more difficult to remove, or because the occasion is more proximate. Would to God that the religious in the house of the Lord may never have the misfortune to commit a grave fault against chastity! Isaias regards such a one as already lost. He says: In the land of the saints he hath done wicked things, and he shall not see the glory of the Lord. Hence those nuns who have charge of the education of young pupils must always be watchful in regard to their conduct, and should not scruple to suspect the worst. When they perceive any attachment or familiarity between two young persons they must separate them at once, and not permit them to go together, and they should continually keep their eyes upon them lest any evil should happen. They should also from time to time exhort them in general to avoid, as they would avoid death, ever concealing through shame any sin in confession, and for this purpose they should relate to them the sad example of persons who had the misfortune of being condemned to hell for having made sacrilegious confessions.

St. Basil prescribed a very severe chastisement for the nuns of his Order who should entertain particular friendships. St. Bernard calls such friendships "Poisoned attachments, and the enemies of the peace of communities." They are a source of disturbance, of murmurings, of irregularities, of factions, and of parties; and sometimes they influence the votes at elections to office in favour not of the most worthy, but of the greatest favourites. Let it be your study to love all and to serve all, so that each will regard you as a friend. But abstain from familiarity with any; let your intimacy be only with God. Be particularly careful to avoid familiarity with all who manifest attachment to you. The way through which you walk in this life is dark and slippery: if you select an imperfect companion who will lead you to the precipice, you are lost.

Beware of all human respect of the accursed fear of what others will say or think of you. "If," you will say, I give up all intercourse with such a secular; if I separate from such a one; if I consecrate myself to retirement, to prayer, and to mortification what will be said of me? I shall be an object of jest and derision to all. Ah, how many religious of both sexes has this accursed weakness of human respect brought to eternal misery? "Oh!" says St. Augustine, "How many has this infirmity precipitated into hell?"—St. Francis Borgia says that he who desires to consecrate himself to God must, in the first place, trample under his feet all regard for what others will say of him. O my God, why do we not ask what Jesus Christ or his holy mother will think of our conduct?

My spouse, says our Lord, is a garden enclosed. To be the true spouse of Jesus, the heart of a religious must be an enclosed garden, excluding every affection that is not for God. Remember that to cherish in the soul any strange affection is, perhaps, of all the defects of nuns the most displeasing to God. He requires the full and undivided possession of the heart of his spouse. Even men cannot bear with any division in the affections of their spouses. In conclusion, I exhort you to endeavor to love God as if he and you were the only beings in existence.

But before finishing, I cannot omit to blame the folly of certain religious who become fond of animals, such as cats and dogs. These they wish to have always with them at table, and even in bed. They often carry them in their arms, kiss them, and say even affectionate words to them. If these animals become sick they are greatly afflicted; if they die they are inconsolable, and are an annoyance to those who may have been the cause of the death. If such an affection is unreasonable even in a person of the world, how much more is it unreasonable in a spouse of Jesus Christ!

Prayer.

My Jesus, I already understand Thee. Thou dost desire my whole heart and all my love; and I desire to consecrate my whole soul and all my affections to Thee. After all the insults which I have offered to Thy majesty, I deserve to be abandoned by Thee. But I feel that Thou dost still call me to Thy love. Thou shall, thou sayest, love the Lord thy God with thy whole heart. I desire, O my God, to obey, and henceforth to love Thee only. Oh that I were wholly consumed for Thee, O my Jesus, who hast been entirely consumed for my salvation! For my sake Thou hast given all Thy blood; for my redemption, Thou hast spent Thy life; and shall I be reserved with Thee? Even a thousand hearts are too little to love Thee, and shall I give a part of this, my miserable heart, to creatures? No Thou dost wish for it entirely; I give it wholly to Thee Accept my being, O my Jesus, my Love, and my Spouse. I am Thine, and entirely Thine: dispose of me as Thou pleasest.

Mary, my hope, unite me with thy Son Jesus; make me belong entirely to him. From thee I desire this favour—from thee I hope for it.

CHAPTER XI

HOLY HUMILITY.

The Advantages of Humility.

HUMILITY has been regarded by the saints as the basis and guardian of all virtues. Although in point of excellence the virtue of humility does not hold the highest rank, still, according to St. Thomas, because it is the foundation of all virtues it has obtained the first place among them. Hence, as in the structure of an edifice, the foundation takes precedence of the walls, and even of the golden ornaments, so, to expel pride, which God resists, humility must, in the edification of the spiritual man, precede all other virtues. "Humility," says the angelic Doctor "Holds the first place, inasmuch as it expels pride, which God resists." Hence St. Gregory asserts that "He who gathers virtues without humility is like the man who carries dust against the wind." His virtues shall be scattered.

There was in the desert a certain hermit who had a high character for sanctity. At the hour of death he sent for the abbot, and asked from him the Viaticum. During the administration of the holy sacrament a public robber ran to the cell; but seized with compunction for his sins, he esteemed himself unworthy to enter, or to be present at so sacred a ceremony, and in the humility of his soul exclaimed: "Oh that I were what you are!" The dying monk heard the words, and, swelled with pride, said: "Happy, indeed, should you be were you as holy as I am." After these words he expired: the robber immediately ran off from the place for the purpose of going to confession; on his way he fell over a precipice and was killed. At the death of the hermit his companion burst into tears; but at the fate of the robber he exulted with joy. Being asked why he wept over the death of the former and rejoiced at the melancholy end of the latter, he replied: Because the robber was saved by contrition for his past sins, but my companion is damned in punishment of his pride. Do not imagine that the hermit yielded to pride only at the hour of death: from his last words it is clear that pride had long before taken root in his heart; by its baneful influence he was brought to a miserable eternity. "Unless," says St. Augustine, "Humility shall have preceded, shall be continued, and shall have followed, pride will wrest the whole from our hands." Yes, the rapacious grasp of pride shall tear from us every good work which is not preceded, accompanied, and followed by humility.

This sublime virtue was but little known, but little loved, and greatly abhorred on earth, where pride, the cause of the ruin of Adam and of his posterity, enjoyed universal sway. Therefore the Son of God came down from heaven to teach it to men by his example as well as by his preaching. To instruct them in humility he came upon earth in the likeness of flesh and in the form of a servant. He emptied himself, says the Apostle, taking the form of a servant. He wished to be treated as the most contemptible of men. Despised, says the Prophet Isaias, and the most abject of men. Behold him in Bethlehem, born in a stable and laid in a manger; in Nazareth, poor, unknown, and employed in the humble occupation of assisting a poor artisan. Look at him in Jerusalem, scourged as a slave, buffeted as the vilest of men, crowned with thorns as a mock king, and in the end suffering as a malefactor the ignominious death of the cross. And with all his humiliations before your eyes hearken to his advice: I have given you an example, that as I have done so you do also. As if he said: My children, I have embraced so much ignominy that you may not refuse abjection. Speaking of the humiliations of the Son of God, St. Augustine says: "If this medicine cure not your pride, I know not what will heal it." Hence in one of his epistles to Dioscorus he tells his friends that it is principally by humility a man is made the disciple of Jesus, and that the soul is prepared for a union with God. "The first," says the saint, "Is humility; the second, humility; the third, humility, and as often as you would ask I should answer, humility."

The proud are objects of hatred and abomination before God. Every proud man, says the Holy Ghost, is an abomination to the Lord. Yes; for the proud man is a robber, and is blind; he is a liar, and the truth is not in him. He is a robber, because he appropriates to himself what belongs to God. What hast thou that thou hast not received? Would it not be the extreme of folly in a brute animal (were it gifted with reason) to glory in the gilded trappings of which it knows it may be stripped at the beck of its master? The proud man is blind, as we learn from the Apocalypse of St. John. Thou sayest I am rich, and knowest not that thou art wretched and blind. And what has man of his own but nothingness and sin? Even the little good that he does, when examined with rigor, will appear full of imperfection. "All our justice," says St.

Bernard, "If rigorously judged, will be found to be injustice." Lastly, the proud man is a liar, and the truth is not in him. For all his advantages, whether of nature—such as health, talent, beauty, and the like; or of grace—such as good desires, a docile heart, and an enlightened mind, are all the gifts of God. By the grace of God, says St. Paul, I am what I am. The same apostle tells us that of ourselves we are not capable of even a good thought. Not that we are sufficient to think anything of ourselves as of ourselves.

Woe to the proud religious! Into a haughty soul the Spirit of God cannot enter; over all its actions the devil exercises the most arbitrary despotism. "With the proud religious," says St. Joseph Calasanctius, "Satan sports himself as with a toy." Cesarius relates that when a demoniac was once brought to a certain monastery, the abbot asked the evil spirit whether he would depart at the command of a certain young monk who was reputed a saint. "No," replied the demon, "I am not afraid of him, because he is proud."

To preserve his servants from pride, the Lord sometimes permits them to be afflicted with the shameful solicitations of the flesh; to their repeated prayers to be delivered from the suggestions of Satan and of their own corruption he appears deaf, and leaves them to combat with the temptation. It was thus he treated St. Paul; and, says the saint, lest the greatness of the revelations should exalt me, there was given to me a sting of the flesh, an angel of Satan to buffet me. For which thing thrice I besought the Lord that it might depart from me, and , he said to me, My grace is sufficient for thee. "To keep him humble," says St. Jerome, "The Almighty refused to deliver the apostle from the molestation of the flesh by which he was tormented." Moreover, to teach them humility, the Lord sometimes permits the elect to fall into sin. Thus, David acknowledges that he sinned because he had not been humble. Before I was humbled, I offended.

"God," says St. Augustine, "Sits on high; you humble yourself, and he descends to you; you exalt yourself, and he flies from you." The royal prophet says that the Lord looketh at the low, and the high he knoweth afar off. He regards the humble with an affectionate eye, but the proud he beholds only at a distance. As we cannot recognize a person whom we see from afar, so the Lord appears to tell the proud, in the words of the Psalmist, that he knows them not. There was in a certain monastery a religious who had the insolence to say to one of her companions: "You and I wear, indeed, the same habit, and sit at the same table; but though my equal in religion, you are not fit to be a servant in my father's house." Oh, how poor and naked before the Lord was this haughty nun!

The proud are hateful before God; he cannot bear them. As soon as the angels yielded to pride, he banished them from paradise and sent them into hell, far distant from his presence. The words of God must be fulfilled: Whosoever, says the Lord, shall exalt himself, shall be humbled. St. Peter Damian relates that a certain proud man had resolved to assert his right to an estate by single combat; before the time appointed for the duel he went to Mass, and hearing in the church the above-mentioned words of the Gospel: Whosoever shall exalt himself, shall be humbled, he exclaimed: This cannot be true: for had I humbled myself I should have lost my property and my character. But when he came to the combat, his sacrilegious tongue was cut across by the sword of his antagonist, and he instantly fell dead on the ground.

God, says St. James, resisteth the proud, and giveth grace to the humble. The Lord has promised to hear the prayers of all. Everyone that asketh, receiveth. The proud he hears not; according to the Apostle, he resists their petitions. But to the humble he is liberal beyond measure: He giveth grace to the humble. To them he opens his hands, and grants whatsoever they ask or desire. Humble thyself to God, says the Holy Ghost, and wait for his hands. Humble your soul before the Lord, and expect from his hands whatever you seek from him.

"Give me, O Lord," exclaims St. Augustine, "The treasure of humility." Humility is a treasure, because upon the humble the Lord pours every blessing in abundance. A heart full of self cannot be replenished with the gifts of God. To receive the divine favors, the soul must be first emptied by the knowledge of her own nothingness. Thou sendest forth, says David, springs in the vales: between the midst of the hills the waters shall pass. God makes the waters of his graces abound in the valleys, that is, in humble souls; but not on the mountains; the emblems of the proud and the haughty. In the midst of these, his graces pass, but remain not upon them. Because, says Mary, he hath regarded the humility of his handmaid. . . . He that is mighty hath done great things to me. The Lord looking upon my humility, and my sense of

211

nothingness, hath bestowed great favors upon me.

St. Teresa relates of herself, that the greatest graces that she received from God were infused into her soul when she humbled herself most before the Lord in prayer. The prayer of him that humbleth himself shall pierce the clouds, and he will not depart till the Most High behold. The humble obtain from God whatever they ask: they need not be afraid of being confounded, or of being left without consolation. Let not, says David, the humble be turned away with confusion. Hence, St. Joseph Calasanctius used to say: "If you wish to be a saint, be humble; if you wish to be a very great saint, be most humble." To St. Francis Borgia, while a secular, a holy man once said: "If you desire to be a saint, never let a day pass without thinking of your miseries." Hence the saint spent every day the first two hours of prayer in the study of his own nothingness, and in sentiments of self-contempt.

St. Gregory says "That pride is the most evident mark of the reprobate; but humility is, on the contrary, the most evident mark of the elect." Seeing the world covered with the toils of the devil, St. Anthony, with; sigh, exclaimed: "Who can escape so many snares!" "Anthony," replied a strange voice, "It is only humility that passes through them with security: the humble man is not in danger of being caught by them." In a word, unless we are like infants, not in years but in humility, we shall never attain salvation. Unless you become as little children, you shall not enter the kingdom of heaven. In the life of St. Palemon it is related that a certain monk who walked on burning coals said to his companions: Which of you can tread on red-hot fire without being burnt. The saint reproved him for his vanity, but the unhappy man did not amend. Puffed up with pride, he afterwards fell into sin, and died without repentance.

To the humble who are despised and persecuted on earth is promised the glory of God's kingdom. Blessed are ye when they shall revile and persecute you, for your reward is very great in heaven. The humble shall be happy in this life as well as in the next. Learn of me, says Jesus, because I am meek and humble of heart; and you shall find rest to your souls. The proud never enjoy peace, because they never receive the respect or attention which a vain opinion of their own greatness makes them regard as their due. When loaded with honors, they are not content; either because they see others still more exalted; or, because they desire some unattainable dignity, the absence of which is to them a source of torture, not to be removed by the gratification arising from all the honors that they enjoy. Great, indeed, was the glory of Aman, in the court of Assuerus, where he sat at the monarchs table. But, because Mardochai would not salute him, he was unhappy. And whereas I have all these things, I think I have nothing so long as I see Mardochai, the Jew, sitting before the king's gate. Being the result of constraint and of human respect, the honor shown to the great does not give true joy. "True glory," says St. Jerome, "Like a shadow, follows virtue: it flies from all who grasp at it, and seeks after those who despise it."

The humble man is always content, because whatever respect is paid to him he deems to be above his merits, and whatever contempt may be offered to him he regards as far short of what is due to his sins. In humiliation he exclaims with holy Job: I have sinned, and indeed I have offended, and I have not received what I have deserved. Previously to a long journey which he was obliged to make, St. Francis Borgia was advised to dispatch a courier, who would secure accommodation for his master at the hotels where he intended to stop. "I never," replied the saint, "Fail to send my courier before me. But do you know who he is? My courier is the thought of hell, which my sins have merited; this thought makes every lodging appear to me a palace in comparison of the dungeon to which I deserve to be condemned."

Prayer.

O my God, after having committed so many sins, how is it possible that such an excess of pride should still reign in my soul? I now see that my faults have not only rendered me ungrateful to Thee, but have also made me proud. Cast me not away from thy face, as I have deserved. Have pity on me: enlighten my soul, and make me feel what I am and what I merit. How many, for fewer sins than I have committed, are now in hell, and have no hope of pardon! I know that Thou dost offer me pardon if I wish for it. Yes, Lord, I desire it: my Redeemer, pardon me all my sins of pride, by which I have not only despised my neighbour, but have also despised Thee, my Sovereign Good. With St. Catharine of Genoa I will say: "My God, no more sins, no more sins." I have sinned enough. I desire never more to abuse Thy patience. I love Thee, O my God, and I desire to spend the remainder of my life only in loving and in pleasing Thee. My Jesus, assist me. The stronger my present desire to belong entirely to Thee, the more violently will the powers of hell tempt me to sin. Assist me, O Lord, and leave me not in my own hands.

Most holy Virgin Mary, thou knowest that in thee I have placed all my hopes; do not cease to assist me by thy prayers, which God never rejects.

II.

The Humility of the Intellect or of the Judgment.

After having maturely considered the great advantages of humility, let us now examine what must be done for its attainment.

There are two sorts of humility: the humility of the intellect, and the humility of the will or of the heart. Here we shall speak of the former, without which the latter cannot be acquired.

Humility of the intellect consists in thinking lowly of ourselves; in esteeming ourselves to be vile and miserable creatures, such as we really are. "Humility," says St. Bernard, "Is a virtue which, by the knowledge of himself, makes a man contemptible in his own estimation." Humility is truth, as St. Teresa has well said, and therefore the Lord greatly loves the humble, because they love the truth. It is too true that we are nothing; that we are ignorant, blind, and unable to do any good. Of our own we have nothing but sin, which renders us worse than nothing; and of ourselves we can do nothing but evil. Whatever good we have or perform belongs to God and comes from his hands. This truth the humble man keeps continually before his eyes; he therefore appropriates to himself only what is evil, deems himself worthy of all sorts of contempt, and cannot bear to hear others attribute to him what he does not deserve. On the contrary, he delights in seeing himself despised and treated according to his deserts; and thus renders his soul most pleasing to God. "A Christian," says St. Gregory, "Becomes estimable before God in proportion as he is despicable in his own eyes." Hence, speaking of nuns, St. Mary Magdalene de Pazzi used to say, that the two foundations of religious perfection are the love of God and the contempt of self. "Because," says the saint, "The nun who will have humbled herself most upon earth shall see God most clearly in heaven."

It is necessary, then, to pray continually in the words of St. Augustine: "May I know myself; may I know Thee, O my God, that thus I may love thee and despise myself." Make me, O Lord, understand what I am and what Thou art. Thou art the source of every good: I am misery itself. Of myself I have nothing, I know nothing, I can do nothing but evil. It is only the humble that truly honor God. He, says the Holy Ghost, is honoured by the humble. Yes, it is only the humble that can give glory to the Lord, for they alone acknowledge him to be the supreme and only good. If, then, you desire to honor God, keep continually in view all your miseries; confess in the sincerity of your soul, that of yourself you are only nothingness and sinfulness, and that whatsoever you possess belongs to God. And convinced of your own wretchedness, consider yourself deserving only of contempt and punishment; and offer yourself to accept all the chastisements with which God will visit you.

As a sequence of these principles we give here the following rules:

I. Be careful never to boast of anything. Far different from yours was the conduct of the saints. It is my continual practice to exhort all to read, for their spiritual reading, the lives of the saints. The great labors and exertions of the saints for God's glory will humble our pride, and make us ashamed of the little we do or have done for him. But how is it possible that we should glory in anything, when we know that all the virtues that we possess are the gifts of God. "Who," says St. Bernard, "Could abstain from laughing, if the clouds boasted of having begotten rain." Whoever glories in any good action deserves to be treated with similar derision. Father M. Avila relates that a certain rich nobleman who had married a peasant, to prevent her from being puffed up with pride at seeing herself attended by servants and dressed in rich apparel, caused the miserable garment which she wore before her marriage to be preserved and to be kept continually before her eyes. You should imitate his example. When you perceive that you have performed a good work or acquired any virtue, look back to your former state; remember what you were, and conclude that all the good that you possess is but an alms from the Almighty. "Whosoever," says St. Augustine, "Reckons up to Thee, O Lord, his own merits, what else does he reckon up but Thy gifts." Whenever St. Teresa performed a good work, or saw an act of virtue performed by others, she immediately burst out into the praises of God, and referred the whole to him as to its author. Hence the saint justly observes, that it is not incompatible with humility to acknowledge the special graces that God has given more abundantly to us than to others. Such an acknowledgment, continues the saint, is not pride; on the contrary, by making us feel that we are more unworthy, and at the same time more favoured, than others, it assists our humility and stimulates our gratitude. The saint adds, that a Christian who does not reflect with gratitude on the sublime graces that he has received, will never resolve to do great things for God. But in contemplating the gifts that God has bestowed upon us we must always distinguish between what belongs to him and what belongs to us. St. Paul scrupled not to assert that for the glory of the Lord Jesus he had done more than all the other apostles. I have he says, labored more abundantly than all they. But he immediately confessed that his labors were not his own works, but the fruit of the divine grace by which he was assisted: Yet not I, but the grace of God with me.

II. Since without the divine aid you can do nothing, be careful never to confide in your own strength; but after the example of St. Philip Neri, endeavor to live in continual and utter distrust of yourself. Like St. Peter, who protested that not even death would induce him to deny his master, the proud man trusts in his own courage, and therefore yields to temptation. Because he confided in himself, the apostle had no sooner entered the house of the high-priest than he denied Jesus Christ, Be careful never to place confidence in your own resolutions or in your present good dispositions; but put your whole trust in God, saying with St. Paul: I can do all things in him who strengtheneth me. If you cast away all self-confidence, and place all your hopes in the Lord, you may then expect to do great things for God. They that hope in the Lord, says the prophet Isaias, shall renew their strength. Yes, the humble, who trust in the Lord, shall renew their strength; distrusting themselves, they shall lay aside their own weakness and put on the strength of God. Hence, St. Joseph Calasanctius used to say, that "Whoever desires to be the instrument of God in great undertakings, should seek to be the lowest of all." Strive to imitate the conduct of St. Catharine of Sienna, who, when tempted to vainglory, would make an act of humility, and when tempted to despair, would make an act of confidence in God. Enraged at her conduct, the devil began one day to curse her and the person who taught her this mode of resisting his temptations; and added, that he "Knew not how to attack her." When, therefore, Satan tells you that you are in no danger of falling, tremble; and reflect that, should God abandon you for a moment, you are lost. When he tempts you to despair, exclaim in the loving words of David: In thee, O Lord, have I hoped: let me never be confounded. In Thee, O Lord, I have placed all my hopes; I trust that I shall not be confounded, deprived of Thy grace, and made the slave of hell.

III. Should you be so unfortunate as to commit a fault, take care not to give way to diffidence, but humble your soul; repent, and with a stronger sense of your own weakness, throw yourself into the arms of the Lord. To be angry with ourselves after having committed a fault, is not an act of humility, but of pride, which makes us wonder how we could have fallen into such a defect. Yes, it is pride and a delusion of the devil, who seeks to draw us away from the path of perfection, to cast us into despair of advancing in virtue, and thus precipitate us into more grievous sins. After a fault we should redouble our confidence in God, and thus take occasion from our infidelity to place still greater hopes in his mercy. To them that love God, says St. Paul, all things work together unto good. "Yes," adds the Gloss,—even sins. The Lord once said to St. Gertrude: "When a person's hands are stained he washes them, and they become cleaner than before they were soiled." So the soul that commits a fault, being purified by repentance, is made more pleasing in the eyes of God than she was before her transgression. To teach them to distrust themselves, and to confide only in him, God who are not well grounded in humility, to fall into some defect. When, then, dear sister, you commit a fault, endeavor to repair it immediately by an act of love and of sorrow; resolve to amend, and redouble your confidence in God; say with St. Catharine of Genoa: "Lord, this is the fruit of my garden; if Thou dost not protect me I shall be guilty of still more grievous offences; but I purpose to avoid this fault for the future, and with the aid of Thy grace, I hope to keep this resolution." Should you ever relapse, act always in the same manner, and never abandon the resolution of becoming a saint.

IV. Should you ever see another commit some grievous sin, take care not to indulge in pride, nor to be surprised at her fall; but pity her misfortune, and trembling for yourself, say with holy David: Unless the Lord had been my helper, my soul had almost dwelt in hell. If the Almighty had not been my protector, I should at this moment be

buried in hell. Beware of even taking vain complacency in the exemption from faults that you perceive in your companions; otherwise, in
chastisement of your pride the Lord will permit you to fall into the
sins which they have committed. Cassian relates that a certain young
monk, being for a long time molested by a violent temptation to impurity, sought advice and consolation from an aged Father. Instead of
receiving encouragement and comfort he was loaded with reproaches.
"What!" said the old man, "Is it possible that a monk should be subject
to so abominable thoughts?" In punishment of his pride the Almighty
permitted the Father to be assailed by the spirit of impurity to such
a degree that he ran like a madman through the monastery. Hearing
of his miserable condition, the Abbot Appollo told him that God had
permitted this temptation to punish his conduct towards the young
monk, and also to teach him compassion for others in similar circumstances. The Apostle tells us that in correcting sinners we should not
treat them with contempt, lest God should permit us to be assailed by
the temptation to which they yielded, and perhaps to fall into the very
sin which we were surprised to see them commit. We should, before
we reprove others, consider that we are as miserable and as liable to
sin as our fallen brethren. Brethren, if any man be overtaken in a fault
. . . instruct such a one in the spirit of meekness, considering thyself
lest thou also be tempted. The same Cassian relates that a certain abbot
called Machete confessed that he himself had miserably fallen into
three faults, of which he had rashly judged his brethren.

V. Consider yourself the greatest sinner on this earth. They who are
truly humble, because they are most perfectly enlightened by God,
possess the most perfect knowledge, not only of the divine perfections,
but also of their own miseries and sins. Hence, notwithstanding their
extraordinary sanctity, the saints, not in the language of exaggeration,
but in the sincerity of their souls, called themselves the greatest sinners in the world. Thus St. Francis of Assisi called himself the worst of
sinners; St. Thomas of Villanova was kept in a state of continual fear
and trembling by the thought of the account he was one day to render
to God of his life; which, though full of virtue, appeared to him very
wicked. St. Gertrude considered it a miracle that the earth did not open
under her feet and swallow her up alive, in punishment of her sins. St.
Paul, the first hermit, was in the habit of exclaiming: "Woe to me, a
sinner, who am unworthy to bear the name of a monk." In the writings
of Father M. Avila we read of a person of great sanctity who besought

the Lord to make known to her the state of her soul. Her prayer was heard; and so deformed and abominable was the appearance of her soul, though stained only with the guilt of venial sins, that, struck with horror, she cried out: "For mercy's sake, O Lord, take away from before my eyes the representation of this monster!"

VI. Beware, then, of ever preferring yourself to anyone. To esteem yourself better than others, is abundantly sufficient to make you worse than all. "Others," says Tritemius, "You have despised; you have therefore become worse than others." Again to entertain a high opinion of your own deserts, is enough to deprive you of all merit. Humility consists principally in a sincere conviction that we deserve only reproach and chastisement. If, by preferring yourself to others, you have abused the gifts and graces which God has conferred upon you, they will only serve for your greater condemnation at the hour of judgment. But it is not enough to abstain from preferring yourself to any one; it is, moreover, necessary to consider yourself the last and worst of all your sisters in religion. First, because in yourself you see with certainty so many sins; but the sins of others you know not, and their secret virtues, which are hidden from your eyes, may render them very dear in the sight of God. You ought to consider also, that by the aid of the lights and graces which you have received from God you should at this moment be a saint. Ah, had they been given to an infidel, he would perhaps have become a seraph, and you are still so miserable and full of defects.
The consideration of your ingratitude should be sufficient to make you always regard yourself as a fit object of scorn to the whole Community: for, as St. Thomas teaches the malice of sin increases in proportion to the ingratitude of the sinner. Hence one of your sins may be more grievous in the sight of God than a hundred sins of another less favoured than you have been. But you know that you have already committed many sins; that your life has been one continued series of voluntary faults; and that whatever good you may have done is so full of imperfection and of self-love, that it is more deserving of punishment than of remuneration.

VII. All these considerations ought to inspire you with the sentiments of humility which St. Mary Magdalene de Pazzi inculcated on her spiritual children, with a continual sense of your unworthiness to kiss the ground on which your sisters walk. You ought to consider that, had you received all imaginable insults, and were you confined in the bottom of hell, under the feet of all the damned, all this would be but little in comparison with what you deserve. And therefore, from the bottomless abyss of your own miseries you should continually cry out, with holy David: Incline unto my aid, O God; O Lord, make haste to help me. Lord, hasten to my assistance, otherwise I am lost, and shall offend Thee more than ever, and more than all sinners. But this prayer must be repeated continually— almost every moment—in the choir, in the cell, in going through the monastery, at the grate, at table, at rising, and going to sleep. You must cry out: "Assist me, O Lord, assist me: Lord have mercy on me." At the very moment you cease to invoke the divine aid you may become the most wicked monster in creation. Shun, as death itself, every, even the most trifling, act or thought of pride. I conclude with that great saying of St. Bernard: "In the soul no humiliation, however great, is to be feared; but the least elation is to be regarded with horror." Yes; for the smallest degree of arrogance may lead us into every evil.

Prayer.

O God of my soul! I thank Thee for making me feel that whatever the world esteems is all folly. Give me grace to detach my heart from all creatures before death separates me from them. Unhappy me, who have been so many years in Thy house; I have left the world to become a saint, and till now, what progress have I made? Alas, how many disgusting wounds do I see in my soul! My Jesus, have pity on me and heal me. Thou art able and willing to heal me if I consent to a change of life. Yes, Lord, I desire to amend. If the sinner repent, Thou hast promised to forget his wickedness. That if the wicked do penance . . . I will not remember all his iniquities. I am sorry, O my God, above all things for having despised Thy love: forget, then, O Lord, all the displeasure I have given Thee. For the future I desire to lose my life sooner than give Thee the smallest offence. My God, I desire to love Thee; if I do not love Thee, whom shall I love? Thou art most worthy of my love: Thou hast called me to religion. Thou hast loaded me with Thy grace. Thou alone, therefore, dost merit all my love; Thee alone do I desire to love.

My Queen and my great advocate, Mary, assist me by Thy intercession, that I may be no longer ungrateful to Thy Son.

III.

Humility of the Heart or of the Will.

Humility of the intellect consists, as we have seen, in esteeming one's self worthy of reproach and scorn: but humility of the will consists in desiring to be despised by others, and in taking pleasure in contempt. The latter is the most meritorious; because acts of the will are more pleasing to God than acts of the intellect.

Speaking of humility of the will, St. Bernard says: "The first degree is, not to wish for power; the second, to wish to be in a state of subjection to authority; the third is, in subjection to bear injuries with equanimity." Such is the humility of the heart which Jesus Christ wished to teach us by his own example. Learn of me, said the Redeemer, because I am meek and humble of heart. Many have humility on their tongue, but not in their heart. "They, indeed," says St. Gregory, "Confess with their lips that they are most wicked and most deserving of all sorts of chastisement; but they believe not what they say. For, when rebuked, they give way to disquietude, and deny that they are guilty of the fault for which they are corrected." To this class belonged a certain monk, who, as Cassian relates, used to say that he was a great sinner, and unworthy to breathe the breath of life. But when the Abbot Serapion corrected him for violating the Rule by idle visits to the cells of the other monks, he became greatly troubled. Seeing him disturbed, the abbot said: "Why, my son, are you so much disquieted? Hitherto you have called yourself a great sinner, and now you cannot bear from me a charitable admonition." Even in convents we sometimes find similar examples of haughty religious. Certain nuns proclaim that they are the most wicked of sinners, that they deserve a thousand hells. But should the abbess or a sister in religion point out to them any particular fault, or speak of their general tepidity, or of the little edification which they give to the Community, they immediately begin to vindicate their conduct, and in a tone of fretfulness exclaim: What evil or scandal have you seen in my conduct? You would do your duty much better by correcting the others who are guilty of faults that I never commit. A little before they confessed that their sins merited a thousand hells, and now they cannot bear a word of admonition. Such religious possess, indeed, humility in words, but know not the humility recommended by Jesus Christ, which is the humility of the heart.

There is, says the Holy Ghost, one that humbleth himself wickedly, and his interior is full of deceit. There are some who humble themselves, not from desire of being rebuked and despised, but through a motive of being esteemed humble and of being praised for their humility. But, according to St. Bernard, to seek praise from voluntary humiliations is not humility, but the destruction of humility, for it changes humility itself into an object of pride. Speculative humility, says St. Vincent de Paul, presents a very beautiful aspect; but practical humility, because it is nothing else than the love of abjection and contempt, is an object of horror to flesh and blood. Hence St. John Climacus observes that the proof of true humility consists, not in confessing our own sinfulness, but in rejoicing in the contempt due to sinners. "Self-disparagement," says the saint, "Is good, but to confirm the dispraise which others cast upon us, not to resent it but to delight in it, is still better." "When," says St. Gregory, "The humble man calls himself a sinner, he does not contradict others who say the same of him." No; when reproved for his faults he reasserts his own sinfulness. In a word, as St. Bernard says, "The truly humble man wishes, indeed, to be held in little estimation, but desires not to be praised for his humility." Instead of seeking to be esteemed for his humility he wishes to be regarded as a man deserving of contempt and full of imperfections; and because he deems himself worthy only of abjection, he delights in the humiliations which are heaped upon him. Hence, as St. Bernard teaches, "He converts humiliation into humility;" and all the humiliations that he receives only serve to render him more humble. St. Joseph Calasanctius used to say that "He who loves God seeks not to be reputed a saint, but to attain sanctity." If, dear sister, you wish to acquire true humility of heart, you must:—

I. In the first place, shun all self-praise, whether it regards your own actions, talents, virtues; the nobility, wealth, or connections of your family. Let another praise thee, says the wise man, and not thy own mouth. Self-praise never fails to earn the contempt, but seldom wins the respect of others. What would you say or think of a nun who would extol the respectability of her family, or who would boast of having better claims than her sisters to certain offices? Remember that if you indulge in empty boasting, others will say and think of you what you would say and think of her. In speaking of your own concerns, seek always to humble and never to exalt yourself. Self-dispraise can do you no injury; but the smallest portion of unmerited self-commendation may be productive of great evil. "To extol yourself slightly above your deserts is," says St. Bernard, "A great evil." He who in passing through a door bends his head more than is necessary, is free from all danger of injury; but he who carries it too high may be seriously hurt. Be careful, then, to speak of yourself humbly rather than boastingly, and to disclose your faults rather than your virtues. The best rule is, never to speak well or ill of yourself, but to regard yourself as unworthy to be even named in conversation. It frequently happens that in saying what tends to our own confusion we indulge a secret and refined pride. For the confusion arising from the voluntary manifestation of our defects excites within us a desire of obtaining the praise or reputation of being humble. This rule is not to be observed in the tribunal of penance: on the contrary, it will be always useful to make known to the confessor your defects, your evil inclinations; and, generally speaking, even the evil thoughts that pass through your mind. It is also very profitable to manifest, on some occasions, certain circumstances that redound to your shame. On such occasions be careful not to abstain from humbling your own pride. Father Villanova, of the Society of Jesus, was not ashamed to tell the whole Community that his brother was a poor laborer. Father Sacchini, likewise a Jesuit, having in a public place met his father, who was a muleteer, instantly ran to embrace him, and exclaimed: "O behold my father!"

Should it ever happen that you are compelled to listen to your own praise, endeavor to humble yourself, at least interiorly, by casting an eye at the grounds of self-contempt that have been already detailed. To the proud, says St. Gregory, praise, however undeserved, is delicious; but to the humble, even well-merited commendation is a source of grief and of affliction. And being exalted, says the Royal Prophet, I have been humbled and troubled. Like holy David, the humble man, says St. Gregory, is troubled at hearing his own praises. He sees that he has no claim to the virtues or to the good qualities that are ascribed to him; and he fears that by taking self-complacency in his good works he may lose whatever merit he has acquired before God, and that the Judge may say to him: Thou didst receive good things in thy lifetime. Whoever takes pleasure in listening to his own praise has already received his reward: he has no claim to any other remuneration. As gold, says the wise man, is tried in the furnace, so a man is tried by the mouth of him that praiseth. Yes, a man's spirit is tried by praise: when the commendation of his virtues excites sentiments, not of pleasure nor of pride, but of shame and confusion, then, indeed, his humility appears. St. Francis Borgia and St. Aloysius were greatly afflicted whenever they heard themselves extolled. When you are praised or treated with respect, humble your soul and tremble lest the honor that you receive should be to you an occasion of sin and of perdition. Consider that the esteem of men may prove your greatest misfortune; by fomenting pride it may contaminate your heart, and thus be the cause of your damnation.

Keep always before your eyes the great saying of St. Francis of Assisi: "What I am before God, that I am, and no more." Are you so foolish as to think that the esteem of men will render you more pleasing in the sight of God? When you are gratified and elated by the praises bestowed upon you, and are by them induced to think yourself better than the other religious, you may be assured that, while men extol your virtues, God shall cut you off. Be persuaded, then, that the praises of others will never make you more holy in the sight of God. St. Augustine says that as the reproach or slander of an enemy cannot deprive a man of the merit of his virtues, so the applause of a friend or admirer will not make him better than he really is. "A bad conscience," says St. Augustine, "Is not healed by the praise of a flatterer, nor a good one wounded by the contumely of the reviler." Whenever, then, you hear your own praises, say in your heart, with St. Augustine: "I know myself better than they do; and God knows me better than I do myself." They, indeed, praise me, but I, who see the state of my own soul better than they do, know that these praises are unmerited; God knows it still better than I do; he sees that I deserve neither honor nor respect, but all the contempt of earth and hell.

II. Secondly, as you ought carefully to refrain from all complacency in the praises that you receive from others, so you must abstain with still greater caution from asking any office of rank or dignity in the convent. "You must," as St. Mary Magdalene de Pazzi says, "Avoid with all possible care every exercise that is apt to attract attention, for it is in such exercises that pride delights." It is necessary to shun, even with horror, every honourable office in the monastery. In the convent of the Most Holy Trinity, in Naples, there was a very exemplary religious called Sister Archangela Sanfelice. The confessor said to her one day: "Sister Archangela, the nuns wish to make you abbess." At first she appeared afflicted and surprised, but afterwards expressed her readiness to accept the office. After signifying her assent, she was suddenly seized with a fit of apoplexy, which nearly deprived her of life, and obliged the nuns to seek another abbess.

"All worldly honor," says St. Hilary, "Is the business of the devil." Worldly honors are the means by which Satan gains many souls for hell. And, if the ambition of honors occasions great ruin in a worldling, it is productive of far greater havoc in a religious. "The body of the Church," says St. Leo, "Is defiled by the contention of the ambitious." Speaking of nuns, St. Teresa says that "Where they attend to punctilios of honor, fervor will never flourish." In another place she says, "The monastery in which points of honor and claims of precedence are attended to, may be considered as lost: from it the Spouse is already banished." Addressing her own Community, she says: "Should a Judas be ever found among you, expel her at once, as a source of infection; and deprive forever of all hope of success in her projects the nun who attempts to seek superiority over her companions. I would rather see this monastery burnt to the ground than ever see ambition enter into it." Similar were the sentiments of St. Jane Frances de Chantal. "I would," says the saint, "Sooner see my monastery buried in the sea, than ambition or the desire of office enter it."

Listen to the wise remarks of Peter de Blois on this subject. In one of his letters he describes the pestiferous effects of ambition, and its frightful ravages in the souls of Christians. Ambition, he says, though full of uncharitableness, puts on the garb of charity. Charity suffers all things for the attainment of eternal goods: ambition, too, endures every hardship, but only for the acquisition of the miserable honors of this world. Charity is kind, but particularly to the poor and the abject; ambition, too, abounds in benevolence, but only to the rich and powerful, who can gratify its cravings. Charity bears all things to please God: ambition submits to every wrong, but only through the vain motive of obtaining honors or office. O God, to what annoyance, inconvenience, fatigues, fears, expenses, and even reproaches and insults, must the ambitious submit, for the attainment of the dignity to which they aspire! Finally, charity believes and hopes all that regards the glory of eternity; but ambition believes and hopes only what regards the empty honors of this life.

But, in the end, what is the fruit of all the labors of the ambitious?

They only attain some empty dignity which contents not the heart, and which renders them, in the eyes of the others, objects of contempt rather than of respect. "By the sole desire of it," says St. Teresa, "Honor is lost: the greater the dignity obtained, the more disgraceful it is to the person who has procured it. For the more he has labored for its attainment, the more he has shown himself unworthy of it." St. Jane Frances de Chantal said that "They who esteem themselves most deserving of office are the most unworthy of it: because they want humility, which is the best disposition for the fulfillment of an office." God grant that the dignity which the ambitious procure may not be the cause of their eternal ruin. Father Vincent Carafa, of the Society of Jesus, having once visited a dying friend, to whom an office of great emolument, but at the same time of great danger, had been given, was requested by the sick man to obtain from God the restoration of his health. No, my friend, replied the Father, I shall not abuse my affection for you: desirous of your salvation, God calls you to another life while you are in the state of grace. I know not whether, if restored, to health, you would save your soul in the office which has been offered to you. The sick man peacefully accepted the stroke of death, and expired with sentiments of joy and resignation. "It is scarcely possible," says St. Bonaventure, "That he who delights in honors should not be in great danger." To take complacency in any dignity, particularly in the office of abbess, of assistant, mistress of novices, or in any other charge to which are annexed serious obligations, exposes a religious to great danger of perdition. But the condition of the nun who through ambition has procured such an office is still more perilous. For she cannot, without great difficulty, refuse any request to the sisters by whom she was promoted, and thus she will probably be lost. Besides, God is not bound to give her the aid necessary for the discharge of the duties of an office which she has procured by her own exertions. How, then, can she, bereft of the divine assistance, fulfill her obligations? Oh, how many shall we see condemned on the Day of Judgment for having obtained offices by their own efforts!

If, dear sister, you desire to preserve humility, do not allow yourself to be seduced by any desire of worldly glory. What shall I say of the nun who, to make a display of pomp and riches, is guilty of extravagance in the discharge of her office? What shall I say of the nun who, though a poor religious, receives with pleasure worldly titles? Were she truly humble, she would tell all, even the servants of her parents, that such titles are neither agreeable nor suited to her. It is certain that to a nun the title of reverend is more honorable than the appellation of noble; because the former is given to her as the spouse of Jesus, but it is only as a person of rank in the world that she can claim the latter. St. Francis Xavier used to say that to desire respect and honor, or to take complacency in them, is unworthy of a Christian, who should have always before his eyes the ignominies of Jesus Christ. How much more unsuited must such foolish ambition be to a religious, the consecrated spouse of the Redeemer, who lived for so many years in obscurity and contempt? St. Mary Magdalene de Pazzi used to say that "The honor of a nun consists in being the lowest of all, and in having a horror of being preferred to any." To surpass all her sisters in humility and in the love of Jesus should, says St. Thomas of Villanova, be the sole object of the ambition of religious. "Let your ambition be to be the most humble and the most dear to Jesus Christ." In entering religion you said, with holy David: I have chosen to be an abject in the house of my God, rather than to dwell in the tabernacles of Sinners. Yes, you then publicly declared your determination to prefer abjection in the house of the Lord, before honor and glory in a wicked world. And why should you be now attached to earthly vanities? St. Bonaventure tells you, that if you desire to be a saint, you must endeavor to lead a life of obscurity and contempt. "Love," says the saint, "To be unknown and despised," so that no attention whatever may be shown to you in the monastery.

Envy not the religious who surpass you in talent and understanding, or who are more highly esteemed by the Community than you are. Envy those only who are your superiors in charity and humility. Humiliation is preferable to all the applause and honor which the world can bestow. For a nun, the most useful of all sciences is that which teaches her to humble and despise herself, and to delight in being treated with contempt. God has not given you great abilities, because they might lead you to perdition. Be content, then, with the little talent that you have received: let the want of talent be to you an occasion of practicing humility, which is the safest, and indeed the only, way to save your soul and to become a saint. If others surpass you in the knowledge of governing, or in the art of acquiring the esteem of the Community, take care to outstrip all in the practice of humility. But, says St. Paul, let each esteem others better than themselves. They who are invested with authority over others are exposed to great danger of being puffed up with pride, of losing the divine light, and of thus becoming like sense-less beasts that seek only the miserable goods of the earth, and never think of the glory of eternity. And, says the Psalmist, when he was in honor he did not understand: he is compared to senseless beasts, and is become like to them.

If you wish to walk in the secure path, shun all posts of honor, and embrace the most abject exercises and offices. A religious who wishes to be a saint should seek only the meanest offices of the convent; and therefore she ought frequently to beg of the Superior, and of them that are in office, to employ her in the occupations that others decline. The spouse of the Canticles presents at one time the character of a solitary, at another of a warrior, and again of the cultivator of the vine; but she always appears full of love. Like her, every religious should perform all her actions through the love of her Spouse, and in all her occupa-tions should appear as a lover of Jesus Christ, and therefore she should not refuse any office or employment. The employments that the world regards as the most contemptible are the most important and exalted in religion, and are most sought after by the saints, because they are most dear to Jesus Christ. Cassian relates that, to shun the respect and veneration shown to him in Egypt, the Abbot Paphnutius fled from that country and betook himself to the monastery of St. Pachomius. Being unknown, he was at first entrusted with the cultivation of the garden, and enjoyed great happiness in his humble employment. As soon as he was recognized, he was removed from so mean a charge. But he wept continually for having lost the treasure that he found in his humilia-tion.

Endeavor also to practice humility by the poverty of your furniture and of your garments. The dress of St. Equitius was so humble, that, as St. Gregory relates, they who had not known him would have scorned to salute him. Oh, what a source of edification is poverty of dress! Of the two Macariuses it is related that, in passing the Nile along with certain seculars richly attired, the poverty of their garments made such an impression on one of the seculars, that he abandoned the world and became a monk. To keep the eyes modestly cast down, and to speak in a low tone of voice, helps to preserve humility. But it must be observed that such external acts assist humility of the heart when they are united with it. Without it they would be acts of pride the most abominable—of pride concealed under the garb of humility. "Pride," says St. Jerome,

"Is far more deformed when it is hidden under the outward appearance of humility."

Prayer.

My Jesus, I am ashamed to appear before Thee. Thou hast loved contempt and opprobrium, so as to die on the cross an object of derision and of scorn; and I cannot bear the smallest affront! Thou, the innocent Lamb of God, hast for my sake been saturated with ignominies, and I, a sinner, am so desirous of praise and honor. Ah, my Spouse, how unlike am I to Thee! This makes me tremble for my eternal salvation; for the predestined must be conformable to Thy image. But I will not distrust Thy mercy. It is from Thee I expect succour and a change of life. With Thy assistance, I purpose henceforward to suffer for the love of Thee all the contempt and all the injuries that shall be offered to me. Ah! Lord, by Thy example, Thou hast rendered ignominies agreeable and delightful to all who love Thee. I love Thee, and desire to do all that I can to please Thee. Pardon me all my sins of pride, of which I now repent with my whole heart; and give me strength to be faithful to the promise that I now make, never more to resent any affront that I may receive.

O Mary, my mother, the model of humility, obtain for me grace to imitate thee as much as possible.

IV.

Continuation of the Same Subject, and especially Patience, in bearing Contempt.

III. In the third place, to preserve humility, you must not allow yourself to be disquieted by reproof or correction. The nun who, when rebuked, yields to disquietude, shows that she has not yet acquired humility, and therefore should beg of God that holy virtue, which is so necessary for salvation. Father Rodriguez says that some religious resemble the hedgehog: when touched they become all thorns, and instantly break out into words of impatience, of reproach, and even of murmuring. "We have known many," says St. Gregory, "Who, when no one accuses them, confess themselves sinners; but when they have been corrected for a fault, they endeavor with all their might to defend themselves, and to remove the imputation of guilt." Such, too, is the practice of certain religious—they ought to attend to the words of the Holy Ghost: He that hateth to be reproved, walketh in the trace of a sinner. Whoever is disturbed by correction, walks not in the way of the just, but in the path of sinners—the road to hell.

St. Bernard says: Some are displeased with the physician who cures them by reproof, and are not angry with the man who wounds them by flattery. Terrible is the threat of the wise man against all who spurn correction: Because they have despised all my reproof, the prosperity of fools shall destroy them. The prosperity of fools consists in the privation or in the contempt of advice, and therefore they are miserably lost. The Venerable Bede gives a frightful account of the fate of two nuns who despised the admonitions of their Superior. Their irregularity became so great that they at length fled from the monastery. When brought back to the convent, they were asked by the abbess, St. Borgontofora, what had led them into such a crime? They answered that it was their inattention to her admonitions. Shortly after their return both were seized with a mortal disease, but could not be induced to confess their sins. Even at the point of death, to those who exhorted them to have recourse to the tribunal of penance they replied, Wait a little— wait; and turning to the religious, they exclaimed: Do you not see the crowd of demons who are come to carry us away? Calling for respite from the demons, they both died miserably without the sacraments.

St. John Chrysostom says that the just man when discovered in a fault weeps for his fall. The sinner, too, says the saint, if detected in a criminal act, weeps—not for his transgression, but because his guilt is known; and instead of repenting, he seeks to defend his conduct, and pours out his indignation on the friend who corrects him. Have you, dear sister, hitherto indulged in anger against those from whose charity you have received correction? And if you have, are you disposed to repeat such conduct? "Sister," says St. Bernard, "Give many thanks to him who has rebuked you: be not sad when he shall have shown you the way of salvation." Is it not most unjust to be displeased with the sister who points out to you the way to eternal life? Could it be done without violating the Rule, you would do well to procure, according to the advice of St. Mary Magdalene de Pazzi, a faithful companion who would remark to you all the faults that you do not perceive. You know that you are full of miseries and defects. The only remedy for them is to humble your soul when you perceive them, or when others make them known to you. "Our humility," says St. Augustine, "Is perfection." Since our manner of practicing the virtues of the Gospel is so full of imperfection, let us at least be perfect in humbling ourselves, and in rejoicing under the confusion occasioned by the reproofs we receive for the faults we have committed. It may be here observed, that to our pride undeserved reproach is more tolerable than well-merited censure, because the latter is more painful to self-love. When justly reproved, be careful to offer to God, in atonement for your transgression, the shame and confusion that you experience. Make use of that confusion as a means of repairing your fault; crush the scorpion on the wound he has inflicted, and be assured that the mercy of the Lord in granting you pardon will be proportioned to your humility in receiving correction.

When corrected for a fault, be careful never to defend or excuse yourself, and thus you will practice an act of humility highly pleasing to God. St. Teresa says that to a nun such an act is more profitable than to be present at ten sermons. Should you, then, ever receive an unmerited reprimand, abstain, in honor of holy humility, from the vindication of your conduct, unless, to prevent scandal to the Community, such vindication be necessary. To a religious who requested her director— Father Anthony Torres—to excuse her to a certain person who had charged her with a fault, the Father replied: "I am astonished at your request. I pity your weakness. I suppose that the occupations in which you were engaged for the last few days must have soon obliterated from your mind the remembrance of the doleful narrative which you so lately heard of the sorrows of your Spouse, who had been called a seducer. It is impossible that you can have remembered the calumnies and the blasphemies that were uttered against him, and at the same time request me to vindicate your character. Filled with sentiments of shame and confusion, and prostrate before the crucifix, implore of your crucified Spouse the pardon of your infidelity. Resolve neither on this nor on any other occasion to justify or excuse your conduct, but always acknowledge, however galling such acknowledgment may be, that you have erred. For your sake the Saviour died on a cross, saturated with opprobrium; and it is by humiliation that you are to obtain the possession of your Spouse."

St. Mary Magdalene de Pazzi says that to excuse one's self, even under a false accusation, is to cease to be a religious. A truly humble religious not only abstains from excusing her faults, but even seeks to make them known to all. In the "Prodigies of Grace" we read that a certain religious of the reformed Order of La Trappe, as soon as he committed a fault, confessed it—first to the abbot, then to the prior, and afterwards before the whole Chapter. St. Mary Magdalene de Pazzi used to say that the nun who manifests her faults merits to be washed from them by the blood of Jesus Christ.

IV. Fourthly, if you wish to acquire perfect humility, accept in peace all the contempt and bad treatment that you receive. These are easily borne by all who truly believe that in punishment of their sins they merit nothing but scoffs and insults. Humiliation is the touchstone of sanctity. St. John Chrysostom says that to receive affronts with meekness is the most certain proof of virtue. In his History of Japan, Father Crasset relates that during the last persecution, in consequence of having received an insult without resenting it, a certain Augustinian missionary, though disguised, was instantly taken for a Christian, and cast into prison by the idolaters, who asserted that no one but a Christian could practice such a virtue.

Some, says St. Francis of Assisi, imagine that sanctity consists in the recital of many prayers or in the performance of works of penance; but, not understanding the great merit of patience under insult, they cannot bear an injurious word. You will acquire more merit by meekly receiving an affront than by fasting ten days on bread and water. It will sometimes happen that a privilege that is refused to you will be conceded to others; that what you say will be treated with contempt, while the words of others are heard with respectful attention; that while the actions of others are the theme of general praise, and they are elected to the offices of honor, you are passed by unnoticed, and your whole conduct is made a subject of derision. If you accept in peace all these humiliations, and if, with a sisterly affection, you recommend to God those from whom you receive the least respect, then indeed, as St. Dorotheus says, it will be manifest that you are truly humble. To them you are particularly indebted, since by their reproaches they cure your pride—the most malignant of all diseases that lead to spiritual death. Because they deem themselves worthy of all honors, the proud convert their humiliations into an occasion of pride. But because the humble consider themselves deserving only of opprobrium, their humiliations serve to increase their humility. "That man," says St. Bernard, "Is truly humble who converts humiliation into humility."

Voluntary humiliations, such as to serve the sick, to kiss the feet of those who imagine, even unjustly, that we have offended them, and similar acts of humility, are very profitable; but to embrace with cheerfulness, for the love of Jesus Christ, the humiliations that come from others, such as reproofs, accusations, insults, and derisions, is still more meritorious. Gold and silver, says the Holy Ghost, are tried in the fire, but acceptable men in the furnace of humiliation. As gold is tried in the fire, so a man's perfection is proved by humiliation. St. Mary Magdalene de Pazzi used to say that "Untried virtue is not virtue." He who does not suffer contempt with a tranquil mind shall never attain the spirit of perfection. My spikenard, says the Spouse, sent forth the odor thereof. The spikenard is an odoriferous plant, whose scent is drawn forth only by friction and trituration. Oh, what an odor of sweetness does the humble religious exhale when she embraces in peace all manner of contempt, and delights in seeing herself maltreated and despised, as the most contemptible among her sisters. A monk of the name of Zachary, being asked the best means of attaining humility, took his cowl, put it under his feet, and, trampling on it, said: "He who takes pleasure in being treated like this cowl is truly humble." Ah, how happy the death of the religious who has lived in abjection in her monastery, and has always borne her humiliations in peace. Her soul shall overflow with feelings, not of dislike, but of thanksgiving, to all who have despised her. St. John Climacus relates that a good monk called Abacyrus, who had for fifteen years been treated contemptuously by others, at the hour of death returned them many thanks for their charity in having afforded him so many occasions of humiliation, and thus expired in celestial peace.

There are some who imagine that they are humble because they feel a strong conviction of their own miseries and a deep sorrow for their past sins. But they will not submit to humiliations, and cannot endure the slightest want of respect or esteem; and therefore they shun all humble offices, and whatever is not flattering to their pride. They acknowledge that they are worthy of all sorts of ignominy, but cannot bear any mark of inattention; on the contrary, they seek continually to be treated with respect and honor. There is, says the Holy Ghost, one that humbleth himself wickedly, and His interior is full of deceit. There are some who practice external humility, by confessing that they are the worst of sinners, but in their hearts they seek after honors and the esteem of men. I hope, dear sister that you do not belong to that class of Christians. If you sincerely believe that you are a greater sinner than any of your sisters, be content to be treated as the lowest among them: love as your best friends all who, by despising you, assist you to practice humility and to detach your heart from earthly glory, and thus to unite your soul more closely to God, and to seek nothing in this life but his holy love.

Consider yourself as only worthy of universal horror; offer yourself to God, professing your readiness to suffer for his sake, and in satisfaction for your offences, all manner of opprobrium, and never permit self-love to complain of the contempt with which you are treated. Remember that they who have dared to despise the Almighty merit far greater contempt; they deserve to be the footstool of the devils for all eternity in hell. "I know no remedy," says St. Bernard, "Better able to heal the wounds of my conscience than opprobrium and contumely." Rejoice, then, blessed spouse of the Lord, when you are humbled, and treated as the last of your sisters; or when you see yourself an object of derision, and regarded by all as the most foolish and contemptible member of the Community. When censured, even without grounds, neither excuse yourself nor seek to be excused by others, unless, as I have already said, you see that your justification is absolutely necessary to prevent scandal. Do not hinder others to disclose your faults to the Superior. When you receive any humiliation, seek not to know the sister who was the occasion of it; and should you discover her name, be careful not to reprove her, not to show that you know it, nor to complain of her conduct: on the contrary, in your prayers for others, pray, in the first place, for her, and for all by whom you have been despised or persecuted.

Be persuaded of the truth of what Father Alvarez used to say, that the time of humiliation is the time for putting off our own miseries and for acquiring great merits. St. Mary Magdalene de Pazzi used to say that crosses and ignominies are the greatest favors that God is accustomed to bestow on his beloved spouses. In conversing with those who are despised she experienced great consolation from the conviction that they were most dear to Jesus Christ. Hence she fervently exhorted the religious to place all their happiness in being treated with contempt.

But, above all, it is necessary to keep before your eyes what the Redeemer has said, that happy is he who is hated and cast out by men. Blessed shall you be when men shall hate you, and when they shall separate you, and shall reproach you, and cast out your name as evil for the Son of Man's sake. The apostle St. Peter adds: If you be reproached for the name of Christ, you shall be blessed: for that which is of the honor, glory, and power of God, and that which is his Spirit, resteth upon you. When you are insulted for the sake of Jesus Christ, then shall you be happy; for then shall the true honor, the true power, and the true Spirit of God rest upon you.

The saints have not been made saints by applause and honor, but by injuries and insults. St. Ignatius Martyr, a bishop, and an object of universal esteem and veneration, was sent to Rome as a criminal, and on his way experienced from the soldiers who conducted him nothing but the most barbarous insolence. In the midst of his suffering and humiliations he joyfully exclaimed: "I now begin to be a disciple of Christ." I now begin to be a true disciple of my Jesus, who endured so many ignominies for my sake. St. Francis Borgia, when travelling, slept one night in the same room with his companion, Father Bustamente, who, in consequence of a severe attack of asthma, spent the whole night in coughing and casting out phlegm unconsciously on the saint, and frequently in his face. In the morning Father Bustamente perceived his mistake, and was greatly afflicted at having given so much cause of pain to the saint. Father, said St. Francis, be not disturbed; for there is no part of this room so fit for the reception of spittle as my face.

O God, what must become of the religious who will not submit to an insult for the love of Jesus Christ! The nun who cannot bear contempt shows that she has lost sight of Jesus crucified. Standing once before the crucifix, Blessed Mary of the Incarnation said to her sisters in religion: Is it possible, dear sisters that we refuse to embrace contempt when we see Jesus Christ reviled and scoffed? A certain holy religious having been affronted, went before the Blessed Sacrament, and said: Lord, I am very poor; I have nothing to present to you: but I offer you the injury that I have just received. Oh, how lovingly does Jesus Christ embrace all that embrace contempt for his sake! He soon consoles and enriches them with his graces. Father Anthony Torres was once unjustly charged with disseminating false doctrines, and in punishment of his supposed transgression was for many years deprived of faculties to hear confessions. But in a letter to a certain friend he says: "Be assured that during the whole time I was calumniated the spiritual consolations that the Lord gave me surpassed any I ever received from him."

To suffer contempt with a serene countenance not only merits a great reward, but also serves to draw others to God. "He," says St. John Chrysostom, "Who is meek is useful to himself and to others." The man who meekly bears affronts is useful to himself and to all who behold him. For nothing is more edifying to a neighbour than the meekness of a man who receives injuries with a tranquil countenance. "Nothing," adds the saint, "Conciliates friends to the Lord so much as to see a man agreeable by his meekness." Father Maffei relates that a Jesuit, while preaching in Japan, having been spit upon by an insolent bystander, removed the spittle with his handkerchief, and continued his sermon as if nothing had happened. One of his auditors exclaimed, that a doctrine that teaches such humility must be true and divine, and was instantly converted to the faith. Thus, also, St. Francis de Sales converted innumerable heretics by his meekness in bearing the insults that he received from them.

A religious who lives in a monastery of relaxed observance, and who wishes to walk in the way of perfection, may be assured that during her whole life she shall be an object of continual derision and persecution. There is no remedy: The wicked, says the Holy Ghost, loathe them that are in the right way. They who walk in the broad road cannot but feel an abhorrence of them that tread in the narrow way. For the lives of the saints are a continual reproach to sinners who wish to see all like themselves. Shunning the grates, assisting in choir, observance of silence, detachment from particular friendships, and almost every good work of a fervent religious will be regarded by the tepid as singularities, or perhaps, as hypocritical acts, performed from a motive of acquiring the reputation of a saint. Should a fervent nun in a convent of relaxed discipline commit a fault (for she has not ceased to be frail, and subject to defects),— should she, for example, yield to a word of slight impatience, or sometimes defend herself against an unjust accusation,—oh, what an outcry is raised against her! Behold the saint, the tepid exclaim. To impose upon others she communicates every morning, she always observes silence, she wears hair-cloth, and remains all day in the choir. They sometimes add falsehood to truth. If she wishes to be a saint, she must be careful to suffer, and to offer to God all these reproaches. Unless she submit to them she will not continue long in the way of perfection; she will soon lose all that she has acquired, and will become as imperfect as the others. In speaking once of a certain religious who was esteemed a saint, St. Bernard said: He indeed is a saint, but he wants the greatest of all blessings—the reputation of a sinner.

Let us then be persuaded that to be persecuted in this life confers the highest excellence on the saints. And, says the Apostle, all that will live godly in Christ Jesus shall suffer persecution. The Redeemer says, If they have persecuted me, they will also persecute you.

Some will say: I attend only to my own concerns, I give offence to no one: why should I be persecuted? But all the saints have been persecuted; Jesus Christ, the head of the saints, has been persecuted: and will you not submit to persecution? But what greater favour, says St. Teresa, can God bestow upon us than to send us the treatment that he wished his beloved Son to suffer on earth? "Believe me," says Father Torres, in a letter to one of his penitents, "That one of the greatest graces that God can confer upon you is to make you worthy to be calumniated by all, without being esteemed by any." When, then, dear sister, you see yourself disregarded and despised by all men, rejoice, and thank your Spouse, who wishes you to be treated in the same manner in which he himself wished to be treated in this life. And to prepare your soul to accept humiliations when they occur, represent to yourself in the time of meditation all the contempt, contradictions, and persecutions which may happen to you, and offer yourself, with a strong desire and resolution to suffer them all for the sake of Jesus Christ, and thus you shall be better prepared to accept them.

V. In the fifth place, you must not only accept humiliations in peace, but must also be glad and exult under them. "A good religious," says St. Joseph Calasanctius, "Despises the world and rejoices in its scoffs." The Venerable Louis de Ponte could not at first conceive how a soul could delight in contempt; but when he became more perfect he experienced the consolations of abjection. By our own strength we certainly cannot rejoice in humiliations, but by the aid of Jesus Christ we can imitate the apostles, who went from the presence of the council, rejoicing that they were accounted worthy to suffer reproach for the name of Jesus. There are some, as St. Joseph Calasanctius says, who suffer reproach, but not with joy. To teach the perfect spirit of humility to St. Mary Magdalene de Pazzi, St. Ignatius came down from heaven and assured her that true humility consists in taking pleasure in whatever inspires self-contempt.

Worldlings do not delight as much in honors as the saints do in contempt. Brother Juniper, of the Order of St. Francis, received insults as he would the most costly gems. When derided by his companions, St. John Francis Regis was not only pleased by their ridicule, but even encouraged it. Thus from the lives of the saints it would appear that sufferings and humiliations were the sole objects of their wishes. With a cross on his shoulder and a crown of thorns on his head the Redeemer once appeared to St. John of the Cross and said: "John, ask of me what thou wilt." "Lord, replied the saint," I desire to suffer and to be despised for Thy sake. As if he said: Lord, seeing you oppressed with sorrow and saturated with opprobrium for the love of me, what can I ask from you but pains and ignominies? The Lord once assured Blessed Angela of Foligno that the surest means by which a soul can ascertain whether its lights are from God is to examine if they have inspired and left behind a strong desire of being despised for his sake. Jesus wishes that under injuries and persecutions we not only be not disquieted, but that we even rejoice and exult in expectation of the great glory that he has prepared for us in heaven as the reward of our sufferings. Blessed are ye when they shall revile and persecute you; . . . be glad and rejoice, for your reward is very great in heaven.

To those who are about to enter religion it is my custom to recommend, above all things, the practice of obedience, and of patience under contempt. I have been anxious to treat the latter at full length. Because I am convinced that without bearing contempt it is impossible for a nun to advance in perfection; and because I hold as certain that the religious who cheerfully embraces humiliations shall become a saint. "A soul humble of heart," says St. Paulinus, "Is the heart of Christ." The nun who is humble of heart or who delights in contempt is transformed into the heart of Jesus Christ. Be assured, then, dear sister, that if you are to be a saint you must suffer humiliations and contempt. Though all your companions were saints, you would notwithstanding, by God's ordinance, meet with frequent contradictions; you will be put below others, held in little esteem, and will frequently have to submit to accusations and reproofs. To render you like himself, Jesus Christ will easily find the means of making you an object of contempt. Hence I entreat you to practice every day the beautiful advice of Father Torres given to his penitents: "Say every day an Our Father and a Hail Mary, in honor of the life of ignominy of Jesus; and offer yourself to suffer not only in peace but even with joy for the love of him all the contradictions and reproaches that he will send you; begging always his assistance to be faithful to him in bearing patiently all injuries and humiliations."

Prayer.

My Jesus, my love, how is it possible that, seeing Thee, my God, humbled unto death, and even the ignominious death of the cross, I should be so proud? Ah, through the merits of Thy ignominies make me know my miseries and deformities that I may abhor myself; and suffer in peace for the love of Thee all the injuries that I shall receive. Ah, my Redeemer, Thou hast rendered ignominies amiable to all who love Thee. Grant that I may understand Thy goodness and Thy love, that thus to please Thee 1 may love and embrace all manner of contempt. Grant that I may banish from my heart all human respect, and that in all my actions I may seek only Thy will and pleasure. I love Thee, O my humbled Jesus; and I purpose with Thy grace not to resent any injuries, nor to complain of any affront that may be offered to me. From Thee I hope for strength to fulfill this resolution.

Mary, my mother, assist me by thy intercession; pray to Jesus for me.

CHAPTER XII

FRATERNAL CHARITY.

The Necessity of this Virtue, and its Practice in our Thoughts and Sentiments.

To love God without at the same time loving our neighbour is impossible. The same precept that prescribes love towards God imposes a strict obligation of fraternal charity. And this commandment we have from God that he who loveth God love also his brother. Hence St. Thomas teaches that the love of God and the love of our neighbour proceed alike from charity. For charity makes us love God and our neighbour, because such is the will of God. Such too was the doctrine of St. John the Evangelist. St. Jerome relates that being asked by his disciples why he frequently recommended fraternal love, that holy apostle replied: "Because it is the precept of the Lord, and the fulfillment of it alone is sufficient."

St. Catharine of Genoa once said to the Lord: "My God, Thou dost command me to love my neighbour; and I can love nothing but Thee." "My child," answered Jesus, "He that loves me, loves whatsoever I love." Indeed, when we love any person we also love his relatives, his servants, his likeness, and even his clothes, because we know that he loves them. And why do we love our neighbors? It is because God loves them. Hence St. John says that if any man say I love God and hateth his brother, he is a liar. But as hatred towards our brethren is incompatible with the love of God, so an act of charity performed in their regard will be accepted by Jesus Christ as if done for himself. I say to you, says the Redeemer, as long as you did it to one of these my brethren you did it to me. St. Catharine of Genoa used to say that our love of God is to be measured by our love for our neighbor.

But holy charity—the beautiful daughter of God, being banished from the world by the greater part of mankind, seeks an asylum in the monasteries of religious. Oh, what then will become of the convent from which charity is exiled! As hell is a land of hatred, so paradise is the kingdom of love, where all the blessed love one another, and each one rejoices at the happiness of the rest as at his own. Oh, what a paradise is the convent in which charity reigns, it is the delight of God himself.

Behold, says the Psalmist, how good and how pleasant it is for brethren to dwell together in unity. The Lord looks with complacency on the charity of brethren and sisters who dwell together in unity, who are united by one will of serving God, and who seek only to sanctify one another that they may be all united one day in the land of bliss. The highest praise bestowed by St. Luke on the first Christians was that they had but one heart and soul. And the multitude of the believers had but one heart and one soul. This unity was the fruit of the prayer of Jesus Christ, who before his Passion besought his eternal Father to make his disciples one by holy charity as he and the Father are one. Holy Father, keep them in thy name—that they may be one as we also are. This unity is one of the principal fruits of redemption, as may be inferred from the prediction of Isaias: The wolf shall dwell with the lamb; and the leopard shall lie down with the kid they shall not hurt, nor shall they kill in all my holy mountain. Yes, the followers of Jesus, though of different countries and of different dispositions, shall live in peace with one another, each seeking by holy charity to accommodate himself to the wishes and inclinations of the other. And as a certain author has well remarked, what does a Community of religious mean, but a union of many by will and desire so as to form but one person. It is charity that maintains union; for it is not possible that all the members of a convent should have congenial dispositions. It is charity that unites their hearts and makes them bear one another burdens, and it is charity that makes each conform to the will of the other.

St. John Climacus relates that in the vicinity of Alexandria there was a celebrated monastery, where, because they loved one another so cordially in holy charity, all the religious enjoyed the peace of paradise. In general the first that perceived a disagreement between two of the religious was able to restore peace by a mere sign. But if they could not be reconciled, both were sent as exiles to a neighboring house, and were told at their departure that the abode of two demons in the monastery could be no longer profitable to the Community. Oh, how delightful is it to see in a convent of nuns each praise, assist, and serve the others, and all love the others with a true sisterly affection. Nuns are called sisters, because they are such not by blood, but by charity, which should unite them in love more closely than all the ties of flesh and blood. "The nun who has not charity," says St. Jane Frances de Chantal, "Is a religious in name, but not in reality. She is a sister in dress, not in affection." Hence because they knew that where there is no union there is no God, almost all the founders and foundresses of religious Orders have with their last breath recommended the practice of holy charity to their spiritual children.

"When," says St. Augustine, "You see the stones of any fabric well bound to the timber, you enter with security, and apprehend no danger." But were the stones detached from the wood, you should shudder at the very thought of approaching the building. Happy the religious house in which all are united by holy charity; but miserable is the monastery in which disunion and party-spirit prevail. "Yes," says St. Jerome, "Such a monastery is not the tabernacle of the Lord, but the abode of Lucifer; it is a house not of salvation, but of perdition." Of what use are riches and magnificence, a splendid church and a beautiful garden, to a monastery from which union and charity are banished? Such a monastery is a hell, where, to prevent the advancement of the rivals, each party decries the other. Suspicions and aversions are always on the increase: they fill the minds, are poured out in conversation, and occupy the thoughts of the religious at mental prayer, at Mass, and at Communion. Hence we may exclaim, O miserable prayers, miserable Masses, miserable Communions! In a word, where there is not charity there is no recollection, no peace, no God.

If, dear sister, factions exist in your convent, prostrate yourself before the Lord, and in his presence pour forth tears of blood and fervent supplications that by his Almighty hand he may remedy the evil. For when the spirit of faction has crept into the cloister, it can be extinguished only by the arm of omnipotence. If it be in your power to restore peace, endeavor with all your might and at all hazards to accomplish so great a good; but if the extinction of discord be beyond your reach, it is your duty at least to remain neutral, and to shun, as you would death itself, every act that may encourage the fell spirit of faction.

Remember, however, that I do not mean to censure those zealous nuns who defend the observance of Rule, and who strenuously oppose all abuses. Whoever seeks the good of the Community belongs to the party of Jesus Christ. Would to God that all were of this party! If, dear sister, you ever see an abuse introduced into the convent, I exhort you to unite with the fervent, and never to abstain from vindicating the cause of God even though you should be left alone. The Lord will reward your efforts for the maintenance of regular observance. To feel careless and to manifest indifference about the relaxation and neglect of discipline is neither virtue nor humility, but is the fruit of pusillanimity, tepidity, and of a want of divine love.

The religious, then, whom I condemn are those who maintain parties for promoting their own interests or particular friendships, or for depressing a rival or resenting an insult. From such parties I exhort you to keep aloof, though, in punishment of your neutrality, you should be reproached with ingratitude, wrongheadedness, or baseness of spirit, and even though you should be deprived of office and doomed to perpetual disgrace. To preserve charity and the common peace you must sacrifice all self-interest. When some of the bishops wished to have St. Gregory Nazianzen for patriarch while others refused to submit to his authority, the saint, to heal their dissensions, exclaimed: "My brothers, I wish to see you in peace, and if the renunciation of my patriarchal dignity be necessary to preserve harmony among you, I am ready to renounce my see." He then gave up the bishopric of Constantinople, and retired into solitude.

But, let us speak in particular of the means that a nun should adopt for the maintenance of charity among her sisters in religion. She must follow the advice of the Apostle to his disciples: Put ye on, therefore, as the elect of God, holy and beloved, the bowels of mercy. As a religious always wears her habit, and as her whole body is covered by it, so in all her actions she must be clothed and encompassed around with charity. Put on the bowels of mercy. A religious should be clothed not only with charity, but with the bowels of charity; that is, she should love each of her sisters as if for each she had the tenderest affections. When a person entertains for others a strong attachment he rejoices at their prosperity and grieves at their misfortunes as at his own. He continually seeks to promote their happiness, to vindicate their character from any imputation that may be cast upon it, to excuse any fault that they may commit, and to extol every good act that they may perform. Now what is the effect of passion in worldlings should be the fruit of holy charity in religious.

PRACTICE OF CHARITY IN OUR THOUGHTS AND SENTIMENTS.

I. To practice charity in thought you must, in the first place, endeavor
243

to banish all rash judgments, suspicions, and doubts. To entertain a rash doubt regarding another is a defect; to indulge a positive suspicion is a greater fault, and to judge with certainty without certain grounds that another has sinned, is still more criminal before God. Whoever judges rashly of his neighbor shall be judged with severity. Judge not, that you may not be judged. For with what judgment you judge you shall be judged. But although it is sinful to judge evil of others without certain grounds, still it is not a violation of the divine law to suspect or even to judge evil of them when we have certain motives for such suspicions or judgments. However, the safest and most charitable rule is to think well of all, and to banish all such judgments and suspicions. Charity, says the Apostle, thinketh no evil. But this rule is not to be observed by the religious who hold the office of Superior, or of Mistress of novices. Because, to prevent evil, it is their duty to suspect whenever there are grounds of suspicion. But if by your office you are not charged with the correction of others, endeavor always to judge favorably of all your sisters. St. Jane Frances de Chantal used to say that "In our neighbor we should observe only what is good." Should you sometimes through mistake praise in others what is censurable, you will never have reason to repent of your error. "Charity," says St. Augustine, "Grieves not when she erroneously thinks well of what is evil." St. Catharine of Bologna once said: "I have lived for many years in religion, and have never thought ill of any of my sisters; because I know that a person who appears to be imperfect may be more dear to God than another whose conduct is much more exemplary." Be careful, then, not to indulge in observing the defects and concerns of others, nor to imitate the example of those who go about asking what others say of them, and thus fill their minds with suspicions and their hearts with bitterness and aversions. Listen not to them who tell you that others have spoken of your defects, and ask not from them the names of those who dispraised you. In such tales there is, in general, a great deal of exaggeration. Let your conduct be such as deserves praise from all, but regard not what is said of you. When told that any one has charged you with a certain fault, let your answer be that others know you but little; and that, were they aware of all your defects, they would say a great deal more of you; or you may say that only God is to be your judge.

II. When our neighbor is visited with any infirmity, loss, or other calamity, charity obliges us to regret his misfortune at least with the superior will. I say with the superior will; for concupiscence always appears to take a certain delight in hearing that a calamity has befallen an enemy. But that delight is not culpable as long as it is resisted by the will. Whenever the inferior appetite solicits the will to rejoice at the misfortune of others, pay no more attention to its criminal solicitations than you would to a dog that barks without reason; but endeavor to excite in the superior will sentiments of regret at their distress. It is indeed sometimes lawful to rejoice at the good effects that are likely to result from the temporal afflictions of others. For example, it is not forbidden to be glad from a motive of his conversion, or of the cessation of scandal, that a notorious and obstinate sinner has been visited with sickness. However, should he have offended us, the joy occasioned by his infirmity may be the fruit of passion as well as of zeal.

III. Charity obliges us to rejoice at a neighbor's good, and to banish envy, which consists in a feeling of regret at the good of others, inasmuch as it is an obstacle to our own.

According to St. Thomas, a person may grieve at the good of others in four ways:

First, when he apprehends that their advancement will be detrimental to himself or to others; and if the loss sustained be unjust, his regret is not envy, and may be blameless. "It may often happen," says St. Gregory, "That without losing charity, we rejoice at the ruin of an enemy; and that without incurring the guilt of envy, we feel sorrow at his exaltation, when by his downfall we think that others will be justly exalted, and when we fear that by his prosperity many will be unjustly oppressed."

Secondly, when a person grieves not because others have been prosperous, but because he himself has not been equally successful. This grief is not envy, but is, on the contrary, an act of virtue when it regards spiritual goods.

Thirdly, when he regrets the success of others, because he deems them unworthy of it; and this sorrow is not sinful, when he believes that the advantages, dignity, or riches that they have acquired will be injurious to their salvation.

Fourthly, when a person regrets the prosperity of others, because it is an obstacle to his own advancement: this is envy, and should not be entertained. The Wise Man says that the envious imitate the devil, who instigated our first parents to sin, because he was grieved to see them destined for that celestial kingdom from which he himself had been expelled.

But, says the Wise Man, by the envy of the devil death came into the world, and they follow him that are of his side. But charity makes us regard the happiness or misery of others as we would our own.

Prayer.

Ah, my Redeemer, how unlike am I to Thee! Thou wast all charity towards Thy persecutors; I am all rancor and hatred towards my neighbor. Thou didst pray with so much love for those who crucified Thee; and I immediately seek revenge against those that offend me. Pardon me, my Jesus: I wish no more to be what I have hitherto been; give me strength to love and to do good to all who injure me. Abandon me not, O Lord to my passions. Oh, what a hell would it be to me, after having received so many of Thy graces, to be again separated from Thee, and deprived of Thy friendship. For the sake of the blood that Thou hast shed for me, permit not such a separation. Eternal Father, through the merits of Thy Son, suffer me not to become Thy enemy. Shouldst Thou see that I will one day offend Thee, take me out of life, now that I hope to be in the state of grace. O God of love, give me Thy love! O in finite power, assist me! O infinite mercy, have pity on me! O infinite goodness, draw me entirely to Thee! I love Thee, O Sovereign Good!

O Mother of God, pray to Jesus for me! Thy protection is my hope.

II.

The Charity to be Practiced in Words.

I. To practice fraternal charity in words, you must above all, abstain from every species of detraction. The talebearer, says the Holy Ghost, shall defile his own soul, and shall be hated by all. Yes; he shall be an object of hatred to God and to men, and even to those who for their own amusement applaud and encourage his slanderous language. Even they shall shun him; because they justly fear that as in their presence he has detracted others, so before others he will slander them. St. Jerome says that some who have renounced other vices cannot abstain from detraction. "They who have abandoned other sins continue to fall into the sin of detraction." Would to God that even in the cloister there were not to be found religious whose tongues are so sharp that they cannot speak without wounding the character of a neighbor! Such persons should be banished from all monasteries, or should at least be separated from the society of their sisters. For they disturb the recollection, silence, devotion, and peace of the whole Community. In a word, they are the ruin of religious houses. God grant that such uncharitable nuns may not meet the fate of a certain slanderer, who, according to Thomas Cantipratensis, died in a fit of rage, and in the act of lacerating his tongue with his teeth. St. Bernard speaks of another slanderer who attempted to defame the character of St. Malachy; his tongue instantly swelled and became filled with worms. In this miserable state the unhappy man died after seven days.

But how dear to God and to men is the nun who speaks well of all! St. Mary Magdalene de Pazzi used to say, that if she knew anyone who had never in his whole life spoken ill of a neighbor, she would have him canonized. Be careful never to utter a word that savors of detraction; be particularly careful to avoid all uncharitableness towards your sisters in religion. But, above all, be on your guard against every expression that is in the slightest degree apt to depress the character of your prelate, abbess, confessor, or any other Superior. By speaking ill of them, you would destroy in your companions the spirit of obedience, by diminishing their respect for the judgment and authority of their Superiors. Should your language excite a suspicion in the mind of the sisters that the Superior is unreasonable in her commands, it will be very difficult to induce them to practice the obedience that is due to her. The sin of detraction is committed, not only by imputing to others what is not true, by exaggerating their defects, or by making known their hidden faults, but also by representing their virtuous actions as defective, or by ascribing them to a bad motive. It is also detraction to deny the good works of others, or to question their claims to the just praise bestowed upon them. To render their calumnies more credible, worldlings sometimes begin by praise and end with slander. Such a person, they say, has a great deal of talent, but he is proud; he is very generous, but at the same time very vindictive.

Let it be your care always to speak well of all. Speak of others as you would wish to be spoken of by others. With regard to the absent, observe the excellent rule of St. Mary Magdalene de Pazzi: "Never to utter in their absence what you would not say in their presence." And should you ever hear a sister speak ill of others, be careful neither to encourage her uncharitableness nor to appear pleased with her language; otherwise you will partake of her guilt. You should either reprove her, or change the subject of conversation, or withdraw from her, or at least pay no attention to her. Hedge in thy ears with thorns, says the Holy Ghost; hear not a wicked tongue. Against detraction, hedge in your ears with thorns, that it may not enter. Whenever, then, you hear a person speak ill of others, it is necessary to show, at least by silence, by a gloomy countenance, or by downcast eyes, that you are not pleased with the conversation. Conduct yourself always in such a way that no one will in future dare attack the character of another in your presence. And when it is in your power, charity requires of you to take the part of the person who is detracted. Thy lips are as a scarlet lace. My spouse, says the Lord, I will have thy lips as a scarlet lace; that is, according to the explanation of St. Gregory of Nyssa, your words must be full of charity, so as to cover as much as possible the defects of others, or at least to excuse their intention, if their actions be inexcusable. "Excuse the intention," says St. Bernard, "If you cannot excuse the act." The Abbot Constabile, as Surius relates, was called "The covering of his brethren." For this holy monk, as often as he heard any one speak of the defects of others, sought to cover and excuse them. Such, too, was the practice of St. Teresa. Of her the nuns used to say, that in her presence their character was secure, because she would defend them.

II. Be careful never to mention to any sister that another has spoken ill of her; for tale-bearing of this kind sometimes occasions disputes and aversions which last for a long time. Oh, how frightful the account which talebearers must render to God! The sowers of discord are objects of abomination in his sight. Six things there are that the Lord hateth, and the seventh his soul detesteth? The seventh is the man that soweth discord among brethren! An uncharitable word that proceeds from passion may be excusable. But how can the Almighty bear with a religious who sows discord and disturbs the peace of a Community? Listen to the advice of the Holy Ghost: Hast thou heard a word against thy neighbor, let it die within thee. The words that you hear of a sister must not only be confined to yourself, but must even die and be buried within you. You must be careful, then, never to give the slightest intimation of what you have heard. For a single word, a nod of the head, a simple hint, may lead others to a knowledge or at least to a suspicion of the faults that were mentioned to you.

Some appear to suffer the pangs of death until they have disclosed the secrets communicated to them; as if these secrets were so many thorns that wound their very heart until they are drawn out. You should never mention the hidden defects of others to anyone except to the Superiors, and not even to them unless the reparation of the injury done to the Community, or the good of the sister herself who has committed the fault, require that her neglect should be known to the Superior.

III. Moreover, in your conversation you must be careful never to wound even by jests the feelings of a sister. Jests that offend a neighbor are opposed to charity, and to the words of Jesus Christ: All things whatsoever you would that men should do to you, do you also to them. You certainly would not like to be made an object of derision and of mockery before your companions. Abstain then from casting ridicule on others.

Endeavor also to avoid as much as possible all disputes. Sometimes trifles give occasion to arguments that end in disputes and injurious language. There are some who violate charity by proposing, through the spirit of contradiction, certain topics of debate which give rise to useless disputation. Strive not, says the Wise Man, in a matter which doth not concern thee.

But you will say that in every debate you defend the right side of the question, and that you cannot listen in silence to assertions utterly destitute of foundation. I answer in the words of Cardinal Bellarmine: "That an ounce of charity is more valuable than a hundred carloads of reason." In all debates, but particularly when the subject is of little importance, give your opinion if you wish to join in the conversation; but be careful never to defend it with obstinacy. It is better to give up your own opinion than to enter into a useless and perhaps dangerous controversy. Blessed Egidius used to say that in such controversies to submit is to conquer; because submission evinces a superiority in virtue and preserves peace. Surely the preservation of peace is of far greater importance than the empty honor of a wordy victory. Hence St. Ephrem used to say that to maintain peace he always yielded to his adversary in disputation. Hence, also, St. Joseph Calasanctius advises "All who desire peace never to contradict anyone."

IV. If you love charity, endeavor to be affable and meek to all. Meekness is the characteristic virtue of the lamb; it is the beloved virtue of Jesus Christ, who through a love of meekness took the appellation of Lamb. In your conversation and intercourse with others be agreeable not only to the Superior and to those who are in office, but to all, and particularly to the sisters who have offended you, who oppose your wishes, or displease you by their roughness of manner, or by their forgetfulness of past favors. Charity is patient: beareth all things. Whoever, then, bears not the defects of his neighbor cannot have true charity. The most perfect souls are not free from all defects. You yourself are subject to faults; and notwithstanding your manifold imperfections you expect to be treated with charity and compassion. You therefore should, according to the advice of the Apostle, compassionate the defects of others. Bear ye one another burdens. A mother, because she loves them, submits in patience to the insolence of her children. It is by the manner in which you bear the burdens of your sisters that you are to judge whether you love them with true charity, which, because it is supernatural, should be stronger than natural affection.

Oh, with what charity did the Redeemer bear with the rudeness and imperfections of his disciples during the whole time that he lived with them! With what charity did he wash the feet of the traitor Judas! With what patience has he borne even to the present moment with your sinfulness and ingratitude! And will you refuse to bear with the defects of your sisters? The physician while he loves a patient loathes his disease; and if you have charity you must love your sisters and at the same time hate their faults. But you will say: What am I to do? I have a natural repugnance to the society of such a sister, and feel it painful to hold intercourse with her. My answer is: Have more fervor and more charity, and all such antipathies will vanish.

Let us come to the practice of meekness.

In the first place, endeavor with all your might to restrain every motion of anger. In the next place, you must be careful to abstain from all disagreeable words, and to avoid all roughness and haughtiness of manner; for rude conduct is sometimes more offensive than insulting language. Should a sister ever treat you with contempt, suffer it in patience for the love of Jesus Christ, who for the love of you has borne with far greater insults. My God, what a misery to see certain religious, who practice mental prayer and frequent the sacraments, so sensitive to every mark of disrespect or inattention! Sister Mary of the Ascension, as often as she received an affront, went immediately before the Blessed Sacrament, and said: My Spouse, I bring you this little present; I beg you to accept it, and to pardon the person by whom I have been offended. Why do you not imitate this holy religious? To preserve charity you must suffer all things. Father Alvarez used to say that virtue is weak till it is proved by maltreatment from others. It is by the manner in which she bears with contempt and insult that a soul shows whether she abounds or fails in charity.

Should anyone ever address you in the language of passion, or even of insult and reproach, answer with sweetness, and her anger will be instantly appeased. A mild answer breaketh wrath St. John Chrysostom says: "Fire cannot be extinguished by fire, nor wrath by anger." Do you imagine that by replying with acrimony to all who speak to you in anger you will calm passion? On the contrary, you will provoke it, and will also violate charity. Let your answer to every word of anger be full of sweetness, and the fire of passion will be instantly extinguished. Sophronius relates that two monks having missed their way on a journey, entered by chance into a field in which seed had been just sown. The man who was intrusted with the care of the field burst into a fit of rage and heaped upon them every epithet of reproach. At first they were silent, but seeing that their silence served only to inflame his anger, they exclaimed: "Brother, we have done wrong: for God's sake pardon us." This humble answer calmed his passion and filled his soul with sorrow for his conduct. He immediately asked pardon of the monks for his injurious language—he even left the world and joined them in the cloister.

You will sometimes think it right and even necessary to repress by a sharp answer the forwardness of a sister, particularly if you are Superior, and she be wanting in respect to you: be assured that such sharpness proceeds from passion rather than from reason. I know that anger is sometimes lawful. Be angry, says the Psalmist, and sin not. But to be angry and not to sin is very difficult in practice. Whoever abandons himself to anger exposes his soul to imminent danger. Hence St. Francis de Sales wisely teaches in his Philothea, that however just the occasions of anger may be, its motions should be repressed. "It is better," says the saint, "To have it said of you that you are never angry, than that you were justly angry." St. Augustine says that anger once allowed to enter the soul is banished with difficulty; and therefore he strongly recommends us to stifle it in its very origin. A certain philosopher, called Agrippinus, having lost his property, said: "If I have lost my goods I will not lose my peace." Let such be your language as often as you receive any offence. Is it not enough for you to have received an affront, do you wish, moreover, to lose the peace of your soul by yielding to anger? The disturbance of mind occasioned by anger will be far more injurious to you than the insult that you have received. St. Augustine says that he who yields to passion on every occasion of insult is his own chastiser. Disquiet of soul, even when it arises from regret for a fault, is always injurious. For, as St. Aloysius used to say, it delights the devil to fish in troubled water.

I have said that when a sister speaks to you in the language or tone of passion or contempt you should answer her with sweetness. But I now say, that whenever the soul is disturbed, it is better to be silent; for passion will then make harsh expressions appear just and reasonable. But when peace returns, you will see that your language was altogether unjustifiable. St. Bernard says that anger draws over the soul a dark veil, which renders her incapable of distinguishing what is right from what is wrong.

When a sister who has offended you comes to ask pardon, be careful not to receive her with a stern countenance, nor to show discontent or want of respect by your words or looks. If you give signs of dissatisfaction, you will violate charity, you will confirm the sister in her dislike towards you, and will give great scandal to the whole Community. You must, then, receive her with affection; and if, through humility, she fall on her knees to ask pardon, you should likewise go on your knees, and say to her: O my sister, why should you ask pardon of me? You know how much I love and esteem you. I ask pardon for having displeased you by my ignorance and negligence, and by my want of attention to you. Have pity, then, on me, and forgive me.

But whenever you offend or displease a sister, endeavor at once, by all means in your power, to make satisfaction to her, and to remove from her heart all feelings of aversion towards you. St. Bernard says "That humility alone is the reparation of wounded charity." Self-humiliation is the most efficacious means of repairing the violation of charity. Whenever, then, you offend against charity, humble yourself immediately, overcome by force your natural repugnance to humiliation: the longer you defer the reparation of the fault you have committed, the more your repugnance to make reparation will increase. If, says the Redeemer, thou offer thy gift at the altar, and there thou remember that thy brother hath anything against thee, leave there thy offering before the altar, and go first to be reconciled to thy brother, and then coming, thou shalt offer thy gift. If you come to the altar to offer your gift, to receive the Holy Eucharist, or to attend Mass, and remember that you have offended a brother, retire from the altar and be reconciled with him. However, if you think that by asking pardon of the sister you have offended, you will only renew her anguish, it is better to wait for a more convenient opportunity, or to ask pardon through another sister But you must, in the mean time, show her particular attention and respect.

Prayer.

O my God, look not on my sins, but on Jesus Thy Son, who has sacrificed his life for my salvation. For the sake of Jesus, have pity on me, and pardon all the offences I have given Thee, but especially those which I have committed by my want of charity to my neighbor. Destroy in me, O Lord, whatever displeases Thee, and give me a sincere desire to please Thee in all things. Ah, my Jesus, my greatest sorrow arises from a conviction that I have been so long in the world, and that I have loved Thee so little. Ah, give me a portion of that sorrow which Thou didst feel for my sins in the garden of Gethsemane. Oh, that I had died before I offended Thee. It consoles me, however, to know that Thou givest me time to love Thee. I desire to spend all that remains of my life in Thy love. I love Thee, O infinite Good! I love Thee, the only love of my soul. Ah, make me entirely Thine before I die. Draw all my affections to Thy love, so that I may never love any object but Thee.

But while I live I am in danger of losing Thee. When shall I be able to say, O my Jesus that I can never lose Thee again! O Jesus, unite me to

Thee, so that I can never be separated from Thee. Grant me this favour, through the love with which Thou didst love me on the cross.

O most holy Virgin, thou art most dear to God, he denies thee nothing; obtain for me the grace never more to offend him, and to love him with my whole heart. I ask no other favour of thee.

III.

The Charity to be Practiced in Works, and towards Whom it is to be Practiced.

With regard to the charity which you ought to practice in works, endeavor to be always ready to assist your sisters in all their necessities. Some religious say that they sincerely and affectionately love all their sisters, but they will not submit to inconvenience for the sake of any of them. My little children, let us not love in word, nor in tongue, but in deed and in truth. To fulfill the precept of charity, it is not enough to love our neighbor in words: we must love him in deed. The just are merciful says the Wise Man. All the saints were full of charity and compassion to all who required their assistance. It is related of St. Teresa, that she was accustomed to perform every day some act of charity towards her sisters; and whenever she was unable to do so by day, she was careful to do so by night, at least by showing light to the sisters who passed in the dark before her cell.

I. Give alms as often as it is in your power. Holy Scripture says, that alms delivers a soul from death; that it purifies her from sin, and obtains for her the divine mercy and eternal salvation. For alms, says Tobias, delivereth from death, and the same is that which purgeth away sins, and maketh to find mercy and life everlasting. St. Cyprian says, that "The Lord commands nothing more frequently than the constant practice of alms." By alms-deeds I mean not only the distribution of money or of temporal goods, but every species of relief given to a neighbor who stands in need of our assistance. He that hath the substance of this world, says St. John, and shall see his brother in need, how doth the charity of God abide in him? When a religious assists her companions in their labors she performs an act of charity very pleasing in the sight of God. St. Theodora, a religious, endeavored to assist all her sisters in performing the duties of their office, but was careful never to seek assistance from anyone in the discharge of her own duties. St. Mary Magdalene de Pazzi not only assisted her sisters in their most laborious duties, but also offered to perform by herself alone every work that required extraordinary labor. Hence it was a common saying in the convent, that she labored more than four lay-sisters. Endeavor as much as possible to imitate her conduct, and when you are overcome by fatigue, look on your Spouse carrying his cross, and embrace with joy any new labor which your duties may require. The aid that you receive from God will be proportioned to the assistance that you give to your companions. And with what measure you mete, says Jesus Christ, it shall be measured to you again. Hence, St. John Chrysostom says that the practice of charity is a powerful means of obtaining great graces from God. "Alms," says the saint, "Is the most lucrative of all arts." St. Mary Magdalene de Pazzi used to say that she felt more happy during the time she assisted her neighbor than when she was rapt in contemplation. "Because," says the saint, "When I am rapt in contemplation, God assists me; but when I relieve a neighbor, I assist God." The Redeemer has declared that what we do to a brother, we do to him. But in assisting others you should not expect either thanks or recompense. You should even rejoice when you receive for your kindness no other reward than inattention and reproach. For then you will have double profit. It is an act of charity to accede to the reasonable requests of others. But should a sister ask you to leave your devotions in order to amuse her by your conversation, you ought to refuse her request, and attend to your devotions. Charity is well ordered. He set in order charity in me, says the Spouse in the Canticles. Hence whatever injures your own spiritual progress, or that of a sister in religion, is not charity.

II. The most perfect charity consists in zeal for your neighbor's spiritual good. To relieve the spiritual necessities of a fellow-man, or to contribute to his spiritual welfare, as far excels the exercise of charity towards his body as the dignity of the soul transcends the lowly condition of the flesh. Charity towards the soul is practiced, in the first place, by correcting our neighbors' faults. St. James declares that he who causes a sinner to be converted from the error of his way, shall save his soul from death, and shall cover a multitude of sins. But, on the other hand, St. Augustine says that he who sees a brother destroying his soul, by giving way to anger against a neighbor, or by insulting him, and neglects to correct him, sins more grievously by his silence than the other does by his insults and contumely. "You," says the saint, "See him perish, and care not; your silence is more criminal than his reproachful language." Do not excuse yourself by saying that you know not how to correct him. St. John Chrysostom tells you that for correcting the faults of others charity is more necessary than wisdom. Make the correction at a seasonable time, with charity and sweetness, and it will be profitable. If you are Superior, you are bound by your office to correct the sisters; if not, you are bound in charity to administer correction as often as you expect fruit from it. Would it not be cruelty in him who should see a blind man walking over a precipice not to admonish him of his danger, and thus rescue him from temporal death? But it would be still greater cruelty in you to neglect, when able, to deliver a sister from eternal death. If you prudently judge that your advice would be unprofitable, be careful at least to make known the fault to the Superior, or to some other person who will be able to apply a remedy. Do not say, This is not my business; I will not take any trouble about it. This was the language of Cain. Am I, said he, my brother's keeper? It is the duty of everyone, when able, to save his neighbor from ruin. And, says Ecclesiasticus, he gave every one of them a commandment concerning his neighbour.

St. Philip Neri says, that when necessary, God wishes that we omit mental prayer in order to assist a neighbor, particularly in his spiritual necessities. St. Gertrude desired one day to entertain herself in prayer, but a work of charity was to be performed, and therefore the Lord said to her: "Tell me, Gertrude, do you intend that I should serve you, or that you should serve me?" "If," says St. Gregory, "You go to God, take care not to come alone to him." And St. Augustine says, "If you love God, draw all to the love of God." If you love God, you should take care not to be alone in loving him, but should labor to bring to his love all your relatives, and all those with whom you have intercourse, but particularly your sisters in religion. Ah, how a holy nun can sanctify the whole Community by her words, by her example, by performing her exercises of devotion with a view to induce others to do the same! Be not afraid of vainglory. Actions that have nothing extraordinary in them, but which become every religious that tends to perfection, according to her obligation, ought to be performed, even with the intention of giving good example, and of drawing the sisters nearer to God. So let your light shine before men, that they may see your good works, and glorify your Father who is in heaven. Hence, to appear devout, mortified, observant of rule, devoted to mental prayer and to frequent Communion, in order to give good example to the other sisters, is not an act of vanity, but an act of charity, very pleasing to God.

III. Endeavor, then, to assist all according to the best of your ability, by words, by works, and particularly by prayers. Every spouse of Jesus Christ should have zeal for his honor, as he himself said to St. Teresa, when he called her his spouse: "Henceforth, as a true spouse, you shall be zealous for my honor." If the spouse of Jesus Christ do not take his part, who will take it? Many Doctors, along with St. Basil, teach, that by the words, Amen I say to you, if you ask the Father anything in my name, he will give it you. Jesus Christ promises to hear our prayers, not only for ourselves, but also for others, provided they do not place a positive obstacle in the way. Hence, in the common prayer, in your thanksgiving after Communion, and your visits to the Blessed Sacrament, you should never omit to recommend to God all poor sinners, infidels, and heretics, and all that live without God.

How pleasing to Jesus Christ are the prayers of his spouses for sinners! He once said to the Venerable Sister Seraphina de Capri: "Assist me, O my daughter, to save souls by your prayers." To Mary Magdalene de Pazzi he said: See, Magdalene, how Christians are in the hands of the devil; unless my elect by their prayers deliver them, they shall be devoured. Hence the saint used to say to her religious: "My sisters, God has not separated us from the world only for our own good, but also for the benefit of sinners." And on another occasion she said: "My sisters, we have to render to God an account of so many lost souls: had we recommended them to God with fervor, perhaps they would not be damned." Hence we read in her life that she did not allow an hour of the day to pass without praying for sinners. That great servant of God, Sister Stephana de Soncino, for forty years performed severe penances, and offered them all for sinners. Oh, how many souls are sometimes converted, not so much by the sermons of priests, as by the prayers of religious! It was once revealed to a preacher that the fruit which he produced was not the effect of his sermons, but of the prayers of a brother who assisted him at the pulpit. Be careful, also, to pray for priests, that they may labor with true zeal for the salvation of souls.

IV. Do not neglect to pray for the souls in purgatory. It is not only a counsel, but also (as a learned author says) a duty of holy charity, to pray for these holy souls who stand in great need of our prayers. St. Thomas teaches that Christian charity extends not only to the living, but also to all who have died in the state of grace. Hence, as we are bound to relieve our living neighbors, who require our aid, so we are obliged to succor these holy prisoners. According to St. Thomas, their sufferings surpass all the pains of this life. They stand in need of our assistance, because they cannot assist themselves. A certain Cistercian monk appeared after death to the sacristan of his monastery, and said to him: "Assist me by your prayers, for I can obtain nothing for myself." If all the faithful ought to assist these holy souls, how much more are religious, placed by God in monasteries, which are so many houses of prayer, bound to succor them by their suffrages. Be careful, then, to recommend to God, every day, in all your prayers, these spouses of the Saviour, who ask your assistance. Be not unwilling to offer for them some fasts and other mortifications. Above all, apply to them the masses that you hear, for this affords great relief to these holy souls who, even in their prison, cannot be ungrateful, and will not fail to obtain great graces for us from God, and still greater when they are admitted into heaven.

V. From what has been already said, you see how much you stand in need of the virtue of charity, in order to be a saint, and even to be saved. You must practice this charity towards all your neighbors, but particularly towards the sisters of your monastery. If you lived in a desert this virtue would not be so necessary. For in order to become a saint in the solitude of a desert it would be sufficient to attend to prayer and penance. But if you have not great charity towards those with whom you live in the cloister, you will commit a thousand defects every day, and will perhaps be lost. Were a vessel in the midst of the ocean tossed by a violent tempest, surely the persons on board would think only of saving one another from shipwreck. Imagine that God has placed you in this monastery as in a ship, where it is your duty to assist one another to escape the shipwreck of eternal death, and to reach heaven, where you hope to be united for eternity in praising God.

Be particularly careful to practice charity towards the sick, whether they are choir nuns or lay-sisters. Father Anthony Torres used to say: "If you wish to know whether the Spirit of God reigns in a Community, ask how the sick are treated." Hence, when Superior, although of a most amiable disposition, he punished with severity the person who had the care of the sick whenever he was wanting in charity to them. Oh, how pleasing to God is charity towards the sick! All religious that tend to perfection practice this charity, either in choir or in the cells of the sick. St. Mary Magdalene de Pazzi, even though not infirmarian, never omitted (when it was in her power) to assist and serve the sick; and she would say that she desired always to live in a hospital in order to be always employed in an office so pleasing to God.

Let it be remembered that the merit of serving the sick is far greater than the merit of serving those who are in health. First, because the sick stand in greater need of assistance. They sometimes find themselves abandoned by all; sometimes tormented by pains, by melancholy, and by fears. Oh, how pleasing is it to God to labor to console them in that state of affliction! There is greater merit also, because there are greater inconveniences in serving them; in their rooms you find a disagreeable smell, and the gloom of melancholy.

Be careful, then, when it is in your power, never to omit to visit a sick companion, even though she be the humblest lay-sister in the monastery. To the lay-sisters you should pay special attention, for they are generally the most abandoned, particularly when their illness is of long duration. Console them, serve them, and even bring them an occasional little present. Do not look for thanks; but bear with their complaints, impatience, and rudeness. The Lord will reward the charity you practice towards them. It is related in the Chronicles of the Teresians, that St. Isabella of the Angels was seen ascending to heaven immediately after her death, carried by angels amid great splendor. And she said to a religious to whom she appeared, that God had bestowed that great glory on her on account of her charity towards the sick.

VI. Lastly, I recommend you, above all, to practice charity towards the sisters who are opposed to you. I am grateful, such a nun says, to all who treat me with kindness. But I cannot bear acts of ingratitude. But, as Jesus Christ says, the infidels are grateful to their benefactors. Christian virtue consists in wishing well to those who hate and injure us. But I say to you, says Jesus Christ, love your enemies, do good to them that hate you, and pray for them that persecute and calumniate you. What a horrible thing must it be in a religious who makes mental prayer every day, and communicates frequently, to entertain aversion or rancor towards a sister! She is even not ashamed to show it; and when she hears others speak of the sister, she endeavors to lessen their esteem for her whenever she can. If she meet the sister, she does not salute her; if the sister speak to her, she turns away. She turns away from a sister, and God turns his back on her. Consider how the Lamb of God must reward such a tiger of hell. But poor and miserable is the nun that lives in a monastery with hatred in her heart! She shall suffer a hell here and another hereafter; she endures, even in this life, the punishment of the damned, because she is constrained to live always with a person whom she cannot bear to see.

But, Father (she replies), this sister is impertinent; it is impossible to bear with her. But it is in bearing with those who are unbearable that the virtue of charity consists. She lessens your character; she thwarts your designs; she even takes away your reputation; but you, as it perfectly ignorant of her conduct, should force yourself, not to show the smallest alienation or coldness: whenever occasion requires, speak to her with a serene countenance. If she appear distant with you, salute her before she salutes you, and endeavor to gain her by sweetness. To act in this manner is not baseness, but the most heroic action that you can perform; because it is very pleasing to God. Do not say that her conduct is unreasonable: listen to what St. Teresa says: "Let her who wishes to bear the cross only when it is reason able, return to the world, where such reasons are admitted." The reason that ought to prevail with you is, to practice charity in order to please God, though you should die of pain.

If the sister goes so far as to do you a positive injury, take revenge on her; but let it be the revenge of the saints. What is the revenge of the saints? St. Paulinus answers, that "To love an enemy is heavenly revenge." The saints have taken revenge by loving, praising, and doing good to all that have done them evil. St. Catharine performed for a long time the offices of a servant for a woman confined by sickness, who had charged the saint with a sin against chastity. St. Acaius sold his goods in order to relieve a man who had taken away his reputation. St. Ambrose assigned to an assassin, who made an attempt on his life, a daily sum, sufficient to enable him to live comfortably. Venustanus, governor of Tuscany, through hatred of the faith, ordered the hands of St. Sabinus, bishop, to be cut off. The tyrant feeling a violent pain in one of his eyes, prayed the saint to apply a remedy. The saint offered a prayer to God, and raising his arm, still streaming blood, blessed the tyrant, restored his health, and saved his soul; for, entering into himself at the sight of the miracle, the governor was converted to the faith. St. John Chrysostom relates that St. Meletius, seeing the people prepared to stone to death the governor who conducted him to exile, stretched his arms over him, and thus saved his life. Father Segneri also relates that in Bologna there was a lady, whose only son was murdered; the murderer came into her house in order to escape the officers of justice. What did she do? She concealed him from them; and said to him: Since I have lost my son, you shall henceforth be my son and heir: take this sum of money, and save yourself elsewhere; for here your life is not secure. In answer to such examples someone may say: These have been saints; I have not strength to imitate their example. Let St. Ambrose answer for me: If you have not strength, ask it of God and he will give it. "If," says the saint, "You are weak, pray: you pray, and God protects you."

He who pardons those who have offended him is secure of forgiveness from God, who says: Forgive, and you shall be forgiven. Blessed Baptista of Verona, a Franciscan nun, used to say: Were I to raise the dead to life, I would not be so certain of being loved by God as I am when I feel inclined to do good to those who have done me evil. Our Lord said to Blessed Angela of Foligno: The strongest proof of a mutual love between me and my servants is the love that they bear to the person who has offended them. If, then, you can do nothing else, at least pray for all who have offended and persecuted you; and recommend them fervently to God, that you may fulfill the command of Jesus Christ: Pray for them that persecute and calumniate you. Blessed Jane of the Cross prayed continually for those who gave her any displeasure. Hence her sisters in religion used to say: Whoever desires the prayers of Mother Jane must offer some insult to her. St. Elizabeth, Queen of Hungary, after having prayed for a person who had offended her, heard from God the following words: Know that you never said a prayer more acceptable to me than that which you have just offered, and on account of this prayer I pardon all your sins. Imitate her example, and you shall certainly obtain the pardon and affection of your divine Spouse.

Prayer.

My Jesus, grant me the gift of Thy love, which will make me embrace
261

all pains and insults in order to please Thee: give me strength to deny myself all things that are not pleasing to Thee, and to accept all that is disagreeable to self-love— sorrows, persecutions, loss of relatives, of health, of self-esteem, and all the crosses that shall come from Thee. I now accept all from Thy hand: I accept all the troubles of my life, and especially the pains of my death. Grant that I may live only to please Thee; and that at death I may sacrifice my life to Thee, with all the affection of my soul. My God, Thou dost command me not to offend Thee; and I dread an offence against Thee more than death. Thou dost command me to love Thee, and I desire only to love Thee. But I know my weakness. Ah, assist me continually with Thy grace: do not leave me in my own hands, if Thou dost, I will betray Thee again. I love Thee, O my Sovereign Good, and I hope always to love Thee.

O Mary, my hope, and my mother, obtain for me the grace to be faithful to God, and to love him as a God of infinite goodness deserves to be loved.

CHAPTER XIII.

PATIENCE.

I.

Patience in General.

Patience hath a perfect work. Patience is a perfect sacrifice that we offer to God; because in suffering tribulations and contradictions we do nothing but accept from his hands the cross that he sends us. A patient man is better than the valiant. He who suffers with patience is better than a valiant man. Some are resolute and courageous in promoting and supporting a pious undertaking, but are not patient in bearing adversity: it would be better for them to be valiant in patience than in the works that they undertake. This earth is a place of merits, and therefore it is not a place of repose, but of toils and pains; for merits are acquired not by rest, but by suffering. All those that live here below (whether saints or sinners) must suffer. Some are in want of one comfort, others of another; some have nobility, but have not property; others abound in riches, but want nobility; others enjoy nobility and wealth, but have not health. In a word, all, even sovereigns, have occasion to suffer; and because they are the most exalted of mortals their cares and troubles are the most harassing and perplexing.

All our good, then, consists in bearing crosses with patience. Hence the Holy Ghost admonishes us not to assimilate ourselves to senseless beasts that break out into a rage when they are unable to indulge their appetites. Do not become like the horse and the mule who have not understanding. What other advantage than to double our misfortunes can we ever derive from giving way to impatience in contradictions? The good and the bad thief both died on the cross and suffered the same pains; but because the one embraced them with patience he was saved, and because the other bore them with impatience he was damned. St. Augustine says that the same affliction sends the just to glory because they accept it with peace and the wicked to fire because they submit to it with impatience.

It often happens that a person who flies from a cross that God sends him meets with another far more afflicting. They, says Job, that fear the hoary frost, the snow shall fall upon them. They who shun the hoar-frost shall be covered with snow. Such a nun may say: Give me any other office, but take from me the one that I hold. But she shall suffer much more in the second office than in the first, and with little or no merit. Be careful not to imitate her: embrace the fatigue and tribulation that God sends you: for you shall thus acquire greater merit, and shall have less to suffer: you will at least suffer with peace, knowing that your sufferings come not from self-will, but from the will of God. Let us be persuaded of the truth of what St. Augustine says, that the whole life of a Christian must be a continual cross. The life of religious who wish to become saints must in a special manner be a continued series of crosses. St. Gregory Nazianzen says that these noble souls place their riches in poverty, their glory in contempt, and their delights in the voluntary privation of earthly pleasures. Hence St. John Climacus asks: Who is truly a religious? It is, he says, the nun that offers continual violence to herself: and when shall this violence cease? When, answers St. Prosper, life shall have an end. Then shall the battle cease when the conquest of the eternal kingdom shall be obtained. If you remember to have hitherto offended God, and if you desire to be saved, you should be consoled when you see that God sends you occasions of suffering. St. John Chrysostom writes: "Sin is an ulcer and chastisement a medicinal iron: therefore the sinner if left unpunished is most miserable." Sin is an imposthume of the soul: if tribulation do not come to extract the putrid humor the soul is lost. Miserable the sinner who is not punished after his sin in this life.

Be persuaded, then, says St. Augustine, that when the Lord sends you suffering he acts as a physician; and that the tribulation that he sends you is not the punishment of your condemnation, but a remedy for your salvation. "Let man understand," says the holy Doctor, "That God is a physician, and that tribulation is a medicine for salvation, not a punishment for damnation." Hence you ought to thank God when he chastises you; for his chastisements are a proof that he loves you, and receives you into the number of his children. Whoever the Lord loveth, says St. Paul, he chastiseth; and he scourgeth every son whom he receiveth. Hence, St. Augustine says: "Do you enjoy consolation, acknowledge a father who caresses you: are you in tribulation, recognize a parent who corrects you." On the other hand, the same holy Doctor says: "Unhappy you, if after you have sinned God exempts you from scourges in this life. It is a sign that he excludes you from the number of his children." Say not, then, for the future, when you find yourself in tribulation, that God has forgotten you; say rather that you have forgotten your sins. He who knows that he has offended God must pray with St. Bonaventure: "Run, O Lord, run, and wound Thy servants with sacred wounds, lest they be wounded with the wounds of death." Run, O Lord, and wound Thy servants with the wounds of love and salvation, that they may escape the wounds of Thy wrath and of eternal death.

Let us rest assured that God sends us crosses not for our perdition but for our salvation; if we know not how to turn them to our own profit it is entirely our own fault. Explaining the words, the house of Israel is become dross to me, all these are . . . iron and lead in the midst of the furnace, St. Gregory says: "As if God should say, I wished to purify them by the fire of tribulation, and sought to make them gold, but in the furnace they have become to me iron and lead." I have endeavoured by the fire of tribulation to change them into gold, but they have been converted into lead. These are the sinners who, after having several times deserved hell when visited with any calamity, break out into impatience and anger; they almost wish to treat God as if he were guilty of injustice and tyranny, and even go so far as to say: But, O Lord, I am not the only one who has offended Thee; it appears that I am the only person whom Thou chastisest: I am weak, I have not strength to bear so great a cross. Miserable man, alas, what do you say? You say to God, I am not the only one who has offended you. If others have offended God, he will punish them also in this life if he wishes to show mercy to them; but do you not know that, according to the words which God himself spoke by Ezekiel, My indignation shall rest in thee, and my jealousy shall depart from thee, and . . . I will be angry no more, the greatest chastisement that God can inflict on sinners is not to chastise them on this earth? I have no more zeal for your soul, and therefore as long as you live you shall never more feel my anger. But St. Bernard says, "God's anger is greatest when he is not angry. I wish, O Father of mercies, that Thou mayest be angry with me." God's wrath against sinners is greatest when he is not angry with them, and abstains from chastising them. Hence the saint prayed the Lord, saying: Lord, I wish that Thou shouldst treat me with the mercy of the Father of mercies, and therefore I wish that Thou shouldst chastise me here for my sins, and thus save me from Thy everlasting vengeance. Do you say, I have not strength to bear this cross? But if you have not strength why do you not ask it of God? He has promised to give his aid to all who pray for it; Ask, and it shall be given you.

When you, dear sister, are visited by God with any infirmity, or loss, or persecution, humble yourself, and say with the good thief, We receive the due reward of our deeds. Lord, I deserve this cross because I have offended Thee. Humble yourself and be comforted: for the chastisement that you receive is a proof that God wishes to pardon the eternal punishment due to your sins. Who will grant me, says Job, . . . that this may be my comfort, that afflicting me with sorrow, He spare not. Let this be my consolation, that the Lord may afflict me and may not spare me here below in order to spare me hereafter. O God, how can he who has deserved hell complain if the Lord send him a cross. Were the pains of hell trifling, still, because they are eternal, we should gladly exchange them for all temporal sufferings that have an end. But no: in hell there are all kinds of pain—they are all intense and everlasting. And though you should have preserved baptismal innocence and have never deserved hell, you have at least merited a long purgatory: and do you know what purgatory is? St. Thomas says that the souls in purgatory are tormented by the very fire that tortures the damned. Hence St. Augustine says that the pain of that fire surpasses every torment that man can suffer in this life. Be content, then, to be chastised in this life rather than in the next; particularly since by accepting crosses with patience in this life your sufferings will be meritorious; but hereafter you will suffer without merit.

Console yourself also in suffering with the hope of paradise. St. Joseph Calasanctius used to say: "To gain heaven all labor is small." And before him the Apostle said: The sufferings of this time are not worthy to be compared with the glory to come, that shall be revealed in us. It would be but little to suffer all the pains of this earth for the enjoyment of a single moment in heaven: how much more, then, ought we to embrace the crosses that God sends us when we know that the short sufferings of this life shall merit for us an eternal felicity. That which is at present momentary and light of our tribulation, worketh for us . . . an eternal weight of glory. We should feel not sadness but consolation of spirit when God sends us sufferings here below. They who pass to eternity with the greatest merits shall receive the greatest reward. It is on this account that the Lord sends us tribulations. Virtues, which are the fountains of merits, are practiced only by acts. They who have the most frequent occasions of annoyance make the most frequent acts of patience; they who are most frequently insulted make most frequent acts of meekness. Hence St. James says, Blessed is the man that endureth temptation; for when he hath been proved, he shall receive the crown of life. Blessed is he who suffers afflictions with peace; for when he shall be thus proved he shall receive the crown of eternal life.

This thought made St. Agapitus, martyr, a boy of fifteen years, say, when the tyrant ordered his head to be encompassed with burning coals, "It is very little to bear the burning of my head, which shall be crowned with glory in heaven." This thought made Job exclaim: If we have received good things at the hand of God, why should we not receive evil? He meant to say, if we have gladly received good things, why should we not also receive with greater joy temporal evils, by which we shall acquire the eternal goods of paradise? This thought also filled with jubilation the hermit whom a soldier found singing in a wood, though his body was covered with ulcers so that his flesh was falling to pieces. The soldier said to him: Is it you that were singing? Yes, I sang, and I had reason to sing; for between me and God there is nothing but the filthy wall of my body. I now see it falling to pieces, and therefore I sing, because I see that the time is at hand when I shall go to enjoy my Lord. This thought made St. Francis of Assisi say. "So great is the good which I expect, that to me every pain gives delight." In a word, the saints feel consoled when they see themselves in tribulation, and are afflicted when they enjoy earthly consolations. We read in the Teresian Chronicles that in reciting these words of the Office: When wilt thou comfort me? Mother Isabella of the Angels used to say them so fast that she would anticipate the other sisters. Being asked why she did so, she answered: "I am afraid that God may console me in this life."

To be in tribulation in this world is a great sign of predestination. "To be afflicted here below," says St. Gregory, "Belongs to the elect, for whom is reserved the beatitude of eternity." Hence we find in the lives of the saints, that all, without exception, have been loaded with crosses. This is precisely what St. Jerome wrote to the virgin Eustochia: "Seek," says the holy Doctor, "And you shall find that every saint has been subject to tribulations: Solomon, alone, lived in the midst of delights, and therefore perhaps he was lost." The Apostle has said that all the predestined must be found like to Jesus Christ: Whom he foreknew, he also predestined to be made conformable to the image of His Son. But the life of Jesus Christ was a life of continual suffering; hence the same Apostle says: Yet so if we suffer with him, that we may be also glorified with him. If we suffer with Jesus Christ, we shall then be glorified with Jesus Christ.

But we shall not be glorified with him unless we suffer with patience like our Saviour, who when he was reviled did not revile: when he suffered he threatened not. St. Gregory says that as to suffer with patience is a mark of predestination, so to suffer with impatience is a presage of damnation. Hence the Lord tells us that we shall attain salvation only by suffering with patience: In your patience you shall possess your souls. And let us be persuaded that God sends us tribulations only because he seeks our welfare; by them he wishes to detach us from earthly pleasures, which may occasion the loss of our eternal salvation. "The world," says St. Augustine, "Is bitter and it is loved; if it were sweet, how ardently, think you, should it be loved." The world is bitter because all its delights do not content the heart of man, and because they all ultimately terminate in bitterness and remorse of conscience; but still it is loved. Imagine, then, says the saint, were it sweet, how intensely should we love it, and how completely would we forget the soul, heaven, and God. To wean an infant, and to give it a horror of taking suck, the mother puts gall on the paps. It is thus God treats us. He makes the very pleasures of this earth become bitter, that, detaching our hearts from them, we may pant after the eternal delights which he prepares in heaven for all those that love him. It was for this end that our loving Saviour came on earth to suffer, that we might not refuse to imitate his example. Christ, says St. Peter, suffered for us, leaving you an example, that you should follow his steps. Behold how he invites us to follow him: If any man will come after me, let him deny himself, and take up his cross and follow me. As if he said, He who wishes not to suffer and refuses the cross let him cease to pretend to be my disciple, or to expect to follow me to paradise.

But the desire of pleasing God is the sublime end which a soul should have in embracing sufferings Ecclesiasticus says that some show friendship only in the time of prosperity, and abandon a friend in his adversity: There is a friend for his own occasion, and he will not abide in the day of thy trouble. But the most certain testimony of love is to suffer with cheerfulness for the person loved. The sacrifice most agreeable to God consists in embracing with patience all the crosses which he sends. Charity is patienth beareth all things. Love bears all things: external crosses, loss of health, loss of property, of honors, of relatives, of friends: interior crosses, anguish, temptations, sorrows, desolation of spirit. By patience virtue is proved. Hence, in the lives of the saints we usually find a description of their patience under afflictions. It is thus the Lord proves our fidelity. The devil tempts us, and God also tempts us. The devil tempts us in order to bring us to perdition, God tempts us in order to prove us: As gold in the furnace he hath proved them. As gold is proved by fire, so God proves the love of his lovers by the fire of tribulation. Hence to be in tribulation is a mark that the soul is dear to God. Because thou wast acceptable to God, said the angel to Tobias, It was necessary that temptation should prove thee. St. Jerome says that when God sends a person an occasion of suffering, he confers a greater favour than if he gave him power to raise the dead to life. Because, adds the saint, when we work miracles we are debtors to God, but when we bear afflictions with patience, God is, in a certain manner, our debtor.

O God, how is it possible for him who looks at the crucifix, and beholds a God dying in a sea of sorrows and insults; how, I say, is it possible for him, if he loves that God, not to bear with cheerfulness, or even not to desire to suffer every pain for his sake? St. Mary Magdalene de Pazzi used to say: "The sharpest pains become sweet when we behold Jesus on the cross." Justus Lipsius once found himself greatly afflicted with pains: a certain person endeavoured to encourage him to bear them with patience by placing before him the patience of the stoics; but he turned to the crucifix and said: There is true patience. He meant to say, that the example of a God who had suffered so much for the love of us is sufficient to animate us to endure all pain for the love of him. "The ignominy of the cross," says St. Bernard, "Is grateful to him who is not ungrateful to a crucified God." To him who loves his crucified Saviour pains and opprobrium are agreeable. When St. Eleazar was asked by his virgin spouse, St. Afra, how he could submit to so many insults from the rabble without seeking revenge, he said: "My spouse, think not that I am insensible to these insults; I feel them strongly; but I turn to Jesus on the cross, and continue to look at him until my soul becomes tranquil." Love, says St. Augustine, makes all things easy. After being wounded with divine love, St. Catharine Genoa used to say that she knew not what it was to suffer. Although she endured the most grievous pains, she felt none of them, because she regarded them as sent by him who loved her so tenderly. Thus also a good religious of the Society of Jesus, when God visited him with any pain, sickness, or persecution, used to say within himself: "Tell me, O pain, sickness, or persecution, who sends you? Does God send you? Welcome, welcome!" Thus he was always in peace.

Let us conclude. Since in this life we must suffer either cheerfully or with reluctance, let us endeavor to suffer with merit, that is, with patience. Patience is a shield that defends us against all the pains arising from persecutions, infirmities, losses, and other afflictions. He who has not this shield, has to bear all these pains.

Let us, then, in the first place, ask this patience of God; without asking it we shall never obtain this great gift. When afflictions come upon us, let us be careful to do violence to ourselves, and not to break out into words of impatience or complaint. The fire that burns in a vessel is soon extinguished when the vessel is closed. To him that over cometh, I will give the hidden manna. When a person does violence to conquer himself in adversity, by instantly embracing the cross that God sends him, oh, what sweetness does the Lord make him afterwards experience in the very tribulation that he suffers—a sweetness hidden from men of the world, but well known to souls that love God. St. Augustine used to say, that to enjoy a good conscience in the midst of afflictions is sweeter than to live with a guilty conscience in the midst of delights. Speaking of herself, St. Teresa said; I have several times experienced that when I generously resolve to do an act, God instantly makes the performance of it pleasant to me. He wishes the soul to feel these terrors in the beginning, that she may have greater merit.

He who resolves to suffer for God, suffers no more pain. Let us read the lives of the saints, and see how they have been enamoured of suffering.

St. Gertrude used to say, that so great was her enjoyment in suffering, that no time was more painful than that in which she was free from pain. St. Teresa used to say, that she did not wish to live without suffering; hence she would often exclaim: "Either to suffer or to die." St. Mary Magdalene de Pazzi went so far as to say: "To suffer and not to die."

When the tyrant was preparing new torments for the martyr Procopius, the saint said to him: "Torment me as much as you please; do you not know that to him who loves Jesus Christ there is nothing more dear than to suffer for Jesus Christ."

St. Gordian, as St. Basil relates, being threatened with great torments if he refused to deny Jesus Christ, answered: "I am sorry that I can die but once for my Saviour, Jesus Christ." He afterwards intrepidly suffered death.

To the tyrant who threatened to make her die in a caldron of boiling pitch, St. Potamiena, virgin, said: I entreat you to let me down into this caldron, not at once, but by degrees, that thus I may suffer more for my Jesus. The tyrant complied with her request: she was let down gradually into the caldron, till the pitch having reached her neck, took away her speech and her life.

Baronius describes the celebrated martyrdom of three holy virgins, called Faith, Hope, and Charity, who when threatened with torments by the tyrant Antiochus courageously said: Do you not know that to Christians nothing is more desirable than to suffer for Jesus Christ? St. Faith was first scourged; her breasts were then cut off, she was afterwards tormented with fire, and finally beheaded. St. Hope was first beaten with the sinews of an ox; her ribs were then torn with iron combs and she was afterwards thrown into a vessel of burning pitch. St. Charity was the youngest; she was not more than nine years old; hence the tyrant expected that she would yield through fear of torments. He said to her, My child, be you at least wise, unless you wish to be tortured like your sisters. The holy child answered: You deceive yourself, O Antiochus; all your torments shall not make me forsake Jesus Christ. The tyrant ordered her to be fastened to a rope, and to be cast several times from a height to the ground, until all her bones were dislocated. He then commanded her members to be pierced with sharp irons, so that she died exhausted of blood.

Let us come to more modern examples.

In Japan a certain married woman called Maxentia was subjected to torments for the faith. One of the executioners wished to alleviate her pains, but she rejected the offer. Seeing her continue firm in confessing the faith, one of her persecutors pointed a sword twice to her cheek in order to terrify her; but she said to him: O God, how do you expect to terrify me with that death which I desire? The way to fill me with terror is to promise me life. After these words she stretched her neck to the executioner, and he cut off her head.

In Japan, also, Father John Baptist Maciado, of the Society of Jesus, was confined in a damp prison, in which he remained for forty days in such intense pain, that he could not rest by night or by day. From this prison he wrote to another religious: My Father, not withstanding all my pains, I would not exchange my condition for that of the first monarch of the earth.

From a prison in which he had a great deal to suffer Father Charles Spinola wrote to his companions: "Oh, how sweet is it to suffer for Jesus Christ! I have received the news of my condemnation. I pray you to thank the divine goodness for the great gift bestowed upon me." In the same letter he added: "Charles Spinola condemned for Jesus Christ." Soon after he was burnt alive on a slow fire. It is said that, in thanksgiving to God, when he was fastened to the stake, he intoned the Psalm, O praise the Lord, all ye nations. Thus he died.

But how, someone may ask with wonder, were the holy martyrs able to suffer with so much joy? Were they not flesh, or did the Lord make them insensible to pain? No, says St. Bernard, their patience and jubilation under suffering, says the saint, were the effect not of insensibility, but of the love which they bore to Jesus Christ; they were not exempt from pain, but through love for their Lord they conquered and despised it. That great servant of God, Father Hippolitus Durazzo, of the Society of Jesus, used to say: "Let God cost what he will, the price is never too great." And St. Joseph Calasanctius said, that he who knows not how to suffer for Jesus Christ knows not how to gain Jesus Christ. Ah, souls that understand the language of love, being convinced that by embracing crosses they please God, know well how to find all their happiness in suffering.

Prayer.

My crucified Jesus, Thou hast suffered so many sorrows and insults for my sake; Thou hast died in order to gain my love, and I have so often renounced Thy love for nothing. Have mercy on me and pardon me. Blessed be Thy mercy which has borne with me so long and with so much patience. During that time I neither loved Thee nor cared to be loved by Thee. I now love Thee with my whole soul; and the greatest of all my pains is that which arises from having offended Thee, who hast loved me so tenderly. Yes, this is my greatest pain. But it is a pain that consoles me, because it gives me confidence that Thou hast already pardoned me. Oh, that I had died rather than have ever offended Thee. My God, if I have not hitherto loved Thee, I now give myself entirely to Thee. I wish to renounce all things to love only Thee, my Saviour, who art worthy of infinite love. I have sinned enough against Thee. The remainder of my life I wish to spend in loving Thy heart, which is so enamoured of me. Tell me all Thou wishest from me: I wish to do it. Give me strength to execute this wish. I love Thee, O infinite Goodness, I love Thee with my whole heart; and for Thy sake I accept all the pains which Thou shalt be pleased to send me.

Mary, my Mother, assist me by thy intercession: in thee I trust.

II.

Patience in Sickness, Poverty, Contempt, Persecutions, and Spiritual Desolation.

1. PATIENCE IN SICKNESS.

We must practice patience in sickness. This is the touchstone by which the spirit of a Christian is found to be of gold or of copper. Some are cheerful, patient, and devout as long as they enjoy health, but when visited by sickness they commit a thousand defects: they appear to be inconsolable; they are impatient to all, even to the person who attends them through charity; they complain of every pain or inconvenience that they suffer; they complain of all,—of the physician, the Superior, the infirmarian,—saying that they are treated with neglect and inattention. Behold, the gold is found to be copper. But, my Father, such a person may say, I suffer so much, and can I not even complain, or tell what I endure? I do not forbid you to make known your pains when they are severe, but when they are trifling it is a weakness to complain of them to all, and to seek sympathy and compassion from everyone who visits you. And should the remedies prescribed not remove your pains, I wish that you yield not to impatience under them, but that you resign yourself in peace to the will of God.

Another may say, But where has charity gone? Behold how my very sisters forget me, and abandon me on the bed of sickness. I pity you; not on account of your bodily infirmities, but on account of your want of patience under them, which makes you doubly sick—in body and soul. The sisters forget you; but you have forgotten Jesus Christ, who died abandoned for your sake on the cross. And what profit do you derive from complaining of the sisters? Complain of yourself because you have but little love for Jesus Christ, and therefore have so little patience. St. Joseph Calasanctius used to say: "If the sick had patience there should be no more complaints." Salvian writes that there are many per sons who, had they good health, could not be saints. With regard to saintly women, we know from their published lives that they were almost all continually afflicted with various infirmities. For forty years St. Teresa was not free from pain for a single day. Hence, Salvian adds, that persons dedicated to the love of Jesus Christ are infirm, and wish to continue in their infirmities.

Another will perhaps say: I do not refuse sickness, but I regret that on account of my infirmities I am not able to be present in choir, to go to Communion, or to make mental prayer, and that I am a burden to the Community. Allow me to answer all these excuses one by one. 1. Tell me, why do you wish to go to the choir in order to recite the Office, or to the church in order to communicate? Is it not to please God? Well, but if it is God's will and pleasure that you go neither to choir to say the Office, nor to the church to communicate, but that you remain in bed to suffer, why should you be troubled? Father M. Avila wrote to a priest labouring under sickness: "Friend, do not stop to examine what you would do if you had health, but be content to remain sick as long as it shall please God. If you seek the will of God, it matters not whether you are in sickness or in health." St. Francis de Sales has even said that "We serve God better by sufferings than by works." 2. You say that in sickness you cannot make mental prayer, and why can you not make mental prayer? I grant that you cannot apply the mind to reflection, but why can you not look at the crucifix, and offer to your crucified Saviour the pains that you suffer? And what prayer can be better than to suffer, and to resign yourself to the divine will, uniting your sufferings to those of Jesus Christ, and presenting them to God in union with the sufferings of his Son? 3. You say that in sickness you are useless, and a burden to the Community. But as you conform yourself to the divine will, so you ought to suppose that your sisters also conform to it, when they see that you are a burden to the monastery, not through your own fault, but by the will of God. Ah, such desires and complaints spring not from the love of God, but from self-love; for we would wish to serve the Lord not in the manner that pleases him, but in the way that is agreeable to ourselves.

Ah, embrace with peace all the infirmities that God sends you, if you truly wish to please him, and wish at the same time to give good example to your sisters. Oh! How great the edification given by the religious, who, in spite of all her pains, and even in the danger of death with which she is threatened, preserves a serene countenance, abstains from all complaints against the physician or the sisters, thanks all for their attendance, whether it be much or little, and accepts in the spirit of obedience the remedies applied, however bitter or painful they may be! St. Lidwina, as Surius relates, lay for thirty-eight years on a board, abandoned, covered with sores, and tortured by pains: she never complained of anything, but peaceably embraced all her sufferings. Blessed Humiliana of Florence, a Franciscan nun, being afflicted with several painful and violent diseases, used to raise her hand to heaven, and say: "Be blessed, my love, be blessed." St. Clare was likewise continually sick for twenty-eight years, and the smallest complaint never escaped her lips. St. Theodore, abbot, had a painful ulcer during his whole life, and he would say that the Lord sent it in order to give him occasion to thank God unceasingly, as he was always accustomed to do. When we suffer any pain, let us cast a glance at so many holy martyrs, whose flesh was torn in pieces with iron hooks, or burnt with red-hot plates, and let us at the sight of their torments take courage to offer to God the pain by which we are afflicted.

Patience under the severity of the seasons accompanies patience in infirmities. When cold or heat is intense, some are disturbed and complain, particularly if they have not the clothes or other comforts that they wish for. Be careful not to imitate their example; but bless these creatures as ministers of the divine will, and say with Daniel, O ye fire and heat, bless the Lord. . . . O ye cold and heat, bless the Lord.

Above all, we should in the time of sickness accept death should it come, and the death that God wills. And what is this life but a continual tempest, in which we are always in danger of being lost? St. Aloysius, though he died in the flower of youth, embraced death with joy, saying: "Now I find myself, as I hope, in the grace of God: I know not what might happen to me hereafter. I therefore gladly quit this earth, if it now pleases God to call me to the other life." But you will say: St. Aloysius was a saint, and I am a sinner. But listen to the answer of Father M. Avila: Everyone who finds himself even moderately well disposed should desire death, in order to escape the danger of losing the grace of God, to which he is always exposed as long as he lives on this earth. What more desirable than, by a good death, to be secure of being no longer able to lose God! But, you reply, hitherto I have gained nothing for my soul: I would wish to live in order to do something before I die. But if God calls you at present to the other life, how do you know that for the future you will not be worse than you were hitherto, and that you will not fall into other sins and be lost?

And if we had no other motive, we ought to embrace death with peace when it comes, because it delivers us from the commission of new sins. In this life no one is exempt from all sins—at least from all venial sins. Hence, St. Bernard says: "Why do we desire life, in which the longer we live the more we sin?" Why do we desire to live, since we know that the greater the number of our days, the more our sins shall be multiplied? Moreover, if we love God, we should sigh to see and to love him face to face in heaven. But, unless death opens the gate to us, we cannot enter into that happy country. Hence the enamoured St. Augustine exclaimed: "Lord take me out of life, that I may be able to go to see Thee."

2. PATIENCE IN POVERTY.

In the second place, it is necessary to practice patience in the inconveniences of poverty when we are in want of temporal goods. "What," says St. Augustine, "Can be sufficient for him for whom God is not sufficient?" They who possess God, though they should want everything else, possess all things. Hence they can say, "My God and my all." Hence, the Apostle says, that though the saints have nothing, they possess all things. As having nothing, and possessing all things. When, then, you want medicines in sickness, when you want food, or fire in the winter, or clothes, say, My God, Thou alone art sufficient for me;

and thus console yourself.

Embrace also the losses of creatures, such as the loss of property, of relatives, of friends. Such a nun loses a trifle, a book, a wax taper, a medal, and she disturbs the whole monastery, and cannot keep herself in peace. Another is inconsolable at the death of a relative. She gives up mental prayer, she abstains from Communion, she is impatient to all her sisters, she shuts herself up in her cell, she will not take food, and sends away those who come to console her. To such a religious I would say: Is this the love that you bear to God? Then it is not true that God is your every good, since it is now manifest, that because you have lost a creature, you no longer enjoy peace, and appear almost to care no more about God? Tell me what advantage do you derive from thus abandoning yourself to melancholy? Do you imagine that you please the person who has died? No; you displease God, and also the deceased relative. How much more pleasing would it be to her, if, conforming yourself to the divine will, you endeavoured to abstain from weeping and howling, and sought to unite yourself more closely to God, and to pray for her if she is in purgatory. To shed an occasional tear at the death of a relative is a pardonable weakness of nature; but immoderate grief proceeds from weakness of spirit and of the love of God. Holy religious also hear of the death of persons most dear to them; but reflecting that God has willed their death, they instantly resign themselves, and go in peace to pray for them. They then make more frequent meditations and Communions, and unite themselves more to God, hoping to go one day to enjoy him in heaven, along with their deceased relatives.

Other nuns, who appear to be the most devout, are not so much afflicted at the loss of relatives and friends as at the loss of their director. They seem as if inclined to complain of God, saying that he has abandoned them by taking away their help and spiritual guide. Oh what folly! It is God and not a confessor that must make us saints. The Lord certainly wishes that we do not leave our confessor as long as we have him to point out to us the will of God in our regard. But when God takes him away he will take care to send another, or to supply in some other way. Hence to be disturbed when we are deprived of our ordinary director is not virtue, but an imperfection, and a great imperfection; for the inquietude arises either from earthly attachment, or at least from a want of confidence in God. Let it be your care, dear sister, to remain always detached from your director, and to be prepared to lose him whenever God wishes. And should he leave you, or should God call him to the other life, say with Job: The Lord hath given and the Lord hath taken away; blessed be the name of the Lord. You can then follow the directions that he has given you though you should have another confessor: however, regulate your conduct, generally, by the advice of your ordinary confessor, who, commonly speaking, may be said to be the most secure guide; because he is assigned to you by God, and the extraordinary director is chosen by yourself.

3. PATIENCE IN CONTEMPT AND PERSECUTIONS.

Thirdly, it is necessary to practice patience in contempt and persecutions. But, you say, I have not failed in anything—why should I receive such an affront, why should I be persecuted? This is not the will of God. But do you not know the answer that Jesus Christ gave to St. Peter, Martyr, who complained of being unjustly imprisoned, saying: O Lord, what evil have I done that I should suffer this mortification? Jesus answered from the cross, And what evil have I done that I should be nailed to this cross. If, then, my dear sister, your Redeemer has voluntarily embraced death for the love of you, it is not too much for you to embrace this mortification for the love of him. It is true that God does not will the sin of the person who insults or persecutes you; but he certainly wishes that you bear this, contradiction for his sake, and also for your own welfare. Although, says St. Augustine, we have not committed the fault that is imputed to us, we have been guilty of other sins that deserve the chastisement we receive, and even far greater chastisement.

All the saints have been persecuted in this world. St. Basil was accused of heresy before St. Damasus, Pope. St. Cyril of Jerusalem was condemned as a heretic by forty bishops, and was deprived of his see. St. Athanasius was charged with the crime of sorcery and St. John Chrysostom with sins against chastity. St. Romuald, at the age of more than a hundred years, was accused of an enormous sin, for which some said that he deserved to be burned alive. St. Francis de Sales was charged with an unchaste familiarity with a secular lady, and remained for three years under the imputation till his innocence was discovered. Of St. Lidwina it is related that one day a woman entered her chamber, and began to insult her in the most atrocious manner; and because the saint preserved her usual tranquility, the tigress becoming more furious began to spit in her face, and seeing the saint still undisturbed, she screamed like a madwoman.

There is no remedy: for, says the Apostle, all who will live godly in Christ Jesus shall suffer persecution. All who wish to follow Jesus Christ shall be persecuted. If, says St. Augustine, you are unwilling to suffer any persecution, tremble lest you have not as yet begun to serve Jesus Christ. Who more innocent and holy than our Saviour? And still he was persecuted by men until he died on a cross, covered with wounds, and overwhelmed with shame. Hence, to animate us to bear persecutions with peace the Apostle exhorts us to keep always before our mind Jesus Christ crucified. Think diligently upon him that endured much opposition from sinners against himself. Let us rest secure that when we suffer persecution in peace God will take up our defense; and should he ever permit us to remain in dishonor here. He will reward our patience with greater honors hereafter.

4. PATIENCE IN SPIRITUAL DESOLATION.

In the fourth and last place, we ought to practice patience in desolation of the spirit, which is the most sensible and the sharpest pain that a soul that loves God can experience on this earth. To a soul assisted by divine consolations, all insults, sorrows, losses, and persecutions are not only not an affliction, but rather a source of consolation, because they give her occasion to offer these pains to her Lord, and by such offerings to unite herself more closely to her beloved. The severest pain of a loving soul consists in seeing herself without devotion, without fervor, without desires, and in finding nothing but disgust and tediousness in meditation and Communion. But, according to St. Teresa, God has the best proof of their love, when without relish, and even with anguish and pain, they persevere patiently in their accustomed exercises. By aridity and temptations, says the saint, God tries his lovers. Blessed Angela of Foligno, finding herself in a state of aridity, complained to God as if he had abandoned her. No, daughter, answered our Lord, I now love you more than before, and I bring you nearer to myself.

In the beginning, some religious, finding themselves in desolation, imagine that God has abandoned them, or that they are not fit for the way of perfection; thus they leave the road in which they began to walk, begin to give liberty to the senses, and thus lose all they have done. Be attentive, do not allow yourself to be deceived by the enemy: when you feel aridity, be constant, and omit none of your ordinary exercises of devotion. Humble yourself, and say that you deserve to be treated in this manner in punishment of your sins. Above all, resign yourself to the divine will, and trust more than ever in God; for that is the time of rendering yourself dear to your divine Spouse. Do you imagine that the saints were always in the enjoyment of consolations and celestial tenderness? Know that they have spent the greater part of their life in desolation and darkness. And to speak the truth, which I have learned by experience, I have but little confidence in the soul that abounds in spiritual sweetness without having first passed through the ordeal of internal sufferings; because it not infrequently happens that such souls go on well as long as the divine consolations continue, but when tried by aridity they give up all, and abandon themselves to a life of tepidity.

But such a nun may say: I do not refuse this cross if it be the will of God; but what afflicts me is that this abandonment may be the chastisement of my infidelities. But I answer: Let it be a chastisement, as you say; to you in a special manner, I say, that if you have failed by attachment to any creature, God, who is jealous of the heart of his spouses, justly withdraws himself. Let it then be a chastisement; is it not a just one? Is it not the will of God that you accept it? Accept it then in peace, and remove the cause of your desolation, take away affections to creatures, take away dissipation of spirit arising from excessive indulgence of the eyes, the tongue, and the ears: give yourself again entirely to God, and he will restore your former fervor. But seek not to be consoled by your former tenderness; but rather ask strength to be faithful to God. Be persuaded that he sends desolation only for our greater profit, and to prove our love. He said to St. Gertrude that he tenderly loves the souls that serve him at their own expense, that is, in aridity and without sensible sweetness.

Love is not proved so much in following one that caresses you as in seeking after him that flies from you. But, says St. Bernard, fear not, O spouse of Jesus, fear not if the Spouse hides his face for a little; know that he does all for your good; he withdraws for your security, lest, finding yourself greatly caressed, you begin to despise your companions by esteeming yourself better than they are; he withdraws also that you may desire him with greater ardor, and seek after him with greater solicitude. You must in the mean time persevere in your pious exercises, though you should suffer in them the agonies of death: far more painful was the agony which your Spouse suffered in the garden of Gethsemane when he was preparing for death and was praying for you. Being in agony he prayed the longer. Be constant, then, in seeking after your Spouse; he will not delay long to come and console you. And should he not come to give you consolations and tenderness, be content with receiving from him courage and strength to love him without the recompense of present delights. God is more pleased with a strong than with a tender love.

5. A FEW PRACTICAL COUNSELS.

Let us conclude with giving a few practical counsels in order to obtain patience and to practice it under every trial.

1. In general, St. Thomas says, that to reflect on them before they happen is a great help to bear all tribulations with fortitude. Jesus Christ said to his disciples: In; the world you shall have distress: but have confidence, I have overcome the world. My children, know that in the world you shall be afflicted and despised; but have confidence in me, who have conquered the world. The reason is, that by reflecting beforehand on tribulation, and embracing it with patience we form to ourselves an idea of it, not as an evil, but as a good conducive to eternal life. Thus the premeditation takes from us the fear of the evil that the tribulation excites. This has been the practice of the saints: they have embraced crosses long before they happened; and thus they have found themselves prepared to bear them in peace when they have come suddenly upon them. Accustom yourself, then, in mental prayer to embrace the tribulations which are likely to come upon you.

2. And when you imagine it to be impossible for you to suffer such a tribulation (should it happen) pray to the Lord to give you his aid to submit to it in case it occurs, and have confidence in him, saying: I can do all things in him who strengtheneth me. And when you do this, doubt not that your prayers will in that case obtain the strength that you do not possess. And how have the holy martyrs obtained courage to bear so many torments and deaths the most painful, except by prayer and by recommending themselves to God? When you find yourself

under the cross have recourse instantly to prayer, If says St. James, any of yon sad, let him pray. Is any of you afflicted with any tribulation or passion, let him pray, and not cease to pray until he finds the peace of his soul restored. Call upon me in the day of trouble: I will deliver thee, and thou wilt glorify me. When you are in tribulation invoke my aid, and I will rescue you from difficulties, and you will give glory to me. When a soul in trouble recommends itself to God, he delivers it from the evil which afflicts it, or gives it grace to bear it with patience, and thus it glorifies the Lord. St. Ignatius of Loyola used to say that the greatest evil that could befall him in this world would be the destruction of the society; but he hoped that, even should such a calamity happen, his peace of mind would be restored by a quarter of an hour's mental prayer.

3. Endeavor also, in the time of tribulation, to communicate more frequently. The ancient Christians in the time of persecution prepared themselves for martyrdom by frequent Communion.

4. Be careful to ask advice from your director, or from some other spiritual person; for a word of comfort gives great help to bear the cross with patience. But beware of explaining your trials to imperfect souls: for they will only add to your troubles and confusion, particularly if you have received an injury, or if you actually suffer persecution.

5. But above all, I say again, have recourse to prayer, have recourse to Jesus in the Most Holy Sacrament, and beg of him to make you in all things conformable to his holy will. He promises to comfort all who are in tribulation when they have recourse to him. Come to me, all you that labor and are burdened, and I will refresh you.

Prayer.

My God, I offer to Thee the pains of Jesus, Thy Son, in satisfaction for my sins. He is the Lamb whom Thou didst one day behold sacrificed for Thy glory, and for our salvation, on the altar of the cross. For the love of that victim, so dear to Thee, pardon me all the offences, whether grievous or venial, which I have offered to Thee: I am sorry for them all with my whole heart, because by them I have offended Thy infinite goodness. Thou, O my God, dost call me to Thy love: behold I leave all things, and I come to Thee, my treasure and my life. For the love of Thee, I renounce all the goods and honors and pleasures of the world. I love Thee, O my Sovereign Good, above every other good. Ah, my Jesus, do not permit me to resist any longer, and to be ungrateful to the tender affection that Thou hast shown me. Ah, make known to me always more and more the greatness of Thy goodness, that I may be enamoured of Thee, who art infinitely amiable. Thou hast shown Thyself enamoured of my soul, and shall I be able to love anything but Thee? No, my Redeemer; for Thee only do I wish to live, Thee only do I wish to love.

O Mary, my mother, assist me, and obtain for me grace to be faithful to this my promise.

III.

Patience in Temptations.

Dear sister in the Lord, your past life does not content either God or yourself; if death came upon you at present, you should certainly die discontented. But since, as I hope, you have resolved to serve him better for the future, prepare yourself to combat with temptations. Behold the admonition of the Holy Ghost: Son, when than contest to the service of God, stand injustice and in fear, and prepare thy soul for temptation. And remember that, as the prophet says, religious are the most acceptable food to the devil. The enemy labors more to gain one religious than a hundred seculars. And why? First, because by making a spouse of Jesus Christ become one of his slaves he gains a greater triumph. Secondly, because by bringing a nun into sin he gains more than one, because by her bad example she will probably draw others with her. On the other hand, the Lord usually permits souls that are most dear to him to be most severely tormented by temptations. While he lived in the solitude of Palestine, in prayer and penitential works, St. Jerome was greatly afflicted with temptations: behold how he himself described them!—"I was alone, and my heart was full of bitterness; my dried and withered members were covered with a sack. My skin became as black as that of a Moor; the hard ground was my bed, which served rather to give pain than rest; my food was very scanty: and still my heart was inflamed against my will with bad desires. I had no other refuge than to have recourse to Jesus, and to implore his aid."

The Lord permits us to be tempted for our greater good. First, that we may be more humble. Ecclesiasticus says: What doth he know that hath not been tried. What does he who has not been tempted know? In truth, no one is better acquainted with his own weakness than the man that is tempted. St. Augustine remarks, that St. Peter, before he had been tempted, presumed on his own strength, boasting that he would have constancy to embrace death rather than deny Jesus Christ; but when tempted he miserably denied his master, and then he became sensible of his weakness. Hence, having favoured St. Paul with celestial revelations, our Lord, in order to preserve him from vain glory, wished him to be molested with an importunate temptation against chastity, which is of all temptations the most humiliating to man. And, says the saint, lest the greatness of the revelations should exalt me, there was given me a sting of my flesh, an angel of Satan, to buffet me.

Secondly, the Lord permits us to be tempted in order to make us rich in merits. Many religious are disturbed by scruples, on account of the bad thoughts that molest them. But they are disturbed in vain; for it is certain that the consent to evil, but not evil thoughts, is a sin. Temptations, however violent they may be, leave no stain on the soul when they happen without any fault of ours, and when we drive them away. St. Catharine of Sienna and Blessed Angela of Foligno were strongly tempted against chastity, but the temptations increased rather than diminished their purity. Every time the soul conquers a temptation she gains a degree of grace, for which she shall be afterwards rewarded with a degree of glory in heaven. Hence we shall receive as many crowns as we resist temptations. "As often." says St. Bernard, "As we conquer, we are crowned." And our Lord said to St. Matilda: "He who is tempted, places as many gems on my head as he overcomes temptations." In the Cistercian Chronicles it is related that a certain monk was one night greatly molested with unchaste temptations, which he overcame. A lay-brother had a vision, in which he saw a most beautiful young man handing to him a crown of gems, saying, Go to such a monk, and bring him this crown, which he has gained this night. The lay-brother related the vision to the abbot, who sent for the monk that had been tempted. When the abbot heard from him the resistance that he had made against the temptations, he understood the reason why the Lord had prepared so great a reward for him in heaven. The divine mother revealed to St. Bridget that for the violence that the saint had done to herself, in order to banish bad thoughts, our Lord would give her a reward, although the thought remained in her mind.

And God is faithful, who will not suffer you to be tempted above that which you are able, but will make also with the temptation issue, that you may be able to bear it. St. Jerome says that to a ship no tempest is more dangerous than too long a calm. He meant to say, that the tempest of temptation prevents a man from rotting in sloth, and makes him unite himself more closely to God, by turning to him to ask his graces, by renewing good purposes, by making good acts of humility, of confidence, and of resignation. In the lives of the ancient Fathers we read that to a certain young man who was constantly and severely assailed by carnal temptations, his spiritual Father, seeing him in great affliction, said: Son, do you wish me to pray to God to deliver you from so many temptations, which do not allow you to live an hour in peace? The young man answered, No, my Father; for though I am greatly molested by these temptations, I derive great advantage from them, for with the divine aid I thus make continual acts of virtue. I now pray more than I did before, I fast more frequently, I watch more, I endeavor to practice greater mortifications of my rebellious flesh. It is better for you to pray to God that he may assist me by his grace to bear these temptations with patience, and thus to advance in perfection. Such temptations, then, we should not desire; but we ought to accept them with resignation, believing that God permits them for our greater good. The Apostle, when molested by similar temptations, several times implored the Lord to deliver him from them. But God answered: My grace is sufficient for thee. For which thing thrice I besought the Lord that it might depart from me. And he said to me: My grace is sufficient for thee: for power is made perfect in infirmity. You will say: But St. Paul was a saint. And St. Augustine answers: By what means, think you, did the saints resist temptations? Was it by their own strength, or by the power of God? The saints have trusted in God, and thus have conquered. Hence the holy Doctor adds: Do you also abandon yourself into the hands of God, and fear not. He who placed you in the combat will not leave you alone, neither will he abandon you to perdition.

But let us come to what is practical, and see with what arms we must fight in order to escape defeat.

I. The first, the principal, and I may say the only, and absolutely necessary means for conquering temptations, is to have recourse to God by prayer. Speaking of the necessity of humility, in order to be true disciples of Jesus Christ, St. Augustine says: "If you ask what holds the first place in the discipline of Christ, I will answer, Humility. What is the second? Humility. What is the third? Humility. And as often as you ask, so often shall I give the same answer." Now, were you to ask what are the means of overcoming temptations, I would answer, The first means is prayer; the second is prayer; the third is prayer; and should you ask me a thousand times, I would always repeat the same.

This means is particularly necessary for conquering temptations against purity; these, as the Wise Man says, are overcome only by recommending ourselves to God. And as I knew that I could not otherwise be continent except God gave it, . . . I went to the Lord and besought him. As soon as I knew that I could not obtain continence unless God gave it, I went to the Lord and asked it from him. Hence, St. Jerome has written, "As soon as lust assails us, let us instantly say: Lord, assist me; do not permit me to offend you." Thus the Abbot Isaias exhorted his disciples always to repeat in such temptations: Incline unto my aid, O God,—and he would add, that this is a secure defense. He had just reason to say so; for God cannot violate his promises to hear all who pray to him: Cry to me, and I will hear thee. Call upon me I will deliver thee. Ask, and it shall be given you; seek, and you shall find. For every one that asketh, receiveth. You shall ask whatever you will, and it shall be done unto you.

In the book of the Sentences of the Fathers it is written that St. Pachomius related to his disciples that he once heard the devils discoursing together; one of them said: My monk, when I tempt him, listens to me he does not turn to God, and therefore I make him fall frequently. Another complained that he could do nothing with his monk, because he instantly asked help from God, and thus was always victorious. Hence, brethren, concluded the holy abbot, resist temptations by always invoking the name of Jesus. But this must be done immediately, without listening to or arguing with the temptation. Another monk, as we find in the lives of the Fathers, complained to an aged Father of being continually tempted to impurity; the good old man prayed for him, and learned by revelation that the monk did not turn away instantly from the temptation, but used to stop to look at it. The Father corrected him for this fault, and the monk was not molested afterwards as much as before. "While the enemy is small," says St. Jerome, "Kill him."

A lion when small is easily killed, but not when he has become large. Unchaste temptations must be instantly shaken off, as we shake from the hand the sparks that fly from the fire. The best means of conquering them is, as I have said, to turn away from them, without listening to them. Were a queen tempted by a Negro slave, what would she do? Would she not indignantly turn away without giving him an answer? Be careful to act in this manner if the devil should molest you; turn away without answering him, and invoke the name of Jesus and of Mary; and if you do this, you will be always sure of not falling into sin. St. Francis de Sales says: "The instant you feel any temptation, imitate children, who, when they see a wolf, run into the arms of their father or mother, or at least cry out to them for assistance. Do you in like manner run with filial confidence to Jesus and Mary."

In temptations it is also very useful to make the sign of the cross. St. Augustine says: "All the machinations of the devil are reduced to nothing by the power of the cross." By giving his life on the cross, Jesus destroyed the powers of hell; and therefore at the sign of that sacred symbol all the machinations of the devil vanish. St. Athanasius relates of St. Anthony, that when the devils assailed him he instantly armed himself with the sign of the cross, and, thus armed, would say to them: Of what use is it to labor to injure me when I am rendered secure by this sign, and by the confidence I have in my Lord? St. Gregory Nazianzen relates what is still more wonderful, that Julian the apostate, knowing the virtue of the sign of the cross, used, when terrified by the devils, to make that holy sign, and the devils would be put to flight.

II. The second means of conquering temptations is to humble yourself, and to distrust your own strength. To make us humble, the Lord often permits us to be assaulted with temptations, and even frequently with temptations the most shameful. Hence, when we see ourselves thus molested, let us humble ourselves and say: I deserve to be thus tormented for the offences I have hitherto offered to you. In the lives of the Fathers, it is related that a virgin and anchoret called Sara was cruelly persecuted in the desert by the spirit of impurity. She never asked God to deliver her from the temptation, but humbled herself, and constantly implored strength. The more violently the devil tempted her, the more she labored to humble herself, and to supplicate the divine aid. Finally, the enemy, not being able to make her fall into sins of impurity, endeavoured to tempt her to vainglory. Hence he said with a loud voice: Sara, you have conquered, you have conquered. The humble servant of God answered: No, wicked spirit, I have not conquered you, but Jesus my God has conquered you.

Thus let us humble ourselves, and at the same time let us have recourse with confidence to God, who protects all that hope in him. He is the protection of all that trust in him. He himself has promised to deliver all those that hope in him. Because he hoped in me, I will deliver him. When, then, we find ourselves tortured by temptations, and fears of losing God, let us say with great courage: In thee, O Lord, have I hoped: let me never be confounded. In thee, O Lord, have I placed my hopes: do not permit me ever to be confounded, or to incur thy enmity. I say, with great courage; for, according to St. Teresa, when the devils see themselves despised, they remain powerless. And when the enemy represents the great difficulty of doing what is necessary to become saints, let us say, with diffidence in ourselves, but with confidence in God: I can do all things in him who strengtheneth me. I can do nothing of myself, but I can do all things with the aid of my Lord.

III. The third means of overcoming temptations is, to make them known to your spiritual Father. Thieves, when discovered, take flight. Hence, St. Philip Neri used to say, that a temptation disclosed is half conquered. St. Antonine relates that Brother Ruffinus, the companion of St. Francis, was assailed by a strong temptation to despair, and to believe that all he did was lost. The afflicted brother concealed the temptation from his Superior, St. Francis; it became more violent, and one day the devil appeared to him in the form of Jesus crucified, and said to him, Know that you and Francis, and all your followers, are damned. Hence, Ruffinus regarded himself as lost. This was revealed to St. Francis, who sent for him; but Ruffinus refused to come; at length he went to the saint and disclosed the temptation. The saint ordered him to despise it. The devil returned, but seeing himself treated with contempt, he fled. And afterwards Jesus crucified appeared to him, and assured him that he was in the state of grace.

IV. The fourth means, which is a very important one, of relieving one's self from temptations is to avoid the occasions of them. St. Basil says that God assists the man who is engaged in the contest against his own will; but he who voluntarily places himself in the battle, does not deserve compassion, and is therefore abandoned by God. And, before him, Ecclesiasticus said: He that loveth danger, shall perish in it. He that loves danger, and goes in search of it, shall perish in it: nor is it of any use to hope for aid from God; to trust in God, and to expose one's self voluntarily to the occasion of sin, is not a holy but a rash confidence, which merits chastisement.

V. Lastly, it is necessary to give in this place two very important admonitions.

1. It is necessary to remark that we must conquer some temptations by contrary acts; for example, temptations to revenge must be overcome by seeking to do good to those who have offended you; temptations to vanity by humbling ourselves; to envy by rejoicing at the good of others; similar temptations must be conquered in the same manner. But it is better to resist other temptations, such as those against faith, or against chastity, or to blasphemy, by despising them, and by making good acts indirectly opposed to the temptations, such as acts of confidence, of contrition, of charity. St. John Climacus relates that a certain monk was greatly tormented with blasphemous temptations. The miserable man was all in confusion: he went to a good Father, and told him all the execrable blasphemies that passed through his mind. Have confidence, said the Father, I take on myself all these sins; do not think of them anymore. The monk followed the advice, and his peace of mind was restored. But with regard to temptations against chastity, it is not advisable for timorous souls to contend directly with the bad thought, saying and repeating, I will not do it, I will not consent to it. For by endeavoring to make these contrary acts, the image of the bad objects presented to the mind becomes more vivid, and thus the struggle is longer and more severe. It is better to renew, in general, the purpose of dying a thousand times rather than offend God. It is also useful to renew your vows, particularly the vow of chastity: you must, then, instantly turn to God for help, making acts of hope and love, as has been already said, and frequently invoking the most holy name of Jesus and of Mary.

2. Secondly, it is necessary to remark that the most dangerous temptations are those that come under the appearance of good, so that a soul, without perceiving it, may find that she has fallen over some precipice. This may easily happen to spiritual persons in particular. "A good man," says St. Bernard, "Is never deceived except by the similitude of

good." The devil deceives souls that have a good intention only by the appearance of good. St. Bonaventure relates that there was a brother so attached to silence that he would not speak even in confession, but wished to explain his sins by signs. The minister-general, in presence of St. Francis, bestowed great praise on the brother for his exact observance of silence. But the saint said: My Father, you deceive yourself: command him to confess his sins twice a week. The minister imposed the precept, but the brother refused to obey, and became so obstinate on this point, that on account of his disobedience he in the end abandoned the religious state.

Still more dangerous would be the temptation which would induce a religious to entertain too great an affection for the spiritual Father or for any other person, because she considers him to be a saint. The devil persuades her that the relations of direction or of friendship to such a one will be conducive to high perfection. He inspires her with an ardent desire to have such an advantage, and she does all that she can to secure it. After this the enemy begins by causing to arise in her heart an affection that appears to be altogether spiritual; then follow mutual confidence, familiarity; then the license of tender words; and finally all ends in allowing themselves to be seduced into base actions or sacrilegious desires. But of this we have already spoken.

I conclude by repeating, that, to overcome temptations, all the means explained in this chapter are very good, but the first, and the one that is absolutely necessary, is to have recourse to God by prayer that he may give us light and strength to conquer. Without asking the divine aid, it is impossible to overcome temptations; and if we ask it we shall certainly be victorious. Praising, I will call upon the Lord; and I shall be saved from my enemies.

Prayer.

Ah, my God, I will no longer resist the love that Thou dost entertain for me. This love made Thee bear me with so much patience when I offended Thee. Ah, my Jesus, through Thy merits do not permit me ever more to offend Thee. O make me cease to be ungrateful to Thee, or make me cease to live. I see that Thou dost wish me to be saved, and I wish to be saved, that I may go to sing Thy mercies for eternity in heaven. Lord, do not abandon me. I know that Thou wilt never abandon me if I do not first abandon Thee; but past experience makes me afraid of my weakness. Ah, through the painful death that Thou didst one day suffer for me on the cross, give me strength in my temptations, and especially the grace to have immediate recourse to Thee. I love Thee, O infinite goodness, and I hope to love Thee always. Ah, bind me with the sweet chains of Thy love, that my soul may never more be separated from Thee.

O Mary, thou art called the mother of perseverance; this great gift is dispensed through thee; thee I ask to obtain it for me: through thy intercession I certainly hope for it.

CHAPTER XIV.

RESIGNATION TO THE WILL OF GOD.

I.

The Merit of Resignation to the Divine Will.

ST. JOHN CHRYSOSTOM says that all the perfection of the love of God consists in resignation to the divine will. As hatred divides the wills of enemies, so love unites the wills of lovers, so that each wishes only what the other desires. "True friendship of persons consists in wishing and not wishing the same thing," says St. Jerome to Demetriades. Hence the Wise Man says: They that are faithful in love shall rest in him. Souls that are faithful in loving God acquiesce in all that he wills.

Since nothing is more dear to us than self-will, the sacrifice of it is the most acceptable offering we can present to the Lord. This is the sacrifice that God himself continually asks of us with so much earnestness. My son, give me thy heart. Son, give me your heart, that is, your will. Nothing else that we offer to God can content him as long as we reserve our own will. I explain myself by this example: If you had two servants, one of whom labored continually, but always according to his own will; the other performed less work, but was obedient to all your directions,—you would certainly entertain a great regard for the latter, and little or no esteem for the former. Oh, how often do we deceive ourselves by desiring to engage in certain undertakings in order to please ourselves without seeing that they are not conformable to the divine will. How often do we act through self-love, saying: But what I wish to do is conducive to the glory of God. But let us be persuaded that the greatest glory that we can give to God is to conform ourselves to his divine will. Blessed Henry Suso used to say: "God is not so much glorified when we abound in lights and spiritual consolations as when we submit to the divine will and pleasure." Hence Blessed Stephana of Soncino saw among the seraphim certain souls whom she had known on earth; and she learned by revelation that they had attained that sublime elevation by the perfect union of their will in this life with the will of God.

All the malice of sin consists in wishing what God does not will; for then, says St. Anselm, we in a certain manner endeavor to rob God of his crown. He who wishes to follow his own will against the will of God takes, as it were forcibly, from God his crown; for as the crown belongs only to the sovereign, so to do his own will (without dependence on others) belongs to God only. Samuel said to Saul that to refuse to conform to the divine will is a species of idolatry. It is like the crime of idolatry to refuse to obey. It is called idolatry because, in refusing to conform to the divine will, man, instead of adoring the will of God, adores his own will. Now, since all the malice of a creature consists in contradicting the Creator, so all the goodness of the creature consists in a union with the will of the Creator. He who conforms himself to the divine will becomes, as the Lord said of David, a man according to God's own heart. I have found David . . . a man according to my own heart, who shall do all my will. The Lord also says: a soul that is conformed to my will shall have for her name my will. Thou shalt be called my pleasure in it. Yes, for in this happy soul, because self-will is dead, only the will of God lives.

Ah, happy the soul that can always say with the sacred Spouse: My soul melted when he spoke. My soul melted as soon as my beloved spoke. Why does she say melted? Listen: what is rendered liquid no longer retains its own shape, but takes the form of the vessel in which it is contained. Thus, loving souls do not retain their own wills, but conform them to whatever their beloved wills. This conformity implies a will docile and pliant in all things pleasing to God, compared with the obdurate will that resists the divine will. An instrument is said to be a good one when it is obedient to the person that employs it; if it refuse to obey, of what use is it? For example, were a pencil to resist the hand of the painter,—if, when drawn to the right, it should turn to the left; if when drawn downwards, it should seek to move upwards,—what would the painter do? Would he not instantly cast it into the fire?

Some place their sanctity in works of penance, others in frequent Communion, others in reciting many vocal prayers. But, no: St. Thomas says that perfection consists not in these things, but in submission to the divine will. "The perfection of the human soul consists in its subjection to God." Works of penance, prayers, Communions, are good, inasmuch as God wills them; hence they serve only as means to unite us to the divine will. But all perfection and sanctity consists in doing

293

the will of God. In a word, the divine will is the rule of all goodness and virtue. Because it is holy, it sanctifies all, even the most indifferent actions, when they are done to please God. The will of God is your sanctification, says the Apostle. The accomplishment of the divine will is the sanctification of your souls.

I know well that men cheerfully conform to the will of God in prosperity, but are afterwards unwilling to submit to it in adversity. But this is great folly; for they thus suffer doubly and without merit from the evils that befall them, since, whether they wish or wish not, the will of God shall be accomplished. My counsel shall stand, and all my will shall be done. When, then, a person in sickness does not accept his pains with patience, but gives way to anger, and complains of every one, what does he do? Does he by his impatience get rid of his pains? No: on the contrary, he increases them, because by resisting the will of God he loses his peace, and still endures the same pains. Who hath resisted him, and hath had peace? But were he to embrace his sufferings in peace, he would feel his pains less sensibly, and would derive consolation from the thought of pleasing God, by accepting crosses from his divine hands.

Oh, what pleasure does he give to the Lord, who in the time of tribulation says with David: I was dumb, and I opened not my mouth, because thou hast done it. My God, I have shut my mouth, and have not dared to speak, because I know that Thou hast done it. No; there is no one that is better able than God to promote our welfare, or that loves us more than our Creator. And let us be persuaded that whatever he does, he does for our good, and because he loves us. Many things appear to us to be misfortunes, and we call them misfortunes; but if we understood the end for which God sends them, we should see that they are graces. It appeared a calamity to King Manasses to be deprived of his kingdom, and to be made a slave of the prince of the Assyrians: but these misfortunes were blessings; for after his downfall he returned to God, and did penance for the wickedness of his life. And after that he was in distress, he prayed to the Lord his God; and did penance exceedingly before the God of his fathers. We labor under a vertigo, and therefore many things appear to us to go to ruin; and we know not that it is our giddy head that makes them appear to us different from what they are in reality. Such a nun may say: How does it happen that everything goes astray with me? No, sister, but you go astray: your will is crooked; for all that happens comes from God. He does all for your welfare, but you know it not.

And whom can we ever find more solicitous for our welfare and for our salvation than God? To make us understand this truth, he likens himself at one time to a shepherd, going through the desert in search of his lost sheep; at another to a mother who cannot forget her own child. Can a woman forget her infant, so as not to have pity on the son of her womb. Again, to a hen gathering and sheltering her chickens under her wings, that they may suffer no injury: Jerusalem, Jerusalem, . . . How often would I have gathered together thy children, as the hen doth gather her chickens under her wing, and thou wouldst not. In a word, according to David, God surrounds us with his goodwill, in order to save us from all the assaults of our enemies. Lord, thou hast crowned us with a shield of thy good will. Why, then, do we not abandon ourselves entirely into the hands of this good Father? Would it not be folly in a blind man, placed in the midst of precipices, to reject the guidance of a father who loves him, and to follow the way suggested by his own caprice?

Happy the soul that permits itself to be conducted in the way in which God leads it. Father St. Jure relates that a certain young man, desirous of entering the Society of Jesus, was rejected because he had only one eye. Who would not have said that the defect was a great misfortune to the poor young man? But that defect was the occasion of the happiest end that he could meet; for on account of it he was received into the Society only on the condition that he would consent to go on the Indian mission. He went to India, and had the happiness of dying for the faith. The Venerable Balthazar Alvarez used to say that "The kingdom of heaven is the kingdom of the lame, the tempted, and the abject." Let us then, as if blind, permit ourselves to be guided by God, through whatever level or steep road by which he may be pleased to conduct us, secure of finding in it eternal salvation. St. Teresa used to say, "Our Lord never sends a cross without rewarding it with some favour, when we accept it with resignation."

Oh, how great the peace of the soul whose will is in all things conformed to the will of God! Because she wishes only what he wills, she always obtains whatsoever she desires; for all that happens in the world, happens by the will of God. Panormitano relates that King

Alphonsus, called the Great, being asked whom he esteemed happy in this life, wisely answered: "He who abandons himself entirely to the divine will of God." And, in reality, does not all our inquietude arise from this cause—that things do not happen according to our wishes, and that we resist the divine will? St. Bernard says: "God justly ordains that they who refuse to be governed by him in peace should rule themselves amid difficulties and troubles." But, on the other hand, they who wish only what God wills, always find their wishes accomplished, and therefore are always in peace, as well in prosperity as in adversity. When, then, you see a person in sadness, tell her that she is sad because she is not resigned to the will of God. The saints, even in the midst of persecutions the most severe and torments the most painful, knew not what it was to be sad. And why? Because they were united to the divine will. Whatsoever shall befall the just man, it shall not make him sad. Hence, Cardinal Petrucci has wisely said that this frail and fleeting world is but a scene of woes. Its most pleasing amusements and pleasures have the appearance of joys, and they are torments. But to follow Christ suffering appears painful and gives true joy.

Speaking of the saints, Salvian says: "If they are humbled, they desire their humiliations; if they are poor, they delight in their poverty: hence in every misfortune which befalls them they are content, and therefore they begin even in this life to enjoy beatitude." Crosses will certainly be painful to the senses, but this pain is in the inferior part: in the superior part of the soul peace shall reign. The saints, says Father Rodriguez, are like Mount Olympus: at the base there are showers of rain and thunderstorms, but at the summit, which is raised above the middle region of the atmosphere, there is a perpetual calm. In a word, they are like Jesus our Saviour, who, in the midst of all the sorrows and ignominies of his Passion, suffered no diminution of his peace. The more the saints suffer, the more they rejoice in spirit, knowing that in accepting their sufferings they please their Lord, whom only they love. This David experienced when he said: Thy rod and thy staff, they have comforted me. St. Teresa says: "And what greater good can we acquire than a testimony that we please God?" Father Avila has written: "One Blessed be God, in adversity, is of greater value than a thousand acts of thanksgiving in prosperity."

But such a religious says: I accept all the crosses that come to me from God, such as losses, pains, and infirmities; but how can I bear so much

296

maltreatment and such unjust persecutions? They that thus persecute me are certainly guilty of sin, and God does not will sin. But, dear sister, do you not know that all comes from God? Good things and evil, life and death, . . . are from God. Prosperity and adversity, life and death, come from the Lord. It is necessary to know that in every action there is a physical entity which belongs to the material part of the action, and a moral entity that appertains to reason: the moral entity of the action, or the sin of the person who persecutes you, belongs to his malice, but the physical entity appertains to the divine concurrence; so that God wills not the sin, but he wills that you suffer the persecution, and it is he that sends it. When his cattle were taken away from Job, God did not will the sin of the plunderers, but he willed that Job should suffer the loss. Hence, Job said: The Lord gave, and the Lord hath taken away as it hath pleased the Lord, so is it done; blessed be the name of the Lord. St. Augustine remarks that Job did not say: The Lord gave and the devil has taken away; but the Lord gave and the Lord has taken away. The Lord did not wish the sin of the Jews who crucified Jesus Christ, but Jesus Christ said to St. Peter, The chalice which my Father hath given me, shall I not drink it? By these words he showed that his death was caused by the hands of the Jews, but that it was sent to him by his eternal Father. St. Dorotheus says that they who when maltreated seek revenge against the man who maltreats them, imitate the dog that bites the stone by which he is struck, without attending to the hand by which it was thrown. In all the injuries that we receive from others, we should recognize the hand of God, that sends the evil to us, and thus resign ourselves to his holy will.

Prayer.

My beloved Saviour, Thou hast suffered so many sorrows and reproaches for my sake, and I, on account of the miseries of this life, have so often turned my back on Thee. I thank Thee for having waited for me till the present moment. Had I died in my sins, I could never more love Thee. Since I am now able to love Thee, I wish to love Thee with my whole heart. Accept me, O my love, now that I return to Thee, full of tenderness and sorrow for the offences 1 have given Thee. But if, when I despised Thy love, Thy didst not cease to seek after me, how can I fear that Thou wilt cast, me off, now that I desire nothing but Thy love. Thou hast borne with me so long that I might love Thee. Yes, I wish to love Thee. I love Thee, my God, with my whole heart, and I feel greater sorrow for having hitherto offended Thee than if I had suffered every other evil. O love of my soul! I wish never more to give Thee any deliberate displeasure; and I wish to do all that Thou dost wish me to do. Thy will shall henceforth be my only love. Make known to me what I must do in order to please Thee: I wish to do it. I wish to love Thee with a true love, and therefore I embrace all the tribulations that Thou wilt send me. Chastise me in this life, that I may be able to love Thee for eternity! My God, give me strength to be faithful to Thee.

Mary, my mother, to thee I recommend myself: do not cease to pray to Jesus for me.

II.

In what Things we Ought, in a Special Manner, to Resign Ourselves.

We have already seen the great efficacy of resignation to the divine will, to render us dear to God and to procure for us great good. Let us now come to the practice. In what things in particular must we resign ourselves?

I. Let it be remembered, in the first place, that it is very useful to resign ourselves in small things; for example, to suffer a painful word, an importunate fly, the barking of a dog, a trip in walking, the extinguishing of a candle, the tearing of a garment, and the like. It is of greater importance to bear these trifles than to submit to great crosses. First, because they are more frequent; secondly, because we thus more easily acquire a habit and facility of resigning ourselves in things that are difficult.

II. Let us be careful to practice resignation in our infirmities. They that desire to please God should desire the occasions of pleasing him, and therefore what the world calls misfortunes, holy souls call graces; and graces so much the more valuable as they are painful and burdensome. The condition of the sick that suffer and are not conformed to the divine will is most pitiable and deplorable, not so much on account of their pains, as because they know not how to appreciate the riches that God offers them in their sufferings. Miserable souls, they convert into poison the remedy of their evils; for bodily maladies are the most efficacious remedies for the cure of spiritual diseases. The blueness of a wound, says the Wise Man, shall wipe away evils. But , Father Balthazar Alvarez says that they who are resigned in afflictions and pains run to a union with God, or draw God to a union with them, as the Lord himself revealed to St. Gertrude, saying, that when he sees a soul in tribulation he feels himself drawn to it, and that his delights consist in remaining with the sick and afflicted. Of this David assures us in several places: The Lord is nigh to them that are of a contrite heart. God rejoices in being near to those who are in tribulation. The Lord himself says: I am with him in tribulation. I am united with those who are in affliction.

In the time of sickness it is lawful, and even a duty, to take the remedies prescribed by the physician, because this is also the will of God; but we should afterwards resign ourselves entirely to the divine will. We may also pray to God for health, in order to employ it in his service; but we should leave ourselves in his hands, that he may do with us what he pleases: and this is the best means of obtaining the restoration of health. They that seek in their prayers not God, but themselves, shall not be heard; but, on the other hand, he who in his petitions seeks God and the divine will, shall certainly obtain what he asks. I sought the Lord and he heard me. Our Lord appeared one day to St. Gertrude, who suffered great torture from fever, and asked if she wished for health. She embraced his heart and said: "This is what I wish for; I desire nothing but Thy holy will."

Oh, how efficacious a remedy for all infirmities is that beautiful prayer, Thy will be done! St. Lidwina, nailed, as it were, to a bed, all sores and pains, used to say: "Lord, my pleasure is that you load me with pains; because my only consolation is to accomplish Thy will." A tepid soul cannot attain to this perfect spirit of resignation, but loving souls easily attain it. Oh, how consoling the sufferings that are borne with love! This is the sour sweet, so palatable to souls enamoured of that God who rendered scourges, racks, and red-hot plates sweet to the martyrs. When, by order of the tyrant, the flesh of St. Epictetus was torn with hooks of iron and his sides burned with lighted torches, the holy martyr repeated unceasingly: Lord, Thy will be done in me! Lord, Thy will be done in me! Thus he endured all his torments with peace. St. Bonaventure relates that at a time when St. Francis was greatly afflicted with pains, a simple-minded brother said to him: Father, ask of God to treat you with a little more tenderness, for his hand appears to be very heavy upon you. St. Francis answered: "Brother, listen to me: did I not know that what you have said comes from simplicity, I would never see you more; for you wish to censure what God does." After these words the saint threw himself on the ground from the bed on which he lay, and kissing the floor, said: "My God, I thank Thee for these pains, and I beseech Thee to increase them, if it be pleasing to Thee; for I desire nothing else than to do Thy will."

III. We should practice conformity to the divine will with regard to our natural defects; such as want of talent, defective memory, bad sight, bad hearing, bad health, little abilities for the offices of the Community. To them who upbraid us with these defects we should say: He made us, and not we ourselves. And thus let us resign ourselves to the divine will. We are poor; we should be content with the alms which the Lord gives us. What would you think of a beggar who should complain that the garment which you give him is not as rich as he wishes, or that the food is not as delicious as he desires. Let us, then, be content with what God has given us, and seek nothing else. Could he not have left us in our nothingness? Could he not ordain that, instead of being men, we should be toads, flies, or blades of grass? Oh, how often has the want of mental acuteness, of corporal beauty, or of other natural gifts contributed to the salvation of many! For too many the possession of such qualifications might be the occasion of their damnation. To how many have great talents, beauty, nobility, and wealth been the cause of pride and haughtiness, and of running headlong into a multitude of crimes? Let us, then, desire only the goods that God wishes to give us, and no more. Blessed Henry Suso used to say: "I would rather be the vilest animal on earth in conformity with the will of God than be a seraph with my own will." And though, on our part, we ought to aspire to the highest sanctity that we can attain, we should be content with that degree of perfection which God gives us.

IV. We ought in a special manner to practice resignation in spiritual desolations, which are the severest trials to a soul that loves God. But be not disturbed at them, nor say: I would not be troubled if I knew that I am in desolation because God wills it; but I fear that the Lord has withdrawn from me in punishment of my sins. Though your desolation be a chastisement, it is the will of God that you bear it; accept it, then, and you shall enjoy peace.

To remove disquietude, it is necessary to know that there are two sorts of aridity—one in the sensible part of the soul, the removal of which does not depend on us. This kind of aridity is not displeasing to God. The other is in the will (this is, properly speaking, voluntary tepidity), and this we can remove. It is needless to treat here of this second kind of aridity, for I have said enough about it. But with regard to the first we should not be disturbed, though we see ourselves unable to raise the heart to God, to make acts of love, of contrition, and of conformity. It is enough to wish to perform them with a prompt will; and though they be made with dryness, without relish, and without feeling, God accepts them, and is pleased with them. When in our darkness we can do nothing else, let us at least annihilate ourselves before God; and confessing our miseries, let us cast ourselves into his hands as we cast a stone from a mountain into a valley without knowing where it may go, and we shall find peace. But in every state in which we find ourselves, whether of darkness or of light, let us pray to God, saying, Lord, conduct me in any way Thou pleasest; make me do Thy will: I wish for nothing else. The soul that is disturbed in aridity shows that it has not entirely abandoned itself to the divine will. St. Teresa used to say: "The sole end of those who practice mental prayer should be to conform their will to the will of God; and let them be persuaded that in this consists the highest perfection. They who practice it best shall receive the greatest gifts from God." Hence St. Mary Magdalene de Pazzi has well said that "The accomplishment of the divine will should be the object of all our prayers."

O blessed spouse of the Lord, accustom yourself in meditation to offer yourself always to God, to suffer for the love of him every spiritual or bodily pain, every desolation, every sorrow, infirmity, dishonour, or persecution; and beg of him always to give you strength to do in all things his holy will. Attend to the excellent admonition given by spiritual masters: When any serious calamity befalls you, there is no better subject for your mental prayer than the tribulation that has come upon you; and in your meditation be careful to make repeated acts of conformity to the divine will. The union of the will with God has been the continual exercise of the saints. Even in going to sleep St. Peter of Alcantara would imagine himself at the point of death, and would repeat: "Lord, Thy will be done in me." He would desire that every respiration during his repose should be an act of resignation. Oh, how pleasing to the Lord are such oblations and acts of conformity; not

301

because he rejoices in our sufferings, but because he then knows how much we love him. When God commanded Abraham to sacrifice his son Isaac, he did not wish the death of the son, but he wished to know if Abraham was ready to do his will.

What God wishes from us all is that we keep our will united to his. Some religious by reading books on mystic theology become desirous of the supernatural or passive union; I would wish that they should desire the active union, that is, perfect conformity to the will of God; in which, according to St. Teresa, the true union of the soul with God consists. They, adds the saint, who have only the active union, may have much greater merit, because this is accompanied with labor on their part, and the Lord conducts them as strong in virtue: he reserves what they do not enjoy here to give it to them all at once in heaven. Cardinal Petrucci also says that without the gift of infused contemplation a soul may, only with the ordinary grace, succeed in annihilating its own will and in transforming it into the will of God. Hence he concludes that we should neither desire nor ask of God any other favour than the accomplishment of his will, in which all sanctity consists. We thus die to ourselves, that is, we renounce all our gratifications and desires in order to make only the divine will live in us. This is what the Apostle said: And I live now, not I, but Christ liveth in me. I live no longer in myself, but Jesus Christ lives in me; because I wish only what he wishes.

Endeavor, then, dear sister, in every occurrence, particularly in things that are painful to the senses, to have always in your mouth the words of our Saviour: Yea, Father, for so hath it seemed good in thy sight. Lord, let what has happened be done, for so it has pleased Thee. A holy monk, as Cesarius relates, performed many miracles; being asked by his Superior what were the extraordinary works for which God had bestowed upon him the gift of miracles, he answered: "I do nothing, except that I endeavor to wish only what God wishes, and to accept everything from his hands." But, said the abbot, were you not disturbed at the great injury we sustained from such an enemy a few days ago? No, replied the monk, because I regarded it as permitted by the divine will. From this the abbot perceived why the good religious was so dear to God. Thus, also, when tormented with the fear of any grievous calamity that may befall you, say immediately: Lord, I wish what Thou wishest; do what Thou pleasest with me, and with all I possess.

302

St. Gregory relates that the devil in the form of a serpent tormented a religious for three years; the religious, though he suffered a great deal, never lost his peace, but would say to the enemy: "Do with me what you wish if such be the will and pleasure of God." Let your continual prayer be: "Thy will be done." At rising in the morning, in going to bed at night, in meditation, at Communion, at the visit to the Most Holy Sacrament, and always, say: "Thy will be done—thy will be done." St. Gertrude used to say three hundred times in the day: "My Jesus, let not my will but Thine be done."

Happy you if you do the same that—is, if you are always resigned to the divine will. Truly happy shall be your life, and still more happy your death. Blosius says that he who, at the moment of death, makes an act of perfect conformity to the divine will, shall be delivered not only from hell, but also from purgatory, though he had been guilty of all the sins of the whole world. The reason is that he who accepts death with perfect resignation acquires merit similar to that of the holy martyrs who spontaneously gave their lives for Jesus Christ. Moreover, he who dies with perfect conformity to the divine will dies in peace and joy, even in the midst of pains. A Cistercian monk was seized with his last illness; his flesh became rotten, and his pains were so excruciating that he suffered a continual death; but the good religious unceasingly thanked the Lord, and enjoyed uninterrupted tranquility and consolation. When near his last breath, and racked with increased torture, he began to sing. The monks that stood round his bed were astonished to see such joy amid so many pains; but his cheerfulness continued to the last moment, and thus, with joy and jubilation, he happily closed his life.

To them that love God, all things work together unto good. To him who loves God all things are an occasion of merit and consolation; for it is certain that God sends us crosses only for our welfare. This he himself said one day to St. Catharine of Sienna: I can wish only what is useful to you. As I have freely created man, so I have loved him infinitely. Hence you will infer that I ordain tribulations for your own good, which I desire more ardently than you yourself wish it. Another holy woman died consumed by an ulcer, which had entirely changed her appearance. The bishop who assisted her in her last moments could not restrain his tears when he saw her agony; but she smiled, and was surprised to see the bishop weeping. The prelate, on the other hand, was astonished to see her smiling, and said to her, Why do you smile? She answered, Tell me, were a princess confined in a dungeon, informed that she could not return to her palace till the prison was destroyed, how great should be her joy at seeing its walls falling to the ground? Thus, because I find myself near my deliverance from this prison of my body, I rejoice and smile.

I do not dilate much on the subject of conformity to the will of God, on which I would never cease to speak, because I have already written a little treatise on it, which I pray you to procure, and to read several times: for it is certainly in uniting ourselves to the divine will that all our salvation, peace, and perfection consist. And life in his good-will.

Lastly, I entreat you to perform all that you do for the sole motive of doing the will of God, for thus you will never be disturbed when things do not happen according to your wishes. Thus you will be always in peace, and will always give pleasure to God. Oh, how delightful a thing it is to please God! Do you wish to know what is meant by giving pleasure to God? I will tell you, in the words of the Venerable Father Anthony Torres: "It means to please that loving heart to which we owe so much; to gratify those divine eyes, always solicitous for our welfare; to satisfy that will, always employed with the love of us. To give pleasure to God is the end for which he has created us, the goal to which our desires should tend; the rule that ought to be the measure of our existence. To give pleasure to God is that which is most ardently sought by the saints; that which moved so many holy virgins to consecrate themselves to him in the cloister that sent so many anchorets to the deserts. This made the persecuted insensible to calumnies and reproaches, and rendered sweet to the martyrs torments and death. To give pleasure to God is that for which an enlightened soul offers itself to every kind of spoliation, to all sorrows—to all, even the worst, calumnies; to all deaths the most painful, and to hell itself. To give pleasure to God is such, that everyone should prefer it to all self-interest, to all felicity. It is such, that if the very blessed in paradise knew that it would give greater pleasure to God that they should be in hell than in heaven, they would all (and the first should be the Most Holy Virgin) cast themselves into hell, there to find, in the midst of these eternal torments, the greater pleasure of God. That is what is meant by giving greater pleasure to God."

Prayer.

My Jesus have mercy on me, miserable that I have been! How often, in order to follow my own will against Thine, have I voluntarily condemned myself to hell? Hadst Thou then taken me out of life, I should now remain in that pit forever, to curse and hate Thy will. But no; I now bless it, I love it; I wish always to love it. My Redeemer, pardon me; I will not contradict Thee anymore; tell me what Thou wishest from me, and give me strength; I wish to do Thy will. Thy will be done. Make me do Thy will perfectly during the remainder of my life, and I ask nothing more. Ah, my sweet love, what else dost Thou wish but my welfare and my salvation? Eternal Father, for the love of Jesus Christ, who has taught me to pray to Thee in his name, I ask this grace of Thee: Thy will be done in me! Thy will be done in me! Thy will be done in me! O happy shall I be if I live and terminate life doing Thy will.

O Mary, happy thou who hast always done the will of God perfectly. O my mother, obtain for me by thy prayers the grace that I may fulfill the divine will during all the remaining moments of my life: this grace I hope for through thy intercession.

CHAPTER XV.

MENTAL PRAYER.

I.

Moral Necessity of Mental Prayer for Religious.

THE life of a religious must be a life of prayer. It is difficult, or to speak more correctly, it is morally impossible for a religious, who is not a lover of mental prayer, to be a good religious. If you see a tepid religious, say that she does not make mental prayer and you will say the truth. The devil labors hard to make religious lose the love for meditation; and should he conquer them in this, he will gain all. St. Philip Neri used to say, "A religious without mental prayer is a religious without reason." I add: she is not a religious, but the corpse of a religious. Let us examine what makes mental prayer so necessary.

I. In the first place, without mental prayer a religious is without light. They, says St. Augustine, who keep their eyes shut, cannot see the way to their country. The eternal truths are all spiritual things that are seen, not with the eyes of the body, but with the eyes of the mind, that is, by reflection and consideration. Now, they who do not make mental prayer do not see these truths, nor do they see the importance of eternal salvation, and the means that they must adopt in order to obtain it. The loss of so many souls arises from the neglect of considering the great affair of our salvation, and what we must do in order to be saved. With desolation says the prophet Jeremias, is all the land made desolate: because there is none that considereth in the heart. On the other hand, the Lord says, that he who keeps before his eyes the truths of faith, that is, death, judgment, and the happy or unhappy eternity that awaits us, shall never fall into sin. In all thy works remember thy last end, and thou shalt never sin. Draw near to God, says David, and you shall be enlightened. Come ye to him and be enlightened. In another place our Saviour says: Let your loins be girt, and lamps burning in your hands. These lamps are, according to St. Bonaventure, holy meditations; for in prayer the Lord speaks to us, and enlightens, in order to show us the way of salvation. Thy word is a lamp to my feet.

St. Bonaventure also says, that mental prayer is, as it were, a mirror, in which we see all the stains of the soul. In a letter to the Bishop of Osma, St. Teresa says: "Although it appears to us that we have no imperfections, still when God opens the eyes of the soul, as he usually does in prayer, our imperfections are then clearly seen." He who does not make mental prayer does not even know his defects, and therefore, as St. Bernard says, he does not abhor them. He does not even know the dangers to which his eternal salvation is exposed, and therefore he does not even think of avoiding them. But he that applies himself to meditation instantly sees his faults, and the dangers of perdition, and seeing them, he will reflect on the remedies for them. By meditating on eternity, David was excited to the practice of virtue, and to sorrow and works of penance for his sins. I thought upon the days of old, and I had in my mind the eternal years, . . . and I was exercised, and I swept my spirit. The spouse in the Canticles said: The flowers have appeared in our land: the time of pruning is come: the voice of the turtle is heard in our land. When the soul, like the solitary turtle, retires and recollects itself in meditation to converse with God, then the flowers, that is, good desires, appear; then comes the time of pruning, that is, the correction of faults that are discovered in mental prayer." Consider," says St. Bernard, "That the time of pruning is at hand, if the time of meditation has gone before." For, says the saint in another place, meditation regulates the affections, directs the actions, and corrects defects.

II. Besides, without meditation there is not strength to resist the temptations of our enemies, and to practice the virtues of the Gospel. Meditation, says the Venerable Bartholomew of the Martyrs, is like fire with regard to iron, which when cold is hard, and can be wrought only with difficulty, but placed in the fire it becomes soft, and the workman gives it any form he wishes. To observe the divine precepts and counsels, it is necessary to have a tender heart—that is, a heart docile and prepared to receive the impressions of celestial inspirations, and ready to obey them. It was this that Solomon asked of God: Give, therefore, to thy servant an understanding heart. Sin has made our heart hard and indocile; for being altogether inclined to sensual pleasures, it resists, as the Apostle complained, the laws of the spirit. But I see another law in my members fighting against the law of my mind. But the soul is rendered docile and tender to the influence of grace that is communicated in mental prayer. By the contemplation of the divine goodness, the great love which God has borne him, and the immense benefits that God has bestowed upon him, man is inflamed with love, his heart

307

is softened, and made obedient to the divine inspirations. But without mental prayer his heart will remain hard and restive and disobedient, and thus he shall be lost. A hard heart shall fare evil at the last. Hence, St. Bernard exhorted Pope Eugene never to omit meditation on account of external occupations. "I fear for you, O Eugene, lest the multitude of affairs (prayer and consideration being intermitted), may bring you to a hard heart, which abhors not itself, because it perceives not."

Some may imagine that the long time which devout souls give to prayer, and which they could spend in useful works, is unprofitable and lost time. But such persons know not that in mental prayer souls acquire strength to conquer enemies and to practice virtue. "From this leisure," says St. Bernard, "Strength comes forth." Hence the Lord commanded that his spouse should not be disturbed. I adjure you . . . that you stir not up, nor awake my beloved till she please. He says, until she please: for the sleep or repose which the soul takes in mental prayer is perfectly voluntary, but is at the same time necessary for its spiritual life. He who does not sleep, has not strength to work, nor to walk, but goes tottering along the way. The soul that does not repose and require strength in meditation is not able to resist temptations, and totters on the road. In the life of the Venerable Sister Mary Crucified we read that while at prayer she heard a devil boasting that he had made a nun omit the common meditation, and that afterwards, because he continued to tempt her, she was in danger of consenting to mortal sin. The servant of God ran to the nun, and with the divine aid rescued her from the criminal suggestion. Behold the danger to which one who omits meditation exposes their soul! St. Teresa used to say that he who neglects mental prayer needs not a devil to carry him to hell, but that he brings himself there with his own hands. And the Abbot Diocles said that "The man who omits mental prayer soon becomes either a beast or a devil."

III. Without petitions on our part God does not grant the divine helps, and without aid from God we cannot observe the commandments; hence the Apostle exhorted his disciples to pray always. Pray without ceasing. We are poor mendicants: I am a beggar and poor. The entire revenue of the poor consists in asking alms from the rich; and our riches also consist in prayer, that is, in the prayer of petition; for by prayer we obtain from God his graces. Without prayer, says St. John Chrysostom, it is absolutely impossible to lead a good life. And, says

308

the learned Monsignor Abelly, what but the neglect of mental prayer can be the cause of the great relaxation of morals that we witness? God has an ardent desire to enrich us with his graces, but, as St. Gregory writes, he wishes to be entreated, and, as it were, forced by our prayers to grant them to us. "God," says the holy Doctor, "Wishes to be asked, he wishes to be compelled, he wishes to be overcome by a certain importunity." According to St. John Chrysostom, it is impossible for him who attends to prayer to fall into sin. And in another place he says that when the devils see that we pray, they immediately cease to tempt us.

From the absolute necessity of the prayer of petition arises the moral necessity of mental prayer; for he who neglects meditation, and is distracted with worldly affairs, will not know his spiritual wants, the dangers to which his salvation is exposed, the means which he must adopt in order to conquer temptations, or even the necessity of the prayer of petition for all men; thus he will give up the practice of prayer, and by neglecting to ask God's graces, he will certainly be lost. The great Bishop Palafox, in his Annotations to the letters of St. Teresa, says; "How can charity last, unless God gives perseverance? How will the Lord give us perseverance if we neglect to ask him for it? And how shall we ask him without mental prayer? Without mental prayer, there is not the communication with God which is necessary for the preservation of virtue." And Cardinal Bellarmine says that for him who neglects meditation, it is morally impossible to live without sin.

Someone may say, I do not make mental prayer, but I say many vocal prayers. But it is necessary to know, as St. Augustine remarks, that to obtain the divine grace it is not enough to pray with the tongue: it is necessary also to pray with the heart. On the words of David: I cried to the Lord with my voice, the holy Doctor says: "Many cry not with their own voice (that is, not with the interior voice of the soul), but with that of the body. Your thoughts are a cry to the Lord. Cry within, where God hears." This is what the Apostle inculcates. Praying at all times in the spirit. In general, vocal prayers are said distractedly with the voice of the body, but not of the heart, especially when they are long, and still more especially when said by a person who does not make mental prayer; and therefore God seldom hears them, and seldom grants the graces asked. Many say the Rosary, the Office of the Blessed Virgin, and perform other works of devotion; but they still continue in sin. But it is impossible for him who perseveres in mental prayer to continue in sin; he will either give up meditation or renounce sin. A great servant of God used to say that mental prayer and sin cannot exist together. And this we see by experience: they who make mental prayer rarely incur the enmity of God; and should they ever have the misfortune of falling into sin, by persevering in mental prayer, they see their misery, and return to God. Let a soul, says St. Teresa, be ever so negligent, if she persevere in meditation, the Lord will bring her back to the haven of salvation.

IV. All the saints have become saints by mental prayer. Mental prayer is the blessed furnace in which souls are inflamed with the divine love. In my meditation, says David, a fire, shall flame out. St. Vincent of Paul used to say, that it would be a miracle if a sinner who attends at the sermons in the mission, or in the spiritual exercises, were not converted. Now, he who preaches and speaks in the exercises is only a man; but it is God himself that speaks to the soul in meditation. I will lead her into the wilderness; and I will speak to her heart St. Catharine of Bologna used to say: "He who does not practice mental prayer deprives himself of the bond that unites the soul to God; hence, finding her alone, the devil will easily make her his own." "How," she would say, "Can I conceive that the love of God is found in the soul that cares but little to treat with God in prayer?"

Where but in meditation have the saints been inflamed with divine love? By means of mental prayer St. Peter of Alcantara was inflamed to such a degree that in order to cool himself he ran into a frozen pool, and the frozen water began to boil like water in a caldron placed on the fire. In mental prayer St. Philip Neri became inflamed, and trembled so that he shook the entire room. In mental prayer St. Aloysius Gonzaga was so inflamed with divine ardor that his very face appeared to be on fire, and his heart beat as strongly as if it wished to fly from the body.

St. Laurence Justinian says: "By the efficacy of mental prayer temptation is banished, sadness is driven away, lost virtue is restored, fervor which has grown cold is excited, and the lovely flame of divine love is augmented." Hence, St. Aloysius Gonzaga has justly said that he who does not make much mental prayer will never attain a high degree of perfection.

A man of prayer, says David, is like a tree planted near the current of waters, which brings forth fruit in due time; all his actions prosper before God. Blessed is the man . . . who shall meditate on his law day and night! And he shall be like a tree which is planted near the running waters, which shall bring forth its fruit in due season, and his leaf shall not fall off: and all, whatsoever he shall do, shall prosper. Mark the words, in due season; that is, at the time when he ought to bear such a pain, such an affront, etc.

St. John Chrysostom compared mental prayer to a fountain in the middle of a garden. Oh, what an abundance of flowers and verdant plants do we see in the garden which is always refreshed with water from the fountain. Such, precisely, is the soul that practices mental prayer: you will see that she always advances in good desires, and that she always brings forth more abundant fruits of virtue. Whence does she receive so many blessings? From meditation, by which she is continually irrigated. Thy plants are a paradise of pomegranates with the fruits of the orchard, . . . the fountain of gardens, the well of living waters, which run with a strong stream from Libanus. But let the fountain cease to water the garden, and, behold, the flowers, plants, and all instantly wither away; and why? Because the water has failed. You will see that as long as such a religious makes mental prayer she is modest, humble, devout, and mortified in all things. But let her omit meditation, and you will instantly find her wanting in modesty of the eyes, proud, resenting every word, in devout, no longer frequenting the sacraments and the church; you will find her attached to vanity, to useless conversations, to pastimes, and to earthly pleasures; and why? The water has failed, and therefore fervor has ceased. My soul is as earth without water unto thee. . . . My spirit hath fainted away. The soul has neglected mental prayer, the garden is therefore dried up, and the miserable soul goes from bad to worse. When a soul abandons meditation St. John Chrysostom regards it not only as sick, but as dead. "He," says the holy Doctor, "Who prays not to God, nor desires to enjoy assiduously his divine conversation, is dead. . . . The death of the soul is not to be prostrated before God."

The same Father says that mental prayer is the root of the fruitful vine. And St. John Climacus writes that "Prayer is a bulwark against the assault of afflictions, the spring of virtues, the procurer of graces." Rufinus asserts that all the spiritual progress of the soul flows from mental prayer. And Gerson goes so far as to say, that he who neglects meditation cannot, without a miracle, lead the life of a Christian.

Speaking of mental prayer, Jeremias says: He shall sit solitary, and hold his peace; because he hath taken it up upon himself. That is, a soul cannot have a relish for God, unless it withdraws from creatures, and sits, that is, stops to contemplate the goodness, the love, the amiableness, of God. But when solitary and recollected in meditation, that is, when it takes away its thoughts from the world, it is then raised above itself, and departs from prayer very different from what it was when it began it.

St. Ignatius of Loyola used to say that mental prayer is the short way to attain perfection. In a word, he who advances most in meditation makes the greatest progress in perfection. In mental prayer the soul is filled with holy thoughts, with holy affections, desires, and holy resolutions, and with love for God. There man sacrifices his passions, his appetites, his earthly attachments, and all the interests of self-love. Moreover, by praying for them in mental prayer we can save many sinners, as was done by St. Teresa, St. Mary Magdalene de Pazzi, and is done by all souls enamoured of God, who never omit in their meditations to recommend to him all infidels, heretics, and all poor sinners; begging him also to give zeal to priests who work in his vineyard, that they may convert his enemies. In mental prayer we can also, by the sole desire of performing them, gain the merit of many good works which we do not perform. For as the Lord punishes bad desires, so, on the other hand, he rewards all our good desires.

It is necessary, above all, to be careful not to go to mental prayer in order to enjoy consolation and tenderness, but for the purpose of pleasing God, and of learning from him how he wishes to be loved and served by us. Father Balthazar Alvarez used to say: The love of God consists not in receiving his favors, but in serving him through the sole motive of pleasing him. And he would say, that divine consolation is like the refreshment that we take on a journey not to rest in it, but in order to go forward with greater vigour. When you feel aridity in meditation, be careful to persevere, in spite of all the tediousness that you experience, and know that you then give great pleasure to your Spouse, and acquire great merits. Say to him then: O my Jesus, why dost Thou treat me thus? Thou hast stripped me of all things, of property, of relatives, of my will, and I have been satisfied with these privations, in order to gain Thee; but why dost Thou now deprive me also of Thyself? Say this to him with an humble affection; he will make thee feel that he does all because he loves thee, and for thy greater good. Father Torres used to say: "To carry the cross with Jesus without consolation, makes the soul run and fly to perfection."

Prayer.

My Jesus, Thou hast loved me in the midst of pains; and in the midst of sufferings I wish to love Thee. Thou hast spared nothing: Thou hast even given Thy blood and Thy life in order to gain my love; and shall I continue as hitherto, to be reserved in loving Thee? No, my Redeemer, it shall not be so; the ingratitude with which I have hitherto treated Thee is sufficient. To Thee I consecrate my whole heart. Thou alone dost deserve all my love. Thee alone do 1 wish to love. My God, since Thou wishest me to be entirely Thine, give me strength to serve Thee as Thou deservest, during the remainder of my life. Pardon my tepidity and my past infidelities. How often have I omitted mental prayer in order to indulge my caprice. Alas, how often, when it was in my power to remain with Thee in order to please Thee, have I remained with creatures so as to offend Thee. Oh, that so many lost years would return! But, since they will not return, the remaining days of my life must be entirely Thine, O my beloved Lord. I love Thee, O my Jesus! I love Thee, O my Sovereign Good! Thou art, and shalt be forever, the only love of my soul.

O mother of fair love, O Mary, obtain for me the grace to love thy Son, and to spend the remainder of my life in his love. Thou dost obtain from Jesus whatsoever thou wishest; through thy prayers I hope for this gift.

II.

The Practice of Mental Prayer.

Having seen the great necessity of mental prayer for religious, and the great blessings that they may draw from it, let us now consider the practice of meditation, with regard to the place, the time, and the manner.

1. THE PLACE SUITABLE FOR MENTAL PRAYER.

With regard to the place, it should be solitary. But, said our Saviour, when thou shalt pray, enter into thy chamber, and having shut the door, pray to thy Father in secret. When you wish to pray, shut yourself up in your chamber, and thus pray to your Father. St. Bernard says that silence and the absence of all noise almost force the soul to think of the goods of heaven.

To make mental prayer, the best place is, as has been said, your own room; but for religious the most appropriate place is the church, in presence of the Blessed Sacrament. The Venerable Father Avila used to say that he knew no sanctuary more desirable than a church in which Jesus Christ remains in the holy Eucharist.

In order to make mental prayer well, it is necessary to unite to the external silence interior silence, that is, detachment from earthly affections. Speaking of certain persons attached to the world, our Lord said one day to St. Teresa: "I would wish to speak to them, but creatures make such a noise in their ears that they do not give me a moment in which I can make them listen to me." But in the next chapter, on the solitude of the heart, we shall speak at length on this point.

We have here two things to consider, namely, the time of the day most suitable for mental prayer, and the time that is to be spent in making it.

2. THE TIME OF MAKING MENTAL PRAYER.

1. With regard to the time of making mental prayer, St. Isidore used to say, that, ordinarily speaking, the fittest time for meditation is the morning and evening. * But according to St. Gregory of Nyssa, the morning is the most seasonable time for prayer; because, says the saint, when prayer precedes business, sin will not gain admission to the soul. The Venerable Father Charles Carafa, founder of the Congregation of the Pious Workers, used to say that a fervent act of love made in the morning during meditation is sufficient to maintain the soul in fervor during the entire day. Prayer, as St. Jerome has written, is also necessary in the evening. Let not the body go to rest before the soul is refreshed by mental prayer, which is the food of the soul. But at all times and in all places religious can pray, even at work, or at recre-

ation; it is enough for them then to raise the mind to God and to make good acts, for in this consists mental prayer.

2. With regard to the time to be spent in mental prayer, the rule of the saints was, to devote to it all the hours that were not necessary for the occupations of human life. St. Francis Borgia employed eight hours in the day in meditation, because his Superiors would not allow him a longer time, and when the eight hours were expired, he earnestly asked permission to remain a little longer at prayer, saying, "Ah, give me another little quarter of an hour." St. Philip Neri was accustomed to spend the entire night in prayer. St. Anthony the Abbot remained the whole night at prayer, and when the sun appeared, which was the time assigned for terminating his prayer, he complained of it for having risen too soon. Father Balthazar Alvarez used to say that a soul that loves God, when not in prayer, is like a stone out of its centre, in a violent state; for in this life we should as much as possible imitate the life of the saints in bliss, who are constantly employed in the contemplation of God.

It is right to observe, that with regard to the posture the fittest one is kneeling; but when it causes pain and distraction, a person may, as St. John of the Cross says, make meditation sitting in a modest posture.

But let us come to the particular time which a religious who seeks perfection should devote to mental prayer. Father Torres prescribed for religious who were his penitents an hour's meditation in the morning, another during the day, and a half-hours meditation in the evening, when they should not be hindered by sickness or by any duty of obedience. If to you this appears too much, I counsel you at least to give to mental prayer an hour in addition to the time devoted to it by the Community.

Sometimes the Lord wishes you to omit prayer in order to perform some work of fraternal charity; but it is necessary to attend to what St. Laurence Justinian says: "When charity requires it, the spouse of Jesus goes to serve her neighbor; but during that time she continually sighs to return to converse with her Spouse in the solitude of her cell." Father Vincent Carafa, General of the Society of Jesus, stole as many little moments of time as he could, and employed them in prayer.

Mental prayer is tedious to the religious who is attached to the world, but not to those who love God only. Now, how can it be said that a religious loves God only, when she feels no tediousness in conversing for two hours with a relative or an acquaintance at the grate, and cannot bring herself to make an hour's meditation, in addition to the meditations made by the Community? Ah, conversation with God is not painful nor tedious to those who truly love him. His conversation has no bitterness, his company produces not tediousness, but joy and gladness. Mental prayer, says St. John Climacus, is nothing else than a familiar conversation and union with God. In prayer, as St. John Chrysostom says, the soul converses with God, and God with the soul. No, the life of holy religious that love prayer and fly from earthly amusements is not a life of bitterness. If you do not believe me, Taste and see that the Lord is sweet. Try it, and you will see how sweet the Lord is to those who leave all things in order to converse with him only. But the end which we ought to propose to ourselves in going to meditation should be, as has been said several times, not spiritual consolation, but to learn from our Lord what he wishes from us, and to divest ourselves of all self-love. "To prepare yourself for prayer," says St. John Climacus, "Put off your own will." To prepare ourselves well for meditation, we must renounce self-will, and say to God: Speak, Lord, for thy servant heareth. Lord, tell me what you wish me to do: I am willing to do it. And it is necessary to say this with a resolute will, for without this disposition the Lord will not speak to us.

3. THE MANNER OF MAKING MENTAL PRAYER.

As to the manner of making mental prayer, I will suppose that you are already instructed in it; but allow me to explain briefly the principal parts of mental prayer for any young beginner into whose hands this book may fall.

Mental prayer contains three parts: the preparation, the meditation, and the conclusion.

1. In the PREPARATION there are three acts: an act of faith, of the presence of God, and of adoration; an act of humility and of sorrow for our sins, and a petition for light. They may be made in the following manner:

My God, I believe Thee present within me; I adore Thee with my whole soul.

Be careful to make this act with a lively faith, for a lively remembrance of the divine presence contributes greatly to remove distractions. Cardinal Carracciolo, Bishop of Aversa, used to say that when a person is distracted in meditation there is reason to think that he has not made a lively act of faith.

2. Lord, I should now be in hell in punishment of the offences I have offered to Thee. I am sorry for them from the bottom of my heart; have mercy on me.

3. Eternal Father, for the sake of Jesus and Mary, give me light in this meditation, that I may draw fruit from it.

We must, then, recommend ourselves to the Blessed Virgin by saying a Hail Mary, to St. Joseph, to our guardian angel, and to our holy patron. These acts, says St. Francis de Sales, ought to be made with fervor, but should be short, that we may pass immediately to the meditation.

II. On entering on the meditation we must take leave of all extraneous thoughts, saying with St. Bernard, "O my thoughts I wait here;" after prayer we shall speak on other matters. Be careful not to allow the mind to wander where it wishes; but should a distracting thought enter, we must not be disturbed, nor seek to banish it with a violent effort, but let us remove it calmly and return to God. Let us remember that the devil labors hard to disturb us in the time of meditation in order to make us abandon it. Let him, then, who omits mental prayer on account of distractions be persuaded that he gives delight to the devil. It is impossible, says Cassian, that our minds should be free from all distractions during prayer. Let us, then, never give up meditation, however great our distractions may be. St. Francis de Sales says that if in mental prayer we should do nothing else than continually banish distractions and temptations, the meditation is well made. And before him St. Thomas taught that involuntary distractions do not take away the fruit of mental prayer. When we perceive that we are deliberately distracted, let us desist from the voluntary defect, and banish the distraction, but let us be careful not to discontinue our meditation.

With regard to the subject-matter of meditation, the best rule is to meditate on the truths or mysteries in which the soul finds most nourishment and devotion. But above all, for a religious who loves perfection the most appropriate subject is the Passion of Jesus Christ. Blosius writes that our Lord revealed to several holy women, to St. Gertrude, St. Bridget, St. Mechtilde, and St. Catharine of Sienna that they who meditate on his Passion are very dear to him. According to St. Francis de Sales, the Passion of our Redeemer should be the ordinary subject of the meditations of every Christian; how much more should it be the subject of the meditations of the spouse of Jesus Christ! Oh, what an excellent book is the Passion of Jesus! There we understand better than in any other book the malice of sin, and also the mercy and love of God for man. You may read for your meditation the devout reflections that I have published on what the holy evangelists have written concerning the Passion of our Saviour. To me it appears that Jesus Christ has suffered so many different pains, the scourging, the crowning with thorns, the crucifixion, etc., that having before our eyes so many painful mysteries we might have a variety of different subjects for meditating on his Passion, by which we might excite sentiments of gratitude and love.

When she is alone at meditation a religious will do well always to make mental prayer with the aid of a book. St. Teresa used a book for seventeen years: she would first read a little, and then meditate for a short time on what she had read. It is useful to meditate in this manner, in imitation of the pigeon that first drinks and then raises its eyes to heaven.

However, let it be remembered that the advantage of mental prayer consists not so much in meditating as in making affections, petitions, and resolutions: these are the three principal fruits of meditation. "The progress of a soul," says St. Teresa, "Does not consist in thinking much of God, but in loving him ardently; and this love is acquired by resolving to do a great deal for him." Speaking of mental prayer, the spiritual masters say that meditation is, as it were, the needle which when it has passed must be succeeded by the golden thread composed, as has been said, of affections, resolutions, and petitions.

1. When you have reflected on the point of meditation, and feel any pious sentiment, raise your heart to God and offer him acts of humil-

ity, of confidence, or of thanksgiving; but above all, repeat in mental prayer acts of contrition and of love.

The act of love, as also the act of contrition, is the golden chain that binds the soul to God. An act of perfect charity is sufficient for the remission of all our sins. Charity covereth a multitude of sins. The Lord has declared that he cannot hate the soul that loves him: I love them that love me. The Venerable Sister Mary Crucified once saw a globe of fire in which some straws that had been thrown into it were instantly consumed. By this vision she was given to understand that a soul by making a true act of love obtains the remission of all its faults. Besides, the Angelic Doctor teaches that by every act of love we acquire a new degree of glory. "Every act of charity," says the saint, "Merits eternal life." Acts of love may be made in the following manner:

My God, I esteem Thee more than all things. I love Thee with my whole heart. I delight in Thy felicity.

I would wish to see Thee loved by all.

I wish only what Thou wishest.

Make known to me what Thou wishest from me, and I will do it.

Dispose as Thou pleasest of me and of all that I possess.

This last act of oblation is particularly pleasing to God. St. Teresa was accustomed to offer herself to God in this manner at least fifty times in the day.

Remember that in this chapter we speak of the ordinary mental prayer; for should a soul feel itself at any time united to God by supernatural or infused recollection, without any particular thought of an eternal truth or of any divine mystery, it should not then labor to perform any other acts than those to which it feels itself sweetly drawn to God. It is then enough to endeavor with loving attention to remain united with God without impeding the divine operation, or forcing one's self to make reflections and acts. But this is to be understood when the Lord calls the soul to this supernatural prayer; but until we receive such a call we should not depart from the ordinary method of mental prayer, but should, as has been said, make use of meditation and affections. However, for persons accustomed to mental prayer it is better to employ themselves in affections than in considerations.

2. Moreover, in mental prayer it is very profitable, and perhaps more useful than any other act, to repeat petitions to God asking with humility and confidence his graces; that is, his light, resignation, perseverance, and the like; but above all, the gift of his holy love. St. Francis de Sales used to say, that by obtaining the divine love we obtain all graces; for a soul that truly loves God with its whole heart will of itself, without being admonished by others, abstain from giving him the smallest displeasure, and will labor to please him to the best of its ability.

When you find yourself in aridity and darkness, so that you feel, as it were, incapable of making good acts, it is sufficient to say: My Jesus, mercy. Lord, for the sake of Thy mercy, assist me. And the meditation made in this manner will be for you, perhaps, the most useful and fruitful.

The Venerable Paul Segneri used to say that until he studied theology he employed himself during the time of mental prayer in making reflections and affections; but "God" (these are his own words) "Afterwards opened my eyes, and thenceforward I endeavoured to employ myself in petitions, and if there is any good in me, I ascribe it to this exercise of recommending myself to God." Do you likewise do the same; ask of God his graces in the name of Jesus Christ, and you shall obtain whatsoever you desire. This our Saviour has promised, and his promise cannot fail: Amen, amen, I say to you, if you ask the Father anything in my name he will give it you.

In a word, for you, religious, all your mental prayer should consist in acts and petitions. Hence the Venerable Sister Mary Crucified, while in an ecstasy, declared that mental prayer is the respiration of the soul; for as by respiration the air is first attracted and afterwards given back, so by petitions the soul first receives grace from God, and then by good acts of oblation and love it gives itself to him.

In finishing the meditation it is necessary to make a particular resolution; as, for example, to avoid some particular defect into which you have more frequently fallen, or to practice some virtue, such as to suffer the annoyance that you receive from a sister, to obey more exactly a certain Superior, to perform some particular act of mortification. We must repeat the same resolution several times until we find that we have got rid of the defect or acquired the virtue. Afterwards reduce to practice the resolutions you have made as soon as an occasion presents itself.

You would also do well, before the conclusion of your prayer, to renew the vows made at your profession. This renewal is most pleasing to God, because by her vows a religious gives herself entirely to God. According to the doctrine of St. Thomas, a religious is absolved from all her sins on the day of her profession, on account of the donation that she makes of herself entirely to God by means of the vows by which she consecrates to him all that she has—her property, her body, and her will. The same favour appears to be obtained by the nun who with a true spirit of self-spoliation renews her religious vows. Hence I advise you to renew them frequently, as well in the common prayer as at Communion, in the visit to the Blessed Sacrament, at rising in the morning, and in going to bed at night.

III. The CONCLUSION of meditation consists of three acts: 1. In thanking God for the lights received; 2. In making a purpose to fulfill the resolutions made; 3. In asking of the eternal Father for the sake of Jesus and Mary grace to be faithful to them.

Be careful never to omit at the end of meditation to recommend to God the souls in purgatory and poor sinners. St. John Chrysostom says that nothing more clearly shows the love of a soul for Jesus Christ than her zeal in recommending her brethren to him.

St. Francis de Sales remarks that in leaving mental prayer we should take with us a nosegay of flowers, in order to smell them during the day; that is, we should remember one or two points in which we felt particular devotion in order to excite our fervor during the day.

The ejaculations that are dearest to God are those of love, of resignation, of oblation of ourselves. Let us endeavor not to perform any action without first offering it to God, and not to allow at the most a quarter of an hour to pass, in whatever occupations we may find ourselves, without raising the heart to the Lord by some good act.

Moreover, in our leisure time, such as when we are waiting for a person, or when we walk in the garden, or are confined to bed by sickness, let us endeavor to the best of our ability to unite ourselves to God. It is also necessary by observing silence, by seeking solitude as much as possible, and by remembering the presence of God, to preserve the pious sentiments conceived in meditation. But I shall-speak more at length on this subject in the following chapter.

I here add, that in order to be a soul of prayer, a religious must resist with fortitude all temptations to continue mental prayer in the time of aridity. St. Teresa has left us very excellent instructions on this point. In one place she says: "The devil knows that he has lost the soul that perseveringly practices mental prayer." In another place she says: "I hold for certain that the Lord will conduct to the haven of salvation the soul that perseveres in mental prayer, in spite of all the sins that the devil may oppose." Again she says: "He that does not stop in the way of mental prayer, reaches the end of his journey, though he should delay a little." The love of God does not consist in experiencing tender affections, but in serving him with courage and humility. Finally she concludes, saying: "By aridity and temptations the Lord proves his lovers. Though aridity should be his for life, let not the soul give up prayer: the time will come when all will be well rewarded."

The Angelic Doctor says that true devotion consists not in feeling, but in the desire and resolution to embrace promptly all that God wills. Such was the prayer that Jesus Christ made in the garden; it was all full of aridity and tediousness, but it was the most devout and meritorious prayer that had ever been offered in this world; it consisted of these words: Not what I will, but what thou wilt.

Dear sister, never give up mental prayer in the time of aridity. Should the tediousness that assails you be very great, divide your meditations into several parts, and employ yourself for the most part in petitions to God, even though you should seem to pray without confidence and without fruit. It will be sufficient to say and repeat: My Jesus, mercy. Lord, have mercy on me. Pray, and doubt not that God will hear you and grant your petitions.

And in going to meditation, never propose to yourself your own pleasure and satisfaction, but only to please God, and to learn what he wishes you to do. And for this purpose pray always that God may make known to you his will, and that he may give you strength to fulfill it. All that we ought to seek in mental prayer is light to know and strength to accomplish the will of God in our regard.

Prayer.

Ah, my Jesus, it appears that Thou couldst do nothing more, in order to gain the love of men. It is enough to know that Thou hast wished to become man; that is, to become like us, a worm. Thou hast wished to lead a painful life, of thirty-three years, amid sorrow and ignominies, and in the end to die on an infamous gibbet. Thou hast also wished to remain under the appearance of bread, in order to become the food of our souls; and how is it possible that Thou hast received so much ingratitude, even from Christians that believe these truths, and still love Thee so little? Unhappy me! I have hitherto been among those ungrateful souls; I have attended only to my pleasures, and have been forgetful of Thee and of Thy love. I now know the evil I have done; but I repent of it with my whole heart; my Jesus, pardon me. I now love Thee; I love Thee so ardently that I choose death, and a thousand deaths, rather than cease to love Thee. I thank Thee for the light that Thou givest me. Give me strength, O God of my soul, always to advance in Thy love. Accept this poor heart to love Thee. It is true that it has once despised Thee, but now it is enamoured of Thy goodness; it loves Thee and desires only to love Thee.

O Mary, Mother of God, assist me; in thy intercession I place great confidence.

CHAPTER XVI.

SILENCE, SOLITUDE, AND THE PRESENCE OF GOD.

CASSIAN says: "The religious prays little who prays only when she is on her knees in the choir or in the cell." To fulfill the obligations of her state, a religious should keep her soul continually united with God; but to maintain this constant union, continual prayer is necessary. There are three means of acquiring the habit of continual prayer; namely, silence, solitude, and the presence of God. These were the means that the angel suggested to St. Arsenius when he said: "If you wish to be saved, fly into solitude, observe silence, and repose in God by always keeping yourself in his presence." We shall speak of each of these means separately.

I. Silence.

In the first place, silence is a great means of acquiring the spirit of prayer, and of disposing the soul to converse continually with God. We rarely find a spiritual soul that speaks much. All souls of prayer are lovers of silence that is called the guardian of innocence, the shield against temptations, and the fountain of prayer. For by silence devotion is preserved, and in silence good thoughts spring up in the soul. St. Bernard says: "Silence and the absence of noise in a certain manner force the soul to think of God and of eternal goods." Hence, the saints fled to the mountains, to caves, and to deserts, in order to find this silence, and escape the tumults of the world, in which, as was said to Elias, God is not found. Theodosius the monk observed silence for thirty-five years. St. John the Silent, who gave up his bishopric and became a monk, observed silence for forty-seven years before his death; and all the saints, even they who were not solitaries, have been lovers of silence.

Oh, how great the blessings that silence brings to the soul! The prophet says that silence shall cultivate justice in the soul; for, on the one hand, it saves us from a multitude of sins by destroying the root of disputes, of detractions, of resentments, and of curiosity; and on the other, it makes us acquire many virtues. How well does the nun practice humility who when others speak listens with modesty and in silence! How well does she practice mortification by not yielding to her inclination

324

or desire to tell a certain anecdote, or to use a witty expression suggested by the conversation! How well does she practice meekness by remaining silent when unjustly censured or offended! Hence the same holy prophet said: In silence and in hope shall be your strength. 3 Your strength shall be in silence and in hope; for by silence we shun the occasions of sin, and by hope we obtain the divine aid to lead a holy life.

But, on the other hand, immense evils flow from speaking too much. In the first place, as devotion is preserved by silence, so it is lost by a multitude of words. However recollected the soul may have been in prayer, if it afterwards indulge in long discourses it will find the mind as distracted and dissipated as if it had not made meditation. When the mouth of the burning furnace is opened the heat soon evaporates. St. Dorotheus says: "Beware of too much speaking, for it banishes from the soul holy thoughts and recollection with God." Speaking of religious that cannot abstain from inquiring after worldly news, St. Joseph Calasanctius said: "The curious religious shows that he has forgotten himself." It is certain that he who speaks too much with men converses but little with God, for the Lord says: I will lead her into the wilderness, and I will speak to her heart. If, then, the soul wishes that God speak to its heart, it must seek after solitude; but this solitude will never be found by religious who do not love silence. "If," said the Venerable Margaret of the Cross, "We remain silent, we shall find solitude." And how will the Lord ever condescend to speak to the religious, who, by seeking after the conversation of creatures, shows that the conversation of God is not sufficient to make her happy?

Besides, the Holy Ghost tells us that in speaking too much we shall not fail to commit some fault. In the multitude of words they shall not want sin. While they speak and prolong conversation without necessity, certain persons think that they are not guilty of any defect; but if they carefully examine themselves they will find some fault against modesty, of detraction, of curiosity, or at least of superfluous words. St. Mary Magdalene de Pazzi used to say that a religious should speak only through necessity. For religious are bound in a special manner to give an account of idle words, for which, according to our Saviour, all men shall have to render an account. But I say unto you, that every idle word that men shall speak, they shall account for it in the Day of Judgment.

I have used the words some defect; but when we speak too much we shall find that we have committed a thousand faults. St. James has called the tongue a universal evil: The tongue is . . . a world of iniquity. For, as a learned author remarks, the greater number of sins arise from speaking or from listening to others. Alas, how many nuns shall we see condemned on the Day of Judgment, on account of having had but little regard for silence! And what is most to be deplored is, that the religious that dissipates her mind by intercourse with creatures, and by too much speaking, will never be able to see her defects, and thus she will go from bad to worse. A man full of tongue shall not be established in the earth. The man that speaks too much shall walk without a guide, and therefore he shall fall into a thousand mistakes without the hope of ever perceiving them. Such a religious appears as if unable to live without speaking continually from morning till evening. She wishes to know what happens in the monastery and in the world; she goes about asking questions from all the others, and afterwards says, What evil am I doing? I answer you, dearly beloved sister, put an end to idle talk; endeavor to recollect yourself a little, and you will see how many defects you have committed by the multitude of your words.

St. Joseph Calasanctius used to say "That a dissipated religious is a source of joy to the devil." And justly, for by her dissipation she not only does not attend to her own sanctification, but is also an obstacle to the advancement of others, by going about the monastery in search of someone to converse with her, by speaking in a loud voice in every place, and by a want of reverence, even in the choir and sacristy. St. Ambrose relates that a certain priest, while at prayer, was disturbed by the cries of a multitude of frogs: he commanded them to be silent, and they instantly obeyed. The holy Doctor then took occasion to say: "Shall senseless animals, then, be silent through respect for prayer, and shall men not be silent?" And I add, will religious refuse to practice silence, after having entered the monastery in order to become saints, to observe their Rule, and to maintain holy recollection; or will they perform the office of the devil, by disturbing their sisters who wish to pray, and to be recollected with God? A certain author justly calls such talkative nuns "The home devils of monasteries," who do great injury to the Community.

According to St. Ignatius of Loyola, to know if there is fervor in a convent, it is enough to ascertain whether silence is observed or violated.

A monastery in which the sisters speak continually is an image of hell; for where there is not silence there must be continual disputes, detractions, complaints, particular friendships, and factions. But, on the other hand, a monastery in which the religious love silence is an image of paradise: it excites devotion not only in all who live in it, but also in those who live in the world. It is related by Father Perez, of the Order of Discalced Carmelites, that while a secular he entered one day into a house of the Order, and was so edified and filled with devotion by the silence of the brethren, that he renounced the world and remained in the convent. Father Natalis, of the Society of Jesus, used to say, that to reform a religious house it is enough to establish in it the observance of silence. Because each of the religious would then practice recollection, and would attend to his own advancement. Hence, also, Gerson says that the holy founders of religious Orders have prescribed and earnestly recommended silence to their religious, because they knew how important its observance is for the maintenance of fervor. In his rules for nuns, St. Basil insists, not once, but frequently, on silence. St. Benedict commanded his monks to endeavor to observe continual silence.

And experience shows that in the monastery in which silence is observed, discipline is maintained; and on the other hand, where silence is neglected, but little fervor is found. Hence few religious become saints, because few love silence. In many monasteries the rule of silence is prescribed by the written rules, and is strongly recommended; but some of the religious appear not to know what silence is, and therefore they unhappily live in dissipation, without fervor, and always in trouble. But, dear sister, do not imagine that the negligence of others will excuse or exempt you from the rule of silence. Blessed Clare of Montefalco used to say that in the time of silence it is difficult to speak without committing a fault.

Someone may excuse herself, saying, that it is sometimes necessary to speak in order to get rid of melancholy; but how can the violation of silence free a religious from melancholy? Let us be persuaded that all the creatures on earth or in heaven cannot console us in our afflictions. God alone is the author of consolation; but will he console us at the very time we offend him? But when there is any necessity for speaking in the time of silence, at least ask permission. Another religious does not seek occasions to speak, but as often as they are presented she allows herself to be led into breaches of silence by others who wish to speak. But her condescension will certainly not excuse her from the fault. It is necessary, then, to do violence to yourself, and to go away, or to remain silent, and sometimes by putting the finger on the mouth to make a sign that it is a time of silence.

And even out of the hours of silence endeavor to practice it as much as possible if you wish to keep yourself recollected with God and free from imperfections; for there is no sin more easily committed than sins of the tongue. He, says Solomon, that keepeth his month keepeth his soul. And St. James says that he who sins not with the tongue is a perfect man: If any man offend not in word, the same is a perfect man. Hence it is the same thing to be a silent religious and a holy religious; for by observing silence she will be punctual to the rules, she will be devoted to prayer, to spiritual reading, and to her visits to the Holy Sacrament. Oh, how dear to God does the religious render herself who loves silence—especially if by her silence on certain extraordinary occasions she offers to God an act of mortification; for example, when she feels greatly annoyed by long solitude, or when any very adverse or prosperous event occurs which she feels strongly impelled to re-late to others. On the other hand, the religious who indulges in much speaking will be generally dissipated, will easily omit her meditations and other devout exercises, and thus will gradually lose all relish for God. St. Mary Magdalene de Pazzi used to say: "The religious that has not a love for silence cannot find pleasure in the things of God." Hence the unhappy soul will abandon itself to worldly amusements, and thus retain nothing but the name and habit of a religious.

However, it is necessary to remark, that in monasteries the virtue of silence consists not in being always silent, but in observing silence when there is no necessity for speaking. Hence Solomon says that there is a time to keep silence, and a time to speak. But St. Gregory of Nyssa remarks that the time for silence is put before the time for speaking, because, as the saint adds, by silence we learn to speak well. By silence we learn to consider well what we shall afterwards say. But for a religious who wishes to become a saint, what is the time for silence and the time for speaking? The hours of silence for her are all the hours in which there is no necessity for speaking. The time for speaking is when necessity or charity obliges her to speak. Behold the excellent rule of St. John Chrysostom: "Then only should we speak when it is more useful to speak than to be silent." Hence the saint gives the following advice: "Either remain silent, or say what is more profitable than silence." Oh, happy he who at death can say what the monk Pambo said: "That he did not remember to have ever uttered a word which he was sorry for having spoken." St. Arsenius used to say that he often repented of having spoken, but never of having remained silent. St. Ephrem gave this excellent lesson to religious: "Speak a great deal with God, and little with men." St. Mary Magdalene de Pazzi used to say the same: "The true servant of Jesus Christ bears all things; she labors much, and speaks little."

From all that has been said, every religious that wishes to live in union with God may see with what care she should shun the parlour. As the air that is breathed in the choir or in the cell is the most salubrious for religious, so the air of the grates is for them the most pestiferous. And what is the parlour but what St. Mary Magdalene de Pazzi called it, a place of distractions, inquietudes, and of temptations. The Venerable Sister Mary Villani one day compelled the devil, on the part of God, to tell in what part of the monastery he gained most. The tempter answered: I gain in the choir, in the refectory, and in the dormitory: in these places I partly gain, and partly lose. But in the parlour I gain all, for the whole place is mine. Hence the Venerable Sister Philippa Cerrina had reason to call the parlor an infected place, in which the contagion of sin is easily caught. St. Bernardine of Sienna relates that a religious in consequence of having heard in the parlor an improper word miserably fell into a grievous sin. Truly happy was the holy virgin St. Fabronia, who afterwards gave her life for the faith at the age of nineteen; she would never allow herself to be seen at the grate by any secular, male or female. St. Teresa appeared after death to one of her spiritual children, and said to her: The religious that wishes to be a great friend of God must be an enemy of the grate.

Would to God that in all monasteries there were grates of perforated iron such as we find in some observant convents! A certain author relates that the Superior of a monastery procured a narrow grate; but the devil, through rage, first bent it, and afterwards sent it rolling through the house. The good Superior placed it, crooked as it was, in the parlor to give the nuns to understand that as the grate was hateful to hell so it was pleasing to God. Oh, what an awful account will the abbess have to give to God who introduces open grates, or who neglects to make the companions attend. In one of her letters St. Teresa wrote this great sentence: "The grates when shut are the gates of heaven; and when open they are the gates of danger," (she did not wish to say hell). And she added: "A monastery of nuns in which there is liberty serves to conduct them to hell rather than to cure their weakness."

What rapid progress in divine love does the religious make who resolves never to go to the grate! When you, dear sister, go to the parlor, be careful at least to conduct yourself like a religious. In your intercourse with seculars you should not only guard with great care against all affectionate expressions, but should also be very grave and reserved in the parlor. St. Mary Magdalene de Pazzi wished her nuns to be "Like the wild deer,"—these are her very words. And the Venerable Sister Hyacinth Marescotti used to say: "The courtesy of nuns consists in being discourteous by cutting short all long discourses in the parlor." This applies, ordinarily speaking, to long discourses even with spiritual persons. Mother Anne of Jesus, a Discalced Carmelite, said: "A nun acquires more fervor in the choir or in the cell than by the longest conferences in the parlor. Show all respect to directors, but you should treat with them only through necessity; despatch your business with them in a few words."

Should you ever happen to hear in the "Parlor an indecent word, go away immediately; or, at least, cast down your eyes, and change the discourse, or give no answer. In a monastery of the Venerable Sister Seraphina de Carpi two women began to speak about a certain marriage: the attendant at the turn heard the voice of Sister Seraphina (who was dead) saying, "Chase away, chase away these women." And whenever it is in your power, endeavor to change all discourses that savour of the world. St. Frances of Rome received a buffet from an angel because she did not change the conversation of certain ladies who spoke of worldly vanities. You should be still more careful to observe silence with your sisters in the monastery: for the occasion of breaking silence with them is more continual. Hence it is necessary to mortify curiosity. The Abbot John used to say: "Let him who wishes to restrain the tongue shut his ears by mortifying the curiosity of hearing news." It is also necessary to avoid the conversation of any religious who speaks frequently. It is, moreover, well to fix some time each day during which you will observe silence, remaining alone in your cell or in some solitary place in order to avoid the occasions of speaking.

Whenever you have to speak, be careful, in conformity with the advice of the Holy Ghost, Make a balance for thy words to examine what you ought to say. Make a balance for your words that you may weigh them before you give expression to them. Hence St. Bernard says that "Before your words come to the tongue, let them pass twice under the file of examination," that you may suppress what you should not utter. The same was said by St. Francis de Sales in other words, namely, that to speak without sin everyone should keep a lock on his lips, that in opening his mouth to speak he might reflect well on what he wishes to say.

Before speaking you should consider—
1. Whether what you intend to say can injure charity, modesty, or exact observance.

2. Examine the motive that impels you to speak; for it sometimes happens that what a person says is good, but her intention is bad; she speaks either to appear spiritual, or to acquire a character for talent.

3. Examine to whom you speak, whether to your Superiors, to companions, or to inferiors: whether in the presence of seculars, or of the postulants, who may perhaps be scandalized at what you say.

4. Examine the time at which you speak, whether at the time of silence or of repose.

5. The place in which you speak, whether in the choir, in the sacristy, or the corridors; at the door or in the parlor.

6. Be careful to speak with simplicity, avoiding all affection; with humility, abstaining from all words of pride or vainglory; with sweetness, never uttering a word that savors of impatience, or that tends to the discredit of a neighbor; with moderation, by not being the first to give your opinion on any question that may be proposed, particularly if you are younger than the others; with modesty, by not interrupting any sister while she is speaking; and also by abstaining from every word that savors of the world, from all improper gestures, and immoderate laughter, and by speaking in a low tone of voice; for St. Bonaventure says that it is a great defect in a religious to speak in a loud voice, particularly at night. And should you, as Superior, be ever obliged to

correct a sister, take care not to reprimand her in a loud voice; for otherwise she will perceive that you speak through impatience, and then the reprimand will be unprofitable.

At recreation, which is the proper time for unbending the mind, speak when the others are silent, but endeavor as often as you can to speak on something that has reference to God. "Let us speak of the Lord Jesus," says St. Ambrose, "Let us always speak of him." And what other enjoyment should a religious seek than to speak of her most amiable Spouse? He who has an ardent love for another, appears unable to speak of anything but of him. They who speak little of Jesus Christ, show that they have but little love for Jesus Christ. On the other hand, it often happens that good religious, after speaking on divine love, feel more fervor than after mental prayer. At the conversations of the servants of God, says St. Teresa, Jesus Christ is always present. Of this, Father Gisolfo, of the Congregation of the "Pious Workers," relates a memorable example, in the life of the Venerable Father Anthony de Collelis. He says that Father Constantine Rossi, the Master of novices, saw one day two of his young disciples, F. D. Anthony Torres, and F. D. Philip Orilia, conversing together, and with them a young man of most beautiful aspect. The Master of novices was surprised that two novices, whom he regarded as most exemplary, should speak to a stranger without permission: he therefore asked who was the young man whom he had seen conversing with them. They said there was no one conversing with them. But he afterwards learned that they were speaking of Jesus Christ, and understood that the person whom he saw in their company was our divine Saviour.

Except in the hours of recreation, and other extraordinary occasions, such as in attending the sick, or in consoling a sister in tribulation, it is always better to be silent. A religious of the Order of St. Teresa, as we find in the Teresian Chronicles, said that it is better to speak with God than to speak of God. But when obedience or charity obliges you to speak, or to have intercourse with creatures, you must always endeavor to find intervals, for at least repairing the losses caused by the distractions attendant on these external occupations; stealing at least as many little moments as possible to recollect yourself with God; thus following the counsel of the Holy Ghost: Let not the part of a good gift overpass thee. Do not allow that particle of time to pass away: give it to God, if you can have no more to give him during the day. But whenever you can abridge the conversation, abridge it under some pretext. A good religious seeks not pretexts, as some do, to prolong conversation, but endeavors to find out some means of shortening it. Let us remember that time is given us not to be spent unprofitably, but to be employed for God, and in acquiring merits for eternity. St. Bernardine of Sienna used to say that a moment of time is of as much value as God, because in each moment we can gain his friendship, or greater degrees of grace.

Prayer.

O my God, may the patience with which Thou hast borne me be forever blessed. Thou hast given me time to love Thee, and I have spent it in offending and displeasing Thee. Were I now to die, with what heartfelt pain should I end my life, at the thought of having spent so many years in the world, and of having done nothing. Lord, I thank Thee for still giving me time to repair my negligence, and so many lost years. O my Jesus, through the merits of Thy Passion assist me. I do not wish to live any longer for myself, but only for Thee, and for Thy love. I know not how much of life remains, whether it is long or short; but were it a hundred or a thousand years, I wish to spend them all in loving and pleasing Thee. I love Thee, my Sovereign Good, and I hope to love Thee for eternity. I do not wish to be ever again ungrateful to Thee. I will no longer resist Thy love, which has so long called me to be entirely Thine. Shall I wait till Thou abandon me, and call me no more?

Mary, my mother, assist me, pray for me, and obtain for me perseverance in my resolution to be faithful to God.

II.

The Love of Solitude, and the Avoiding of Idleness.

1. THE LOVE OF SOLITUDE.

Whosoever loves God, loves solitude; there the Lord communicates himself more familiarly to souls, because there he finds them less entangled in worldly affairs, and more detached from earthly affections. Hence, St. Jerome exclaimed: "O solitude, in which God speaks and converses familiarly with his servants! O blessed solitude, in which God speaks and converses with his beloved spouses with familiarity, with great love and confidence! God speaks not at the grates, nor in the belvedere, nor in any other place in which religious indulge in useless laughter and idle talk. The Lord is not in the earthquake. But where is he? I will lead her into the wilderness, and I will speak to her heart. He speaks in solitude, and there he speaks to the heart in words that inflame it with his holy love, as the sacred spouse attests: My soul melted when my beloved spoke. St. Eucherius relates that a certain man, desirous of becoming a saint, asked a servant of God where he should find God. The servant of God conducted him to a solitary place, and said: "Behold where God is found!" By these words he meant to say that God is found not amid the tumults of the world, but in solitude.

Virtue is easily preserved in solitude; and, on the other hand, it is easily lost by intercourse with the world, where God is but little known, and therefore his love, and the goods that he gives to those who leave all things for his sake, are but little esteemed. St. Bernard says that he learned more among the trees of the forest than from books and masters. Hence the saints, in order to live in solitude and far from tumult, have so ardently loved the caves, the mountains, and the woods. The land that was desolate and impassable shall be glad, and the wilderness shall rejoice, and shall flourish like the lily; it shall bud forth and blossom. . . . They shall see the glory of the Lord and the beauty of our God. The wilderness shall be a perennial fountain of joy and gladness to the soul that seeks it; it shall flourish like the lily in whiteness and innocence of life, and shall produce fruits of every virtue. These happy souls shall in the end be raised on high to see the glory and infinite beauty of the Lord. It is certain that to keep the heart united with God we must preserve in the soul the thoughts of God, and of the immense goods that he prepares for those who love him; but when we hold intercourse with the world, it presents to us earthly things that cancel spiritual impressions and pious sentiments. Hence, for a nun that delights in receiving visits and letters, in reading the newspapers, and in speaking frequently of the things of the world, it is impossible to be a good religious. Every time that she unnecessarily holds intercourse with seculars, she will suffer a diminution of fervor.

There is no one more deserving of pity than a nun who, being unable to go into the world, brings the world to herself by spending a great part of the day in vain amusements, in conversing with seculars at the grate, or in diverting herself with the sisters, laughing, talking, censuring others, and by seeking to learn what happens in the neighbourhood. Shall a spouse of Jesus Christ, who should have no other pleasure than that of conversing with her God, place her consolation in a life of distraction, and of intercourse with seculars, who by their conversation will infect her heart with the corrupt maxims of the world? Shall she thus spend the time that the Lord gives her in order to become a saint? O God, how can she squander that time the moments of which the saints would have purchased even at the cost of their blood? Alas, when one day she finds herself at the hour of death, what would she give for a day, or even for one of the many hours that she now loses! A certain religious said at the end of her life: "Oh that I had more time I would give it all to God!" But the unhappy soul desired time when for her time was no more.

Besides, I say to you, dear sister, God in his goodness has rescued you from the dangers of the world, and has given you the courage to forsake it; why, then, should you expose yourself to the same dangers by again holding intercourse with the world? Tertullian says that "We have escaped once from the waves of the world (in which so many perish); let us not voluntarily cast ourselves again into the midst of them," and expose our souls to the danger of perdition. The religious who wishes to become a saint should seek neither to know nor be known by the world; she should endeavor to the utmost of her ability neither to see nor to be seen by seculars. Blessed Clare of Montefalco spoke even to her brother with the veil drawn down; the abbess said that in conversing with her brother she might raise the veil. She answered: "Mother, since I speak only with the tongue, allow me to remain covered." The words of the Venerable Sister Frances Farnese are also very remarkable. "My sisters," said she, "We are shut up within these walls, not to see and to be seen, but to hide ourselves from creatures. The more we hide ourselves from them, the more Jesus Christ will unveil himself to us."

Worldlings shun solitude, and with good reason; for in solitude they feel more acutely the remorse of conscience, and therefore they go in search of the conversations and tumults of the world, that the noise of these occupations may stifle the stings of remorse. The religious, then, who flies from solitude shows that she, too, is a disorderly soul, who, in order to extinguish the remorse caused by her irregularities, seeks after the noise and bustle of the world. On the other hand, religious who live with a tranquil conscience cannot but love solitude; and when they find themselves out of it, they feel like fish out of water—they enjoy no peace, and are, as it were, in a violent state. It is true that man loves society; but what society preferable to the society of God? Ah, to withdraw from creatures and to converse in solitude with our Creator brings neither bitterness nor tediousness. Of this the Wise Man assures us: For her conversation hath no bitterness, nor her company any tediousness, but joy and gladness. The Venerable Father Vincent Carafa, General of the Society of Jesus (as has been said in another place), said that he desired nothing in this world, and that were he to desire anything, he would wish only for a little grotto, along with a morsel of bread, and a spiritual book, in order to live there always in solitude.

It is not true that a life of solitude is a life of melancholy: it is a foretaste and beginning of the life of the saints in bliss, who are filled with an immense joy in the sole occupation of loving and praising their God. Thus St. Jerome said, that flying from Rome he went to shut himself up in the cave of Bethlehem, in order to enjoy solitude. Hence he afterwards wrote: "To me solitude is a paradise." The saints in solitude appear to be alone, but they are not alone. St. Bernard said: "I am never less alone than when I find myself alone;" for I am then in the company of my Lord, who gives me more content than I could derive from the conversation of all creatures. They appear to be in sadness, but they are not sad. The world, seeing them far away from earthly amusements, regard them as miserable and disconsolate; but they are not so; they, as the Apostle attests, enjoy an immense and continual peace. As sorrowful, yet always rejoicing. The prophet Isaias attested the same when he said: The Lord therefore, will comfort Sion, and will comfort all the ruins thereof; and He will make her desert as a place, of pleasure, and her wilderness as the garden of the Lord. Joy and gladness shall be found therein, thanksgiving and the voice of praise. The Lord well knows how to console the solitary soul, and will give a thousand fold compensation for all the temporal pleasures which it has forfeited: he will render its solitude a garden of his delights. There joy and gladness shall be always found, and nothing shall be heard but the voice of thanksgiving and praise to the divine goodness. Hence, Cardinal Petrucci describes the happiness of a solitary heart in the following words: "It appears to be sad, and it is filled with celestial joy. Though it treads on the earth, its dwelling is in heaven. It asks nothing for itself, because in its bosom it contains an immense treasure. It appears to be agitated and overwhelmed by the tempest, and it is always in a secure harbour."

In order to find this happy solitude, it is not necessary for you, dear sister, to hide yourself in a cave or in a desert; even in the monastery, you can, whenever you wish, find the solitude which you desire. Shun the grates, shun useless conversations and discourses; love the choir and the cell; remain in the choir or cell whenever obedience or charity does not call you elsewhere; and thus you will find the solitude that is suited to you, and that God wishes from you. Thus David found it, even in the midst of the great concerns of a kingdom, and therefore he said: Lo, I have gone far off, flying away; and I abode in the wilderness. St. Philip Neri desired to retire into a desert, but God gave him to understand that he should not leave Rome, but that he should live there as in a desert. The Lord wishes the same from religious, whom he desires to be his true spouses; he wishes them to be enclosed in gardens, that in them he may be able to find his delights. My sister—my spouse is a garden enclosed. But Gilbert well remarks: "He knows not how to be a garden, that does not wish to be enclosed." The nun who is unwilling to be enclosed, that is, careful not to bring into her heart the thoughts and dangers of the world by frequent intercourse with worldlings, cannot be the garden of Jesus Christ.

"Live therefore as a solitary," says St. Bernard, "Retire not merely in body, but in spirit." Even when you are with the sisters at work, or at the common recreation, endeavor not to leave your solitude; be careful to keep yourself as much as possible recollected with God; and if you cannot withdraw in body from conversation, withdraw at least in affection and intention, by intending to remain there only because it is God's will that you should remain. Since you must sometimes have intercourse with creatures, you ought to act like a tender woman, who, being accustomed to remain always in a close room, far from the society of men, endeavors, when obliged to go into the street, to return as quickly as possible in order to escape the cold and bustle. It is thus that holy religious act when by duty or charity they are forced to converse with the sisters or with externs; they suffer a species of martyrdom, partly on account of their repugnance to hold intercourse with creatures, and partly through fear of committing some fault, and therefore they seek to abridge the conversation as much as possible.

When external occupations last for a long time, it is very difficult to escape defects. Even when they were employed in the conversion of sinners, Jesus Christ wished the holy apostles to retire from time to time into a solitary place, in order to give some repose to the spirit. Come apart into a desert place, and rest a little. Yes; for in external occupations, even of a spiritual nature, the soul falls into distractions, disquietudes, coldness of divine love, and imperfections; hence repose is always necessary to remove the stains contracted, and to acquire strength to walk better for the future. It is not necessary, then, to remain always in solitude; but, as St. Laurence Justinian has written, we ought to procure it whenever we can, and when we cannot, we ought to love it. Hence, when a religious is obliged to interrupt her retirement in order to serve the Community, or to relieve the necessity of a sister, she must do it with liberty of soul, without disturbing herself: otherwise she will show attachment to solitude, which is a great defect. But in going to treat with creatures her object must not be to amuse herself by their conversation, but to practice obedience or charity. Then, as soon as the occupation is over, she ought instantly to retire to her beloved solitude.

Hitherto we have spoken of the solitude of the body; we must now say something on the solitude of the heart, which is more necessary than the solitude of the body. "Of what use," says St. Gregory, "Is the solitude of the body without the solitude of the heart?" That is, of what use is it to live in the desert if the heart is attached to the world? A soul detached and free from earthly affections, says St. Peter Chrysologus, finds solitude even in the public streets and highways. On the other hand, of what use is it to observe silence in the choir or in the cell, if affections to creatures are entertained in the heart, and by their noise render the soul unable to listen to the divine inspirations? I here repeat the words of our Lord to St. Teresa: "Oh, how gladly would I speak to many souls, but the world makes such a noise in their heart that my voice cannot be heard. Oh, that they would retire a little from the world!"

Let us then understand what is meant by solitude of the heart. It consists in expelling from the soul every affection that is not for God, by seeking nothing in all our actions but to please his divine eyes. It consists in saying with David: What have I in heaven, and besides thee, what do I desire upon earth? . . . Thou art the God of my heart, and the God that is my portion forever. O my God, except Thee, what is there on earth or in heaven that can content me? Thou alone art the Lord of my heart, and Thou shalt always be my only treasure. In fine, solitude of the heart implies that you can say with sincerity, My God, I wish for Thee alone, and for nothing else.

Such a religious complains that she does not find God; but listen to what St. Teresa says: "Detach the heart from all things—seek God, and then you will find him." God can neither be sought nor found if he is not first known; but how can a soul attached to creatures comprehend God and his divine beauty? The light of the sun cannot enter a crystal vessel filled with earth; and in a heart occupied with affections to pleasures, to wealth, and to honors, the divine light cannot shine. Hence the Lord says: Be still, and see that I am God. The soul, then, that wishes to see God must remove the world from her heart, and keep it shut against all earthly affections. This is precisely what Jesus Christ gave us to understand under the figure of a closed chamber, when he said: But when thou shalt pray, enter into thy chamber, and having shut the door, pray to thy Father in secret. That is, the soul, in order to unite itself with God in prayer, must retire into its heart (which, according to St. Augustine, is the chamber of which our Lord speaks), and shut the door against all earthly affections.

This is also the meaning of the words of Jeremiah: He shall sit solitary, and hold his peace; because he hath taken it upon himself. The solitary soul, that is, the soul that is free from all attachments, and in which earthly affections are silent, will unite itself with God in mental prayer by holy desires, by oblations of itself, and by acts of love: and then it will find itself raised above all created objects, so that it will smile at the worldling who sets so high a value on the goods of this earth, and submits to so many toils in order to secure their enjoyment, while it regards them as trifles, and utterly unworthy of the love of a heart created to love God, who is an infinite good. Hence Cardinal Petrucci says, that the love of a heart dedicated to the divine love is raised above all that is spread over the theatre of the world.

2. THE AVOIDING OF IDLENESS.

But remember that by solitude I do not mean pure leisure, as if a religious were to be free from all occupations and from all care. God wishes that his spouses be solitary, but not idle. Some nuns lead a hidden and retired life, but in their retreat they either remain idle, without applying themselves to any work, or spend their time in vain reading, or in other useless occupations. They remain silent, but of this useless silence St. Basil says they shall render an account to God. Idle solitude is the solitude of beasts; solitude devoted to curious studies is worldly solitude; religious solitude is neither idle nor useless, but is all fruitful and holy. Religious should remain in their cells, like the bee, which in its little cell never ceases to make honey; and hence they should not waste their time, but should be employed either in prayer, or in reading spiritual books, or in manual works that will not hinder them to keep the mind on God. St. John Chrysostom says that in solitude the soul is not idle, but occupied in God. In a certain convent of St. Francis there was an idle brother who was always going about the house—now troublesome to one, and again to another. The saint called him Brother Fly. Would to God that in monasteries there were no Sister Fly, constantly going about, observing who is at the grate or at confession; who sends or receive presents, and the like. Such religious would deserve, like flies, to be expelled from the house, or at least to be shut up in a prison that they might cease to disturb others.

It is a common saying, that idleness is the parent of all vices, and it is founded on the oracle of the Holy Ghost: Idleness hath taught much evil. St. Joseph Calasanctius says: "The devil goes in pursuit of idle religious." And, according to St. Bonaventure, a religious assiduously employed is molested with one temptation, but an idle religious shall be assailed by a thousand. It is certain that to a nun the cell is a great help to practice recollection with God. But the same St. Joseph Calasanctius said that a religious "Makes a bad use of her cell when while in it she neither speaks with God nor labors for God." We cannot be always at prayer, and therefore in this life it is necessary for religious to be employed in manual occupations. She hath sought wool and flax, and hath wrought by the counsel of her hands. Hence, St. Jerome prescribed to Demetriade to have wool always in her hands. All holy women, particularly religious, have employed themselves in manual work. St. Mary Magdalene de Pazzi, though so infirm and weak, took part in all the labors of the monastery, as well for the choir nuns as for the lay-sisters. She worked now in the kitchen, and again in the refectory; at one time she swept the convent, at another she carried water from the well. She labored so hard in making bread, that she distorted one of the bones of the hand. In a word, the author of her life says that she performed more work than four lay-sisters together.

And let it be observed, that it is an error to imagine that labor is injurious to bodily health, for it is certain that manual employment contributes greatly to the preservation of health, and this is the reason why lay- sisters ordinarily enjoy better health than the choir nuns. Ah, it is frequently not so much the danger of health, as the desire of escaping the pain attendant on labor, that makes us excuse ourselves from manual work. But the religious who looks at the crucifix will not endeavor to shun labor. Sister Frances of St. Angelo of the Carmelite Order complained one day to Jesus on the cross, that by severity of labor she had injured her hands. Jesus answered: "Frances, look at my hands, and then complain."

Besides, manual work contributes greatly to relieve the tediousness of solitude, and also to overcome temptations, which are very frequent in solitude. St. Anthony found himself one day so molested with immodest thoughts and so weary of solitude that he knew not what to do. An angel appeared and conducted the saint to a little garden. There he took the mattock and began to dig, and afterwards to pray; he next resumed the work, and again returned to prayer. From the conduct of the angel the saint learned that he was to live in solitude, and at the same time defend himself against temptations by passing from prayer to work and from work to prayer. A person should not be always employed at work; but it is impossible for a religious to be always at prayer without affecting her brain, and rendering herself utterly unfit for all spiritual exercises. Hence St. Teresa after death appeared to Sister Paula Mary of Jesus, and exhorted her not to fail to exercise herself in corporal works under the delusive pretext of devoting herself more to holy occupations; and the saint added that these manual exercises are a great help to eternal salvation.

Besides, manual works when performed without solitude and passion do not hinder us from praying. Sister Margaret of the Cross, Archduchess of Austria, a discalced nun, used to perform the most laborious offices of the monastery, and would say that labor is not only useful but necessary for nuns, since it does not hinder them from raising the heart to God. It is related that St. Bernard one day saw a monk who while he worked did not cease to pray. The saint said to him: "My brother, continue to do always what you do at present, and be of good cheer; for by acting in this manner you shall after death be exempt even from purgatory." The saint afterwards practiced the same, as we read in his life. He did not neglect his external works, but he was at the same time wholly recollected in God. And thus every religious, while she works with her hands, should not neglect to keep her heart occupied with God; otherwise, all her external employments shall be without spiritual fruit, and shall be full of imperfections. Hence the Spouse of the Canticles says to the soul: Place me as a seal upon thy heart, as a seal upon thy arm. He first tells her to place him as a seal upon her heart, and afterwards upon her arm; because if she has not God in the heart she cannot have him upon the arm; that is, her external works cannot be pleasing to him. But, on the other hand, St. Teresa says that "Works of the active life, when they spring from divine love, are the highest perfection."

Hence it is an error in a religious to wish to remain always in solitude, or to shun all external occupations. But it is also an error in her to undertake voluntarily such a multiplicity of employments that she afterwards has not time to recollect herself with God. My son, meddle not with many matters; and if thou be rich thou shalt not be free from sin. Son, says the Lord, do not burden yourself with so many concerns; for if you wish to attend to them all, you may indeed succeed, but not without sin.

There are others who, when they undertake any business apply, themselves so closely to it that they render themselves unable to think of anything else. What has been undertaken should be done with diligence, but with tranquility and without passion, so that the soul may have liberty to turn to God from time to time. You should labor; but you who are a religious should not work like a secular, toiling night and day in order to accumulate money. And for what purpose? In order to make presents, or to gratify vanity or caprice. It is necessary to work, but to work like a religious: hence attend first to the business of the soul; and afterwards to that of the body, employing yourself in ex-

342

ternal exercises, with a pure intention either of practising obedience or of assisting the Community, or of relieving your own pressing wants, and of avoiding idleness; but always without avidity or solicitude, which may hinder you from raising the heart to God. St. Antonine says that in every external occupation, however urgent, we must always keep a secret little corner within, in which we may take refuge and turn to God when we find ourselves oppressed and overwhelmed with business. Hence it is of great importance to take care in the beginning as well as in the progress of our work to raise the heart several times to God by an act of love, of oblation, of resignation, or by a petition for his graces. Why, for example, can you not, when employed in embroidering or in sewing, make at every moment an act of the love of God, or of oblation of yourself? I conclude this point. Fervent nuns in all their works are recollected in spirit, unite themselves more closely to God, and always acquire merit. But the tepid and negligent fabricate cobwebs; for they labor and toil through earthly motives, and thus lose all.

Prayer.

My Jesus, grant that I may love Thee ardently during the remainder of my life, and that I may be entirely Thine. I curse the days in which I have loved creatures so as to displease Thee. Henceforth I wish to love nothing but Thee. I entreat Thee to give me strength to detach my heart from all things that divert me from Thy love. Grant that my heart may be employed in regarding only Thee as the only object worthy of love. O Incarnate Word! Thou hast come into the world to dwell in our souls that Thou hast redeemed with Thy blood. Let my heart, then, be all Thine. Take possession of it and watch over all my wants; illuminate my soul, inflame me, and make me promptly obey all Thy wishes. My Jesus, my Sovereign Good, I love Thee and I esteem Thee above every good. I give myself entirely to Thee: accept me to serve Thee forever but to serve Thee not through fear, but through love. Thy majesty deserves to be feared, but Thy goodness deserves still more to be loved.

O Mary, my Mother and my refuge, obtain for me the grace to belong entirely to Jesus.

III.

The Presence of God.

1. EFFECTS PRODUCED BY THIS HOLY EXERCISE.

The practice of the presence of God is justly called by spiritual masters the foundation of a spiritual life, which consists in three things: the avoidance of sin, the practice of virtue, and union with God. These three effects the presence of God produces: it preserves the soul from sin, leads it to the practice of virtue, and moves it to unite itself to God by means of holy love.

I. As to the first effect, the avoidance of sin, there is no more efficacious means of subduing the passions, of resisting temptations, and consequently of avoiding sin, than the remembrance of God's presence. The angelic Doctor says: "If we always thought that God was looking at us, we would never, or scarcely ever, do what is displeasing in his eyes." And St. Jerome has written that the remembrance of God's presence closes the door against all sins. "The remembrance of God," says the holy Doctor, "Shuts out all sins." And if men will not dare in their presence to transgress the commands of princes, parents, or Superiors, how could they ever violate the laws of God if they thought that he was looking at them? St. Ambrose relates that a page of Alexander the Great, who held in his hand a lighted torch whilst Alexander was offering sacrifice in the temple, suffered his hand to be burnt sooner than be guilty of irreverence by allowing the torch to fall. The saint adds, that if reverence to his sovereign could conquer nature in a boy, how much more will the thought of the divine presence make a faithful soul overcome every temptation, and suffer every pain rather than insult the Lord before his face!

All the sins of men flow from their losing sight of the divine presence. "Every evil," says St. Teresa, "Happens to us because we do not reflect that God is present with us, but imagine that he is at a distance." And before her David said the same: God is not before, his eyes; his ways are filthy at all times. Sinners forget that God sees them, and therefore they offend him at all times. The Abbot Diocles went so far as to say that "He who distracts himself from the remembrance of the presence of God becomes either a beast or a devil." And justly; for he shall be instantly assailed by carnal or diabolical desires which he will not have strength to resist.

On the other hand, the saints by the thought that God was looking at them have bravely repelled all the assaults of their enemies. This thought gave courage to holy Susanna to resist the temptations of the Elders, and even to despise their threats against her life. Hence she courageously said to them: It is better for me to fall into your hands without doing it than to sin in the sight of the Lord. It is better to fall into your hands and to die without sin than to offend God before his face. This thought also converted a wicked woman who dared to tempt St. Ephrem; the saint told her that if she wished to sin she must meet him in the middle of the city. But, said she, how is it possible to commit sin before so many persons? And how, replied the saint, is it possible to sin in the presence of God, who sees us in every place? At these words she burst into tears, and falling prostrate on the ground asked pardon of the saint, and besought him to point out to her the way of salvation. St. Ephrem placed her in a monastery, where she led a holy life, weeping over her sins till death. The same happened to the abbot Paphnutius and a sinner called Thais. She tempted him one day, saying that there was no one to see them but God. The saint with a stern voice said to her: "Then you believe that God sees you, and will you commit sin?" Thais was thunderstruck, and filled with horror for her sinful life: she gathered together all her riches,, clothes, and jewels which she had earned by her infamous practices, burned them in the public square, and retired into a monastery, where she fasted on bread and water every day for three successive years, always repeating this prayer: "O Thou who hast made me, have mercy on me! My God, who hast created me, have pity on me!" After these three years she happily ended her life by a holy death. It was afterwards revealed to Paul, a disciple of St. Anthony, that this happy penitent was placed among the saints on an exalted throne of glory.

Behold the efficacy of the remembrance of the divine presence to make us avoid sins. Let us then always pray to the Lord, saying with Job: Set me beside thee, and let any man's hand fight against me My God, place me in Thy presence; that is, remind me in every place that Thou seest me, and then let all my enemies assail me: I shall always defeat them. Hence St. Chrysostom concludes: "If we keep ourselves always in the presence of God, the thought that he sees all our thoughts, that he hears all our words, and observes all our actions will preserve us from thinking any evil, from speaking any evil, and from doing any evil."

II. As to the second effect, the practice of virtue, the presence of God is also a great means. Oh, what valour does a soldier exhibit in the presence of his sovereign! The sole thought that his prince by whom he shall be punished or rewarded is present inspires him with great courage and strength. Thus also when such a religious is in the presence of her Superior, with what exterior recollection does she pray, with what modesty and humility does she treat the sisters; with what care does she execute the directions that she receives! Hence if they reflected that God was looking at all their actions, all religious would do all things well, with a pure intention, without seeking to please anyone but God, and without any regard to human respect. St. Basil says that were a person to find himself in the presence of a king and a peasant, his sole concern would be to please the king without any regard to the wishes of the peasant. Thus he that walks in the divine presence is regardless of the pleasure of creatures, and seeks only to please God, who sees him always.

III. Finally, as to the third effect of the divine presence, that is, to unite the soul to God, it is an infallible rule that love is always increased by the presence of the object loved. This happens even among men, although the more they converse together, the more their defects are discovered. How much more shall the love of a soul for God increase if it keep him before its eyes, for the more it converses with him, the better it comprehends his beauty and amiableness. The morning and the evening meditation are not sufficient to keep the soul united with God. St. John Chrysostom says, that even water, if removed from the fire, soon returns to its natural temperature; and therefore after prayer it is necessary to preserve fervor by the presence of God, and by renewing our affections.

St. Bernard says of himself, that in the beginning of his conversion, when he found himself disturbed, or his fervor cooled, peace and the ardor of divine love were instantly restored by the remembrance of a deceased or absent saint. Now, how much greater the effect which must be produced on a soul that loves God, by remembering that he is present, and that he is asking her love. David said that by the remembrance of his God he was filled with joy and consolation. I remembered God, and was delighted. However great the affliction and desolation of a soul may be, if it loves God it will be consoled and freed from its affliction by remembering its beloved Lord. Hence, souls enamoured of God live always with a tranquil heart and in continual peace; because, like the sunflower that always turns its face to the sun, they in all events and in all their actions seek always to live and act in the presence of God. "A true lover," says St. Teresa, "Always remembers her beloved."

2. PRACTICE OF THE PRESENCE OF GOD.

Let us now come to the practice of this excellent exercise of the divine presence. This exercise consists partly in the operation of the under-standing, and partly in the operation of the will: of the understanding, in beholding God present; of the will, in uniting the soul to God, by acts of humiliation, of adoration, of love, and the like: of the latter we shall speak more particularly hereafter.

I. With regard to the intellect, the presence of God may be practiced in four ways:

1. By imagining that our Redeemer, Jesus Christ, is present, that he is in our company, and that he sees us in whatsoever place we may be. We can at one time represent him in one mystery, and again in another: for example, now an infant lying in the manger of Bethlehem, and again a pilgrim flying into Egypt; now a boy working in the shop of Nazareth, and again suffering as a criminal in his Passion in Jerusa-lem, scourged, or crowned with thorns, or nailed to a cross. St. Teresa praises this method of practising the presence of God. But it is neces-sary to remark, that though this method is good, it is not the best, nor is it always profitable: first, because it is not conformable to truth; for Jesus Christ, as God and man together, is present with us only after Communion, or when we are before the Blessed Sacrament. Besides, this mode is liable to illusion, or may at least injure the head by the efforts of the imagination. Hence, should you wish to practice it, you must do it sweetly, only when you find it useful, and without labour-ing to represent in the mind the peculiar features of our Saviour, his countenance, his stature, or colour. It is enough to represent him in a confused manner, as if he were observing all we do.

2. The second method, which is more secure and more excellent, is founded on the truth of faith, and consists in beholding with eyes of faith God present with us in every place, in considering that he en-

compasses us, that he sees and observes whatever we do. We indeed do not see him with the eyes of the flesh. Nor do we see the air, yet we know for certain that it surrounds us on every side, that we live in it; for without it we could neither breathe nor live. We do not see God, but our holy faith teaches that he is always present with us. Do not I fill heaven and earth, saith the Lord? Is it not true, says God, that I fill heaven and earth by my presence. And as a sponge in the midst of the ocean is encompassed and saturated with water, so, says the Apostle, we live in God, we move in God, and have our being in God. And our God, says St. Augustine, observes every action, every word, every thought of each of us, as if he forgot all his other creatures, and had to attend only to us. Hence, observing all we do, say, and think, he marks and registers all, in order to demand an account on the day of accounts, and to give us then the reward or the chastisement that we have deserved.

This second mode of practising the divine presence does not fatigue the mind; for the exercise of it we need only enliven our faith with an affectionate act of the will, saying: My God, I believe firmly that Thou art here present. To this act we can easily add the acts of love, or of resignation, or of purity of intention, and the like.

3. The third means of preserving the remembrance of the presence of God is to recognize him in his creatures, which have from him their being, and their power of serving us. God is in the water to wash us, in the fire to warm us, in the sun to enlighten us, in food to nourish us, in clothes to cover us, and in like manner in all other things that he has created for our use. When we see a beautiful object, a beautiful garden, or a beautiful flower, let us think that there we behold a ray of the infinite beauty of God, who has given existence to that object. If we converse with a man of sanctity and learning, let us consider that it is God who imparts to him a small portion of his own holiness and wisdom. Thus, also, when we hear harmonious sounds, when we feel a fragrant odour, or taste delicious meat or drink, let us remember that God is the being who by his presence imparts to us these delights, that by them we may be induced to aspire to the eternal delights of paradise.

Let us accustom ourselves to behold in every object God, who presents himself to us in every creature; and let us offer him acts of thanksgiving and of love, remembering that from eternity he has thought of creating so many beautiful creatures that we might love him. St. Augustine says: Learn to love your Creator in creatures; and fix not your affection on what God has made, lest you should become attached to creatures and lose him by whom you, too, have been created.

This was the practice of the saint. At the sight of creatures he was accustomed to raise his heart to God; hence he exclaimed with love: Heaven and earth and all things tell me to love Thee. When he beheld the heavens, the stars, the fields, the mountains, he seemed to hear them say: Augustine, love God, for he has created you for no other end than that you might love him.

Thus, likewise, St. Teresa, when she beheld the plains, the sea, the rivers, or other beautiful creatures, felt as if they reproached her with ingratitude to God. Thus also St. Mary Magdalene de Pazzi, holding in her hand a flower or an apple, and looking at it, became enraptured with divine love, saying within herself: Then my God has thought from eternity of creating this fruit for my sake, and to give me a proof of the love that he bears me! It is also related of St. Simon Salo, that when in walking through the fields he saw flowers or herbs, he would strike them with his staff, saying: "Be silent, be silent, you reproach me with not loving that God who has made you so beautiful for my sake, that I might be induced to love him: I have already heard you; cease; reprove me no longer; be silent."

4. The fourth and most perfect means of remembering the divine presence is to consider God within us. We need not ascend to heaven to find our God; let us be recollected within ourselves, and in ourselves we shall find him. To treat in prayer with God as at a distance, causes great distraction. St. Teresa used to say: "I never knew how to make mental prayer as it ought to be made till God taught me this manner of praying: in this recollection within myself I have always found great profit."

To come to what is practical: It is necessary to know that God is present in us, in a manner different from that in which he is present in other creatures; in us he is present as in his own temple and his own house. Know you not, says the Apostle, that you are the temple of God, and that the Spirit of God dwelleth in you. Hence our Saviour says, that into a soul that loves God, he comes with the Father and Holy Ghost, not to remain there for a short time, but to dwell in it forever, and there to establish an everlasting habitation. If, any one love me, . . . my Father will love him, and we will come to him, and will make our abode with him.

The kings of the earth, though they have their great palaces, have, notwithstanding, their particular apartments in which they generally live. God is in all places; his presence fills heaven and earth; but he dwells in a particular manner in our souls, and there, as he himself tells us by the mouth of the Apostle, he delights to remain as in so many gardens of pleasure. I will dwell in them, and will walk among them, and I will be their God: There he wishes us to love him and to pray to him: for he remains in us full of love and mercy, to hear our supplications, to receive our affections, to enlighten us, to govern us, to bestow on us his gifts, and to assist us in all that can contribute to our eternal salvation. Let us then often endeavor, on the one hand, to enliven our faith in this great truth, and annihilate ourselves at the sight of the great majesty that condescends to dwell within us; and on the other, let us be careful to make acts at one time of confidence, at another of oblation, and again of love of his infinite goodness; now thanking him for his favors, at another time rejoicing in his glory; and again asking counsel in our doubts; consoling ourselves always in the possession of this Sovereign Good within us, certain that no created power can deprive us of him, and that he will never depart from us unless we first voluntarily banish him from our hearts.

This was the little cell that St. Catharine of Sienna built within her heart, in which she lived always retired, always engaged in loving colloquies with God; thus she defended herself against the persecution of her parents, who had forbidden her to retire any more to her chamber for the purpose of praying. And in this little cell the saint made greater progress than she did by retiring to her room; for she was obliged to leave her chamber several times in the day. This interior cell she never left, but remained in it always recollected with God. Hence St. Teresa, speaking of the divine presence in our interior, said: "I believe that they who are able to lock themselves up in this little heaven in their souls, where he who created them is always present, walk in an excellent path, because they make great progress in a short time."

In a word, by this exercise of the presence of God the saints have succeeded in acquiring great treasures of merits. I set the Lord always in my sight says the royal prophet, for he is at my right hand that I be not moved. I endeavor to consider God always present, and observing all my actions. Blessed Henry Suso applied himself with so much attention to this holy exercise that he performed all his actions in the divine presence, and thus continually conversed with God by tender affections. St. Gertrude acquired the habit of this exercise so perfectly, that our Lord said of her to St. Mechtilde: "This beloved spouse always walks in my presence, seeking always to do my will, and directing all her works to my glory." This was also the practice of St. Teresa; for in whatever occupation she found herself she never lost sight of her beloved Lord.

If, then, you ask me how often in the day you should remember the presence of God, I will answer you with St. Bernard that you ought to remember it every moment. As there is not a moment, says the saint, in which we do not enjoy the benefits of God, so there is not a moment in which we should not remember God, and prove our gratitude. If you knew that the king was always thinking of you and of your welfare, though he should confer no real benefit, still you could not remember his affection without feeling an interior love for him. It is certain that your God is always thinking of you, and that he incessantly confers favors on you at one time by his lights, at another by internal helps, and again by loving visits. Is it not ingratitude in you to be forgetful of him for any length of time? It is then a duty to endeavor to remember always, or at least as often as we can, the divine presence.

This was the advice of the Lord to Abraham: Walk before me, and be perfect. Endeavor to walk always in my presence, and you shall be perfect. Tobias gave the same advice to his son: All the days of thy life have God in thy mind. My son, during your whole life keep God always before your eyes. The exercise of the divine presence St. Dorotheus recommended in a most special manner to his disciple, St. Dositheus, who besought him to tell him what he should do in order to be a saint: "Consider that God is always present, and that he is looking at you." St. Dorotheas relates that the good disciple was so faithful to the advice, that in all his occupations, and even in the severe infirmities with which he was visited, he never lost sight of God. Thus after being a soldier, and a dissolute young man, he attained in five years so high a degree of sanctity, that after death he was seen in heaven seated on a throne of glory equal to that of the most holy among the anchorets.

The great servant of God, Father Joseph Anchieta, who by the exercise of the divine presence arrived at such perfection, used to say that nothing else but our inattention to it can divert us from so holy an exercise. The prophet Micheas says: I will show thee, O man, what is good, and what the Lord requireth of thee, . . . to walk solicitous with thy God. O man, I will show you in what your welfare consists, and what the Lord demands of you; behold it: he wishes you to be solicitous, and that your whole concern be to do all your actions in his presence; because then all shall be well done. Hence, St. Gregory Nazianzen has written: "So often should we remember God as we draw breath." He adds, that by doing this we shall do all things. Another devout author says that meditation may in some cases be omitted; for example, in the time of sickness, or of important business, which cannot be deferred; but the exercise of the presence of God must be always practiced by acts of purity of intention, of oblation, and the like, as will be more fully explained hereafter.

II. Hitherto we have spoken of the operation of the intellect; allow me to speak of the application of the will to the holy exercise of the divine presence. And it is necessary, first, to know that to remain always before God, with the mind always fixed on him, is the happy lot of the saints; but in the present state it is morally impossible to keep up the presence of God without interruption. Hence we should endeavor to practice it to the best of our ability, not with a solicitous inquietude and indiscreet effort of the mind, but with sweetness and tranquility.

There are three means of facilitating the application of the will to this exercise.

1. The first method consists in frequently raising the heart to God, by short but fervent ejaculations, or loving affections towards God, present with us. These may be practiced in all places and in all times, in walking, at work, at meals, and at recreation. These affections may be acts of election, of desire, of resignation, of oblation, of love, of renunciation, of thanksgiving, of petition, of humiliation, of confidence, and the like. In whatever occupation you find yourself, you can very easily turn to God from time to time and say to him:

My God, I wish only for Thee, and nothing else.

I desire nothing but to be all Thine.
Dispose as Thou pleasest of me, and of all that I possess.

I give myself entirely to Thee.

I love Thee more than myself.

I wish only what Thou wishest.

I renounce all things for the love of Thee.

I thank Thee for the great graces Thou hast bestowed upon me.

Assist me, have mercy on me.

Give me Thy holy love.

Lord, I should be at this moment in hell.

I delight in Thy felicity.

I would wish that all men loved Thee.

Do not permit me to be separated from Thee.

In Thee I place all my confidence.

When shall I see Thee and love Thee face to face.

Let all that I do and suffer be done and suffered for Thee. May Thy holy will be always done!

The ancient Fathers set great value on all these short prayers, by which we can practice the presence of God more easily than by long prayers. And St. John Chrysostom used to say, that he that makes use of these short prayers or acts shuts the door against the devil, and prevents him from coming to molest him with bad thoughts.

At certain special times it is necessary more particularly to enliven our faith in the divine presence. First, in the morning when we awake, by saying: My God, I believe that Thou art here present, and that Thou wilt be present with me in every place to which I shall go this day; watch over me, then, in all places, and do not permit me to offend Thee before Thy divine eyes. Secondly, at the beginning of all our prayers, whether mental or vocal. The Venerable Cardinal Caracciolo, Bishop of Aversa, used to say, .that he that makes mental prayer with distractions, shows that he has been negligent in making the act of faith in the presence of God. Thirdly, on occasion of any temptation against patience or chastity; for example, if you are seized with any sharp pain, or receive any grievous insult, or if any scandalous object be presented to you, instantly arm yourself with the divine presence, and excite your courage by remembering that God is looking at you. It was thus that David prepared himself to resist temptations. My eyes are ever towards the Lord; for he shall pluck my feet out of the snare. I will keep my eyes on my God, and he will deliver me from the snares of my enemies. You must do the same when you have occasion to perform any very difficult act of virtue; you must imitate the valorous Judith, who, after having unsheathed the sword, and taken Holofernes, who was asleep, by the hair of the head, turned to God before she gave the stroke, and said: Strengthen me, O Lord, in this hour. Thus she courageously cut off his head.

2. The second method of preserving the presence of God by acts of the will is to renew always in distracting employments the intention of performing them all with the intention of pleasing God. And therefore, in the beginning of every action or occupation, whether you apply yourself to work, go to table, or to recreation, or to repose, say: Lord, I do not intend in this work my pleasure, but only the accomplishment of Thy will. In the course of the action endeavor to renew your intention, saying: My God, may all be for Thy glory. By these acts the presence of God is preserved without fatiguing the mind; for the very desire of pleasing God is a loving remembrance of his presence. It is also useful to fix certain times, or particular signs, in order to remember the divine presence; as when the clock strikes, when you look at the crucifix, when you enter or leave the cell. Some are accustomed to keep in their room some particular sign, to remind them of the presence of God.

3. The third method is, when you find yourself very much distracted during the day, and the mind oppressed with business, to procure leave from the Superior to retire, at least for a little, to the choir or to the

cell, in order to recollect yourself with God. Were you on any day to feel bodily weakness, arising from excess of labor and long fasting, would you not take some refreshment in order to be able to proceed with the work? How much more careful should you be to treat the soul in a similar manner, when it begins to fail in courage, and to grow cold in divine love, in consequence of being a long time without food; that is, without prayer and recollection with God? I again repeat what Father Balthasar Alvarez used to say, that a soul out of prayer is like a fish out of water; the soul is, as it were, in a state of violence. Hence, after being a long time engaged in business and distracting occupations, a Christian should retire (if I may use the expression), to take breath in solitude, recollecting himself there with God, by affections and petitions. The life of bliss in heaven consists in seeing and loving God, and therefore I infer that the felicity of a soul on this earth consists also in loving and seeing God, not openly as in paradise, but with the eyes of faith, by which it beholds him always present with it; and thus acquires great reverence, confidence, and love towards its beloved Lord. He that lives in this manner, begins, even in this valley of tears, to live like the saints in heaven, who always see God. They always see the face of my Father, and therefore they cannot cease to love him. Thus he that lives in the divine presence will despise all earthly things, knowing that before God all is misery and smoke; and will begin in this life to possess that Sovereign Good who contents the heart more than all other goods.

Prayer.

My adored Jesus, Thou hast not refused to give all Thy blood for me; and shall I refuse to give Thee all my love? No, my beloved Redeemer, I offer myself entirely to Thee; accept me and dispose of me as Thou pleasest. But since Thou givest me the desire of Thy pure love, teach me what I ought to do, and I will do it. Grant that this heart that was once miserably deprived of Thy love may now neither love nor seek anything but Thee. Grant that my will may wish only what Thou wishest. Unhappy me! I once, for the sake of my pleasures, despised Thy will, and forgot Thee. Grant that from this day forward I may forget all things, even myself, to think only of loving and pleasing Thee. O my God, amiable above every good, how bitterly do I regret that hitherto I have had so little regard for Thee! Lord, pardon me, draw me entirely to Thyself; do not permit me to love Thee but little, or to love anything but Thee. I hope for all things from Thy goodness, and from Thy merits, O my Jesus!

And I place all confidence in thee, O my Queen, my advocate, and my Mother, Mary. Have pity on me, and recommend me to thy Son, who hears thy prayers, and refuses thee nothing.

The End

Other Titles Available from
St Athanasius Press
www.stathanasiuspress.com

Be sure to check our web site for the newest titles being offered and
for our latest contact information!

A Book of Essays
by Msgr Robert Hugh Benson

A Commonitory for the Antiquity and Universality
of the Catholic Faith Against the
Profane Novelties of all Heresies
by Vincent of Lerins

A Golden Book of Three Tabernacles:
Poverty, Humility and Patience
by Thomas A Kempis

A Little Book of Eternal Wisdom
by Blessed Henry Suso

A Short Catechism of Cardinal Bellarmine
by Cardinal Robert Bellarmine

A Thought from St Ignatius Loyola
for Each Day of the Year
by St Ignatius Loyola

A Thought From Thomas A Kempis
for Each Day of the Year
by Thomas A Kempis

A Treatise of Discretion
by St Catherine of Siena

A Treatise of Divine Providence
& A Treatise of Obedience
by St Catherine of Siena

357

A Treatise of Prayer
by St Catherine of Siena

A Treatise on the Particular Examen of Conscious
by Fr Luis De La Palma, SJ

Catholic An Essential and Exclusive Attribute
of the True Church
by Rt Rev Msgr Capel

Christ in the Church:
A Volume of Religious Essays
by Fr Robert Hugh Benson

Christ Our Rest and King
by Henry Edward Manning

Cochems Explanation of the Holy Sacrifice of the Mass
by Fr Martin Cochem

Collection of Catholic Prayers and Devotions

Collection of Thomas A Kempis Classics
by Thomas A Kempis

Confession
by Rev John Furniss, CSSR

Confessions of a Convert
by Fr Robert Hugh Benson

Darts of Fire
by St Alphonsus M Liguori, CSSR

Devotion to the Nine Choirs of Angels
by Henri Marie Boudon

Devotion to the Sacred Heart of Jesus
by Fr John Croiset, SJ

Dignity and Duties of the Priest or Selva
by St Alphonsus M Liguori, CSSR

Enchiridion on Faith, Hope and Love
by St Augustine

Explanation of the Psalms & Canticles
in the Divine Office
by St Alphonsus M Liguori, CSSR

For Passion Sunday
by Thomas A Kempis

General Catholic Devotions
Compiled by Rev Bonaventure Hammer, OFM

God and His Perfections
by Rev John Furniss, CSSR

Hell:
The Dogma of Hell, Illustrated by Facts
Taken from Profane and Sacred History
by Rev. Father Francois Xavier Schouppe, S.J.

Holiness of Life
Being St Bonaventure's Treatise
De Perfectione Vitae ad Sorores
by St Bonaventure

Humility of Heart
by Fr Cajetan Mary da Bergamo

Indifferentism or
Is One Religion as Good as Another?
by John Maclaughlin

Life of St Leonard of Port Maurice
by Fr Dominic Devas, OFM

Martyrs of the Early Church
by St Alphonsus M Liguori, CSSR

Mental Prayer and the Exercises of a Retreat
by St Alphonsus M Liguori, CSSR

Miscellany
by St Alphonsus M Liguori, CSSR

Modernism
by Cardinal Mercier

On Cleaving to God English/Latin
by St Albert the Great

On Contempt for the World or
De Contemptu Mundi
by St Eucherius of Lyon

On Divine Love and the Means of Acquiring It
by St Alphonsus M Liguori, CSSR

On Loving God
by St Bernard of Clairvaux

Paradoxes of Catholicism
by Robert Hugh Benson

2 Volume Set
Personal Recollections of Joan of Arc
by Mark Twain

Prayer: The Key of Salvation
by Fr Michael Muller, CSSR

Preaching
by St Alphonsus M Liguori, CSSR

Preparation for Death
by St Alphonsus M Liguori, CSSR

Poems
by Fr Robert Hugh Benson

Reasonableness of Catholic Ceremonies and Practices
by Rev John J. Burke

Religious Orders of Women
in the United States (1930 Photos included)
by Elinor Tong Dehey

Saint Athanasius:
The Father of Orthodoxy
by F. A. Forbes

Saint Vincent de Paul
by F. A. Forbes

Sermons for All the Sundays in the Year
by St Alphonsus M Liguori, CSSR

Sermons Upon Various Subjects
by St Alphonsus M Liguori, CSSR

Spiritual Maxims
by John Nicholas Grou, SJ

St Alphonsus Liguori on the Council of Trent
by St Alphonsus M Liguori, CSSR

St Charity: A True Life Catholic Pro Life Story
by Mel Waller

Ten Reasons Proposed to His Adversaries
for Disputation in the Name of the Faith
by St Edmund Campion

The Art of Dying Well
by St Robert Bellarmine

The Autobiography of St Ignatius Loyola
by St Ignatius Loyola

The Blessed Eucharist
Our Greatest Treasure
by Fr Michael Müller, CSSR

The Catholic Dogma
by Michael Müller, CSSR

The Choice of a State of Life and the
Vocation to the Religious State
by St Alphonsus M Liguori, CSSR

The Confessions of St Augustine
by Saint Augustine

The Cross and the Shamrock
by Hugh Quigley

The Cure of Ars
by Kathleen O'Meara

The Dialogue of the Seraphic Virgin
St Catherine of Siena
by St Catherine of Siena

The Douay Catechism of 1649
by Henry Tuberville, D.D.

The Eternal Happiness of the Saints
by St Robert Bellarmine

The Friendship of Christ
by Robert Hugh Benson

The Grace of Prayer is Given to All
by St Alphonsus M Liguori, CSSR

The Great Evil
by Rev John Furniss, CSSR

The Great Means of Salvation and of Perfection
by St Alphonsus M Liguori, CSSR

The Great Question
by Rev John Furniss, CSSR

The History of Heresies
by St Alphonsus M Liguori, CSSR

The Holy Eucharist
by St Alphonsus M Liguori, CSSR

The Holy Ways of the Cross
by Henri Marie Boudon

The Incarnation, Birth and Infancy of Jesus Christ
by St Alphonsus M Liguori, CSSR

The Life and Miracles of Saint Philomena, Virgin and Martyr
by Unknown Author

The Life of Blessed John B. Marie Vianney, Cure of Ars
by Anonymous

The Life of St Dominic Savio
by St John Bosco

The Life of Saint Columba
by F. A. Forbes

The Life of Saint Monica
by F. A. Forbes

The Life of St Veronica Giuliani
by Filippo Maria Salvatori

The Life of Our Most Holy Father St Benedict
by St Gregory the Great

The Little Kempis
or Short Sayings and Prayers
by Thomas A Kempis

The Love of Souls Or
Reflections and Affections
on the Passion of Jesus Christ
by St Alphonsus M Liguori, CSSR

The Martyrs of Japan
by St Alphonsus M Liguori, CSSR

The Maxims and Sayings of St Philip Neri
by St Philip Neri

The Mind's Road to God
by St Bonaventure

The Mysteries of the Faith:
The Redemption
by St Alphonsus M Liguori, CSSR

3 Volume Set
The Practice of Christian and Religious Perfection
by Fr Alphonsus Rodriguez, SJ

The Practice of the Love of Jesus Christ
by St Alphonsus M Liguori, CSSR

The Practice of the Presence of God
by Brother Lawrence (Nicholas Herman of Lorraine)
Carmelite Lay Brother

The Psalter of the Blessed Virgin Mary
by St Bonaventure

The Raccolta or A Manual of Indulgences
1957 Edition

The Religion of the Plain Man
by Fr Robert Hugh Benson

The Roman Index of Forbidden Books
by Francis S Betten, SJ

The Sacrifice of Jesus Christ
by St Alphonsus M Liguori, CSSR

The Sight of Hell
by Rev John Furniss, CSSR

The Spiritual Conflict and Conquest
by Dom J Castaniza, OSB

The Treatise on Purgatory
by St Catherine of Genoa

The Triumph of the Cross
by Fra Girolamo Savonarola

The True Spouse of Jesus Christ Vol I
by St Alphonsus M Liguori, CSSR

The Valley of Lilies & The Little Garden of Roses
by Thomas A Kempis

The Way of Salvation and Perfection
by St Alphonsus M Liguori, CSSR

Treatise on Prayer
by St Alphonsus M Liguori, CSSR

Triumph of the Blessed Sacrament or
History of Nicola Aubry
by Fr Michael Muller, CSSR

Trustful Surrender to Divine Providence
by Fr. Jean Baptiste Saint-Jure &
St. Claude de la Colombiere

Utopia
by St Thomas More

Vera Sapentia or True Wisdom
Thomas A Kempis

Victories of the Martyrs
by St Alphonsus M Liguori, CSSR

Visits to the Most Holy Sacrament
and the Blessed Virgin Mary
by St Alphonsus M Liguori, CSSR

Vocations Explained
by A Vincentian Father

Where We Got the Bible
by Henry G Graham

New Titles are Being Added Often!

CPSIA information can be obtained
at www.ICGtesting.com
Printed in the USA
BVHW072356240420
578457BV00001B/68

9 781484 984192